ILLUSTRATED COURSE GUIDES

Microsoft® Excel® 2010

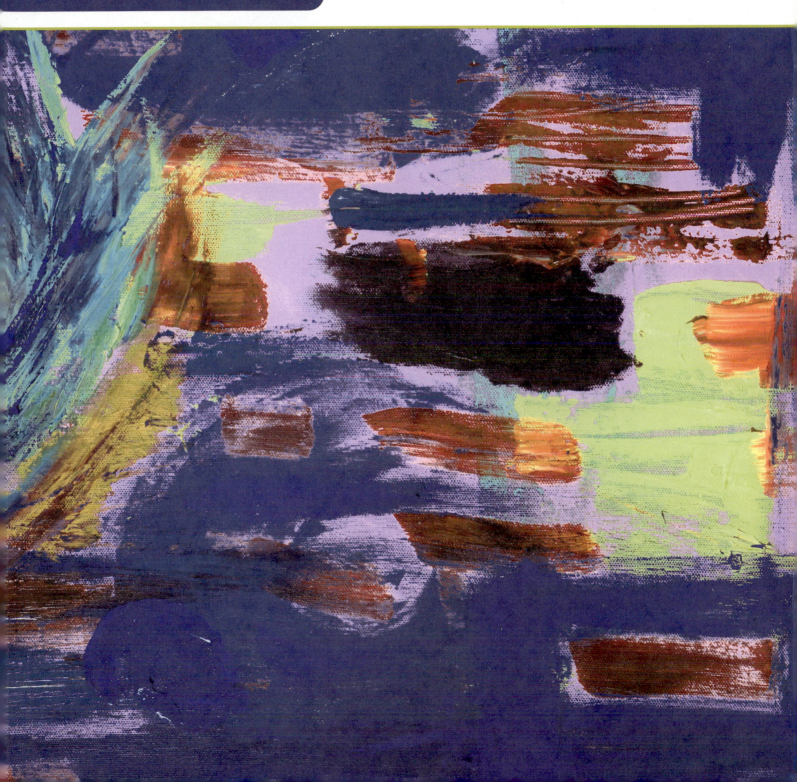

Basic

ILLUSTRATED COURSE GUIDES

Microsoft® Excel® 2010

Basic

Elizabeth Eisner Reding/Lynn Wermers

Australia • Brazil • Japan • Korea • Mexico • Singapore • Spain • United Kingdom • United States

Illustrated Course Guide: Microsoft® Excel® 2010 Basic

Elizabeth Eisner Reding/Lynn Wermers

Vice President, Publisher: Nicole Jones Pinard

Executive Editor: Marjorie Hunt

Associate Acquisitions Editor: Brandi Shailer

Senior Product Manager: Christina Kling Garrett

Associate Product Manager: Michelle Camisa

Editorial Assistant: Kim Klasner

Director of Marketing: Cheryl Costantini

Senior Marketing Manager: Ryan DeGrote

Marketing Coordinator: Kristen Panciocco

Contributing Author: Carol Cram

Developmental Editors: Barbara Clemens, Jeanne Herring

Content Project Manager: Danielle Chouhan

Copy Editor: Mark Goodin

Proofreader: Vicki Zimmer

Indexer: BIM Indexing and Proofreading Services

QA Manuscript Reviewers: Nicole Ashton, John Frietas, Serge Palladino, Susan Pedicini, Jeff Schwartz, Danielle Shaw, Marianne Snow

Print Buyer: Fola Orekoya

Cover Designer: GEX Publishing Services

Cover Artist: Mark Hunt

Composition: GEX Publishing Services

Library of Congress Control Number: 2010935817

ISBN-13: 978-0-538-74836-0
ISBN-10: 0-538-74836-2

Course Technology
20 Channel Center Street
Boston, MA 02210
USA

Cengage Learning is a leading provider of customized learning solutions with office locations around the globe, including Singapore, the United Kingdom, Australia, Mexico, Brazil, and Japan. Locate your local office at:
international.cengage.com/region

Cengage Learning products are represented in Canada by Nelson Education, Ltd.

To learn more about Course Technology, visit **www.cengage.com/coursetechnology**

To learn more about Cengage Learning, visit **www.cengage.com**

Purchase any of our products at your local college store or at our preferred online store **www.cengagebrain.com**

Printed in the United States of America
2 3 4 5 6 7 8 9 18 17 16 15 14 13 12 11

Brief Contents

Contents

Web Apps

Preface

Welcome to *Illustrated Course Guide: Microsoft® Excel® 2010 Basic*. If this is your first experience with the Illustrated Course Guides, you'll see that this book has a unique design: each skill is presented on two facing pages, with steps on the left and screens on the right. The layout makes it easy to learn a skill without having to read a lot of text and flip pages to see an illustration.

This book is an ideal learning tool for a wide range of learners—the "rookies" will find the clean design easy to follow and focused with only essential information presented, and the "hotshots" will appreciate being able to move quickly through the lessons to find the information they need without reading a lot of text. The design also makes this a great reference after the course is over! See the illustration on the right to learn more about the pedagogical and design elements of a typical lesson.

What's New In This Edition

- **Fully Updated.** Highlights the new features of Microsoft Excel 2010 including creating sparklines, using Paste Preview, and the new Backstage view. A new appendix covers cloud computing concepts and using Microsoft Office Web Apps.
- **Maps to SAM 2010.** This book is designed to work with SAM (Skills Assessment Manager) 2010. **SAM Assessment** contains performance-based, hands-on SAM exams for each unit of this book, and **SAM Training** provides hands-on training for skills covered in the book. Some exercises are available in **SAM Projects**, which is auto-grading software that provides both learners and instructors with immediate, detailed feedback (SAM sold separately.) See page xii for more information on SAM.

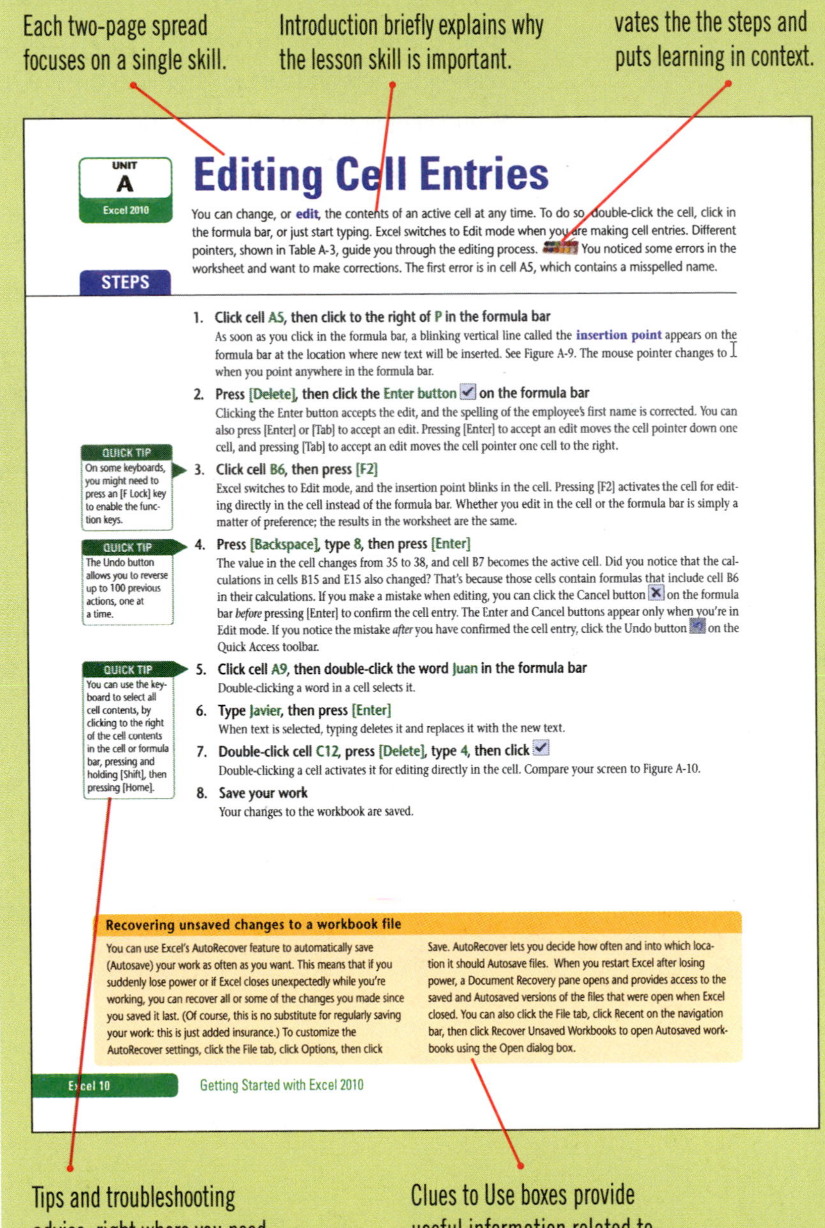
Each two-page spread focuses on a single skill.
Introduction briefly explains why the lesson skill is important.
A case scenario motivates the the steps and puts learning in context.
Tips and troubleshooting advice, right where you need it–next to the step itself.
Clues to Use boxes provide useful information related to the lesson skill.

UNIT A Excel 2010

Editing Cell Entries

You can change, or **edit**, the contents of an active cell at any time. To do so, double-click the cell, click in the formula bar, or just start typing. Excel switches to Edit mode when you are making cell entries. Different pointers, shown in Table A-3, guide you through the editing process. You noticed some errors in the worksheet and want to make corrections. The first error is in cell A5, which contains a misspelled name.

STEPS

1. **Click cell A5, then click to the right of P in the formula bar**
   As soon as you click in the formula bar, a blinking vertical line called the **insertion point** appears on the formula bar at the location where new text will be inserted. See Figure A-9. The mouse pointer changes to I when you point anywhere in the formula bar.
2. **Press [Delete], then click the Enter button ✓ on the formula bar**
   Clicking the Enter button accepts the edit, and the spelling of the employee's first name is corrected. You can also press [Enter] or [Tab] to accept an edit. Pressing [Enter] to accept an edit moves the cell pointer down one cell, and pressing [Tab] to accept an edit moves the cell pointer one cell to the right.
3. **Click cell B6, then press [F2]**
   Excel switches to Edit mode, and the insertion point blinks in the cell. Pressing [F2] activates the cell for editing directly in the cell instead of the formula bar. Whether you edit in the cell or the formula bar is simply a matter of preference; the results in the worksheet are the same.
4. **Press [Backspace], type 8, then press [Enter]**
   The value in the cell changes from 35 to 38, and cell B7 becomes the active cell. Did you notice that the calculations in cells B15 and E15 also changed? That's because those cells contain formulas that include cell B6 in their calculations. If you make a mistake when editing, you can click the Cancel button ✗ on the formula bar *before* pressing [Enter] to confirm the cell entry. The Enter and Cancel buttons appear only when you're in Edit mode. If you notice the mistake *after* you have confirmed the cell entry, click the Undo button on the Quick Access toolbar.
5. **Click cell A9, then double-click the word Juan in the formula bar**
   Double-clicking a word in a cell selects it.
6. **Type Javier, then press [Enter]**
   When text is selected, typing deletes it and replaces it with the new text.
7. **Double-click cell C12, press [Delete], type 4, then click ✓**
   Double-clicking a cell activates it for editing directly in the cell. Compare your screen to Figure A-10.
8. **Save your work**
   Your changes to the workbook are saved.

QUICK TIP: On some keyboards, you might need to press an [F Lock] key to enable the function keys.

QUICK TIP: The Undo button allows you to reverse up to 100 previous actions, one at a time.

QUICK TIP: You can use the keyboard to select all cell contents, by clicking to the right of the cell contents in the cell or formula bar, pressing and holding [Shift], then pressing [Home].

Recovering unsaved changes to a workbook file

You can use Excel's AutoRecover feature to automatically save (Autosave) your work as often as you want. This means that if you suddenly lose power or if Excel closes unexpectedly while you're working, you can recover all or some of the changes you made since you saved it last. (Of course, this is no substitute for regularly saving your work: this is just added insurance.) To customize the AutoRecover settings, click the File tab, click Options, then click Save. AutoRecover lets you decide how often and into which location it should Autosave files. When you restart Excel after losing power, a Document Recovery pane opens and provides access to the saved and Autosaved versions of the files that were open when Excel closed. You can also click the File tab, click Recent on the navigation bar, then click Recover Unsaved Workbooks to open Autosaved workbooks using the Open dialog box.

Excel 10 Getting Started with Excel 2010

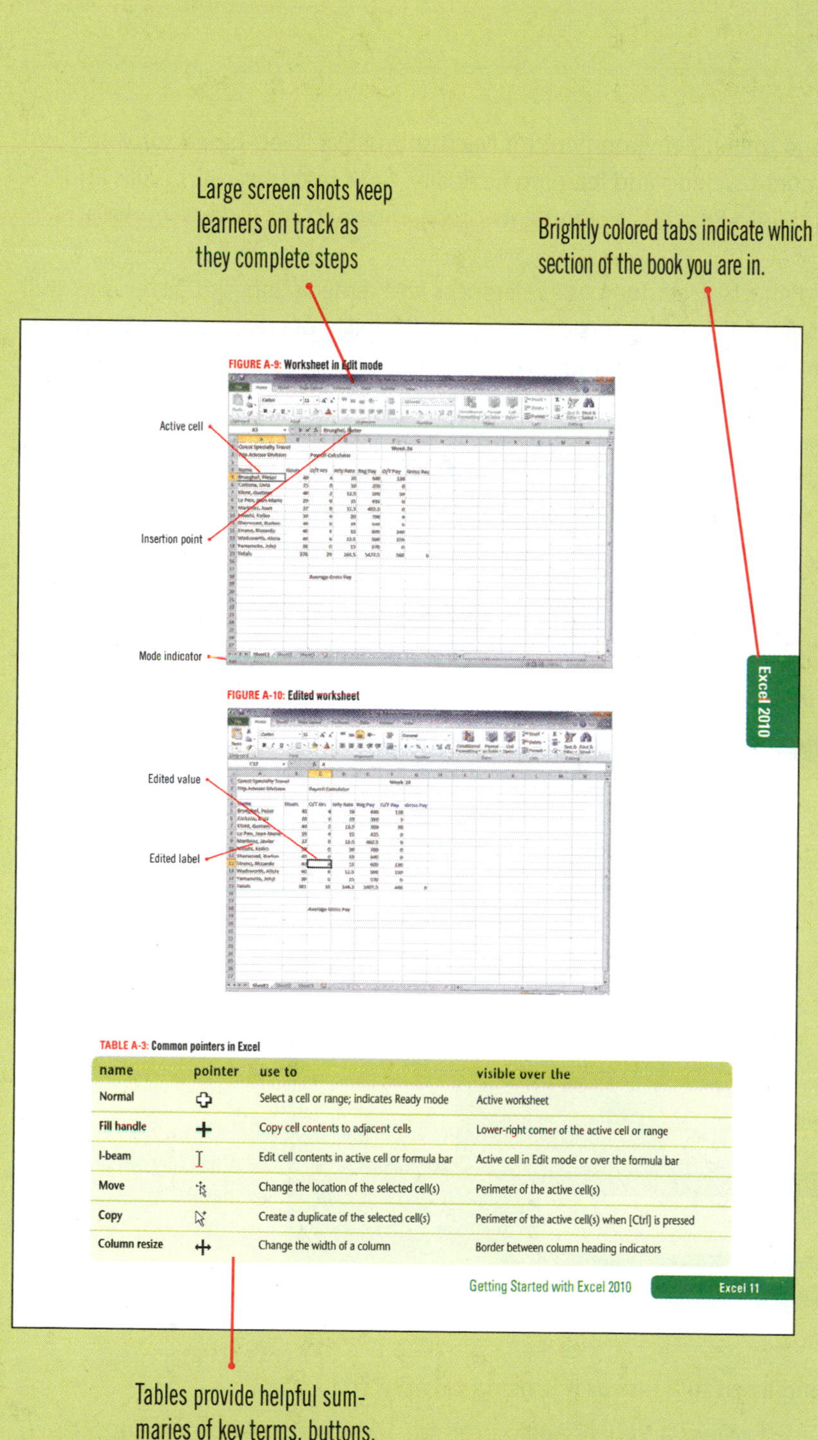

name	pointer	use to	visible over the
Normal	✣	Select a cell or range; indicates Ready mode	Active worksheet
Fill handle	+	Copy cell contents to adjacent cells	Lower-right corner of the active cell or range
I-beam	I	Edit cell contents in active cell or formula bar	Active cell in Edit mode or over the formula bar
Move	✥	Change the location of the selected cell(s)	Perimeter of the active cell(s)
Copy	⇱	Create a duplicate of the selected cell(s)	Perimeter of the active cell(s) when [Ctrl] is pressed
Column resize	↔	Change the width of a column	Border between column heading indicators

Assignments

The lessons use Quest Specialty Travel, a fictional adventure travel company, as the case study. The assignments on the light yellow pages at the end of each unit increase in difficulty. Assignments include:

- **Concepts Review** consist of multiple choice, matching, and screen identification questions.
- **Skills Reviews** are hands-on, step-by-step exercises that review the skills covered in each lesson in the unit.
- **Independent Challenges** are case projects requiring critical thinking and application of the unit skills. The Independent Challenges increase in difficulty, with the first one in each unit being the easiest. Independent Challenges 2 and 3 become increasingly open-ended, requiring more independent problem solving.
- **SAM Projects** is live-in-the-application autograding software that provides immediate and detailed feedback reports to learners and instructors. Some exercises in this book are available in SAM Projects. (Purchase of a SAM Projects pincode is required.)
- **Real Life Independent Challenges** are practical exercises in which learners create documents to help them with their every day lives.
- **Advanced Challenge Exercises** set within the Independent Challenges provide optional steps for more advanced learners.
- **Visual Workshops** are practical, self-graded capstone projects that require independent problem solving.

About SAM

SAM is the premier proficiency-based assessment and training environment for Microsoft Office. Web-based software along with an inviting user interface provide maximum teaching and learning flexibility. SAM builds learners' skills and confidence with a variety of real-life simulations, and SAM Projects' assignments prepare learners for today's workplace.

The SAM system includes Assessment, Training, and Projects, featuring page references and remediation for this book as well as Course Technology's Microsoft Office textbooks. With SAM, instructors can enjoy the flexibility of creating assignments based on content from their favorite Microsoft Office books or based on specific course objectives. Instructors appreciate the scheduling and reporting options that have made SAM the market-leading online testing and training software for over a decade. Over 2,000 performance-based questions and matching Training simulations, as well as tens of thousands of objective-based questions from many Course Technology texts, provide instructors with a variety of choices across multiple applications. SAM Projects is auto-grading software that lets learners complete projects using Microsoft Office and then receive detailed feedback on their finished projects.

SAM Assessment

- Content for these hands-on, performance-based tasks includes Word, Excel, Access, PowerPoint, Internet Explorer, Outlook, and Windows. Includes tens of thousands of objective-based questions from many Course Technology texts.

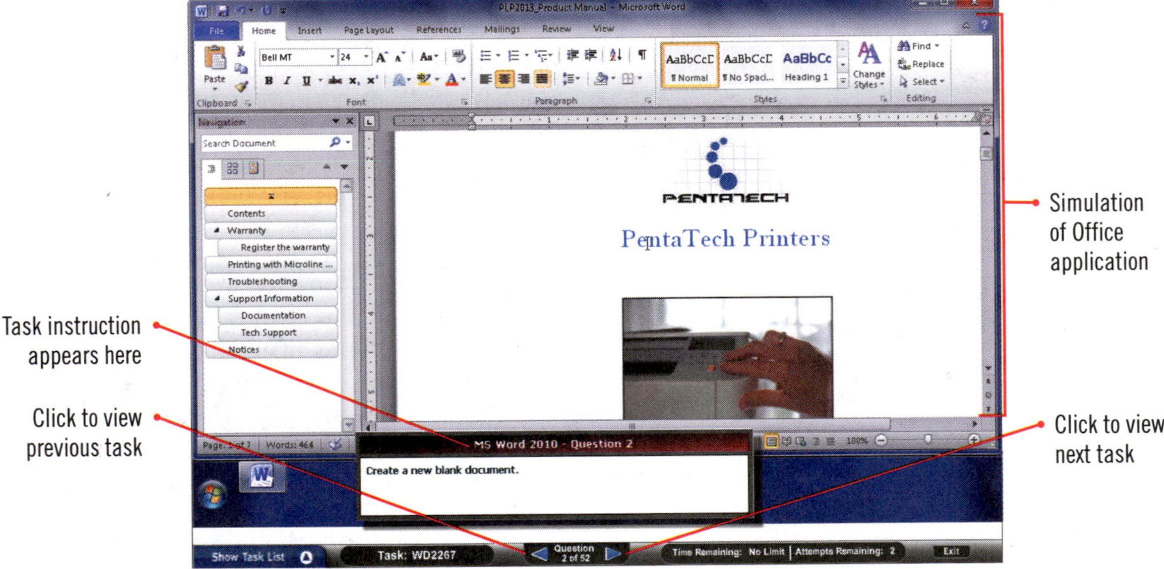

SAM Training

- Observe mode allows the learners to watch and listen to a task as it is being completed.
- Practice mode allows the learner to follow guided arrows and hear audio prompts to help visual learners know how to complete a task.
- Apply mode allows the learner to prove what they've learned by completing a project using on-screen instructions.

SAM Projects

- Live-in-the-application assignments in Word, Excel, Access and PowerPoint allow learners to create a project using the Microsoft Office software and then receive immediate, detailed feedback on their completed project.
- Learners receive detailed feedback on their project within minutes.
- Unique anti-cheating detection feature is encrypted into the data files to ensure learners complete their own assignments.

Instructor Resources

The Instructor Resources CD is Course Technology's way of putting the resources and information needed to teach and learn effectively into your hands. With an integrated array of teaching and learning tools that offer you and your learners a broad range of technology-based instructional options, we believe this CD represents the highest quality and most cutting edge resources available to instructors today. The resources available with this book are:

- **Instructor's Manual**—Available as an electronic file, the Instructor's Manual includes detailed lecture topics with teaching tips for each unit.
- **Sample Syllabus**—Prepare and customize your course easily using this sample course outline.
- **PowerPoint Presentations**—Each unit has a corresponding PowerPoint presentation that you can use in lecture, distribute to your learners, or customize to suit your course.
- **Figure Files**—The figures in the text are provided on the Instructor Resources CD to help you illustrate key topics or concepts. You can create traditional overhead transparencies by printing the figure files. Or you can create electronic slide shows by using the figures in a presentation program such as PowerPoint.
- **Solutions to Exercises**—Solutions to Exercises contains every file learners are asked to create or modify in the lessons and end-of-unit material. Also provided in this section, there is a document outlining the solutions for the end-of-unit Concepts Review, Skills Review, and Independent Challenges. An Annotated Solution File and Grading Rubric accompany each file and can be used together for quick and easy grading.
- **Data Files for Learners**—To complete most of the units in this book, learners will need Data Files. You can post the Data Files on a file server for learners to copy. The Data Files are available on the Instructor Resources CD-ROM, the Review Pack, and can also be downloaded from cengagebrain.com. For more information on how to download the Data Files, see the inside back cover.

  Instruct learners to use the Data Files List included on the Review Pack and the Instructor Resources CD. This list gives instructions on copying and organizing files.
- **ExamView**—ExamView is a powerful testing software package that allows you to create and administer printed, computer (LAN-based), and Internet exams. ExamView includes hundreds of questions that correspond to the topics covered in this text, enabling learners to generate detailed study guides that include page references for further review. The computer-based and Internet testing components allow learners to take exams at their computers, and also saves you time by grading each exam automatically.

Content for Online Learning.

Course Technology has partnered with the leading distance learning solution providers and class-management platforms today. To access this material, visit www.cengage.com/webtutor and search for your title. Instructor resources include the following: additional case projects, sample syllabi, PowerPoint presentations, and more. For additional information, please contact your sales representative. For learners to access this material, they must have purchased a WebTutor PIN-code specific to this title and your campus platform. The resources for learners might include (based on instructor preferences): topic reviews, review questions, practice tests, and more.

Acknowledgements

Instructor Advisory Board

We thank our Instructor Advisory Board who gave us their opinions and guided our decisions as we updated our texts for Microsoft Office 2010. They are as follows:

Terri Helfand, Chaffey Community College

Barbara Comfort, J. Sargeant Reynolds Community College

Brenda Nielsen, Mesa Community College

Sharon Cotman, Thomas Nelson Community College

Marian Meyer, Central New Mexico Community College

Audrey Styer, Morton College

Richard Alexander, Heald College

Xiaodong Qiao, Heald College

Student Advisory Board

We also thank our Student Advisory Board members, who shared their experiences using the book and offered suggestions to make it better: **Latasha Jefferson**, Thomas Nelson Community College, **Gary Williams**, Thomas Nelson Community College, **Stephanie Miller**, J. Sargeant Reynolds Community College, **Sarah Styer**, Morton Community College, **Missy Marino**, Chaffey College

Author Acknowledgements

Elizabeth Eisner Reding Creating a book of this magnitude is a team effort. I would like to thank my husband, Michael, as well as Christina Kling Garrett, the product manager, and my development editor, Jeanne Herring, for her suggestions and corrections. I would also like to thank the production and editorial staff for all their hard work that made this project a reality. Many talented people at Course Technology worked tirelessly to shape this book—thank you all. I am especially grateful to Pam Conrad, editor extraordinaire, whose dedication, wisdom, and precision are evident on every page.

Lynn Wermers Thanks to Barbara Clemens for her insightful contributions, invaluable feedback, great humor, and patience. Thanks also to Christina Kling Garrett for her encouragement and support in guiding and managing this project.

Read This Before You Begin

Frequently Asked Questions

What are Data Files?

A Data File is a partially completed Excel spreadsheet or another type of file that you use to complete the steps in the units and exercises to create the final document that you submit to your instructor. Each unit opener page lists the Data Files that you need for that unit.

Where are the Data Files?

Your instructor will provide the Data Files to you or direct you to a location on a network drive from which you can download them. For information on how to download the Data Files from cengagebrain.com, see the inside back cover.

What software was used to write and test this book?

This book was written and tested using a typical installation of Microsoft Office 2010 Professional Plus on a computer with a typical installation of Microsoft Windows 7 Ultimate.

The browser used for any Web-dependent steps is Internet Explorer 8.

Do I need to be connected to the Internet to complete the steps and exercises in this book?

Some of the exercises in this book require that your computer be connected to the Internet. If you are not connected to the Internet, see your instructor for information on how to complete the exercises.

What do I do if my screen is different from the figures shown in this book?

This book was written and tested on computers with monitors set at a resolution of 1024 × 768. If your screen shows more or less information than the figures in the book, your monitor is probably set at a higher or lower resolution. If you don't see something on your screen, you might have to scroll down or up to see the object identified in the figures.

The Ribbon—the blue area at the top of the screen—in Microsoft Office 2010 adapts to different resolutions. If your monitor is set at a lower resolution than 1024 × 768, you might not see all of the buttons shown in the figures. The groups of buttons will always appear, but the entire group might be condensed into a single button that you need to click to access the buttons described in the instructions.

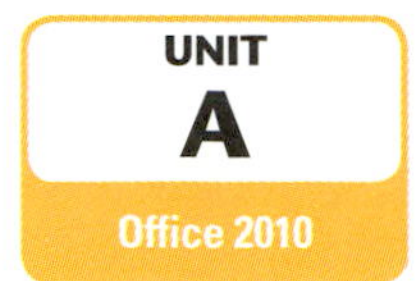

Getting Started with Microsoft Office 2010

Microsoft Office 2010 is a group of software programs designed to help you create documents, collaborate with coworkers, and track and analyze information. Each program is designed so you can work quickly and efficiently to create professional-looking results. You use different Office programs to accomplish specific tasks, such as writing a letter or producing a sales presentation, yet all the programs have a similar look and feel. Once you become familiar with one program, you'll find it easy to transfer your knowledge to the others. This unit introduces you to the most frequently used programs in Office, as well as common features they all share.

OBJECTIVES

- Understand the Office 2010 suite
- Start and exit an Office program
- View the Office 2010 user interface
- Create and save a file
- Open a file and save it with a new name
- View and print your work
- Get Help and close a file

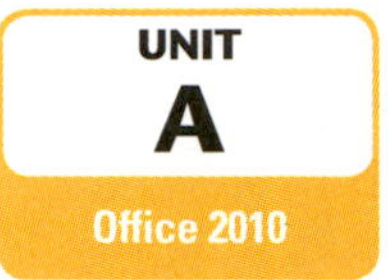
UNIT
A
Office 2010

Understanding the Office 2010 Suite

Microsoft Office 2010 features an intuitive, context-sensitive user interface, so you can get up to speed faster and use advanced features with greater ease. The programs in Office are bundled together in a group called a **suite** (although you can also purchase them separately). The Office suite is available in several configurations, but all include Word, Excel, and PowerPoint. Other configurations include Access, Outlook, Publisher, and other programs. Each program in Office is best suited for completing specific types of tasks, though there is some overlap in capabilities.

DETAILS

The Office programs covered in this book include:

- **Microsoft Word 2010**

  When you need to create any kind of text-based document, such as a memo, newsletter, or multipage report, Word is the program to use. You can easily make your documents look great by inserting eye-catching graphics and using formatting tools such as themes, which are available in most Office programs. **Themes** are predesigned combinations of color and formatting attributes you can apply to a document. The Word document shown in Figure A-1 was formatted with the Solstice theme.

- **Microsoft Excel 2010**

  Excel is the perfect solution when you need to work with numeric values and make calculations. It puts the power of formulas, functions, charts, and other analytical tools into the hands of every user, so you can analyze sales projections, calculate loan payments, and present your findings in style. The Excel worksheet shown in Figure A-1 tracks personal expenses. Because Excel automatically recalculates results whenever a value changes, the information is always up to date. A chart illustrates how the monthly expenses are broken down.

- **Microsoft PowerPoint 2010**

  Using PowerPoint, it's easy to create powerful presentations complete with graphics, transitions, and even a soundtrack. Using professionally designed themes and clip art, you can quickly and easily create dynamic slide shows such as the one shown in Figure A-1.

- **Microsoft Access 2010**

  Access helps you keep track of large amounts of quantitative data, such as product inventories or employee records. The form shown in Figure A-1 was created for a grocery store inventory database. Employees use the form to enter data about each item. Using Access enables employees to quickly find specific information such as price and quantity without hunting through store shelves and stockrooms.

Microsoft Office has benefits beyond the power of each program, including:

- **Common user interface: Improving business processes**

  Because the Office suite programs have a similar **interface**, or look and feel, your experience using one program's tools makes it easy to learn those in the other programs. In addition, Office documents are **compatible** with one another, meaning that you can easily incorporate, or **integrate**, an Excel chart into a PowerPoint slide, or an Access table into a Word document.

- **Collaboration: Simplifying how people work together**

  Office recognizes the way people do business today, and supports the emphasis on communication and knowledge sharing within companies and across the globe. All Office programs include the capability to incorporate feedback—called **online collaboration**—across the Internet or a company network.

FIGURE A-1: Microsoft Office 2010 documents

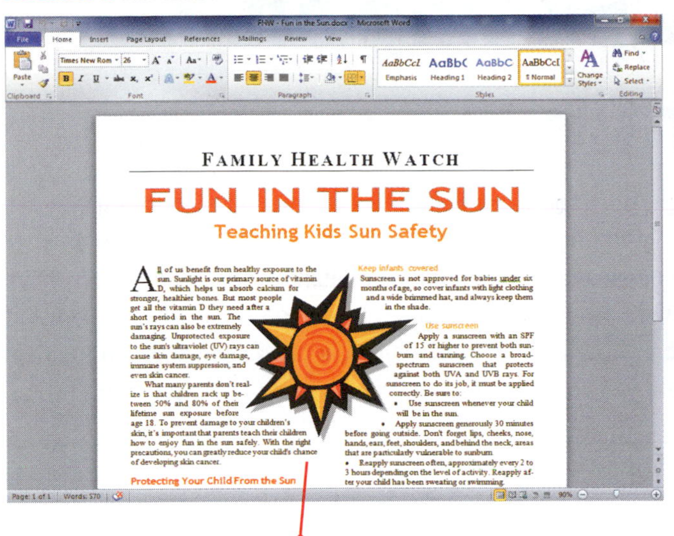

Newsletter created in Word

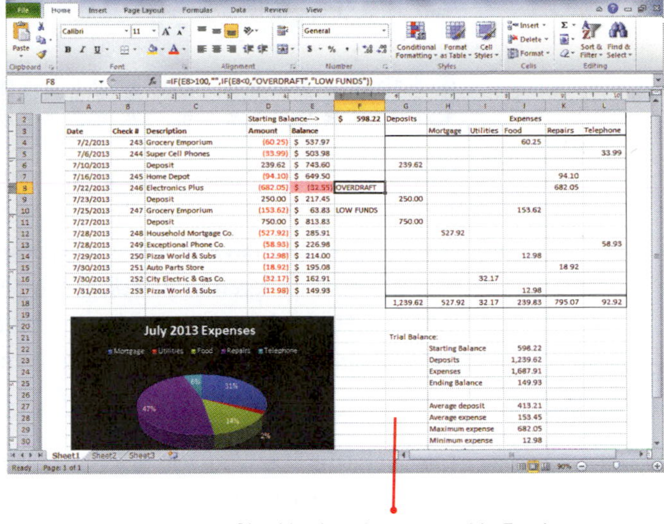

Checkbook register created in Excel

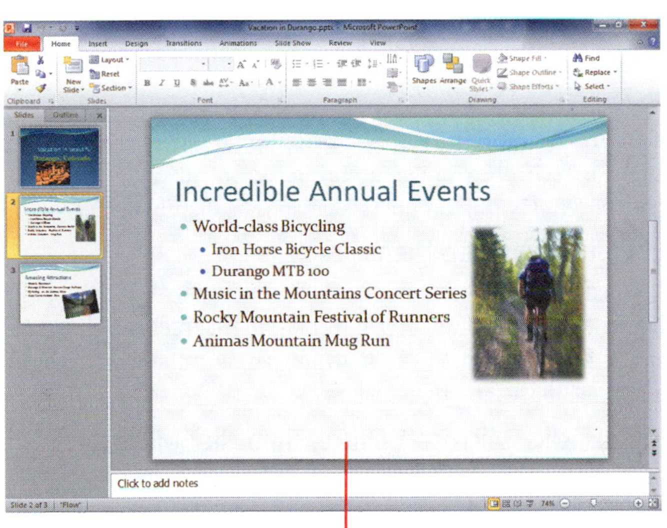

Tourism presentation created in PowerPoint

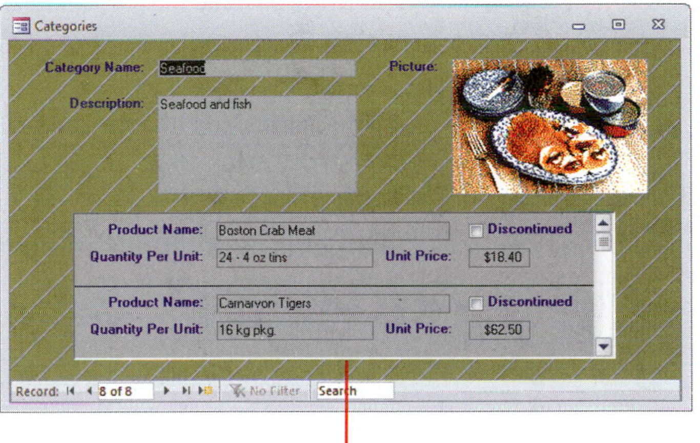

Store inventory form created in Access

Deciding which program to use

Every Office program includes tools that go far beyond what you might expect. For example, although Excel is primarily designed for making calculations, you can use it to create a database. So when you're planning a project, how do you decide which Office program to use? The general rule of thumb is to use the program best suited for your intended task, and make use of supporting tools in the program if you need them. Word is best for creating text-based documents, Excel is best for making mathematical calculations, PowerPoint is best for preparing presentations, and Access is best for managing quantitative data. Although the capabilities of Office are so vast that you *could* create an inventory in Excel or a budget in Word, you'll find greater flexibility and efficiency by using the program designed for the task. And remember, you can always create a file in one program, and then insert it in a document in another program when you need to, such as including sales projections (Excel) in a memo (Word).

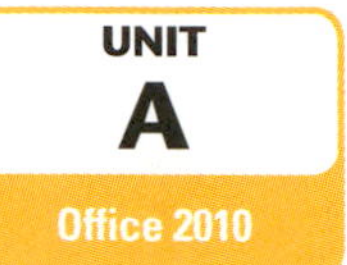

Starting and Exiting an Office Program

The first step in using an Office program is to open, or **launch**, it on your computer. The easiest ways to launch a program are to click the Start button on the Windows taskbar or to double-click an icon on your desktop. You can have multiple programs open on your computer simultaneously, and you can move between open programs by clicking the desired program or document button on the taskbar or by using the [Alt][Tab] keyboard shortcut combination. When working, you'll often want to open multiple programs in Office and switch among them as you work. Begin by launching a few Office programs now.

STEPS

QUICK TIP
You can also launch a program by double-clicking a desktop icon or clicking the program name on the Start menu.

1. **Click the Start button on the taskbar**
   The Start menu opens. If the taskbar is hidden, you can display it by pointing to the bottom of the screen. Depending on your taskbar property settings, the taskbar may be displayed at all times, or only when you point to that area of the screen. For more information, or to change your taskbar properties, consult your instructor or technical support person.
2. **Click All Programs, scroll down if necessary in the All Programs menu, click Microsoft Office as shown in Figure A-2, then click Microsoft Word 2010**
   Word 2010 starts, and the program window opens on your screen.

QUICK TIP
It is not necessary to close one program before opening another.

3. **Click on the taskbar, click All Programs, click Microsoft Office, then click Microsoft Excel 2010**
   Excel 2010 starts, and the program window opens, as shown in Figure A-3. Word is no longer visible, but it remains open. The taskbar displays a button for each open program and document. Because this Excel document is **active**, or in front and available, the Excel button on the taskbar appears slightly lighter.
4. **Point to the Word program button on the taskbar, then click**
   The Word program window is now in front. When the Aero feature is turned on in Windows 7, pointing to a program button on the taskbar displays a thumbnail version of each open window in that program above the program button. Clicking a program button on the taskbar activates that program and the most recently active document. Clicking a thumbnail of a document activates that document.

QUICK TIP
As you work in Windows, your computer adapts to your activities. You may notice that after clicking the Start button, the name of the program you want to open appears in the Start menu above All Programs; if so, you can click it to start the program.

5. **Click on the taskbar, click All Programs, click Microsoft Office, then click Microsoft PowerPoint 2010**
   PowerPoint 2010 starts and becomes the active program.
6. **Click the Excel program button on the taskbar**
   Excel is now the active program.

TROUBLE
If you don't have Access installed on your computer, proceed to the next lesson.

7. **Click on the taskbar, click All Programs, click Microsoft Office, then click Microsoft Access 2010**
   Access 2010 starts and becomes the active program. Now all four Office programs are open at the same time.
8. **Click Exit on the navigation bar in the Access program window, as shown in Figure A-4**
   Access closes, leaving Excel active and Word and PowerPoint open.

Using shortcut keys to move between Office programs

As an alternative to the Windows taskbar, you can use a keyboard shortcut to move among open Office programs. The [Alt][Tab] keyboard combination lets you either switch quickly to the next open program or file or choose one from a gallery. To switch immediately to the next open program or file, press [Alt][Tab]. To choose from all open programs and files, press and hold [Alt], then press and release [Tab] without releasing [Alt]. A gallery opens on screen, displaying the filename and a thumbnail image of each open program and file, as well as of the desktop. Each time you press [Tab] while holding [Alt], the selection cycles to the next open file or location. Release [Alt] when the program, file, or location you want to activate is selected.

FIGURE A-2: Start menu

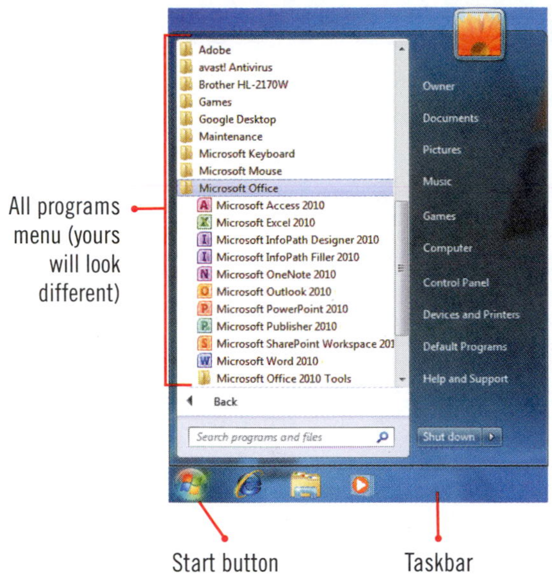

All programs menu (yours will look different)

Start button

Taskbar

FIGURE A-3: Excel program window and Windows taskbar

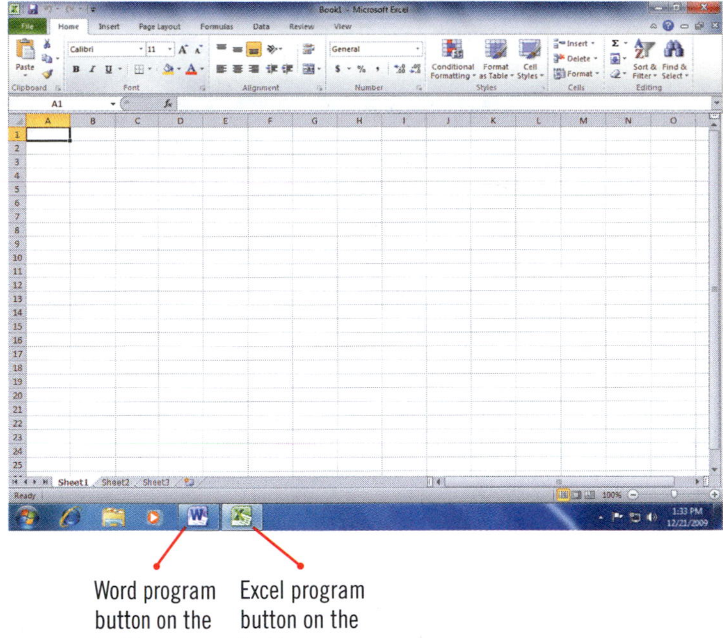

Word program button on the taskbar

Excel program button on the taskbar

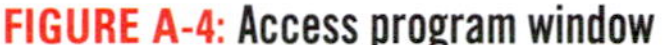

FIGURE A-4: Access program window

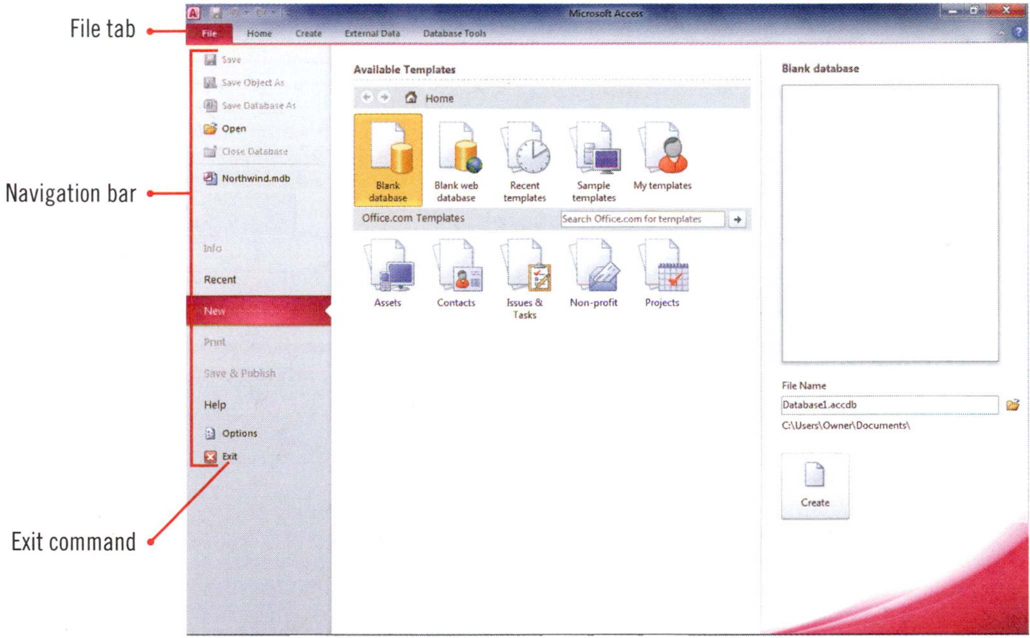

File tab

Navigation bar

Exit command

Windows Live and Microsoft Office Web Apps

All Office programs include the capability to incorporate feedback—called online collaboration—across the Internet or a company network. Using **cloud computing** (work done in a virtual environment), you can take advantage of Web programs called Microsoft Office Web Apps, which are simplified versions of the programs found in the Microsoft Office 2010 suite. Because these programs are online, they take up no computer disk space and are accessed using Windows Live SkyDrive, a free service from Microsoft. Using Windows Live SkyDrive, you and your colleagues can create and store documents in a "cloud" and make the documents available to whomever you grant access. To use Windows Live SkyDrive, you need a free Windows Live ID, which you obtain at the Windows Live Web site. You can find more information in the "Working with Windows Live and Office Web Apps" appendix.

Viewing the Office 2010 User Interface

One of the benefits of using Office is that the programs have much in common, making them easy to learn and making it simple to move from one to another. Individual Office programs have always shared many features, but the innovations in the Office 2010 user interface mean even greater similarity among them all. That means you can also use your knowledge of one program to get up to speed in another. A **user interface** is a collective term for all the ways you interact with a software program. The user interface in Office 2010 provides intuitive ways to choose commands, work with files, and navigate in the program window. Familiarize yourself with some of the common interface elements in Office by examining the PowerPoint program window.

STEPS

QUICK TIP
In addition to the standard tabs on the Ribbon, **contextual tabs** open when needed to complete a specific task; they appear in an accent color and close when no longer needed. To minimize the display of the buttons and commands on tabs, click the Minimize the Ribbon button on the right end of the Ribbon.

1. **Click the PowerPoint program button on the taskbar**
   PowerPoint becomes the active program. Refer to Figure A-5 to identify common elements of the Office user interface. The **document window** occupies most of the screen. In PowerPoint, a blank slide appears in the document window, so you can build your slide show. At the top of every Office program window is a **title bar** that displays the document name and program name. Below the title bar is the **Ribbon**, which displays commands you're likely to need for the current task. Commands are organized onto **tabs**. The tab names appear at the top of the Ribbon, and the active tab appears in front. The Ribbon in every Office program includes tabs specific to the program, but all Office programs include a File tab and Home tab on the left end of the Ribbon.

2. **Click the File tab**
   The File tab opens, displaying **Backstage view**. The navigation bar on the left side of Backstage view contains commands to perform actions common to most Office programs, such as opening a file, saving a file, and closing the current program. Just above the File tab is the **Quick Access toolbar**, which also includes buttons for common Office commands.

3. **Click the File tab again to close Backstage view and return to the document window, then click the Design tab on the Ribbon**
   To display a different tab, you click the tab on the Ribbon. Each tab contains related commands arranged into **groups** to make features easy to find. On the Design tab, the Themes group displays available design themes in a **gallery**, or visual collection of choices you can browse. Many groups contain a **dialog box launcher**, an icon you can click to open a dialog box or task pane from which to choose related commands.

QUICK TIP
Live Preview is available in many galleries and menus throughout Office.

4. **Move the mouse pointer over the Angles theme in the Themes group as shown in Figure A-6, but do not click the mouse button**
   The Angles theme is temporarily applied to the slide in the document window. However, because you did not click the theme, you did not permanently change the slide. With the **Live Preview** feature, you can point to a choice, see the results right in the document, and then decide if you want to make the change.

QUICK TIP
If you accidentally click a theme, click the Undo button on the Quick Access toolbar.

5. **Move away from the Ribbon and towards the slide**
   If you had clicked the Angles theme, it would be applied to this slide. Instead, the slide remains unchanged.

QUICK TIP
You can also use the Zoom button in the Zoom group on the View tab to enlarge or reduce a document's appearance.

6. **Point to the Zoom slider on the status bar, then drag to the right until the Zoom level reads 166%**
   The slide display is enlarged. Zoom tools are located on the status bar. You can drag the slider or click the Zoom In or Zoom Out buttons to zoom in or out on an area of interest. **Zooming in**, or choosing a higher percentage, makes a document appear bigger on screen, but less of it fits on the screen at once; **zooming out**, or choosing a lower percentage, lets you see more of the document but at a reduced size.

7. **Drag on the status bar to the left until the Zoom level reads 73%**

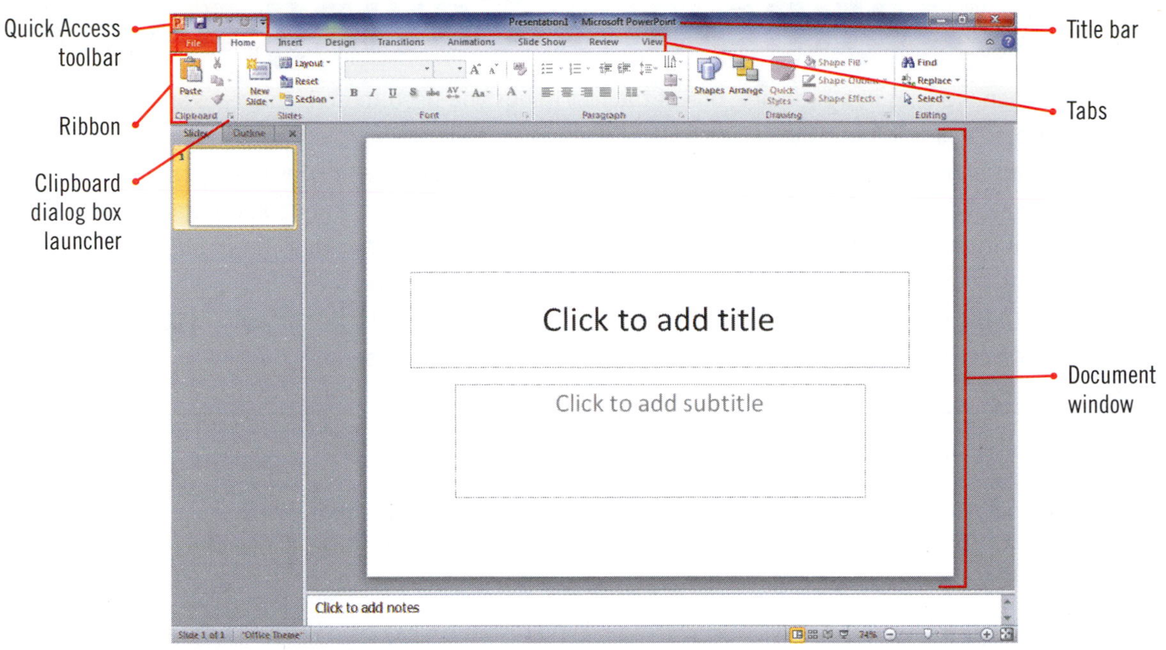

FIGURE A-5: PowerPoint program window

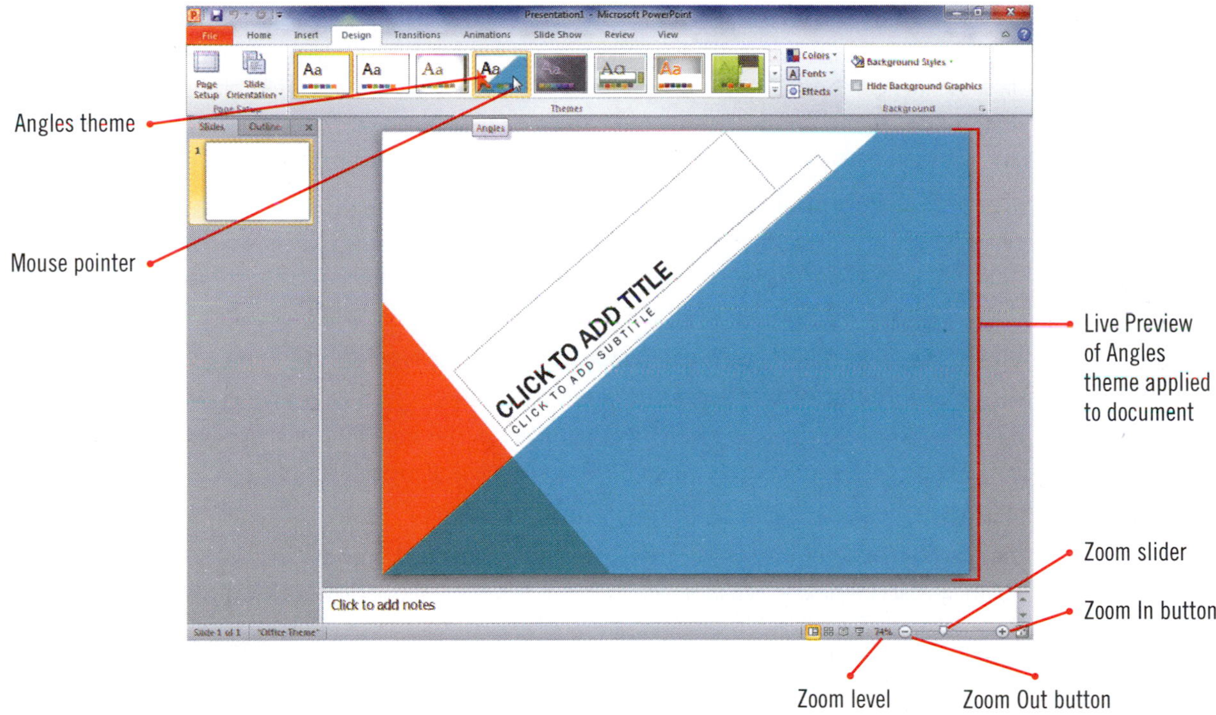

FIGURE A-6: Viewing a theme with Live Preview

Using Backstage view

Backstage view in each Microsoft Office program offers "one stop shopping" for many commonly performed tasks, such as opening and saving a file, printing and previewing a document, defining document properties, sharing information, and exiting a program. Backstage view opens when you click the File tab in any Office program, and while features such as the Ribbon, Mini toolbar, and Live Preview all help you work *in* your documents, the File tab and Backstage view help you work *with* your documents.

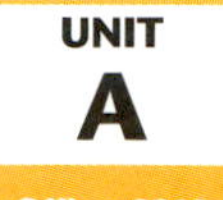

Creating and Saving a File

When working in a program, one of the first things you need to do is to create and save a file. A **file** is a stored collection of data. Saving a file enables you to work on a project now, then put it away and work on it again later. In some Office programs, including Word, Excel, and PowerPoint, a new file is automatically created when you start the program, so all you have to do is enter some data and save it. In Access, you must expressly create a file before you enter any data. You should give your files meaningful names and save them in an appropriate location so that they're easy to find. Use Word to familiarize yourself with the process of creating and saving a document. First you'll type some notes about a possible location for a corporate meeting, then you'll save the information for later use.

STEPS

1. **Click the Word program button on the taskbar**
2. **Type Locations for Corporate Meeting, then press [Enter] twice**

   The text appears in the document window, and the **insertion point** blinks on a new blank line. The insertion point indicates where the next typed text will appear.
3. **Type Las Vegas, NV, press [Enter], type Orlando, FL, press [Enter], type Boston, MA, press [Enter] twice, then type your name**

   Compare your document to Figure A-7.
4. **Click the Save button on the Quick Access toolbar**

   Because this is the first time you are saving this document, the Save As dialog box opens, as shown in Figure A-8. The Save As dialog box includes options for assigning a filename and storage location. Once you save a file for the first time, clicking saves any changes to the file *without* opening the Save As dialog box, because no additional information is needed. The Address bar in the Save As dialog box displays the default location for saving the file, but you can change it to any location. The File name field contains a suggested name for the document based on text in the file, but you can enter a different name.
5. **Type OF A-Potential Corporate Meeting Locations**

   The text you type replaces the highlighted text. (The "OF A-" in the filename indicates that the file is created in Office Unit A. You will see similar designations throughout this book when files are named. For example, a file named in Excel Unit B would begin with "EX B-" .)
6. **In the Save As dialog box, use the Address bar or Navigation Pane to navigate to the drive and folder where you store your Data Files**

   Many students store files on a flash drive, but you can also store files on your computer, a network drive, or any storage device indicated by your instructor or technical support person.
7. **Click Save**

   The Save As dialog box closes, the new file is saved to the location you specified, then the name of the document appears in the title bar, as shown in Figure A-9. (You may or may not see the file extension ".docx" after the filename.) See Table A-1 for a description of the different types of files you create in Office, and the file extensions associated with each.

QUICK TIP
A filename can be up to 255 characters, including a file extension, and can include upper- or lowercase characters and spaces, but not ?, ", /, \, <, >, *, |, or :.

QUICK TIP
Saving a file to the Desktop creates a desktop icon that you can double-click to both launch a program and open a document.

QUICK TIP
To create a new blank file when a file is open, click the File tab, click New on the navigation bar, then click Create near the bottom of the document preview pane.

TABLE A-1: Common filenames and default file extensions

file created in	is called a	and has the default extension
Word	document	.docx
Excel	workbook	.xlsx
PowerPoint	presentation	.pptx
Access	database	.accdb

FIGURE A-7: Document created in Word

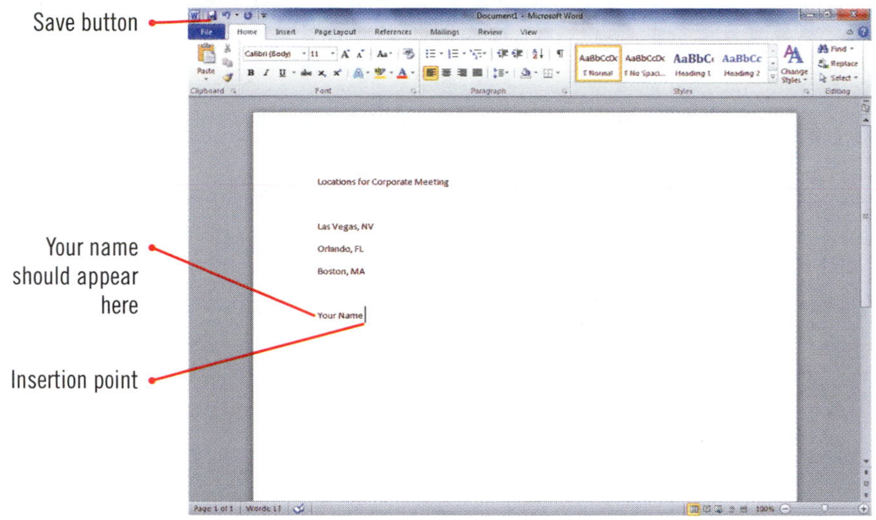

FIGURE A-8: Save As dialog box

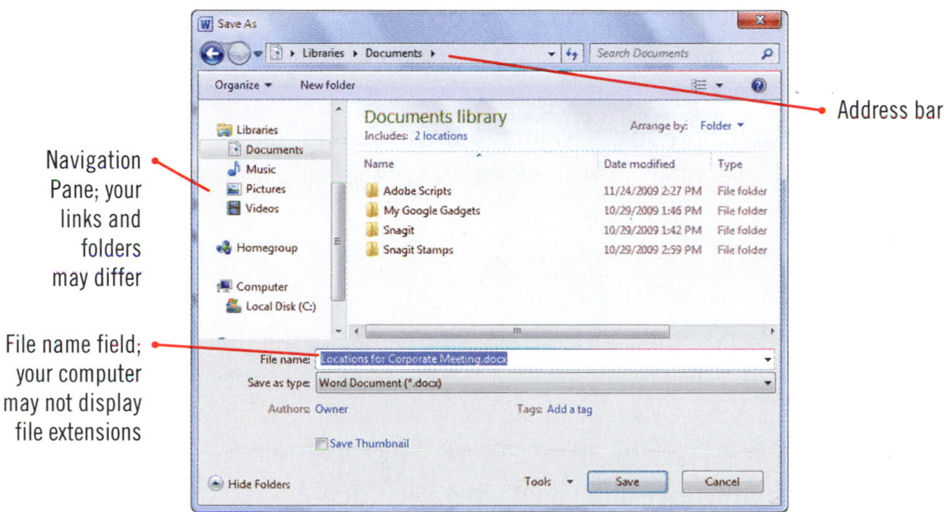

FIGURE A-9: Saved and named Word document

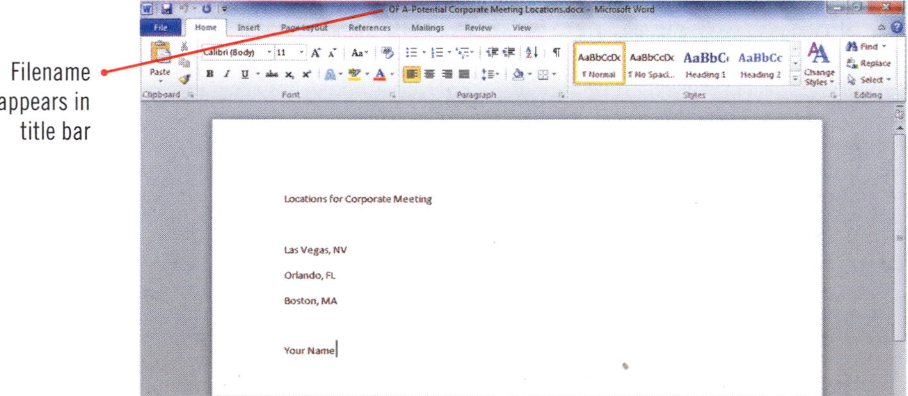

Using the Office Clipboard

You can use the Office Clipboard to cut and copy items from one Office program and paste them into others. The Office Clipboard can store a maximum of 24 items. To access it, open the Office Clipboard task pane by clicking the dialog box launcher in the Clipboard group on the Home tab. Each time you copy a selection, it is saved in the Office Clipboard. Each entry in the Office Clipboard includes an icon that tells you the program it was created in. To paste an entry, click in the document where you want it to appear, then click the item in the Office Clipboard. To delete an item from the Office Clipboard, right-click the item, then click Delete.

Opening a File and Saving It with a New Name

In many cases as you work in Office, you start with a blank document, but often you need to use an existing file. It might be a file you or a coworker created earlier as a work in progress, or it could be a complete document that you want to use as the basis for another. For example, you might want to create a budget for this year using the budget you created last year; you could type in all the categories and information from scratch, or you could open last year's budget, save it with a new name, and just make changes to update it for the current year. By opening the existing file and saving it with the Save As command, you create a duplicate that you can modify to your heart's content, while the original file remains intact. Use Excel to open an existing workbook file, and save it with a new name so the original remains unchanged.

STEPS

QUICK TIP
Click Recent on the navigation bar to display a list of recent workbooks; click a file in the list to open it.

1. **Click the Excel program button on the taskbar, click the File tab, then click Open on the navigation bar**
   The Open dialog box opens, where you can navigate to any drive or folder accessible to your computer to locate a file.
2. **In the Open dialog box, navigate to the drive and folder where you store your Data Files**
   The files available in the current folder are listed, as shown in Figure A-10. This folder contains one file.

TROUBLE
Click Enable Editing on the Protected View bar near the top of your document window if prompted.

3. **Click OFFICE A-1.xlsx, then click Open**
   The dialog box closes, and the file opens in Excel. An Excel file is an electronic spreadsheet, so it looks different from a Word document or a PowerPoint slide.
4. **Click the File tab, then click Save As on the navigation bar**
   The Save As dialog box opens, and the current filename is highlighted in the File name text box. Using the Save As command enables you to create a copy of the current, existing file with a new name. This action preserves the original file and creates a new file that you can modify.

QUICK TIP
The Save As command works identically in all Office programs, except Access; in Access, this command lets you save a copy of the current database object, such as a table or form, with a new name, but not a copy of the entire database.

5. **Navigate to the drive and folder where you store your Data Files if necessary, type OF A-Budget for Corporate Meeting in the File name text box, as shown in Figure A-11, then click Save**
   A copy of the existing workbook is created with the new name. The original file, Office A-1.xlsx, closes automatically.
6. **Click cell A19, type your name, then press [Enter], as shown in Figure A-12**
   In Excel, you enter data in cells, which are formed by the intersection of a row and a column. Cell A19 is at the intersection of column A and row 19. When you press [Enter], the cell pointer moves to cell A20.
7. **Click the Save button on the Quick Access toolbar**
   Your name appears in the workbook, and your changes to the file are saved.

Working in Compatibility Mode

Not everyone upgrades to the newest version of Office. As a general rule, new software versions are **backward compatible**, meaning that documents saved by an older version can be read by newer software. To open documents created in older Office versions, Office 2010 includes a feature called Compatibility Mode. When you use Office 2010 to open a file created in an earlier version of Office, "Compatibility Mode" appears in the title bar, letting you know the file was created in an earlier but usable version of the program. If you are working with someone who may not be using the newest version of the software, you can avoid possible incompatibility problems by saving your file in another, earlier format. To do this in an Office program, click the File tab, click Save As on the navigation bar, click the Save as type list arrow in the Save As dialog box, then click an option on the list. For example, if you're working in Excel, click Excel 97-2003 Workbook format in the Save as type list to save an Excel file so that it can be opened in Excel 97 or Excel 2003.

FIGURE A-10: Open dialog box

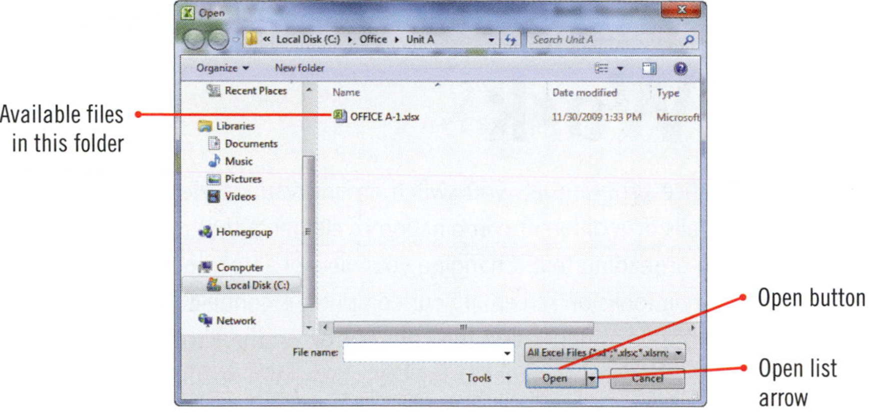

FIGURE A-11: Save As dialog box

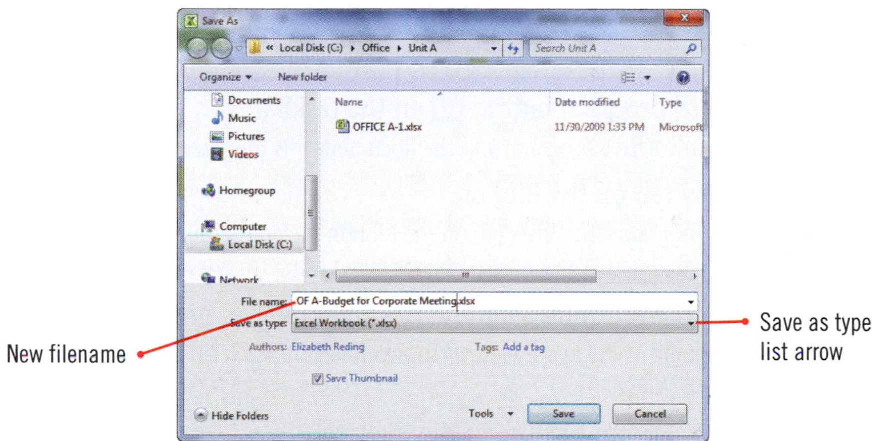

FIGURE A-12: Your name added to the workbook

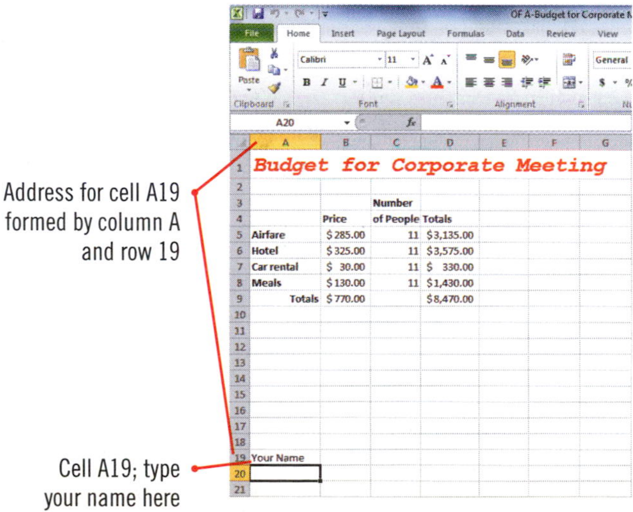

Exploring File Open options

You might have noticed that the Open button on the Open dialog box includes an arrow. In a dialog box, if a button includes an arrow you can click the button to invoke the command, or you can click the arrow to choose from a list of related commands. The Open list arrow includes several related commands, including Open Read-Only and Open as Copy. Clicking Open Read-Only opens a file that you can only save with a new name; you cannot save changes to the original file. Clicking Open as Copy creates a copy of the file already saved and named with the word "Copy" in the title. Like the Save As command, these commands provide additional ways to use copies of existing files while ensuring that original files do not get changed by mistake.

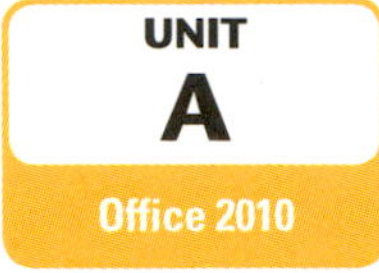

Viewing and Printing Your Work

Each Microsoft Office program lets you switch among various **views** of the document window to show more or fewer details or a different combination of elements that make it easier to complete certain tasks, such as formatting or reading text. Changing your view of a document does not affect the file in any way, it affects only the way it looks on screen. If your computer is connected to a printer or a print server, you can easily print any Office document using the Print button on the Print tab in Backstage view. Printing can be as simple as **previewing** the document to see exactly what a document will look like when it is printed and then clicking the Print button. Or, you can customize the print job by printing only selected pages or making other choices. Experiment with changing your view of a Word document, and then preview and print your work.

STEPS

1. **Click the Word program button on the taskbar**
   Word becomes the active program, and the document fills the screen.
2. **Click the View tab on the Ribbon**
   In most Office programs, the View tab on the Ribbon includes groups and commands for changing your view of the current document. You can also change views using the View buttons on the status bar.
3. **Click the Web Layout button in the Document Views group on the View tab**
   The view changes to Web Layout view, as shown in Figure A-13. This view shows how the document will look if you save it as a Web page.
4. **Click the Print Layout button on the View tab**
   You return to Print Layout view, the default view in Word.
5. **Click the File tab, then click Print on the navigation bar**
   The Print tab opens in Backstage view. The preview pane on the right side of the window automatically displays a preview of how your document will look when printed, showing the entire page on screen at once. Compare your screen to Figure A-14. Options in the Settings section enable you to change settings such as margins, orientation, and paper size before printing. To change a setting, click it, and then click the new setting you want. For instance, to change from Letter paper size to Legal, click Letter in the Settings section, then click Legal on the menu that opens. The document preview is updated as you change the settings. You also can use the Settings section to change which pages to print and even the number of pages you print on each sheet of printed paper. If you have multiple printers from which to choose, you can change from one installed printer to another by clicking the current printer in the Printer section, then clicking the name of the installed printer you want to use. The Print section contains the Print button and also enables you to select the number of copies of the document to print.
6. **Click the Print button in the Print section**
   A copy of the document prints, and Backstage view closes.

QUICK TIP

You can add the Quick Print button to the Quick Access toolbar by clicking the Customize Quick Access Toolbar button, then clicking Quick Print. The Quick Print button prints one copy of your document using the default settings.

Customizing the Quick Access toolbar

You can customize the Quick Access toolbar to display your favorite commands. To do so, click the Customize Quick Access Toolbar button in the title bar, then click the command you want to add. If you don't see the command in the list, click More Commands to open the Quick Access Toolbar tab of the current program's Options dialog box. In the Options dialog box, use the Choose commands from list to choose a category, click the desired command in the list on the left, click Add to add it to the Quick Access toolbar, then click OK. To remove a button from the toolbar, click the name in the list on the right in the Options dialog box, then click Remove. To add a command to the Quick Access toolbar on the fly, simply right-click the button on the Ribbon, then click Add to Quick Access Toolbar on the shortcut menu. To move the Quick Access toolbar below the Ribbon, click the Customize Quick Access Toolbar button, and then click Show Below the Ribbon.

FIGURE A-13: Web Layout view

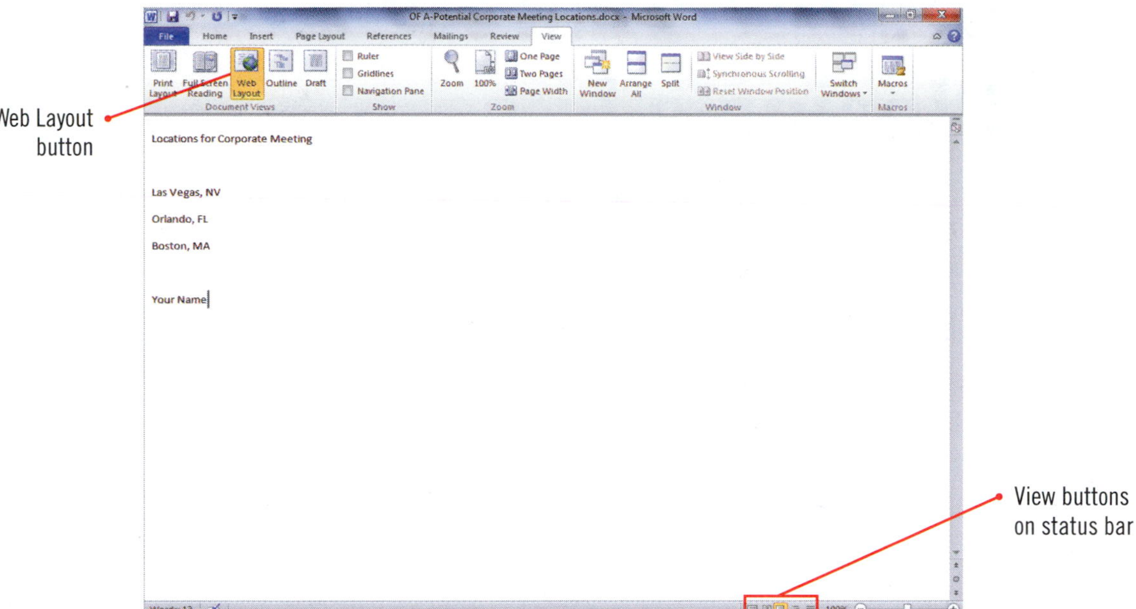

FIGURE A-14: Print tab in Backstage view

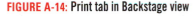

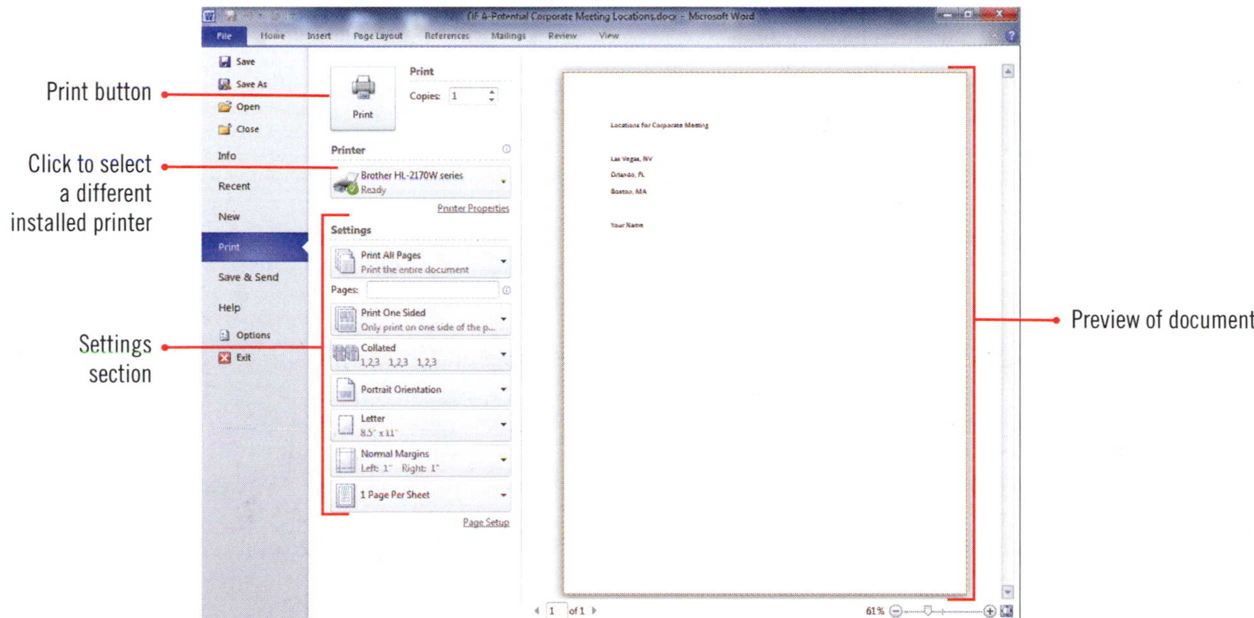

Creating a screen capture

A **screen capture** is a digital image of your screen, as if you took a picture of it with a camera. For instance, you might want to take a screen capture if an error message occurs and you want Technical Support to see exactly what's on the screen. You can create a screen capture using features found in Windows 7 or Office 2010. Windows 7 comes with the Snipping Tool, a separate program designed to capture whole screens or portions of screens. To open the Snipping Tool, click it on the Start menu or click All Programs, click Accessories, then click Snipping Tool. After opening the Snipping Tool, drag the pointer on the screen to select the area of the screen you want to capture. When you release the mouse button, the screen capture opens in the Snipping Tool window, and you can save, copy, or send it in an e-mail. In Word, Excel, and PowerPoint 2010, you can capture screens or portions of screens and insert them in the current document using the Screenshot button on the Insert tab. And finally, you can create a screen capture by pressing [PrtScn]. (Keyboards differ, but you may find the [PrtScn] button in or near your keyboard's function keys.) Pressing this key places a digital image of your screen in the Windows temporary storage area known as the **Clipboard**. Open the document where you want the screen capture to appear, click the Home tab on the Ribbon (if necessary), then click the Paste button on the Home tab. The screen capture is pasted into the document.

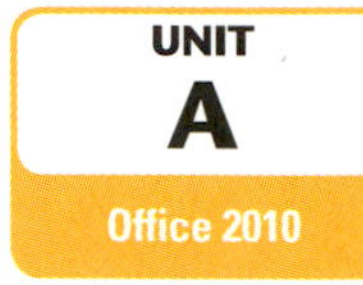
UNIT A Office 2010

Getting Help and Closing a File

You can get comprehensive help at any time by pressing [F1] in an Office program. You can also get help in the form of a ScreenTip by pointing to almost any icon in the program window. When you're finished working in an Office document, you have a few choices regarding ending your work session. You can close a file or exit a program by using the File tab or by clicking a button on the title bar. Closing a file leaves a program running, while exiting a program closes all the open files in that program as well as the program itself. In all cases, Office reminds you if you try to close a file or exit a program and your document contains unsaved changes. Explore the Help system in Microsoft Office, and then close your documents and exit any open programs.

STEPS

TROUBLE

If the Table of Contents pane doesn't appear on the left in the Help window, click the Show Table of Contents button on the Help toolbar to show it.

QUICK TIP

You can also open the Help window by clicking the Microsoft Office Word Help button to the right of the tabs on the Ribbon.

QUICK TIP

You can print the entire current topic by clicking the Print button on the Help toolbar, then clicking Print in the Print dialog box.

1. **Point to the Zoom button on the View tab of the Ribbon**
   A ScreenTip appears that describes how the Zoom button works and explains where to find other zoom controls.
2. **Press [F1]**
   The Word Help window opens, as shown in Figure A-15, displaying the home page for help in Word on the right and the Table of Contents pane on the left. In both panes of the Help window, each entry is a hyperlink you can click to open a list of related topics. The Help window also includes a toolbar of useful Help commands and a Search field. The connection status at the bottom of the Help window indicates that the connection to Office.com is active. Office.com supplements the help content available on your computer with a wide variety of up-to-date topics, templates, and training. If you are not connected to the Internet, the Help window displays only the help content available on your computer.
3. **Click the Creating documents link in the Table of Contents pane**
   The icon next to Creating documents changes, and a list of subtopics expands beneath the topic.
4. **Click the Create a document link in the subtopics list in the Table of Contents pane**
   The topic opens in the right pane of the Help window, as shown in Figure A-16.
5. **Click Delete a document under "What do you want to do?" in the right pane**
   The link leads to information about deleting a document.
6. **Click the Accessibility link in the Table of Contents pane, click the Accessibility features in Word link, read the information in the right pane, then click the Help window Close button**
7. **Click the File tab, then click Close on the navigation bar; if a dialog box opens asking whether you want to save your changes, click Save**
   The Potential Corporate Meeting Locations document closes, leaving the Word program open.
8. **Click the File tab, then click Exit on the navigation bar**
   Word closes, and the Excel program window is active.
9. **Click the File tab, click Exit on the navigation bar to exit Excel, click the PowerPoint program button on the taskbar if necessary, click the File tab, then click Exit on the navigation bar to exit PowerPoint**
   Excel and PowerPoint both close.

FIGURE A-15: Word Help window

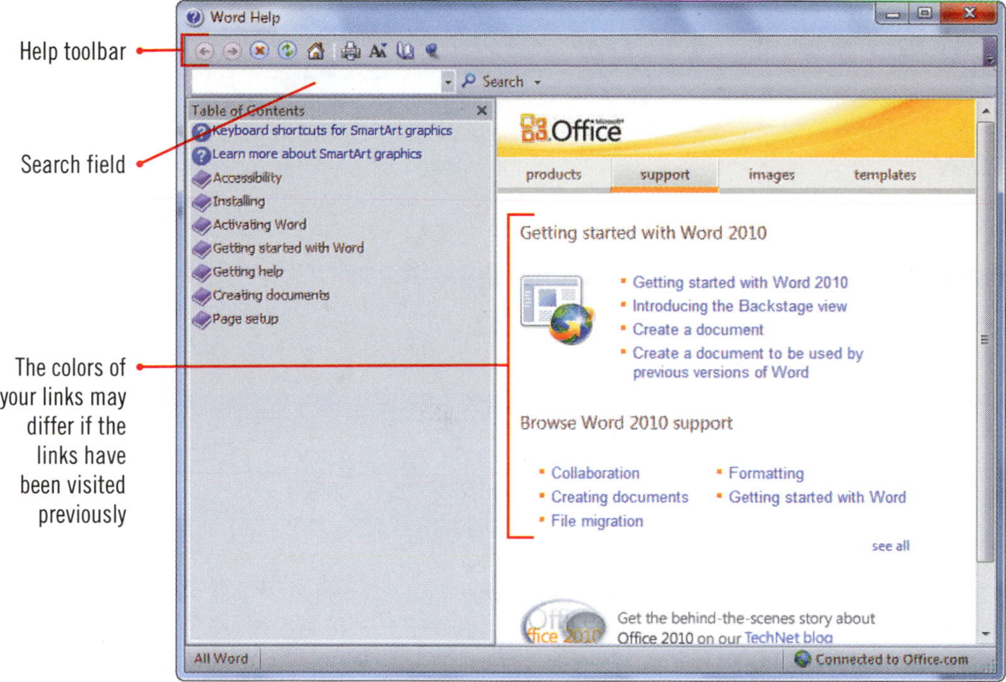

FIGURE A-16: Create a document Help topic

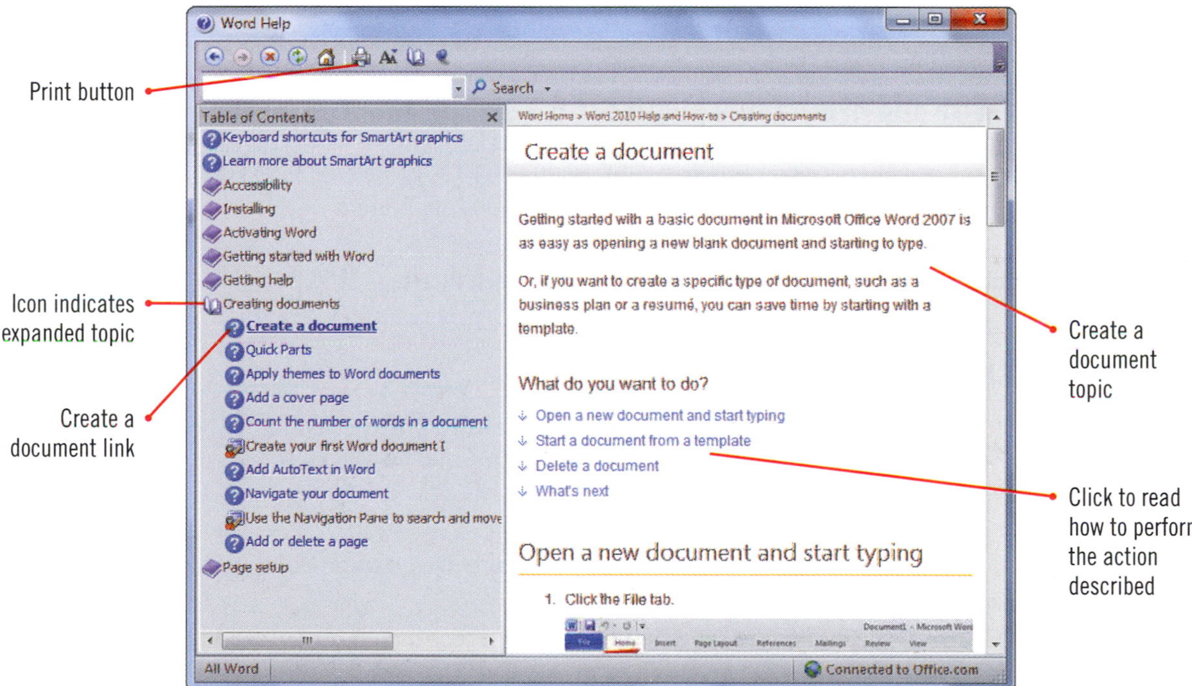

Recovering a document

Each Office program has a built-in recovery feature that allows you to open and save files that were open at the time of an interruption such as a power failure. When you restart the program(s) after an interruption, the Document Recovery task pane opens on the left side of your screen displaying both original and recovered versions of the files that were open. If you're not sure which file to open (original or recovered), it's usually better to open the recovered file because it will contain the latest information. You can, however, open and review all versions of the file that were recovered and save the best one. Each file listed in the Document Recovery task pane displays a list arrow with options that allow you to open the file, save it as is, delete it, or show repairs made to it during recovery.

Practice

For current SAM information, including versions and content details, visit SAM Central (http://www.cengage.com/samcentral). If you have a SAM user profile, you may have access to hands-on instruction, practice, and assessment of the skills covered in this unit. Since various versions of SAM are supported throughout the life of this text, check with your instructor for the correct instructions and URL/Web site for accessing assignments.

Concepts Review

Label the elements of the program window shown in Figure A-17.

FIGURE A-17

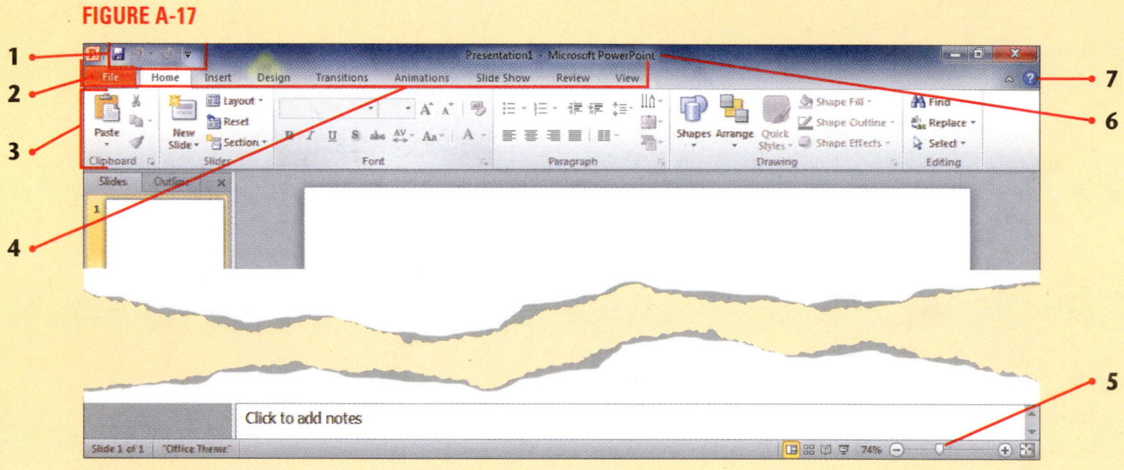

Match each project with the program for which it is best suited.

8. Microsoft Access	**a.** Corporate convention budget with expense projections
9. Microsoft Excel	**b.** Business cover letter for a job application
10. Microsoft Word	**c.** Department store inventory
11. Microsoft PowerPoint	**d.** Presentation for city council meeting

Independent Challenge 1

You just accepted an administrative position with a local independently owned produce vendor that has recently invested in computers and is now considering purchasing Microsoft Office for the company. You are asked to propose ways Office might help the business. You produce your document in Word.

- **a.** Start Word, then save the document as **OF A-Microsoft Office Document** in the drive and folder where you store your Data Files.
- **b.** Type **Microsoft Word**, press [Enter] twice, type **Microsoft Excel**, press [Enter] twice, type **Microsoft PowerPoint**, press [Enter] twice, type **Microsoft Access**, press [Enter] twice, then type your name.
- **c.** Click the line beneath each program name, type at least two tasks suited to that program (each separated by a comma), then press [Enter].

Advanced Challenge Exercise

- Press the [PrtScn] button to create a screen capture.
- Click after your name, press [Enter] to move to a blank line below your name, then click the Paste button in the Clipboard group on the Home tab.

- **d.** Save the document, then submit your work to your instructor as directed.
- **e.** Exit Word.

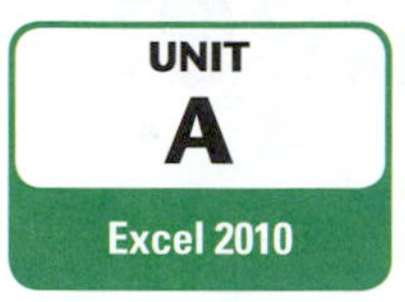

Getting Started with Excel 2010

Files You Will Need:

EX A-1.xlsx
EX A-2.xlsx
EX A-3.xlsx
EX A-4.xlsx
EX A-5.xlsx

In this unit, you will learn how spreadsheet software helps you analyze data and make business decisions, even if you aren't a math pro. You'll become familiar with the different elements of a spreadsheet and learn your way around the Excel program window. You will also work in an Excel worksheet and make simple calculations. You have been hired as an assistant at Quest Specialty Travel (QST), a company offering tours that immerse travelers in regional culture. You report to Grace Wong, the vice president of finance. As Grace's assistant, you create worksheets to analyze data from various divisions of the company, so you can help her make sound decisions on company expansion and investments.

OBJECTIVES

- Understand spreadsheet software
- Tour the Excel 2010 window
- Understand formulas
- Enter labels and values and use the Sum button
- Edit cell entries
- Enter and edit a simple formula
- Switch worksheet views
- Choose print options

Understanding Spreadsheet Software

Microsoft Excel is the electronic spreadsheet program within the Microsoft Office suite. An **electronic spreadsheet** is an application you use to perform numeric calculations and to analyze and present numeric data. One advantage of spreadsheet programs over pencil and paper is that your calculations are updated automatically, so you can change entries without having to manually recalculate. Table A-1 shows some of the common business tasks people accomplish using Excel. In Excel, the electronic spreadsheet you work in is called a **worksheet**, and it is contained in a file called a **workbook**, which has the file extension .xlsx. At Quest Specialty Travel, you use Excel extensively to track finances and manage corporate data.

DETAILS

When you use Excel, you have the ability to:

- **Enter data quickly and accurately**

  With Excel, you can enter information faster and more accurately than with pencil and paper. Figure A-1 shows a payroll worksheet created using pencil and paper. Figure A-2 shows the same worksheet created using Excel. Equations were added to calculate the hours and pay. You can use Excel to recreate this information for each week by copying the worksheet's structure and the information that doesn't change from week to week, then entering unique data and formulas for each week. You can also quickly create charts and other elements to help visualize how the payroll is distributed.

- **Recalculate data easily**

  Fixing typing errors or updating data is easy in Excel. In the payroll example, if you receive updated hours for an employee, you just enter the new hours and Excel recalculates the pay.

- **Perform what-if analysis**

  The ability to change data and quickly view the recalculated results gives you the power to make informed business decisions. For instance, if you're considering raising the hourly rate for an entry-level tour guide from $12.50 to $15.00, you can enter the new value in the worksheet and immediately see the impact on the overall payroll as well as on the individual employee. Any time you use a worksheet to ask the question "What if?" you are performing **what-if analysis**. Excel also includes a Scenario Manager where you can name and save different what-if versions of your worksheet.

- **Change the appearance of information**

  Excel provides powerful features for making information visually appealing and easier to understand. You can format text and numbers in different fonts, colors, and styles to make it stand out.

- **Create charts**

  Excel makes it easy to create charts based on worksheet information. Charts are updated automatically in Excel whenever data changes. The worksheet in Figure A-2 includes a 3-D pie chart.

- **Share information**

  It's easy for everyone at QST to collaborate in Excel using the company intranet, the Internet, or a network storage device. For example, you can complete the weekly payroll that your boss, Grace Wong, started creating. You can also take advantage of collaboration tools such as shared workbooks, so that multiple people can edit a workbook simultaneously.

- **Build on previous work**

  Instead of creating a new worksheet for every project, it's easy to modify an existing Excel worksheet. When you are ready to create next week's payroll, you can open the file for last week's payroll, save it with a new filename, and modify the information as necessary. You can also use predesigned, formatted files called **templates** to create new worksheets quickly. Excel comes with many templates that you can customize.

FIGURE A-1: Traditional paper worksheet

Quest Specialty Travel
Trip Advisor Division Payroll Calculator

Name	Hours	O/T Hrs	Hrly Rate	Reg Pay	O/T Pay	Gross Pay
Brueghel, Pieter	40	4	16–	640–	128–	768–
Cortona, Livia	35	0	10–	350–	0–	350–
Klimt, Gustave	40	2	12.50	500–	50–	550–
Le Pen, Jean-Marie	29	0	15–	435–	0–	435–
Martinez, Juan	37	0	12.50	462.50	0–	462.50
Mioshi, Keiko	39	0	20–	780–	0–	780–
Sherwood, Burton	40	0	16–	640–	0–	640–
Strano, Riccardo	40	8	15–	600–	240–	840–
Wadsworth, Alicia	40	5	12.50	[illegible]	[illegible]	625–
[illegible]	[illegible]	0	[illegible]			

FIGURE A-2: Excel worksheet

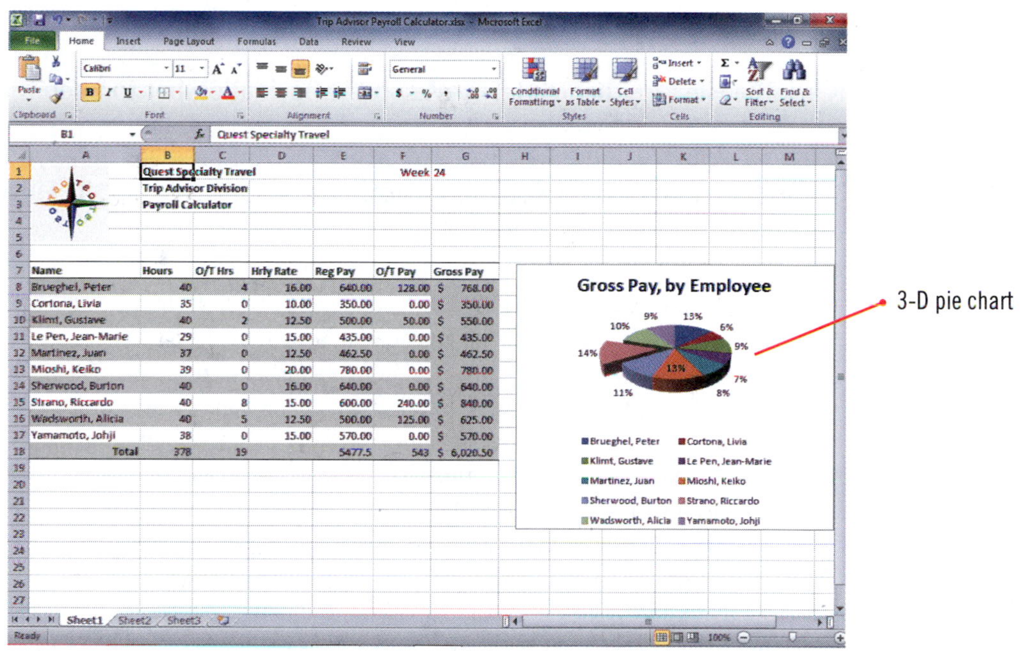

Name	Hours	O/T Hrs	Hrly Rate	Reg Pay	O/T Pay	Gross Pay
Brueghel, Peter	40	4	16.00	640.00	128.00	$ 768.00
Cortona, Livia	35	0	10.00	350.00	0.00	$ 350.00
Klimt, Gustave	40	2	12.50	500.00	50.00	$ 550.00
Le Pen, Jean-Marie	29	0	15.00	435.00	0.00	$ 435.00
Martinez, Juan	37	0	12.50	462.50	0.00	$ 462.50
Mioshi, Keiko	39	0	20.00	780.00	0.00	$ 780.00
Sherwood, Burton	40	0	16.00	640.00	0.00	$ 640.00
Strano, Riccardo	40	8	15.00	600.00	240.00	$ 840.00
Wadsworth, Alicia	40	5	12.50	500.00	125.00	$ 625.00
Yamamoto, Johji	38	0	15.00	570.00	0.00	$ 570.00
Total	378	19		5477.5	543	$ 6,020.50

TABLE A-1: Business tasks you can accomplish using Excel

you can use spreadsheets to:	by:
Perform calculations	Adding formulas and functions to worksheet data; for example, adding a list of sales results or calculating a car payment
Represent values graphically	Creating charts based on worksheet data; for example, creating a chart that displays expenses
Generate reports	Creating workbooks that combine information from multiple worksheets, such as summarized sales information from multiple stores
Organize data	Sorting data in ascending or descending order; for example, alphabetizing a list of products or customer names, or prioritizing orders by date
Analyze data	Creating data summaries and short lists using PivotTables or AutoFilters; for example, making a list of the top 10 customers based on spending habits
Create what-if data scenarios	Using variable values to investigate and sample different outcomes, such as changing the interest rate or payment schedule on a loan

Touring the Excel 2010 Window

To start Excel, Microsoft Windows must be running. Similar to starting any program in Office, you can use the Start button on the Windows taskbar, or you may have a shortcut on your desktop you prefer to use. If you need additional assistance, ask your instructor or technical support person. You decide to start Excel and familiarize yourself with the worksheet window.

STEPS

QUICK TIP

For more information on starting a program or opening and saving a file, see the unit "Getting Started with Microsoft Office 2010."

TROUBLE

If you don't see the extension .xlsx on the filenames in the Save As dialog box, don't worry; Windows can be set up to display or not to display the file extensions.

1. **Start Excel, click the File tab, then click Open on the navigation bar to open the Open dialog box**

2. **In the Open dialog box, navigate to the drive and folder where you store your Data Files, click EX A-1.xlsx, then click Open**

   The file opens in the Excel window.

3. **Click the File tab, then click Save As on the navigation bar to open the Save As dialog box**

4. **In the Save As dialog box, navigate to the drive and folder where you store your Data Files if necessary, type EX A-Trip Advisor Payroll Calculator in the File name text box, then click Save**

   Using Figure A-3 as a guide, identify the following items:
   - The **Name box** displays the active cell address. "A1" appears in the Name box.
   - The **formula bar** allows you to enter or edit data in the worksheet.
   - The worksheet window contains a grid of columns and rows. Columns are labeled alphabetically and rows are labeled numerically. The worksheet window can contain a total of 1,048,576 rows and 16,384 columns. The intersection of a column and a row is called a **cell**. Cells can contain text, numbers, formulas, or a combination of all three. Every cell has its own unique location or **cell address**, which is identified by the coordinates of the intersecting column and row.
   - The **cell pointer** is a dark rectangle that outlines the cell you are working in. This cell is called the **active cell**. In Figure A-3, the cell pointer outlines cell A1, so A1 is the active cell. The column and row headings for the active cell are highlighted, making it easier to locate.
   - **Sheet tabs** below the worksheet grid let you switch from sheet to sheet in a workbook. By default, a workbook file contains three worksheets—but you can use just one, or have as many as 255, in a workbook. The Insert Worksheet button to the right of Sheet 3 allows you to add worksheets to a workbook. **Sheet tab scrolling buttons** let you navigate to additional sheet tabs when available.
   - You can use the **scroll bars** to move around in a worksheet that is too large to fit on the screen at once.
   - The **status bar** is located at the bottom of the Excel window. It provides a brief description of the active command or task in progress. The **mode indicator** in the lower-left corner of the status bar provides additional information about certain tasks.

5. **Click cell A4**

   Cell A4 becomes the active cell. To activate a different cell, you can click the cell or press the arrow keys on your keyboard to move to it.

6. **Click cell B5, press and hold the mouse button, drag ✚ to cell B14, then release the mouse button**

   You selected a group of cells and they are highlighted, as shown in Figure A-4. A selection of two or more cells such as B5:B14 is called a **range**; you select a range when you want to perform an action on a group of cells at once, such as moving them or formatting them. When you select a range, the status bar displays the average, count (or number of items selected), and sum of the selected cells as a quick reference.

FIGURE A-3: Open workbook

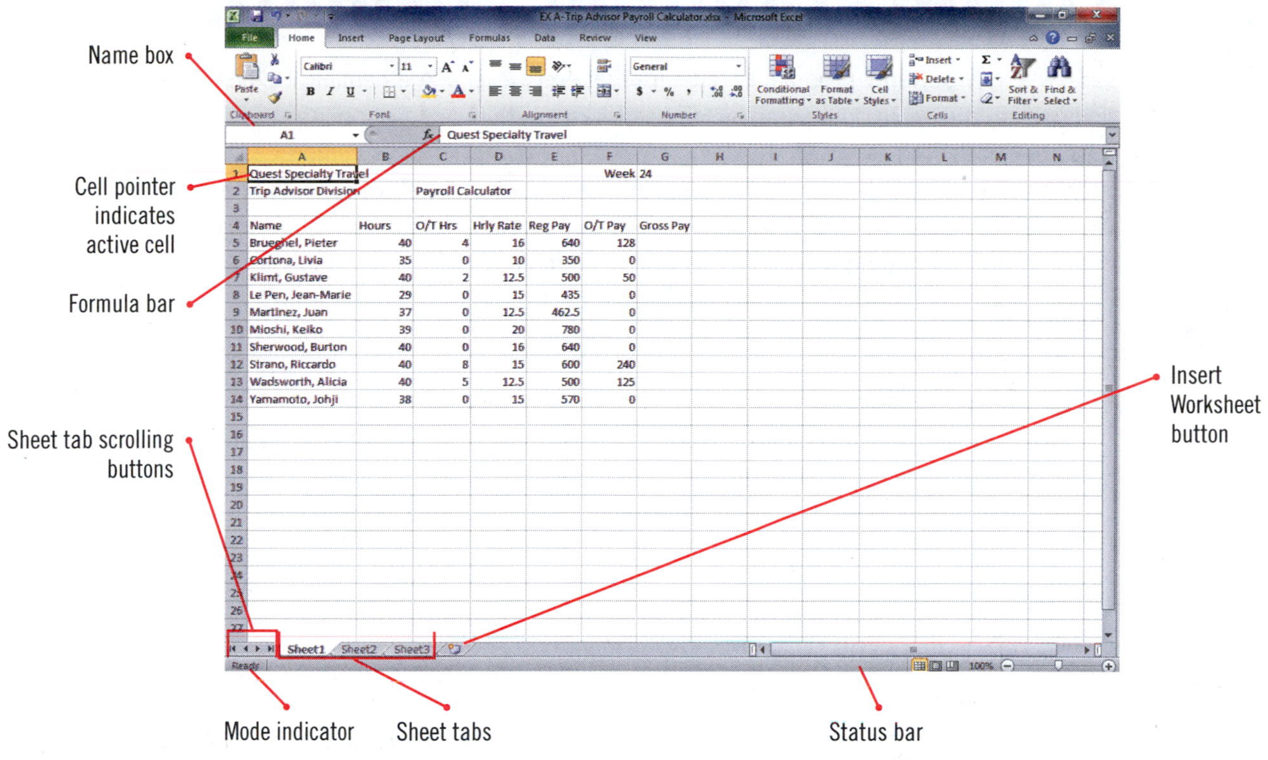

FIGURE A-4: Selected range

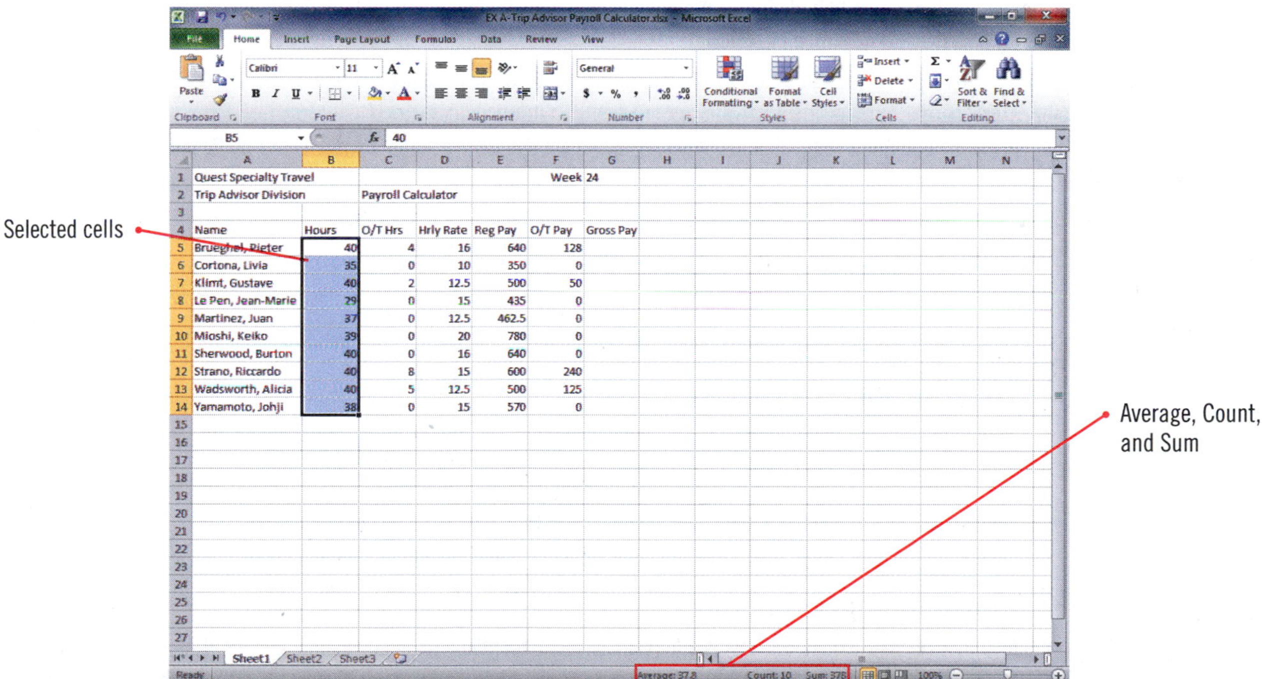

Windows Live and Microsoft Office Web Apps

All Office programs include the capability to incorporate feedback—called online collaboration—across the Internet or a company network. Using **cloud computing** (work done in a virtual environment), you can take advantage of Web programs called Microsoft Office Web Apps, which are simplified versions of the programs found in the Microsoft Office 2010 suite. Because these programs are online, they take up no computer disk space and are accessed using Windows Live SkyDrive, a free service from Microsoft. Using Windows Live SkyDrive, you and your colleagues can create and store documents in a "cloud" and make the documents available to whomever you grant access. To use Windows Live SkyDrive, you need a free Windows Live ID, which you obtain at the Windows Live Web site. You can find more information in the "Working with Windows Live and Office Web Apps" appendix.

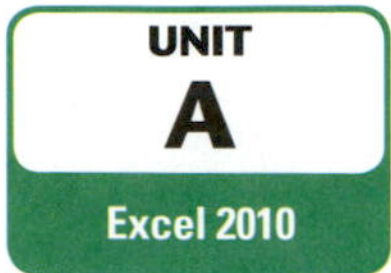

Understanding Formulas

Excel is a truly powerful program because users at every level of mathematical expertise can make calculations with accuracy. To do so, you use formulas. A **formula** is an equation in a worksheet. You use formulas to make calculations as simple as adding a column of numbers, or as complex as creating profit-and-loss projections for a global corporation. To tap into the power of Excel, you should understand how formulas work. Managers at QST use the Trip Advisor Payroll Calculator workbook to keep track of employee hours prior to submitting them to the Payroll Department. You'll be using this workbook regularly, so you need to understand the formulas it contains and how Excel calculates the results.

STEPS

1. **Click cell E5**

   The active cell contains a formula, which appears on the formula bar. All Excel formulas begin with the equal sign (=). If you want a cell to show the result of adding 4 plus 2, the formula in the cell would look like this: =4+2. If you want a cell to show the result of multiplying two values in your worksheet, such as the values in cells B5 and D5, the formula would look like this: =B5*D5, as shown in Figure A-5. While you're entering a formula in a cell, the cell references and arithmetic operators appear on the formula bar. See Table A-2 for a list of commonly used arithmetic operators. When you're finished entering the formula, you can either click the Enter button on the formula bar or press [Enter].

2. **Click cell F5**

   An example of a more complex formula is the calculation of overtime pay. At QST, overtime pay is calculated at twice the regular hourly rate times the number of overtime hours. The formula used to calculate overtime pay for the employee in row 5 is:

   O/T Hrs times (2 times Hrly Rate)

   In the worksheet cell, you would enter: =C5*(2*D5), as shown in Figure A-6. The use of parentheses creates groups within the formula and indicates which calculations to complete first—an important consideration in complex formulas. In this formula, first the hourly rate is multiplied by 2, because that calculation is within the parentheses. Next, that value is multiplied by the number of overtime hours. Because overtime is calculated at twice the hourly rate, managers are aware that they need to closely watch this expense.

DETAILS

In creating calculations in Excel, it is important to:

- **Know where the formulas should be**

  An Excel formula is created in the cell where the formula's results should appear. This means that the formula calculating Gross Pay for the employee in row 5 will be entered in cell G5.

- **Know exactly what cells and arithmetic operations are needed**

  Don't guess; make sure you know exactly what cells are involved before creating a formula.

- **Create formulas with care**

  Make sure you know exactly what you want a formula to accomplish before it is created. An inaccurate formula may have far-reaching effects if the formula or its results are referenced by other formulas.

- **Use cell references rather than values**

  The beauty of Excel is that whenever you change a value in a cell, any formula containing a reference to that cell is automatically updated. For this reason, it's important that you use cell references in formulas, rather than actual values, whenever possible.

- **Determine what calculations will be needed**

  Sometimes it's difficult to predict what data will be needed within a worksheet, but you should try to anticipate what statistical information may be required. For example, if there are columns of numbers, chances are good that both column and row totals should be present.

FIGURE A-5: Viewing a formula

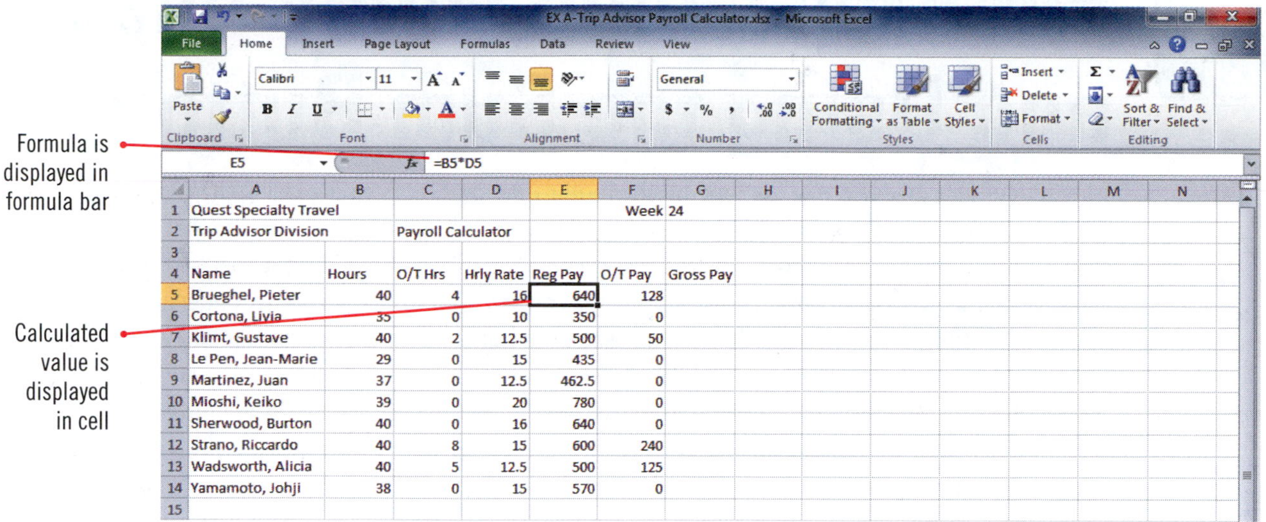

FIGURE A-6: Formula with multiple operators

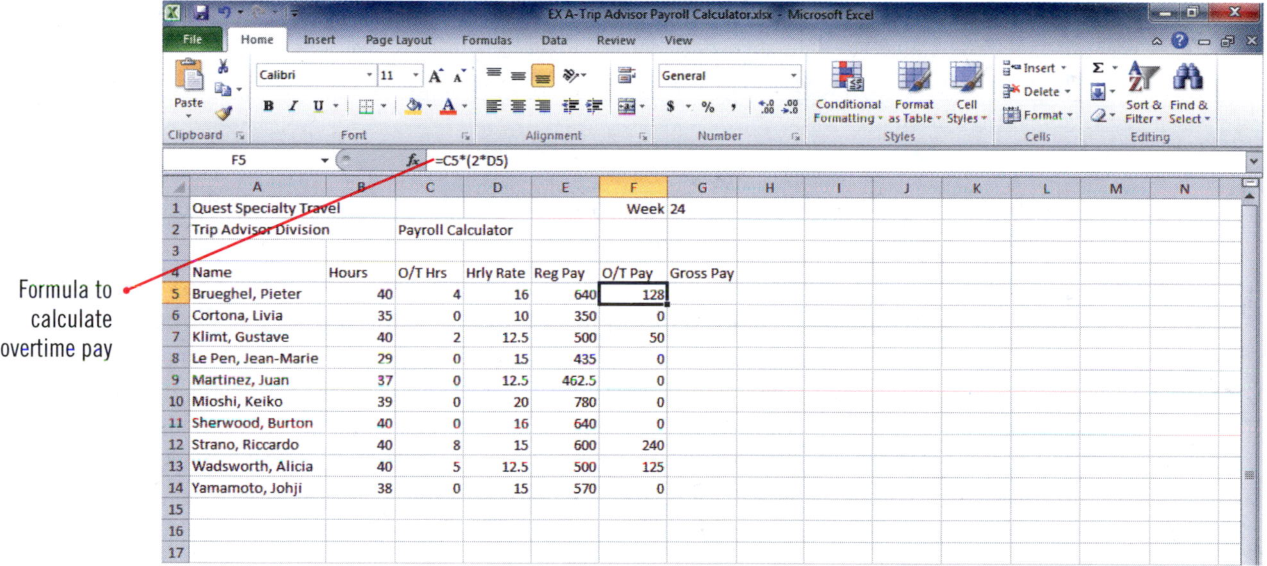

TABLE A-2: Excel arithmetic operators

operator	purpose	example
+	Addition	=A5+A7
-	Subtraction or negation	=A5-10
*	Multiplication	=A5*A7
/	Division	=A5/A7
%	Percent	=35%
^ (caret)	Exponent	=6^2 (same as 6^2)

Entering Labels and Values and Using the Sum Button

To enter content in a cell, you can type on the formula bar or directly in the cell itself. When entering content in a worksheet, you should start by entering all the labels first. **Labels** are entries that contain text and numerical information not used in calculations, such as "2011 Sales" or "Travel Expenses." Labels help you identify data in worksheet rows and columns, making your worksheet easier to understand. **Values** are numbers, formulas, and functions that can be used in calculations. To enter a calculation, you type an equal sign (=) plus the formula for the calculation; some examples of an Excel calculation are "=2+2" and "=C5+C6." Functions are Excel's built-in formulas; you learn more about them in the next unit. You want to enter some information in the Trip Advisor Payroll Calculator workbook, and use a very simple function to total a range of cells.

STEPS

1. **Click cell A15, then click in the formula bar**
   Notice that the **mode indicator** on the status bar now reads "Edit," indicating you are in Edit mode. You are in Edit mode any time you are entering or changing the contents of a cell.

QUICK TIP
If you change your mind and want to cancel an entry in the formula bar, click the Cancel button ✕ on the formula bar.

2. **Type Totals, then click the Enter button ✓ on the formula bar**
   Clicking the Enter button accepts the entry. The new text is left-aligned in the cell. Labels are left-aligned by default, and values are right-aligned by default. Excel recognizes an entry as a value if it is a number or it begins with one of these symbols: +, -, =, @, #, or $. When a cell contains both text and numbers, Excel recognizes it as a label.

3. **Click cell B15**
   You want this cell to total the hours worked by all the trip advisors. You might think you need to create a formula that looks like this: =B5+B6+B7+B8+B9+B10+B11+B12+B13+B14. However, there's an easier way to achieve this result.

4. **Click the Sum button Σ in the Editing group on the Home tab on the Ribbon**
   The SUM function is inserted in the cell, and a suggested range appears in parentheses, as shown in Figure A-7. A **function** is a built-in formula; it includes the **arguments** (the information necessary to calculate an answer) as well as cell references and other unique information. Clicking the Sum button sums the adjacent range (that is, the cells next to the active cell) above or to the left, though you can adjust the range if necessary by selecting a different range before accepting the cell entry. Using the SUM function is quicker than entering a formula, and using the range B5:B14 is more efficient than entering individual cell references.

QUICK TIP
You can create formulas in a cell even before you enter the values to be calculated; the results will be recalculated as soon as the data is entered.

5. **Click ✓ on the formula bar**
   Excel calculates the total contained in cells B5:B14 and displays the result, 378, in cell B15.The cell actually contains the formula =SUM(B5:B14), and the result is displayed.

6. **Click cell C13, type 6, then press [Enter]**
   The number 6 replaces the cell's contents, the cell pointer moves to cell C14, and the value in cell F13 changes.

QUICK TIP
You can also press [Tab] to complete a cell entry and move the cell pointer to the right.

7. **Click cell C18, type Average Gross Pay, then press [Enter]**
   The new label is entered in cell C18. The contents appear to spill into the empty cells to the right.

8. **Click cell B15, position the pointer on the lower-right corner of the cell (the fill handle) so that the pointer changes to +, drag the + to cell G15, then release the mouse button**
   Dragging the fill handle across a range of cells copies the contents of the first cell into the other cells in the range. In the range B15:F15, each filled cell now contains a function that sums the range of cells above, as shown in Figure A-8.

9. **Save your work**

FIGURE A-7: Creating a formula using the Sum button

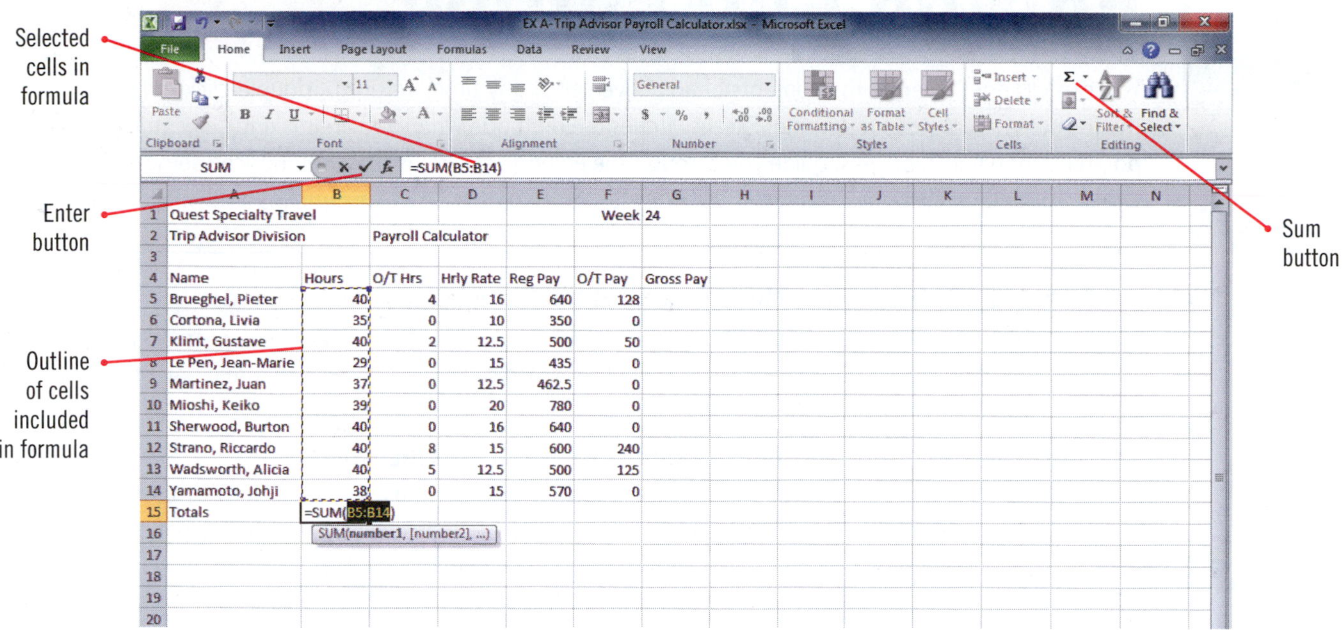

FIGURE A-8: Results of copied SUM functions

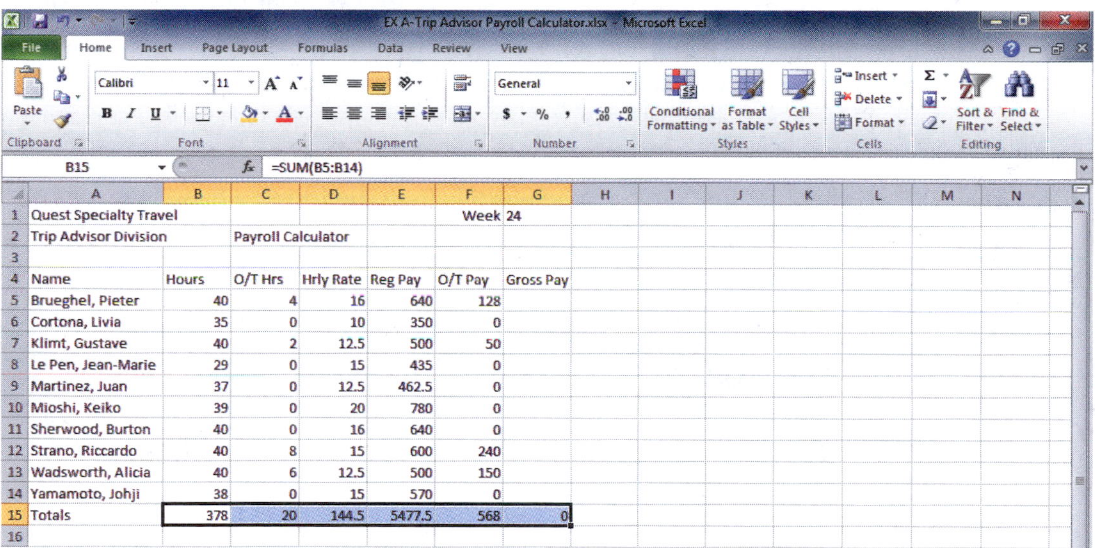

Navigating a worksheet

With over a million cells available in a worksheet, it is important to know how to move around in, or **navigate**, a worksheet. You can use the arrow keys on the keyboard [↑],[↓], [→], or [←] to move one cell at a time, or press [Page Up] or [Page Down] to move one screen at a time. To move one screen to the left press [Alt][Page Up]; to move one screen to the right press [Alt][Page Down]. You can also use the mouse pointer to click the desired cell. If the desired cell is not visible in the worksheet window, use the scroll bars or use the Go To command by clicking the Find & Select button in the Editing group on the Home tab on the Ribbon. To quickly jump to the first cell in a worksheet press [Ctrl][Home]; to jump to the last cell, press [Ctrl][End].

Editing Cell Entries

You can change, or **edit**, the contents of an active cell at any time. To do so, double-click the cell, click in the formula bar, or just start typing. Excel switches to Edit mode when you are making cell entries. Different pointers, shown in Table A-3, guide you through the editing process. You noticed some errors in the worksheet and want to make corrections. The first error is in cell A5, which contains a misspelled name.

STEPS

1. **Click cell A5, then click to the right of P in the formula bar**

   As soon as you click in the formula bar, a blinking vertical line called the **insertion point** appears on the formula bar at the location where new text will be inserted. See Figure A-9. The mouse pointer changes to I when you point anywhere in the formula bar.

2. **Press [Delete], then click the Enter button ✓ on the formula bar**

   Clicking the Enter button accepts the edit, and the spelling of the employee's first name is corrected. You can also press [Enter] or [Tab] to accept an edit. Pressing [Enter] to accept an edit moves the cell pointer down one cell, and pressing [Tab] to accept an edit moves the cell pointer one cell to the right.

QUICK TIP

On some keyboards, you might need to press an [F Lock] key to enable the function keys.

3. **Click cell B6, then press [F2]**

   Excel switches to Edit mode, and the insertion point blinks in the cell. Pressing [F2] activates the cell for editing directly in the cell instead of the formula bar. Whether you edit in the cell or the formula bar is simply a matter of preference; the results in the worksheet are the same.

QUICK TIP

The Undo button allows you to reverse up to 100 previous actions, one at a time.

4. **Press [Backspace], type 8, then press [Enter]**

   The value in the cell changes from 35 to 38, and cell B7 becomes the active cell. Did you notice that the calculations in cells B15 and E15 also changed? That's because those cells contain formulas that include cell B6 in their calculations. If you make a mistake when editing, you can click the Cancel button ✕ on the formula bar *before* pressing [Enter] to confirm the cell entry. The Enter and Cancel buttons appear only when you're in Edit mode. If you notice the mistake *after* you have confirmed the cell entry, click the Undo button on the Quick Access toolbar.

QUICK TIP

You can use the keyboard to select all cell contents by clicking to the right of the cell contents in the cell or formula bar, pressing and holding [Shift], then pressing [Home].

5. **Click cell A9, then double-click the word Juan in the formula bar**

   Double-clicking a word in a cell selects it.

6. **Type Javier, then press [Enter]**

   When text is selected, typing deletes it and replaces it with the new text.

7. **Double-click cell C12, press [Delete], type 4, then click ✓**

   Double-clicking a cell activates it for editing directly in the cell. Compare your screen to Figure A-10.

8. **Save your work**

   Your changes to the workbook are saved.

Recovering unsaved changes to a workbook file

You can use Excel's AutoRecover feature to automatically save (Autosave) your work as often as you want. This means that if you suddenly lose power or if Excel closes unexpectedly while you're working, you can recover all or some of the changes you made since you saved it last. (Of course, this is no substitute for regularly saving your work: this is just added insurance.) To customize the AutoRecover settings, click the File tab, click Options, then click Save. AutoRecover lets you decide how often and into which location it should Autosave files. When you restart Excel after losing power, a Document Recovery pane opens and provides access to the saved and Autosaved versions of the files that were open when Excel closed. You can also click the File tab, click Recent on the navigation bar, then click Recover Unsaved Workbooks to open Autosaved workbooks using the Open dialog box.

FIGURE A-9: Worksheet in Edit mode

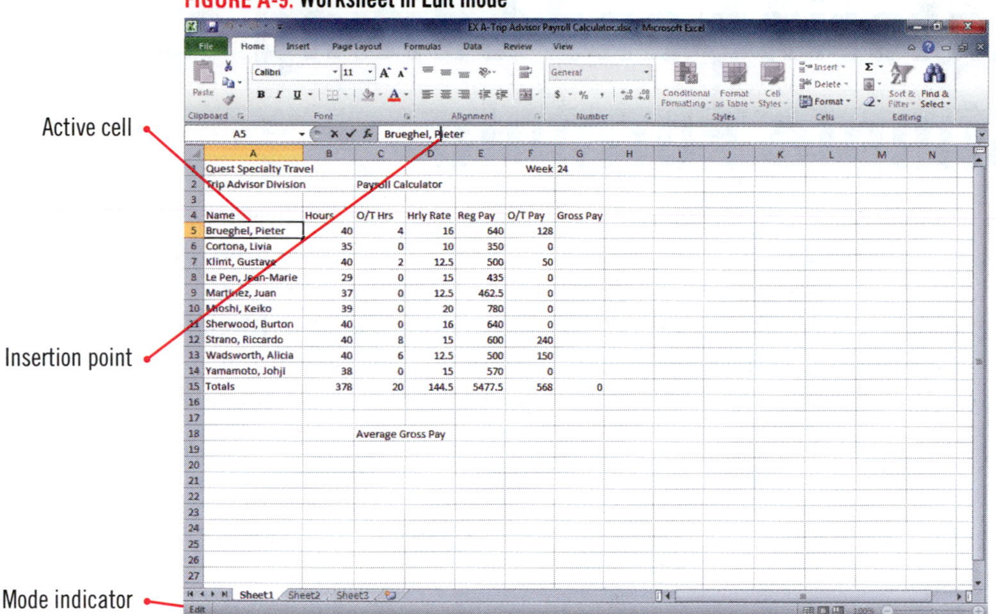

FIGURE A-10: Edited worksheet

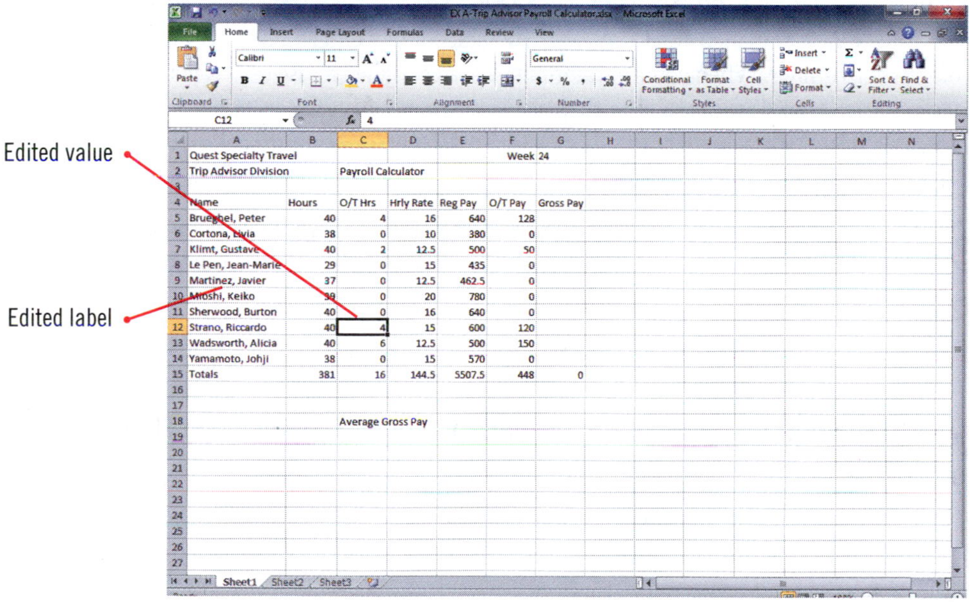

TABLE A-3: Common pointers in Excel

name	pointer	use to	visible over the
Normal	✚	Select a cell or range; indicates Ready mode	Active worksheet
Fill handle	+	Copy cell contents to adjacent cells	Lower-right corner of the active cell or range
I-beam	I	Edit cell contents in active cell or formula bar	Active cell in Edit mode or over the formula bar
Move	✥	Change the location of the selected cell(s)	Perimeter of the active cell(s)
Copy	↖+	Create a duplicate of the selected cell(s)	Perimeter of the active cell(s) when [Ctrl] is pressed
Column resize	↔	Change the width of a column	Border between column heading indicators

Entering and Editing a Simple Formula

You use formulas in Excel to perform calculations such as adding, multiplying, and averaging. Formulas in an Excel worksheet start with the equal sign (=), also called the **formula prefix**, followed by cell addresses, range names, values, and calculation operators. **Calculation operators** indicate what type of calculation you want to perform on the cells, ranges, or values. They can include **arithmetic operators,** which perform mathematical calculations (see Table A-2 in the "Understanding Formulas" lesson); **comparison operators**, which compare values for the purpose of true/false results; **text concatenation operators**, which join strings of text in different cells; and **reference operators**, which enable you to use ranges in calculations. You want to create a formula in the worksheet that calculates gross pay for each employee.

STEPS

1. **Click cell G5**

   This is the first cell where you want to insert the formula. To calculate gross pay, you need to add regular pay and overtime pay. For employee Peter Brueghel, regular pay appears in cell E5 and overtime pay appears in cell F5.

2. **Type =, click cell E5, type +, then click cell F5**

   Compare your formula bar to Figure A-11. The blue and green cell references in cell G5 correspond to the colored cell outlines. When entering a formula, it's a good idea to use cell references instead of values whenever you can. That way, if you later change a value in a cell (if, for example, Peter's regular pay changes to 615), any formula that includes this information reflects accurate, up-to-date results.

QUICK TIP

You can reference a cell in a formula either by typing the cell reference or clicking the cell in the worksheet; when you click a cell to add a reference, the Mode indicator changes to "Point."

3. **Click the Enter button ✓ on the formula bar**

   The result of the formula =E5+F5, 768, appears in cell G5. This same value appears in cell G15 because cell G15 contains a formula that totals the values in cells G5:G14, and there are no other values now.

4. **Click cell F5**

   The formula in this cell calculates overtime pay by multiplying overtime hours (C5) times twice the regular hourly rate (2*D5). You want to edit this formula to reflect a new overtime pay rate.

5. **Click to the right of 2 in the formula bar, then type .5 as shown in Figure A-12**

   The formula that calculates overtime pay has been edited.

6. **Click ✓ on the formula bar**

   Compare your screen to Figure A-13. Notice that the calculated values in cells G5, F15, and G15 have all changed to reflect your edits to cell F5.

7. **Save your work**

Understanding named ranges

It can be difficult to remember the cell locations of critical information in a worksheet, but using cell names can make this task much easier. You can name a single cell or range of contiguous, or touching, cells. For example, you might name a cell that contains data on average gross pay "AVG_GP" instead of trying to remember the cell address C18. A named range must begin with a letter or an underscore. It cannot contain any spaces or be the same as a built-in name, such as a function or another object (such as a different named range) in the workbook. To name a range, select the cell(s) you want to name, click the Name box in the formula bar, type the name you want to use, then press [Enter]. You can also name a range by clicking the Formulas tab, then clicking the Define Name button in the Defined Names group. Type the new range name in the Name text box in the New Name dialog box, verify the selected range, then click OK. When you use a named range in a formula, the named range appears instead of the cell address. You can also create a named range using the contents of a cell already in the range. Select the range containing the text you want to use as a name, then click the Create from Selection button in the Defined Names group. The Create Names from Selection dialog box opens. Choose the location of the name you want to use, then click OK.

FIGURE A-11: Simple formula in a worksheet

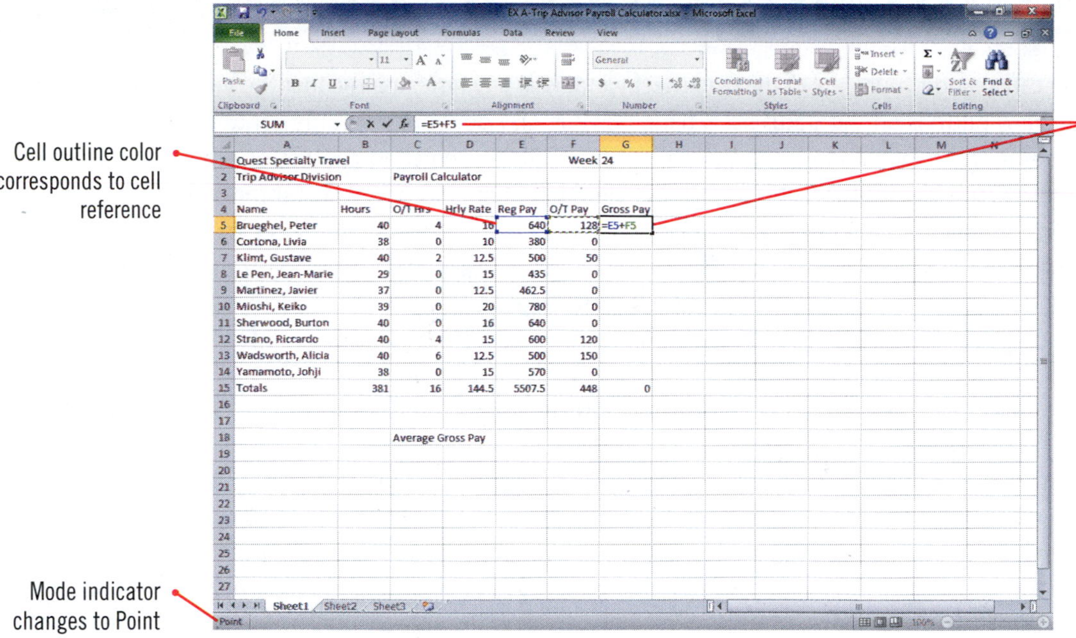

FIGURE A-12: Edited formula in a worksheet

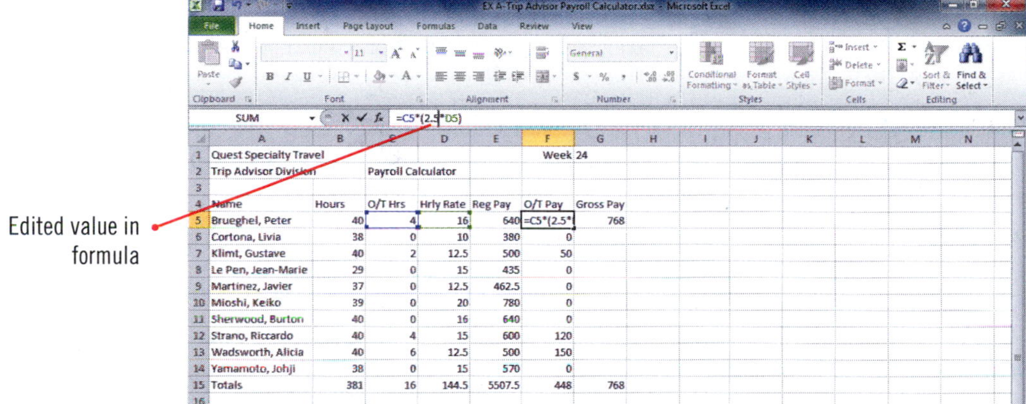

FIGURE A-13: Edited formula with changes

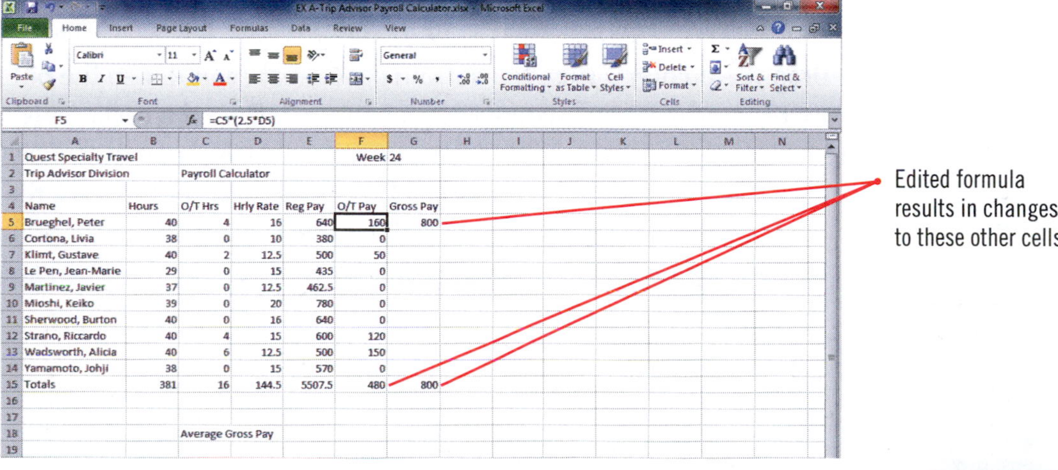

Switching Worksheet Views

You can change your view of the worksheet window at any time, using either the View tab on the Ribbon or the View buttons on the status bar. Changing your view does not affect the contents of a worksheet; it just makes it easier for you to focus on different tasks, such as entering content or preparing a worksheet for printing. The View tab includes a variety of viewing options, such as View buttons, zoom controls, and the ability to show or hide worksheet elements such as gridlines. The status bar offers fewer View options but can be more convenient to use. You want to make some final adjustments to your worksheet, including adding a header so the document looks more polished.

STEPS

QUICK TIP
Although a worksheet can contain more than a million rows and thousands of columns, the current document contains only as many pages as necessary for the current project.

1. **Click the View tab on the Ribbon, then click the Page Layout button in the Workbook Views group**

   The view switches from the default view, Normal, to Page Layout view. **Normal view** shows the worksheet without including certain details like headers and footers, or tools like rulers and a page number indicator; it's great for creating and editing a worksheet, but may not be detailed enough when you want to put the finishing touches on a document. **Page Layout view** provides a more accurate view of how a worksheet will look when printed, as shown in Figure A-14. The margins of the page are displayed, along with a text box for the header. A footer text box appears at the bottom of the page, but your screen may not be large enough to view it without scrolling. Above and to the left of the page are rulers. Part of an additional page appears to the right of this page, but it is dimmed, indicating that it does not contain any data. A page number indicator on the status bar tells you the current page and the total number of pages in this worksheet.

2. **Drag the pointer over the header *without clicking***

   The header is made up of three text boxes: left, center, and right. Each text box is highlighted blue as you pass over it with the pointer.

QUICK TIP
You can change header and footer information using the Header & Footer Tools Design tab that opens on the Ribbon when a header or footer is active. For example, you can insert the date by clicking the Current Date button in the Header & Footer Elements group, or insert the time by clicking the Current Time button.

3. **Click the left header text box, type Quest Specialty Travel, click the center header text box, type Trip Advisor Payroll Calculator, click the right header text box, then type Week 24**

   The new text appears in the text boxes, as shown in Figure A-15.

4. **Select the range A1:G2, then press [Delete]**

   The duplicate information you just entered in the header is deleted from cells in the worksheet.

5. **Click the View tab if necessary, click the Ruler check box in the Show group, then click the Gridlines check box in the Show group**

   The rulers and the gridlines are hidden. By default, gridlines in a worksheet do not print, so hiding them gives you a more accurate image of your final document.

6. **Click the Page Break Preview button on the status bar, then click OK in the Welcome to Page Break Preview dialog box, if necessary**

   Your view changes to **Page Break Preview**, which displays a reduced view of each page of your worksheet, along with page break indicators that you can drag to include more or less information on a page.

7. **Drag the pointer from the bottom page break indicator to the bottom of row 21**

   See Figure A-16. When you're working on a large worksheet with multiple pages, sometimes you need to adjust where pages break; in this worksheet, however, the information all fits comfortably on one page.

QUICK TIP
Once you view a worksheet in Page Break Preview, the page break indicators appear as dotted lines after you switch back to Normal view or Page Layout view.

8. **Click the Page Layout button in the Workbook Views group, click the Ruler check box in the Show group, then click the Gridlines check box in the Show group**

   The rulers and gridlines are no longer hidden. You can show or hide View tab items in any view.

9. **Save your work**

FIGURE A-14: Page Layout view

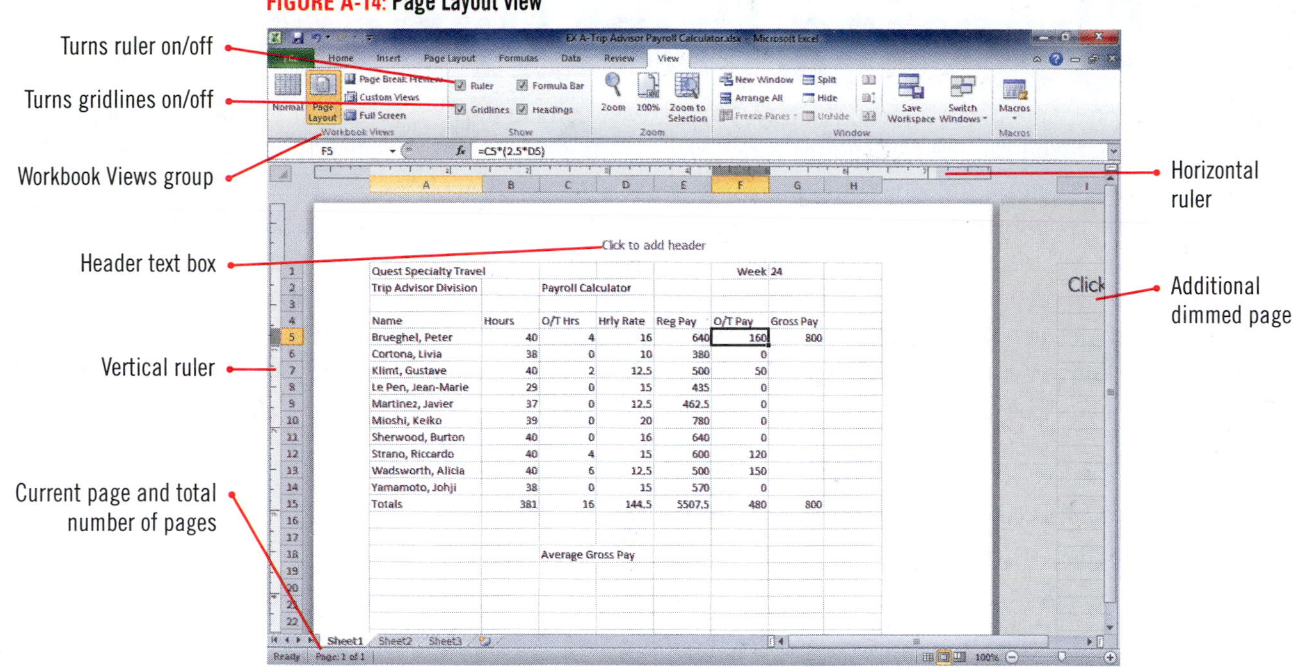

FIGURE A-15: Header text entered

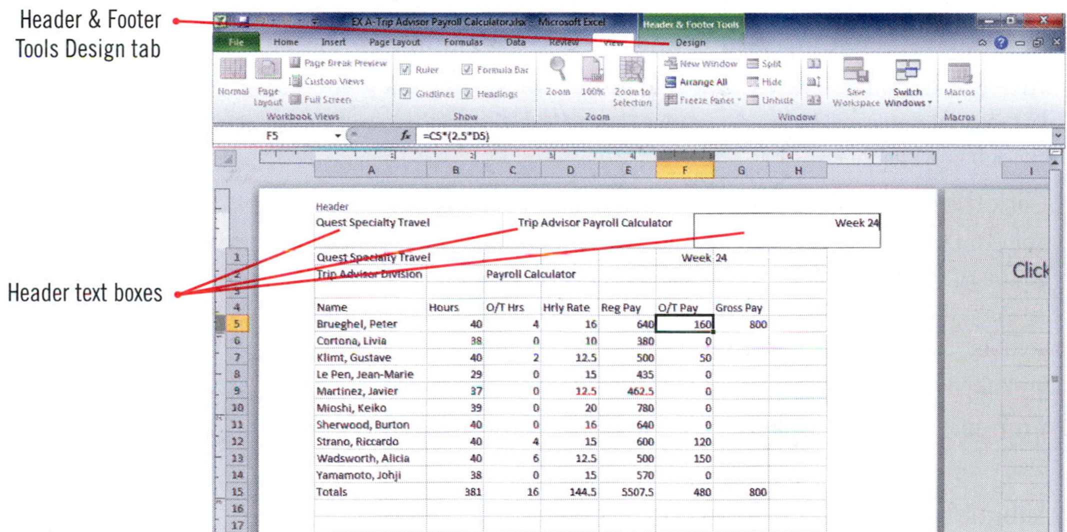

FIGURE A-16: Page Break Preview

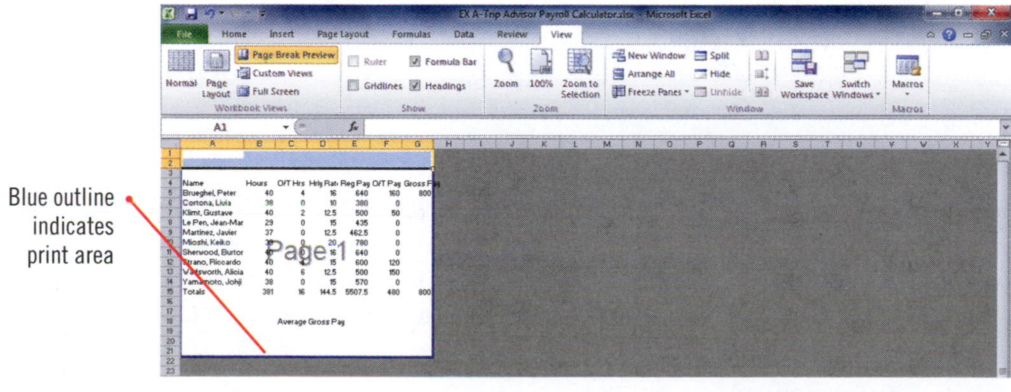

Excel 2010

UNIT A Excel 2010

Choosing Print Options

Before printing a document, you may want to review it using the Page Layout tab to fine-tune your printed output. You can use tools on the Page Layout tab to adjust print orientation (the direction in which the content prints across the page), paper size, and location of page breaks. You can also use the Scale to Fit options on the Page Layout tab to fit a large amount of data on a single page without making changes to individual margins, and to turn gridlines and column/row headings on and off. When you are ready to print, you can set print options such as the number of copies to print and the correct printer, and you can preview your document in Backstage view using the File tab. You can also adjust page layout settings from within Backstage view and immediately see the results in the document preview. You are ready to prepare your worksheet for printing.

STEPS

1. **Click cell A21, type your name, then press [Enter]**
2. **Click the Page Layout tab on the Ribbon**
   Compare your screen to Figure A-17. The dotted line indicates the default **print area**, the area to be printed.
3. **Click the Orientation button in the Page Setup group, then click Landscape**
   The paper orientation changes to **landscape**, so the contents will print across the length of the page instead of across the width.
4. **Click the Orientation button in the Page Setup group, then click Portrait**
   The orientation returns to **portrait**, so the contents will print across the width of the page.
5. **Click the Gridlines View check box in the Sheet Options group on the Page Layout tab, click the Gridlines Print check box to select it if necessary, then save your work**
   Printing gridlines makes the data easier to read, but the gridlines will not print unless the Gridlines Print check box is checked.
6. **Click the File tab, then click Print on the navigation bar**
   The Print tab in Backstage view displays a preview of your worksheet exactly as it will look when it is printed. To the left of the worksheet preview, you can also change a number of document settings and print options. To open the Page Setup dialog box and adjust page layout options, click the Page Setup link in the Settings section. Compare your preview screen to Figure A-18. You can print from this view by clicking the Print button, or return to the worksheet without printing by clicking the File tab again.
7. **Compare your settings to Figure A-18, then click the Print button**
   One copy of the worksheet prints.
8. **Submit your work to your instructor as directed, then exit Excel**

QUICK TIP
You can use the Zoom slider on the status bar at any time to enlarge your view of specific areas of your worksheet.

QUICK TIP
To change the active printer, click the current printer in the Printer section in Backstage view, then choose a different printer.

QUICK TIP
If the Quick Print button appears on the Quick Access Toolbar, you can print your worksheet using the default settings by clicking it.

Printing worksheet formulas

Sometimes you need to keep a record of all the formulas in a worksheet. You might want to do this to see exactly how you came up with a complex calculation, so you can explain it to others. To prepare a worksheet to show formulas rather than results when printed, open the workbook containing the formulas you want to print. Click the Formulas tab, then click the Show Formulas button in the Formula Auditing group to select it. When the Show Formulas button is selected, formulas rather than resulting values are displayed in the worksheet on screen and when printed.

FIGURE A-17: Worksheet with portrait orientation

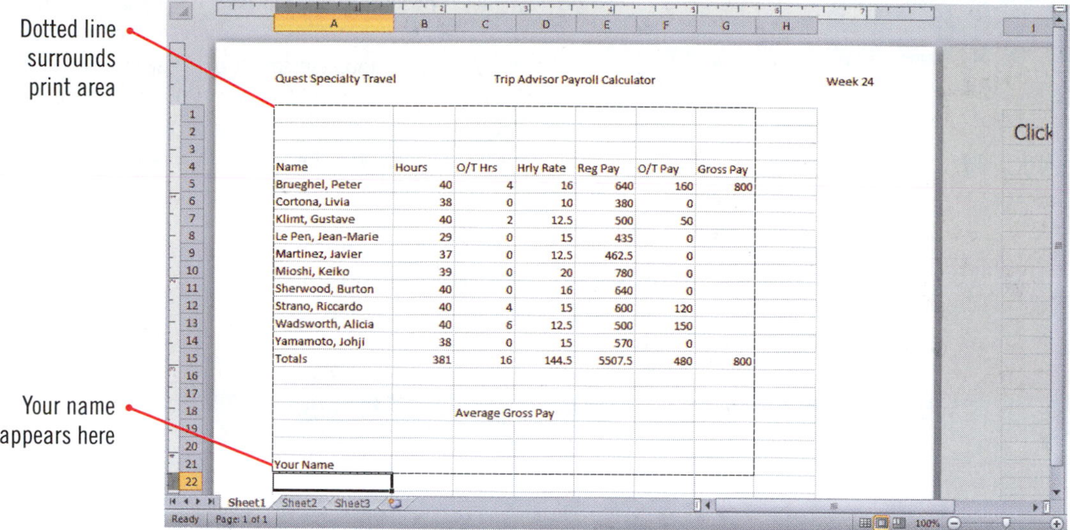

Name	Hours	O/T Hrs	Hrly Rate	Reg Pay	O/T Pay	Gross Pay
Brueghel, Peter	40	4	16	640	160	800
Cortona, Livia	38	0	10	380	0	
Klimt, Gustave	40	2	12.5	500	50	
Le Pen, Jean-Marie	29	0	15	435	0	
Martinez, Javier	37	0	12.5	462.5	0	
Mioshi, Keiko	39	0	20	780	0	
Sherwood, Burton	40	0	16	640	0	
Strano, Riccardo	40	4	15	600	120	
Wadsworth, Alicia	40	6	12.5	500	150	
Yamamoto, Johji	38	0	15	570	0	
Totals	381	16	144.5	5507.5	480	800

FIGURE A-18: Print tab in Backstage view

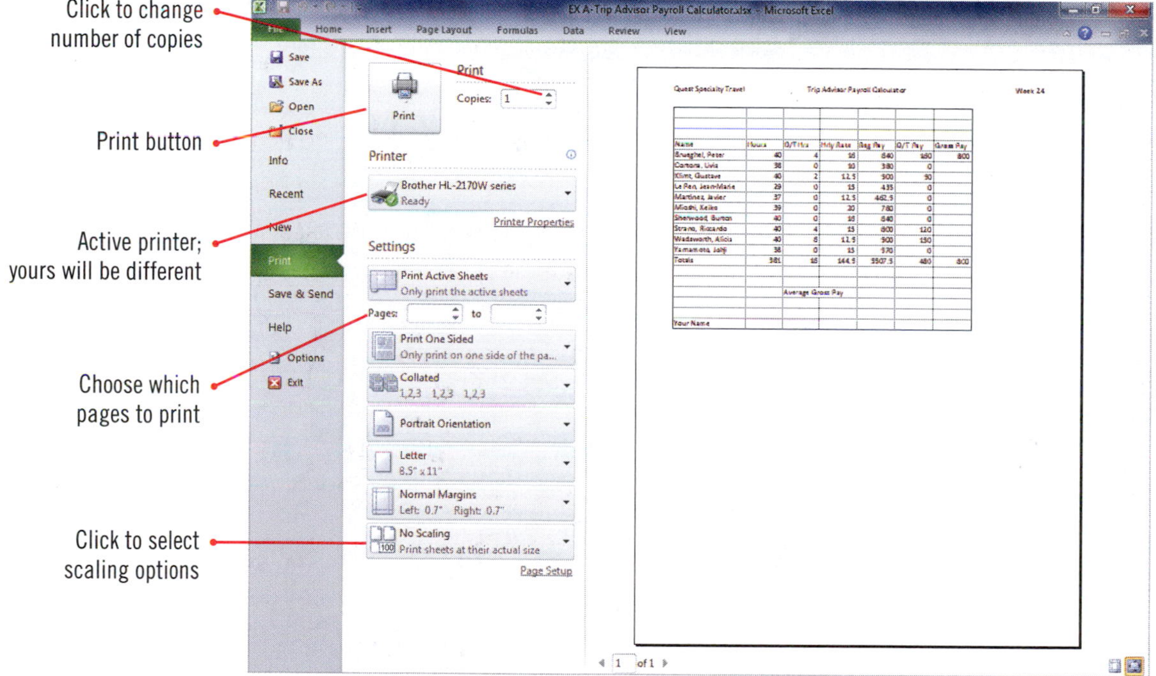

Scaling to fit

If you have a large amount of data that you want to fit to a single sheet of paper, but you don't want to spend a lot of time trying to adjust the margins and other settings, you have several options. You can easily print your work on a single sheet by clicking the No Scaling list arrow in the Settings section on the Print tab in Backstage view, then clicking Fit Sheet on One Page. Another method for fitting worksheet content onto one page is to click the Page Layout tab, then change the Width and Height settings in the Scale to Fit group each to 1 Page. You can also use the Fit to option in the Page Setup dialog box to fit a worksheet on one page. To open the Page Setup dialog box, click the dialog box launcher in the Scale to Fit group on the Page Layout tab, or click the Page Setup link on the Print tab in Backstage view. Make sure the Page tab is selected in the Page Setup dialog box, then click the Fit to option button.

Practice

For current SAM information, including versions and content details, visit SAM Central (http://www.cengage.com/samcentral). If you have a SAM user profile, you may have access to hands-on instruction, practice, and assessment of the skills covered in this unit. Since various versions of SAM are supported throughout the life of this text, check with your instructor for the correct instructions and URL/Web site for accessing assignments.

Concepts Review

Label the elements of the Excel worksheet window shown in Figure A-19.

FIGURE A-19

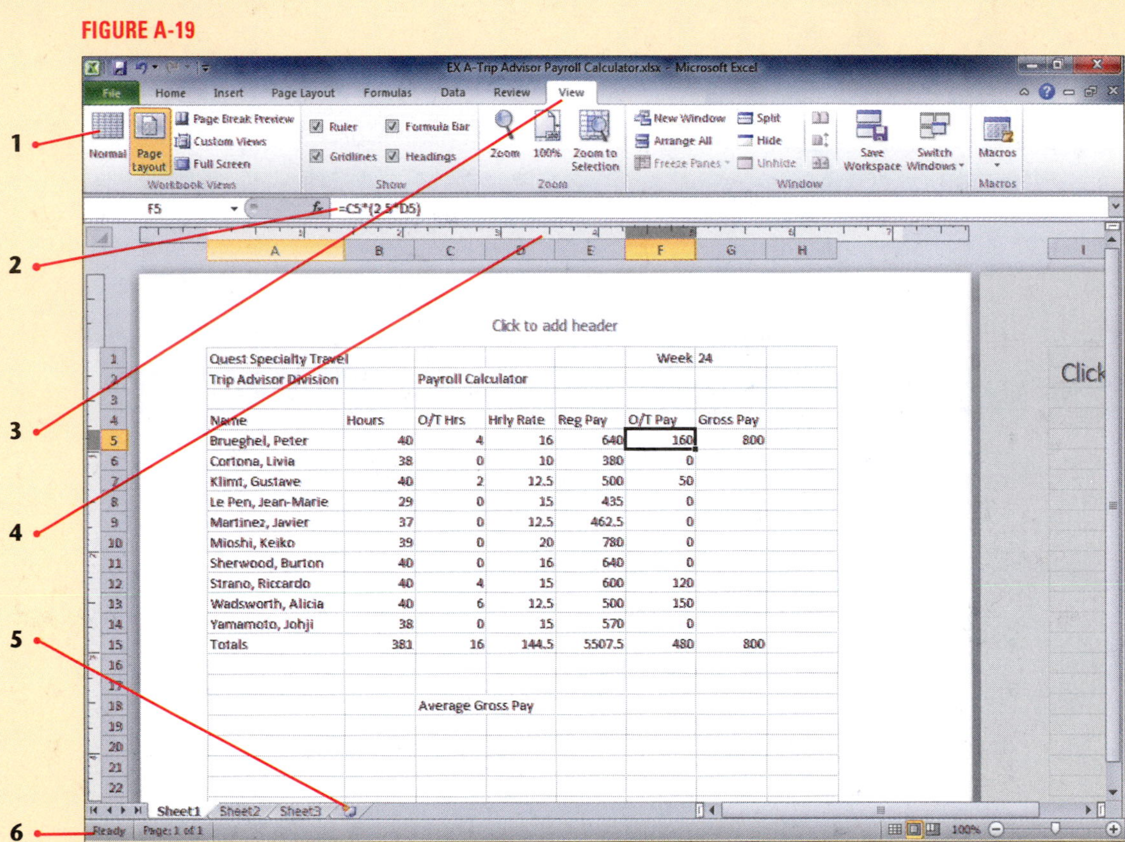

Match each term with the statement that best describes it.

7. **Formula prefix**
8. **Normal view**
9. **Name box**
10. **Cell**
11. **Orientation**
12. **Workbook**

- **a.** Default view in Excel
- **b.** Direction in which contents of page will print
- **c.** Equal sign preceding a formula
- **d.** File consisting of one or more worksheets
- **e.** Intersection of a column and a row
- **f.** Part of the Excel program window that displays the active cell address

Select the best answer from the list of choices.

13. The maximum number of worksheets you can include in a workbook is:

a. 3.
b. 250.
c. 255.
d. Unlimited.

14. Using a cell address in a formula is known as:

a. Formularizing.
b. Prefixing.
c. Cell referencing.
d. Cell mathematics.

15. Which feature could be used to print a very long worksheet on a single sheet of paper?

a. Show Formulas
b. Scale to fit
c. Page Break Preview
d. Named Ranges

16. A selection of multiple cells is called a:

a. Group.
b. Range.
c. Reference.
d. Package.

17. Which worksheet view shows how your worksheet will look when printed?

a. Page Layout
b. Data
c. Review
d. View

18. Which key can you press to switch to Edit mode?

a. [F1]
b. [F2]
c. [F4]
d. [F6]

19. Which view shows you a reduced view of each page of your worksheet?

a. Normal
b. Page Layout
c. Thumbnail
d. Page Break Preview

20. In which area can you see a preview of your worksheet?

a. Page Setup
b. Backstage view
c. Printer Setup
d. View tab

21. In which view can you see the header and footer areas of a worksheet?

a. Normal view
b. Page Layout view
c. Page Break Preview
d. Header/Footer view

Excel 2010

Skills Review

1. Understand spreadsheet software.

a. What is the difference between a workbook and a worksheet?
b. Identify five common business uses for electronic spreadsheets.
c. What is what-if analysis?

2. Tour the Excel 2010 window.

a. Start Excel.
b. Open the file EX A-2.xlsx from the drive and folder where you store your Data Files, then save it as **EX A-Weather Statistics**.
c. Locate the formula bar, the Sheet tabs, the mode indicator, and the cell pointer.

3. Understand formulas.

a. What is the average high temperature of the listed cities? (*Hint*: Select the range B5:G5 and use the status bar.)
b. What formula would you create to calculate the difference in altitude between Denver and Phoenix? Enter your answer (as an equation) in cell D13.

4. Enter labels and values and use the Sum button.

a. Click cell H8, then use the Sum button to calculate the total snowfall.
b. Click cell H7, then use the Sum button to calculate the total rainfall.
c. Save your changes to the file.

Skills Review (continued)

5. **Edit cell entries.**
   a. Use [F2] to correct the spelling of SanteFe in cell G3 (the correct spelling is Santa Fe).
   b. Click cell A17, then type your name.
   c. Save your changes.
6. **Enter and edit a simple formula.**
   a. Change the value 41 in cell C8 to **52**.
   b. Change the value 37 in cell D6 to **35.4**.
   c. Select cell J4, then use the fill handle to copy the formula in cell J4 to cells J5:J8
   d. Save your changes.
7. **Switch worksheet views.**
   a. Click the View tab on the Ribbon, then switch to Page Layout view.
   b. Add the header **Average Annual Weather Statistics** to the center header text box.
   c. Add your name to the right header box.
   d. Delete the contents of cell A1.
   e. Delete the contents of cell A17.
   f. Save your changes.
8. **Choose print options.**
   a. Use the Page Layout tab to change the orientation to Portrait.
   b. Turn off gridlines by deselecting both the Gridlines View and Gridlines Print check boxes (if necessary) in the Sheet Options group.
   c. Scale the worksheet so all the information fits on one page. (*Hint*: Click the Width list arrow in the Scale to Fit group, click 1 page, click the Height list arrow in the Scale to Fit group, then click 1 page.) Compare your screen to Figure A-20.
   d. Preview the worksheet in Backstage view, then print the worksheet.
   e. Save your changes, submit your work to your instructor as directed, then close the workbook and exit Excel.

FIGURE A-20

Independent Challenge 1

A local executive relocation company has hired you to help them make the transition to using Excel in their office. They would like to list their properties in a workbook. You've started a worksheet for this project that contains labels but no data.

If you have a SAM 2010 user profile, an autogradable SAM version of this assignment may be available at http://www.cengage.com/sam2010. Check with your instructor to confirm that this assignment is available in SAM. To use the SAM version of this assignment, log into the SAM 2010 Web site and download the instruction and start files.

a. Open the file EX A-3.xlsx from where you store your Data Files, then save it as **EX A-Property Listings**.
b. Enter the data shown in Table A-4 in columns A, C, D, and E (the property address information should spill into column B).

TABLE A-4

Property Address	Price	Bedrooms	Bathrooms
1507 Pinon Lane	475000	4	2.5
32 Zanzibar Way	325000	3	4
60 Pottery Lane	475500	2	2
902 Excelsior Drive	295000	4	3

Independent Challenge 1 (continued)

c. Use Page Layout view to create a header with the following components: the title **Property Listings** in the center and your name on the right.

d. Create formulas for totals in cells C6:E6.

e. Save your changes, then compare your worksheet to Figure A-21.

f. Submit your work to your instructor as directed.

g. Close the worksheet and exit Excel.

FIGURE A-21

Property Listings   Your Name

Property Address	Price	Bedrooms	Bathrooms
1507 Pinon Lane	475000	4	2.5
32 Zanzibar Way	325000	3	4
60 Pottery Lane	475500	2	2
902 Excelsior Drive	295000	4	3
Total	1570500	13	11.5

Independent Challenge 2

You are the General Manager for Prestige Import Motors, a small auto parts supplier. Although the company is just 5 years old, it is expanding rapidly, and you are continually looking for ways to save time. You recently began using Excel to manage and maintain data on inventory and sales, which has greatly helped you to track information accurately and efficiently.

a. Start Excel.

b. Save a new workbook as **EX A-Prestige Import Motors** in the drive and folder where you store your Data Files.

c. Switch to an appropriate view, then add a header that contains your name in the left header text box and the title **Prestige Import Motors** in the center header text box.

d. Using Figure A-22 as a guide, create labels for at least seven car manufacturers and sales for three months. Include other labels as appropriate. The car make should be in column A and the months should be in columns B, C, and D. A Total row should be beneath the data, and a Total column should be in column E.

FIGURE A-22

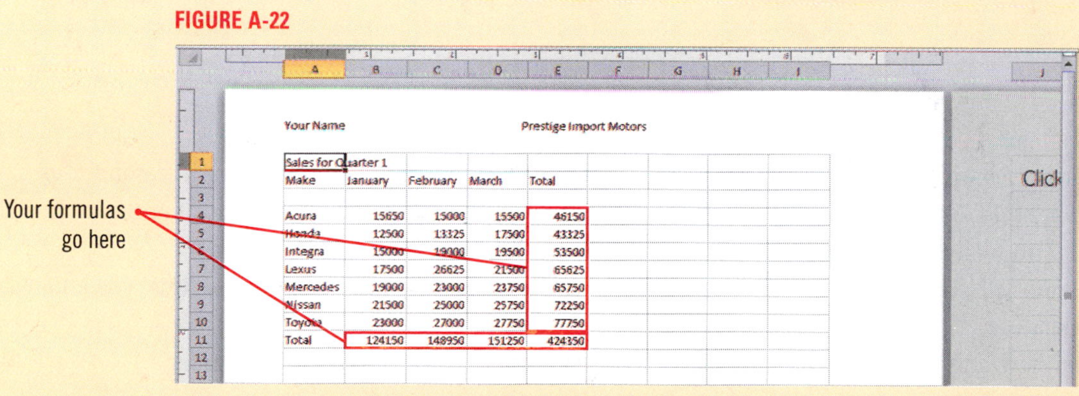
Your Name   Prestige Import Motors

Sales for Quarter 1

Make	January	February	March	Total
Acura	15650	15000	15500	46150
Honda	12500	13325	17500	43325
Integra	15000	19000	19500	53500
Lexus	17500	26625	21500	65625
Mercedes	19000	23000	23750	65750
Nissan	21500	25000	25750	72250
Toyota	23000	27000	27750	77750
Total	124150	148950	151250	424350

e. Enter values of your choice for the monthly sales for each make.

f. Add formulas in the Total column to calculate total quarterly sales for each make. Add formulas at the bottom of each column of values to calculate the total for that column. Remember that you can use the Sum button and the fill handle to save time.

g. Save your changes, preview the worksheet in Backstage view, then submit your work to your instructor as directed.

Independent Challenge 2 (continued)

Advanced Challenge Exercise

- Create a label two rows beneath the data in column A that says **15% increase**.
- Create a formula in each of cells B13, C13, and D13 that calculates monthly sales plus a 15% increase.
- Display the formulas in the worksheet, then print a copy of the worksheet with formulas displayed.
- Save the workbook.

h. Close the workbook and exit Excel.

Independent Challenge 3

This Independent Challenge requires an Internet connection.

Your office is starting a branch in Paris, and you think it would be helpful to create a worksheet that can be used to convert Fahrenheit temperatures to Celsius, to help employees who are unfamiliar with this type of temperature measurement.

a. Start Excel, then save a blank workbook as **EX A-Temperature Conversions** in the drive and folder where you store your Data Files.

b. Create column headings using Figure A-23 as a guide. (*Hint*: You can widen column B by clicking cell B1, clicking the Format button in the Cells group on the Home tab, then clicking AutoFit Column Width.)

FIGURE A-23

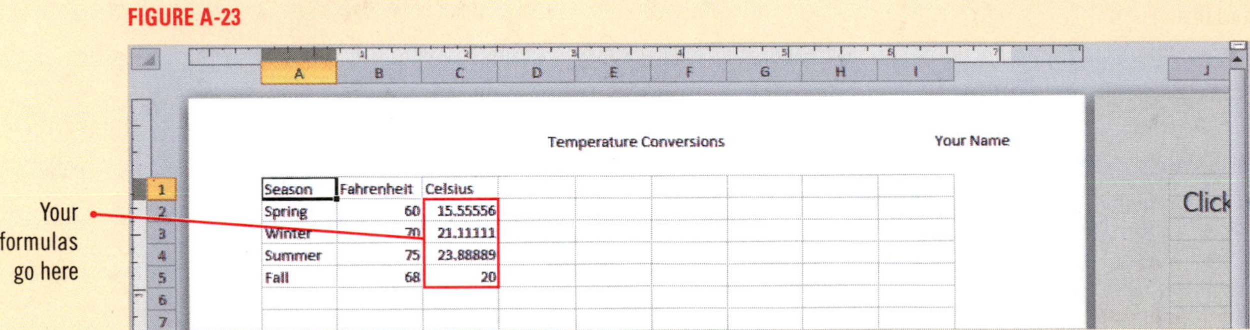

c. Create row labels for each of the seasons.

d. In the appropriate cells, enter what you determine to be a reasonable indoor temperature for each season.

e. Use your Web browser to find out the conversion rate for Fahrenheit to Celsius. (*Hint*: Use your favorite search engine to search on a term such as **temperature conversion formula**.)

f. In the appropriate cells, create a formula that calculates the conversion of the Fahrenheit temperature you entered into a Celsius temperature.

g. In Page Layout View, add your name and the title **Temperature Conversions** to the header.

h. Save your work, then submit your work to your instructor as directed.

i. Close the file, then exit Excel.

Real Life Independent Challenge

You've decided to finally get your life organized. You're going to organize your personal finances so you can begin saving money, and you're going to use Excel to keep track of your expenses.

a. Start Excel, open the file EX A-4.xlsx from the drive and folder where you store your Data Files, then save it as **EX A-Personal Checkbook**.
b. Type check numbers (using your choice of a starting number) in cells A5 through A9.
c. Create sample data for the date, item, and amount in cells B5 through D9.
d. Save your work.

Advanced Challenge Exercise

- Use Help to find out about creating a series of numbers.
- Delete the contents of cells A5:A9.
- Create a series of numbers in cells A5:A9.
- In cell C15, type a brief description of how you created the series.
- Save the workbook.

e. Create formulas in cells E5:E9 that calculate a running balance. (*Hint*: For the first check, the running balance equals the starting balance minus a check; for the following checks, the running balance equals the previous balance value minus each check value.)
f. Create a formula in cell D10 that totals the amount of the checks.
g. Enter your name in cell C12, then compare your screen to Figure A-24.
h. Save your changes to the file, submit your work to your instructor, then exit Excel.

Excel 2010

FIGURE A-24

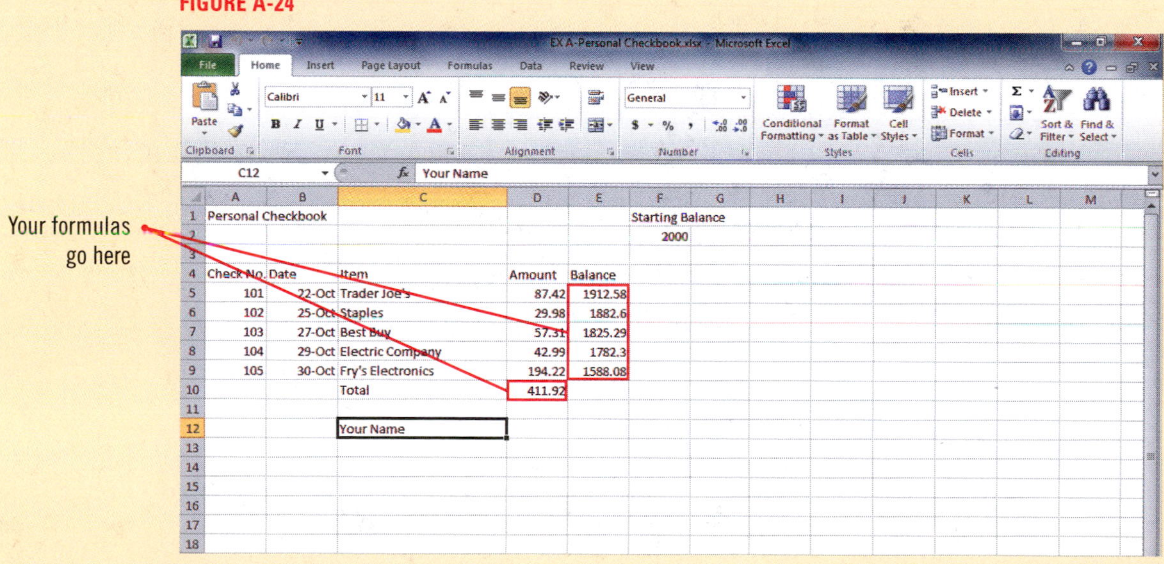

Visual Workshop

Open the file EX A-5.xlsx from the drive and folder where you store your Data Files, then save it as **EX A-Inventory Items**. Using the skills you learned in this unit, modify your worksheet so it matches Figure A-25. Enter formulas in cells D4 through D13 and in cells B14 and C14. Use the Sum button and fill handle to make entering your formulas easier. Add your name in the left header text box, then print one copy of the worksheet with the formulas displayed.

FIGURE A-25

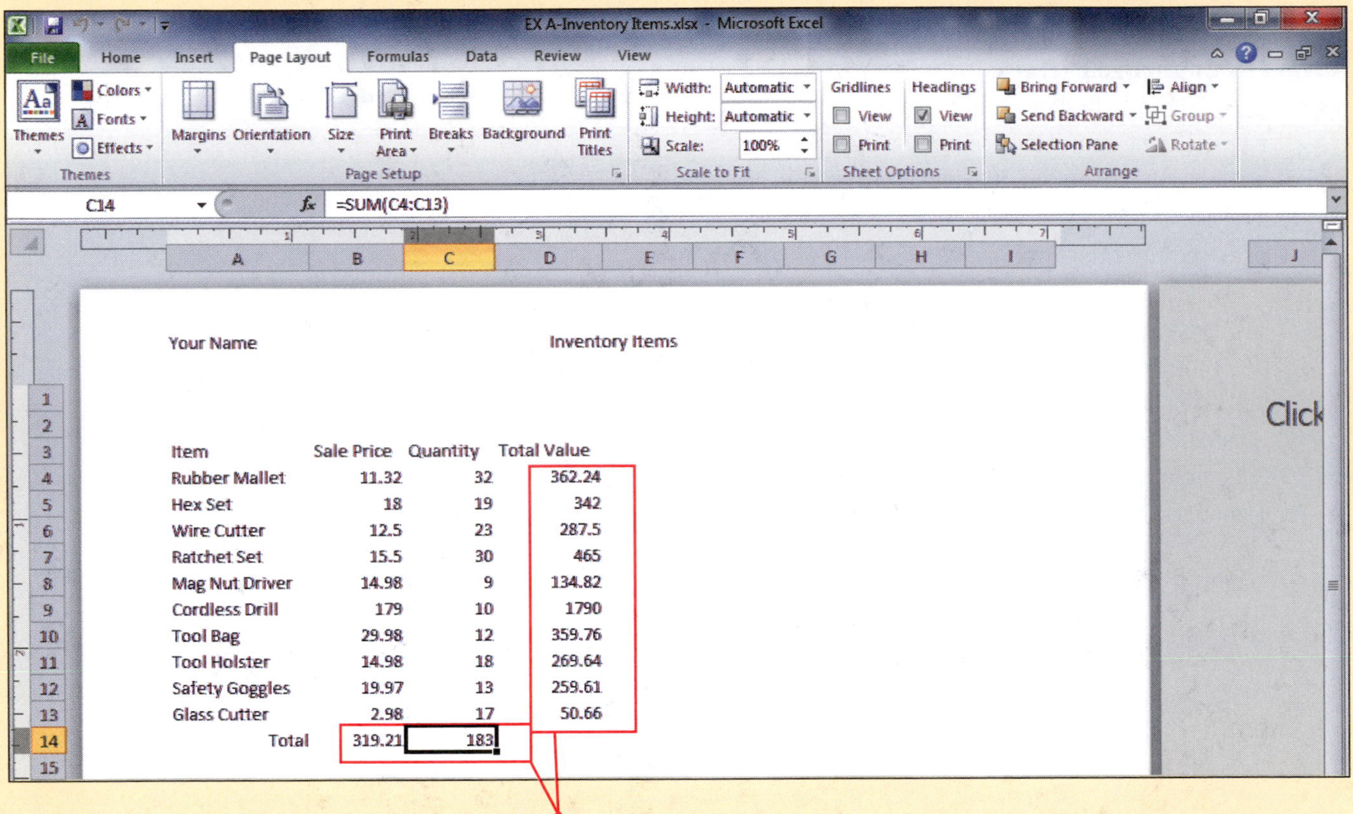

EX A-Inventory Items.xlsx - Microsoft Excel
File
Home
Insert
Page Layout
Formulas
Data
Review
View
C14
=SUM(C4:C13)
Your Name
Inventory Items
Item
Sale Price
Quantity
Total Value
Rubber Mallet 11.32 32 362.24
Hex Set 18 19 342
Wire Cutter 12.5 23 287.5
Ratchet Set 15.5 30 465
Mag Nut Driver 14.98 9 134.82
Cordless Drill 179 10 1790
Tool Bag 29.98 12 359.76
Tool Holster 14.98 18 269.64
Safety Goggles 19.97 13 259.61
Glass Cutter 2.98 17 50.66
Total 319.21 183
Your formulas go here

UNIT
B
Excel 2010

Working with Formulas and Functions

Files You Will Need:

EX B-1.xlsx
EX B-2.xlsx
EX B-3.xlsx
EX B-4.xlsx

Using your knowledge of Excel basics, you can develop your worksheets to include more complex formulas and functions. To work more efficiently, you can copy and move existing formulas into other cells instead of manually retyping the same information. When copying or moving, you can also control how cell references are handled so that your formulas always reference the intended cells. Grace Wong, vice president of finance at Quest Specialty Travel, needs to analyze tour expenses for the current year. She has asked you to prepare a worksheet that summarizes this expense data and includes some statistical analysis. She would also like you to perform some what-if analysis, to see what quarterly expenses would look like with various projected increases.

OBJECTIVES

- Create a complex formula
- Insert a function
- Type a function
- Copy and move cell entries
- Understand relative and absolute cell references
- Copy formulas with relative cell references
- Copy formulas with absolute cell references
- Round a value with a function

UNIT
B
Excel 2010

Creating a Complex Formula

A **complex formula** is one that uses more than one arithmetic operator. You might, for example, need to create a formula that uses addition and multiplication. In formulas containing more than one arithmetic operator, Excel uses the standard **order of precedence** rules to determine which operation to perform first. You can change the order of precedence in a formula by using parentheses around the part you want to calculate first. For example, the formula =4+2*5 equals 14, because the order of precedence dictates that multiplication is performed before addition. However, the formula =(4+2)*5 equals 30, because the parentheses cause 4+2 to be calculated first. You want to create a formula that calculates a 20% increase in tour expenses.

STEPS

> **QUICK TIP**
> When the mode indicator on the status bar says "Point," cells you click are added to the formula.

> **QUICK TIP**
> You can also copy the formulas by selecting the range C14:E14, clicking the Fill button in the Editing group on the Home tab, then clicking Right.

1. **Start Excel, open the file EX B-1.xlsx from the drive and folder where you store your Data Files, then save it as EX B-Tour Expense Analysis**
2. **Click cell B14, type =, click cell B12, then type +**

   In this first part of the formula, you are using a reference to the total expenses for Quarter 1.
3. **Click cell B12, then type *.2**

   The second part of this formula adds a 20% increase (B12*.2) to the original value of the cell (the total expenses for Quarter 1). Compare your worksheet to Figure B-1.
4. **Click the Enter button ✓ on the formula bar**

   The result, 41058.996, appears in cell B14.
5. **Press [Tab], type =, click cell C12, type +, click cell C12, type *.2, then click ✓**

   The result, 41096.916, appears in cell C14.
6. **Drag the fill handle from cell C14 to cell E14**

   The calculated values appear in the selected range, as shown in Figure B-2. Dragging the fill handle on a cell copies the cell's contents or continues a series of data (such as Quarter 1, Quarter 2, etc.) into adjacent cells. This option is called **Auto Fill**.
7. **Save your work**

Reviewing the order of precedence

When you work with formulas that contain more than one operator, the order of precedence is very important because it affects the final value. If a formula contains two or more operators, such as 4+.55/4000*25, Excel performs the calculations in a particular sequence based on the following rules: Operations inside parentheses are calculated before any other operations. Reference operators (such as ranges) are calculated first. Exponents are calculated next, then any multiplication and division—progressing from left to right. Finally, addition and subtraction are calculated from left to right. In the example 4+.55/4000*25, Excel performs the arithmetic operations by first dividing 4000 into .55, then multiplying the result by 25, then adding 4. You can change the order of calculations by using parentheses. For example, in the formula (4+.55)/4000*25, Excel would first add 4 and .55, then divide that amount by 4000, then finally multiply by 25.

FIGURE B-1: Formula containing multiple arithmetic operators

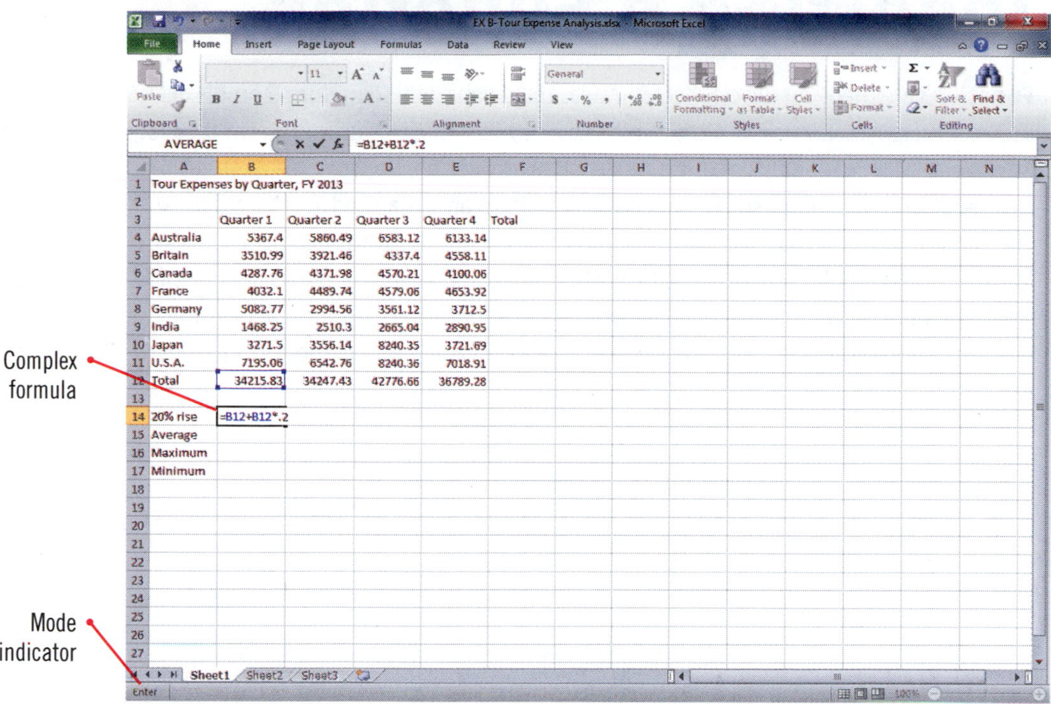

FIGURE B-2: Complex formulas in worksheet

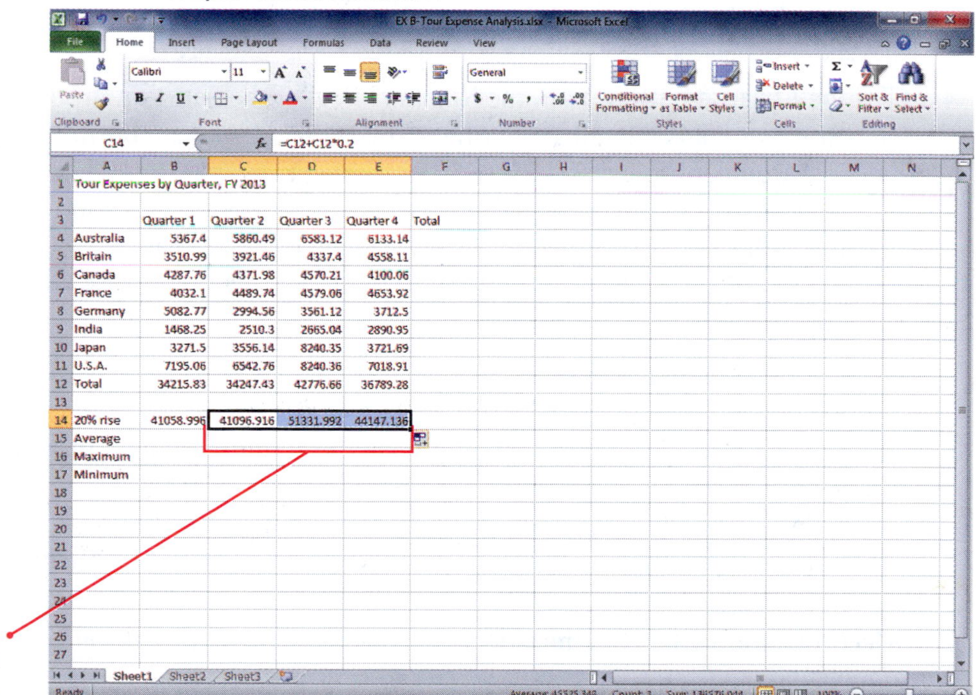

Excel 2010

UNIT
B
Excel 2010

Inserting a Function

Functions are predefined worksheet formulas that enable you to perform complex calculations easily. You can use the Insert Function button on the formula bar to choose a function from a dialog box. You can quickly insert the SUM function using the Sum button on the Ribbon, or you can click the Sum list arrow to enter other frequently used functions, such as AVERAGE. Functions are organized into categories, such as Financial, Date & Time, and Statistical, based on their purposes. You can insert a function on its own or as part of another formula. For example, you have used the SUM function on its own to add a range of cells. You could also use the SUM function within a formula that adds a range of cells and then multiplies the total by a decimal. If you use a function alone, it always begins with an equal sign (=) as the formula prefix. You need to calculate the average expenses for the first quarter of the year, and decide to use a function to do so.

STEPS

QUICK TIP
When using the Insert Function button or the Sum list arrow, it is not necessary to type the equal sign (=); Excel adds it as necessary.

QUICK TIP
To learn about a function, click it in the Select a function list. The arguments and format required for the function appear below the list.

QUICK TIP
When selecting a range, remember to select all the cells between and including the two references in the range.

1. **Click cell B15**
   This is the cell where you want to enter the calculation that averages expenses per country for the first quarter. You want to use the Insert Function dialog box to enter this function.
2. **Click the Insert Function button on the formula bar**
   An equal sign (=) is inserted in the active cell and in the formula bar, and the Insert Function dialog box opens, as shown in Figure B-3. In this dialog box, you specify the function you want to use by clicking it in the Select a function list. The Select a function list initially displays recently used functions. If you don't see the function you want, you can click the Or select a category list arrow to choose the desired category. If you're not sure which category to choose, you can type the function name or a description in the Search for a function field. The AVERAGE function is a statistical function, but you don't need to open the Statistical category because this function already appears in the Most Recently Used category.
3. **Click AVERAGE in the Select a function list if necessary, read the information that appears under the list, then click OK**
   The Function Arguments dialog box opens, in which you define the range of cells you want to average.
4. **Click the Collapse button in the Number1 field of the Function Arguments dialog box, select the range B4:B11 in the worksheet, then click the Expand button in the Function Arguments dialog box**
   Clicking the Collapse button minimizes the dialog box so you can select cells in the worksheet. When you click the Expand button, the dialog box is restored, as shown in Figure B-4. You can also begin dragging in the worksheet to automatically minimize the dialog box; after you select the desired range, the dialog box is restored.
5. **Click OK**
   The Function Arguments dialog box closes, and the calculated value is displayed in cell B15. The average expenses per country for Quarter 1 is 4276.97875.
6. **Click cell C15, click the Sum list arrow Σ in the Editing group on the Home tab, then click Average**
   A ScreenTip beneath cell C15 displays the arguments needed to complete the function. The text "number1" is shown in boldface type, telling you that the next step is to supply the first cell in the group you want to average. You want to average a range of cells.
7. **Select the range C4:C11 in the worksheet, then click the Enter button ✓ on the formula bar**
   The average expenses per country for the second quarter appears in cell C15.
8. **Drag the fill handle from cell C15 to cell E15**
   The formula in cell C15 is copied to the rest of the selected range, as shown in Figure B-5.
9. **Save your work**

FIGURE B-3: Insert Function dialog box

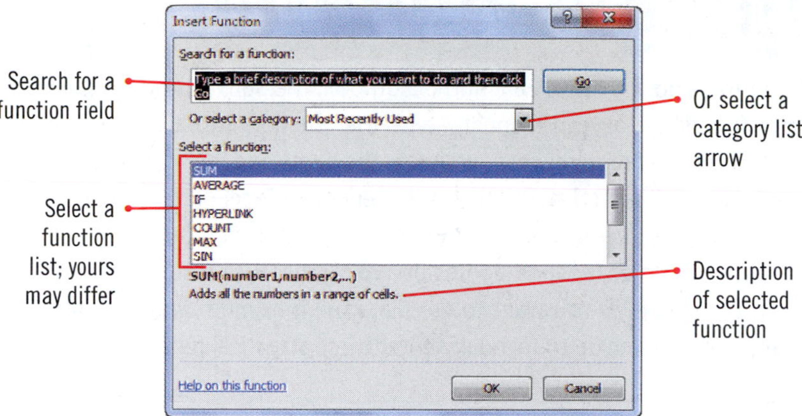

FIGURE B-4: Expanded Function Arguments dialog box

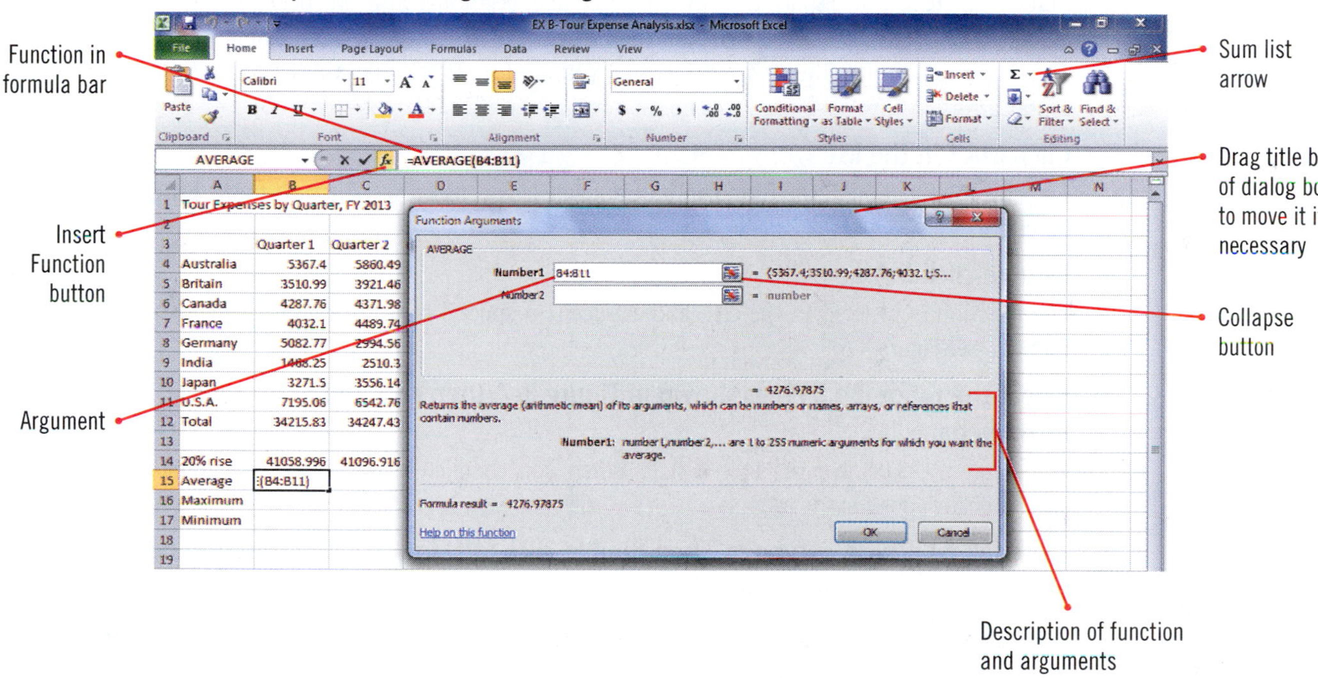

FIGURE B-5: Average functions used in worksheet

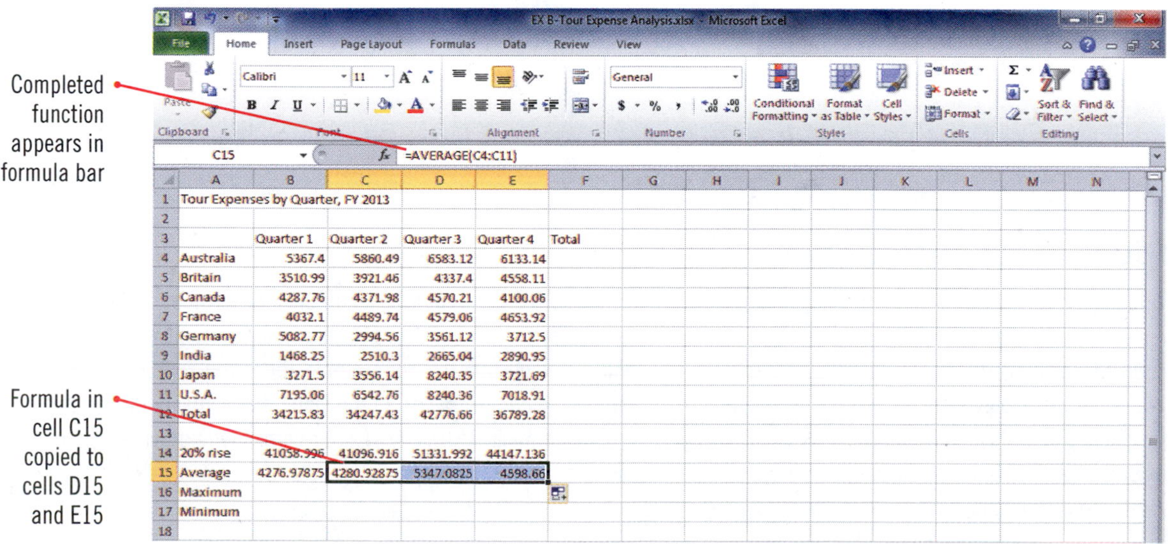

	A	B	C	D	E	F
1	Tour Expenses by Quarter, FY 2013					
2						
3		Quarter 1	Quarter 2	Quarter 3	Quarter 4	Total
4	Australia	5367.4	5860.49	6583.12	6133.14	
5	Britain	3510.99	3921.46	4337.4	4558.11	
6	Canada	4287.76	4371.98	4570.21	4100.06	
7	France	4032.1	4489.74	4579.06	4653.92	
8	Germany	5082.77	2994.56	3561.12	3712.5	
9	India	1468.25	2510.3	2665.04	2890.95	
10	Japan	3271.5	3556.14	8240.35	3721.69	
11	U.S.A.	7195.06	6542.76	8240.36	7018.91	
12	Total	34215.83	34247.43	42776.66	36789.28	
13						
14	20% rise	41058.996	41096.916	51331.992	44147.136	
15	Average	4276.97875	4280.92875	5347.0825	4598.66	
16	Maximum					
17	Minimum					

UNIT
B
Excel 2010

Typing a Function

In addition to using the Insert Function dialog box, the Sum button, or the Sum list arrow on the Ribbon to enter a function, you can manually type the function into a cell and then complete the arguments needed. This method requires that you know the name and initial characters of the function, but it can be faster than opening several dialog boxes. Experienced Excel users often prefer this method, but it is only an alternative, not better or more correct than any other method. Excel's Formula AutoComplete feature makes it easier to enter function names by typing, because it suggests functions depending on the first letters you type. You want to calculate the maximum and minimum quarterly expenses in your worksheet, and you decide to manually enter these statistical functions.

STEPS

1. **Click cell B16, type =, then type m**

   Because you are manually typing this function, it is necessary to begin with the equal sign (=). The Formula AutoComplete feature displays a list of function names beginning with "M" beneath cell B16. Once you type an equal sign in a cell, each letter you type acts as a trigger to activate the Formula AutoComplete feature. This feature minimizes the amount of typing you need to do to enter a function and reduces typing and syntax errors.

2. **Click MAX in the list**

   Clicking any function in the Formula AutoComplete list opens a ScreenTip next to the list that describes the function.

3. **Double-click MAX**

   The function is inserted in the cell, and a ScreenTip appears beneath the cell to help you complete the formula. See Figure B-6.

4. **Select the range B4:B11, as shown in Figure B-7, then click the Enter button ✓ on the formula bar**

   The result, 7195.06, appears in cell B16. When you completed the entry, the closing parenthesis was automatically added to the formula.

5. **Click cell B17, type =, type m, then double-click MIN in the list of function names**

   The MIN function appears in the cell.

6. **Select the range B4:B11, then press [Enter]**

   The result, 1468.25, appears in cell B17.

7. **Select the range B16:B17, then drag the fill handle from cell B17 to cell E17**

   The maximum and minimum values for all of the quarters appear in the selected range, as shown in Figure B-8.

8. **Save your work**

COUNT BLANK

Using the COUNT and COUNTA functions

When you select a range, a count of cells in the range that are not blank appears in the status bar. For example, if you select the range A1:A5 and only cells A1 and A2 contain data, the status bar displays "Count: 2." To count nonblank cells more precisely, or to incorporate these calculations in a worksheet, you can use the COUNT and COUNTA functions. The COUNT function returns the number of cells in a range that contain numeric data, including numbers, dates, and formulas. The COUNTA function returns the number of cells in a range that contain any data at all, including numeric data, labels, and even a blank space. For example, the formula =COUNT(A1:A5) returns the number of cells in the range that contain numeric data, and the formula =COUNTA(A1:A5) returns the number of cells in the range that are not empty.

FIGURE B-6: MAX function in progress

13						
14	20% rise	41058.996	41096.916	51331.992	44147.136	
15	Average	4276.97875	4280.92875	5347.0825	4598.66	
16	Maximum	=MAX(				
17	Minimum	MAX(number1, [number2], ...)				
18						

FIGURE B-7: Completing the MAX function

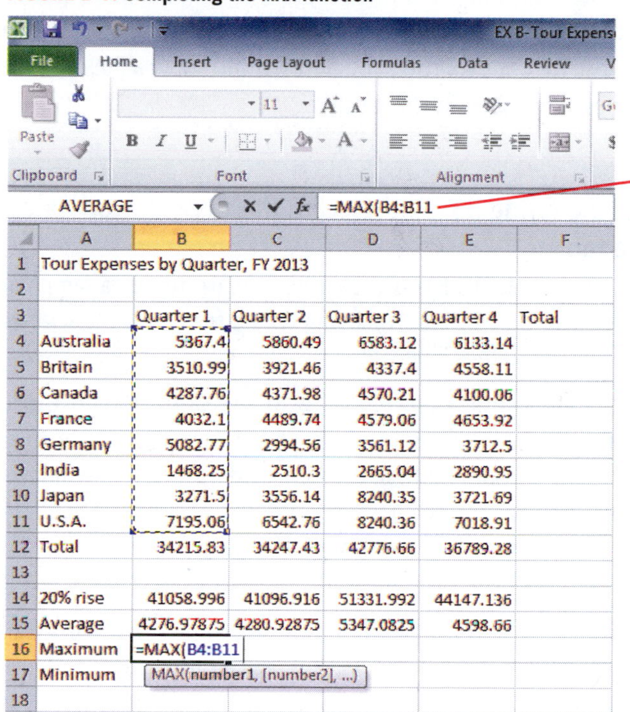

	A	B	C	D	E	F
1	Tour Expenses by Quarter, FY 2013					
2						
3		Quarter 1	Quarter 2	Quarter 3	Quarter 4	Total
4	Australia	5367.4	5860.49	6583.12	6133.14	
5	Britain	3510.99	3921.46	4337.4	4558.11	
6	Canada	4287.76	4371.98	4570.21	4100.06	
7	France	4032.1	4489.74	4579.06	4653.92	
8	Germany	5082.77	2994.56	3561.12	3712.5	
9	India	1468.25	2510.3	2665.04	2890.95	
10	Japan	3271.5	3556.14	8240.35	3721.69	
11	U.S.A.	7195.06	6542.76	8240.36	7018.91	
12	Total	34215.83	34247.43	42776.66	36789.28	
13						
14	20% rise	41058.996	41096.916	51331.992	44147.136	
15	Average	4276.97875	4280.92875	5347.0825	4598.66	
16	Maximum	=MAX(B4:B11				
17	Minimum	MAX(number1, [number2], ...)				
18						

FIGURE B-8: Completed MAX and MIN functions

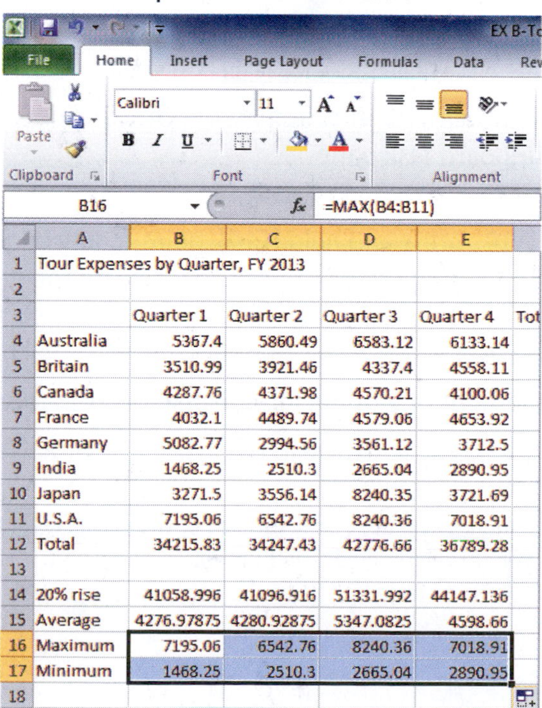

	A	B	C	D	E
1	Tour Expenses by Quarter, FY 2013				
2					
3		Quarter 1	Quarter 2	Quarter 3	Quarter 4
4	Australia	5367.4	5860.49	6583.12	6133.14
5	Britain	3510.99	3921.46	4337.4	4558.11
6	Canada	4287.76	4371.98	4570.21	4100.06
7	France	4032.1	4489.74	4579.06	4653.92
8	Germany	5082.77	2994.56	3561.12	3712.5
9	India	1468.25	2510.3	2665.04	2890.95
10	Japan	3271.5	3556.14	8240.35	3721.69
11	U.S.A.	7195.06	6542.76	8240.36	7018.91
12	Total	34215.83	34247.43	42776.66	36789.28
13					
14	20% rise	41058.996	41096.916	51331.992	44147.136
15	Average	4276.97875	4280.92875	5347.0825	4598.66
16	Maximum	7195.06	6542.76	8240.36	7018.91
17	Minimum	1468.25	2510.3	2665.04	2890.95
18					

UNIT
B
Excel 2010

Copying and Moving Cell Entries

There are three ways you can copy or move cells and ranges (or the contents within them) from one location to another: the Cut, Copy, and Paste buttons on the Home tab on the Ribbon; the fill handle in the lower-right corner of the active cell or range; or the drag-and-drop feature. When you copy cells, the original data remains in the original location; when you cut or move cells, the original data is deleted from its original location. You can also cut, copy, and paste cells or ranges from one worksheet to another. In addition to the 20% rise in tour expenses, you also want to show a 30% rise. Rather than retype this information, you copy and move the labels in these cells.

STEPS

QUICK TIP
To cut or copy selected cell contents, activate the cell, then select the characters within the cell that you want to cut or copy.

1. **Select the range B3:E3, then click the Copy button in the Clipboard group on the Home tab**
   The selected range (B3:E3) is copied to the **Clipboard**, a temporary Windows storage area that holds the selections you copy or cut. A moving border surrounds the selected range until you press [Esc] or copy an additional item to the Clipboard.

2. **Click the dialog box launcher in the Clipboard group**
   The Office Clipboard opens in the Clipboard task pane, as shown in Figure B-9. When you copy or cut an item, it is cut or copied both to the Clipboard provided by Windows and to the Office Clipboard. Unlike the Windows Clipboard, which holds just one item at a time, the Office Clipboard contains up to 24 of the most recently cut or copied items from any Office program. Your Clipboard task pane may contain more items than shown in the figure.

QUICK TIP
Once the Office Clipboard contains 24 items, the oldest existing item is automatically deleted each time you add an item.

3. **Click cell B19, then click the Paste button in the Clipboard group**
   A copy of the contents of range B3:E3 is pasted into the range B19:E19. When pasting an item from the Office Clipboard or Clipboard into a worksheet, you only need to specify the upper-left cell of the range where you want to paste the selection. Notice that the information you copied remains in the original range B3:E3; if you had cut instead of copied, the information would have been deleted from its original location once it was pasted.

4. **Press [Delete]**
   The selected cells are empty. You have decided to paste the cells in a different row. You can repeatedly paste an item from the Office Clipboard as many times as you like, as long as the item remains in the Office Clipboard.

QUICK TIP
You can also close the Office Clipboard pane by clicking the dialog box launcher in the Clipboard group.

5. **Click cell B20, click the first item in the Office Clipboard, then click the Close button on the Clipboard task pane**
   Cells B20:E20 contain the copied labels.

6. **Click cell A14, press and hold [Ctrl], point to any edge of the cell until the pointer changes to , drag cell A14 to cell A21, release the mouse button, then release [Ctrl]**
   The copy pointer continues to appear as you drag, as shown in Figure B-10. When you release the mouse button, the contents of cell A14 are copied to cell A21.

7. **Click to the right of 2 in the formula bar, press [Backspace], type 3, then press [Enter]**

8. **Click cell B21, type =, click cell B12, type *1.3, click the Enter button on the formula bar, then save your work**
   This new formula calculates a 30% increase of the expenses for Quarter 1, though using a different method from what you previously used. Anything you multiply by 1.3 returns an amount that is 130% of the original amount, or a 30% increase. Compare your screen to Figure B-11.

FIGURE B-9: Copied data in Office Clipboard

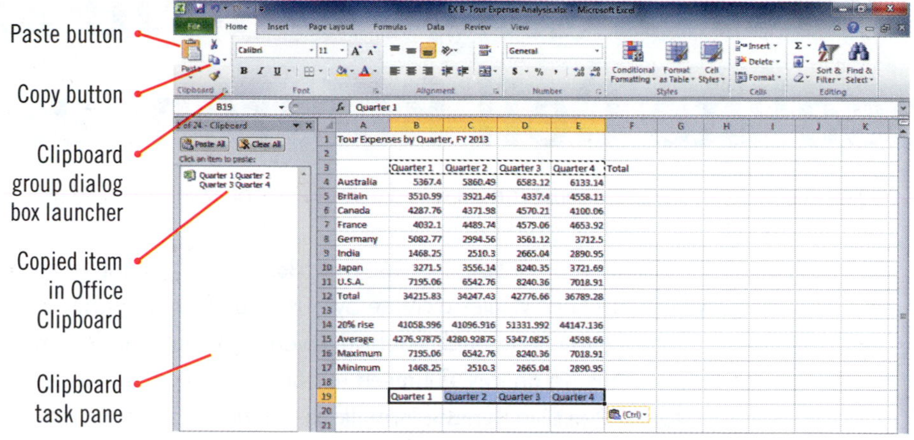

FIGURE B-10: Copying cell contents with drag-and-drop

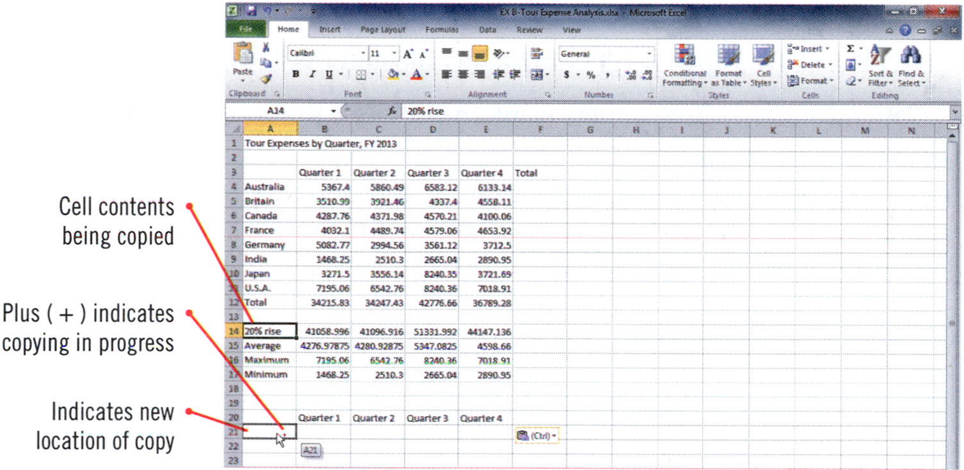

FIGURE B-11: Formula entered to calculate a 30% increase

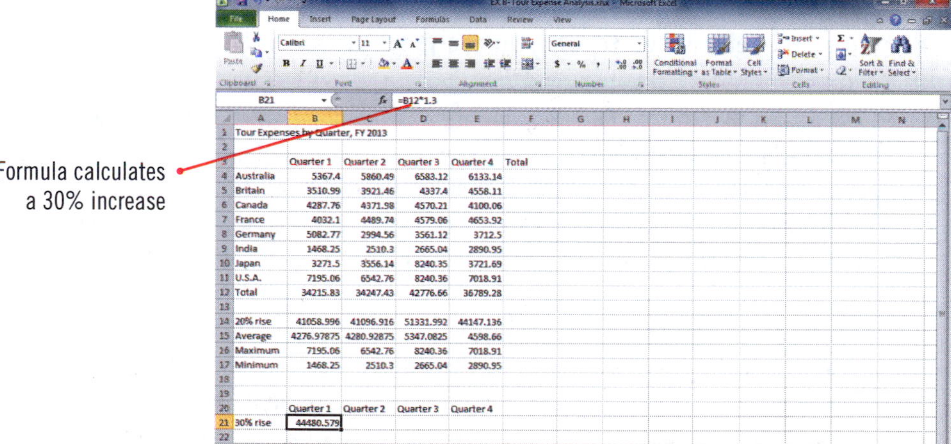

Inserting and deleting selected cells

As you add formulas to your workbook, you may need to insert or delete cells. When you do this, Excel automatically adjusts cell references to reflect their new locations. To insert cells, click the Insert list arrow in the Cells group on the Home tab, then click Insert Cells. The Insert dialog box opens, asking if you want to insert a cell and move the current active cell down or to the right of the new one. To delete one or more selected cells, click the Delete list arrow in the Cells group, click Delete Cells, and in the Delete dialog box, indicate which way you want to move the adjacent cells. When using this option, be careful not to disturb row or column alignment that may be necessary to maintain the accuracy of cell references in the worksheet. Click the Insert button or Delete button in the Cells group to insert or delete a single cell.

Understanding Relative and Absolute Cell References

As you work in Excel, you may want to reuse formulas in different parts of a worksheet to reduce the amount of data you have to retype. For example, you might want to include a what-if analysis in one part of a worksheet showing a set of sales projections if sales increase by 10%. To include another analysis in another part of the worksheet showing projections if sales increase by 50%, you can copy the formulas from one section to another and simply change the "1" to a "5". But when you copy formulas, it is important to make sure that they refer to the correct cells. To do this, you need to understand the difference between relative and absolute cell references. You plan to reuse formulas in different parts of your worksheets, so you want to understand relative and absolute cell references.

DETAILS

Consider the following when using relative and absolute cell references:

- **Use relative references when you want to preserve the relationship to the formula location**

  When you create a formula that references another cell, Excel normally does not "record" the exact cell address for the cell being referenced in the formula. Instead, it looks at the relationship that cell has to the cell containing the formula. For example, in Figure B-12, cell F5 contains the formula: =SUM(B5:E5). When Excel retrieves values to calculate the formula in cell F5, it actually looks for "the four cells to the left of the formula," which in this case is cells B5:E5. This way, if you copy the cell to a new location, such as cell F6, the results will reflect the new formula location, and will automatically retrieve the values in cells B6, C6, D6, and E6. These are **relative cell references**, because Excel is recording the input cells *in relation to* or *relative to* the formula cell.

  In most cases, you want to use relative cell references when copying or moving, so this is the Excel default. In Figure B-12, the formulas in F5:F12 and in B13:F13 contain relative cell references. They total the "four cells to the left of" or the "eight cells above" the formulas.

- **Use absolute cell references when you want to preserve the exact cell address in a formula**

  There are times when you want Excel to retrieve formula information from a specific cell, and you don't want the cell address in the formula to change when you copy it to a new location. For example, you might have a price in a specific cell that you want to use in all formulas, regardless of their location. If you use relative cell referencing, the formula results would be incorrect, because Excel would use a different cell every time you copy the formula. Therefore you need to use an **absolute cell reference**, which is a reference that does not change when you copy the formula.

  You create an absolute cell reference by placing a $ (dollar sign) in front of both the column letter and the row number of the cell address. You can either type the dollar sign when typing the cell address in a formula (for example, "=C12*$B$16"), or you can select a cell address on the formula bar and then press [F4] and the dollar signs are added automatically. Figure B-13 shows formulas containing both absolute and relative references. The formulas in cells B19 to E26 use absolute cell references to refer to a potential sales increase of 50%, shown in cell B16.

FIGURE B-12: Formulas containing relative references

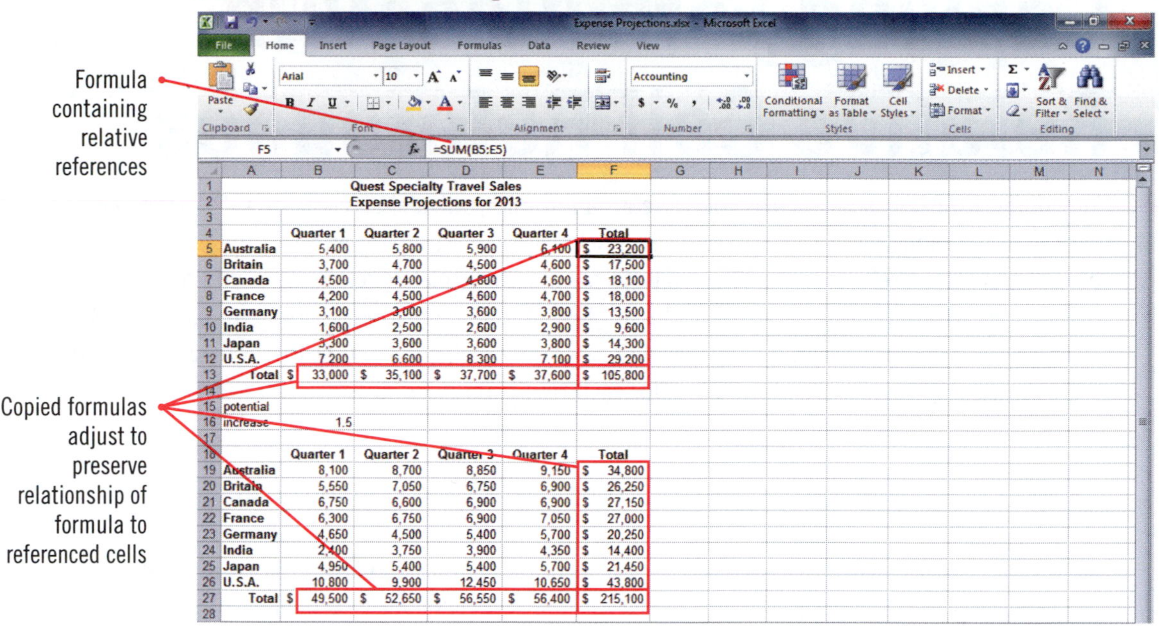
Formula containing relative references
Copied formulas adjust to preserve relationship of formula to referenced cells

FIGURE B-13: Formulas containing absolute and relative references

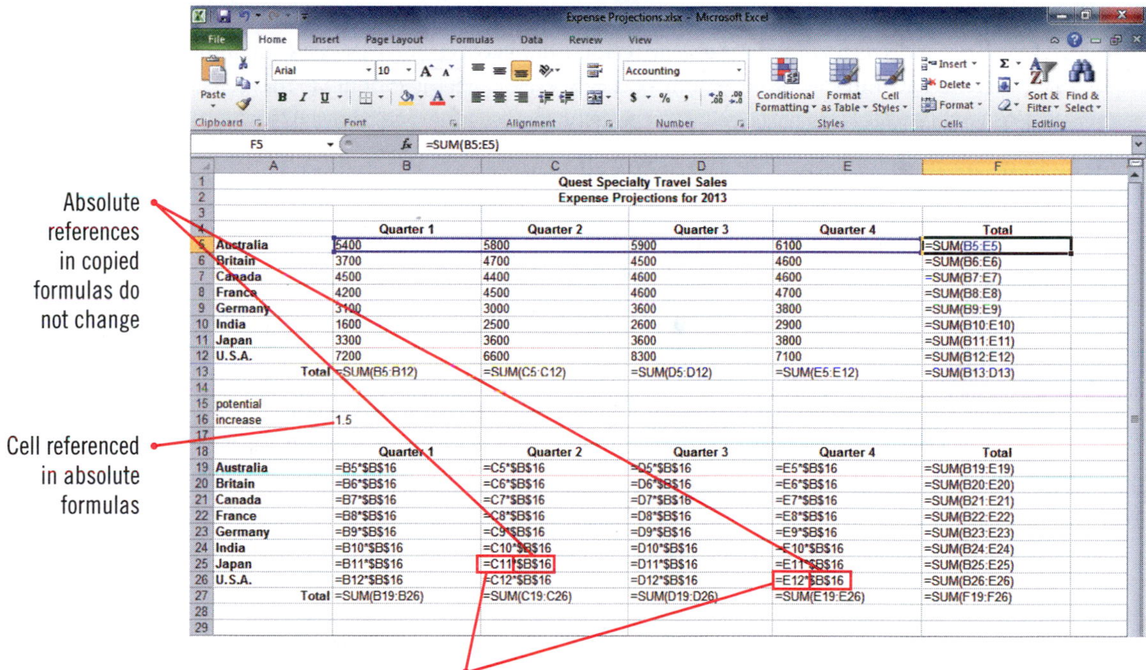
Absolute references in copied formulas do not change
Cell referenced in absolute formulas
Relative references in copied formulas adjust to the new location

Using a mixed reference

Sometimes when you copy a formula, you want to change the row reference, but keep the column reference the same. This type of cell referencing combines elements of both absolute and relative referencing and is called a **mixed reference**. For example, when copied, a formula containing the mixed reference C$14 would change the column letter relative to its new location, but not the row number. In the mixed reference $C14, the column letter would not change, but the row number would be updated relative to its location. Like an absolute reference, a mixed reference can be created by pressing the [F4] function key with the cell reference selected. With each press of the [F4] key, you cycle through all the possible combinations of relative, absolute, and mixed references ($C$14, C$14, $C14, and C14).

UNIT B

Excel 2010

Copying Formulas with Relative Cell References

Copying and moving a cell allows you to reuse a formula you've already created. Copying cells is usually faster than retyping the formulas in them and helps to prevent typing errors. If the cells you are copying contain relative cell references and you want to maintain the relative referencing, you don't need to make any changes to the cells before copying them. You want to copy the formula in cell B21, which calculates the 30% increase in quarterly expenses for quarter 1, to cells C21 through E21. You also want to create formulas to calculate total expenses for each tour country.

STEPS

1. **Click cell B21, if necessary, then click the Copy button in the Clipboard group on the Home tab**

   The formula for calculating the 30% expense increase during Quarter 1 is copied to the Clipboard. Notice that the formula =B12*1.3 appears in the formula bar, and a moving border surrounds the active cell.

2. **Click cell C21, then click the Paste button *(not the list arrow)* in the Clipboard group**

   The formula from cell B21 is copied into cell C21, where the new result of 44521.659 appears. Notice in the formula bar that the cell references have changed, so that cell C12 is referenced in the formula. This formula contains a relative cell reference, which tells Excel to substitute new cell references within the copied formulas as necessary. This maintains the same relationship between the new cell containing the formula and the cell references within the formula. In this case, Excel adjusted the formula so that cell C12—the cell reference nine rows above C21—replaced cell B12, the cell reference nine rows above B21.

3. **Drag the fill handle from cell C21 to cell E21**

   A formula similar to the one in cell C21 now appears in cells D21 and E21. After you use the fill handle to copy cell contents, the **Auto Fill Options button** appears, as seen in Figure B-14. You can use the Auto Fill Options button to fill the cells with only specific elements of the copied cell if you wish.

4. **Click cell F4, click the Sum button in the Editing group, then click the Enter button on the formula bar**

5. **Click in the Clipboard group, select the range F5:F6, then click the Paste button**

   See Figure B-15. After you click the Paste button, the **Paste Options button** appears, which you can use to paste only specific elements of the copied selection if you wish. The formula for calculating total expenses for tours in Britain appears in the formula bar. You would like totals to appear in cells F7:F11. The Fill button in the Editing group can be used to copy the formula into the remaining cells.

6. **Select the range F6:F11**

7. **Click the Fill button in the Editing group, then click Down**

   The formulas containing relative references are copied to each cell. Compare your worksheet to Figure B-16.

8. **Save your work**

QUICK TIP

To paste only specific components of a copied cell or range, click the Paste list arrow in the Clipboard group, then click Paste Special. You can selectively copy formulas, values, or other choices using options in the Paste Special dialog box.

Using Paste Preview

You can selectively copy formulas, values, or other choices using the Paste list arrow, and you can see how the pasted contents will look using the Paste Preview feature. When you click the Paste list arrow, a gallery of paste option icons opens. When you point to an icon, a preview of how the content will be pasted using that option is shown in the worksheet. Options include pasting values only, pasting values with number formatting, pasting formulas only, pasting formatting only, pasting transposed data so that column data appears in rows and row data appears in columns, and pasting with no borders (to remove any borders around pasted cells).

FIGURE B-14: Formula copied using the fill handle

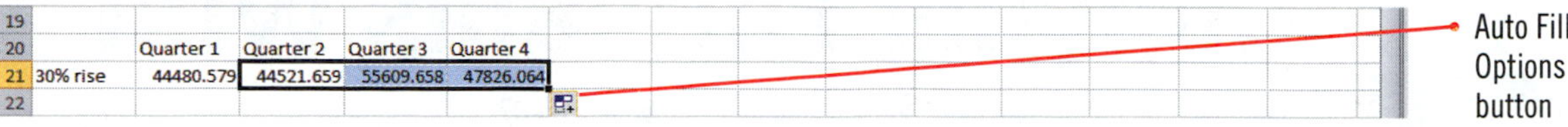

FIGURE B-15: Formulas pasted in the range F5:F6

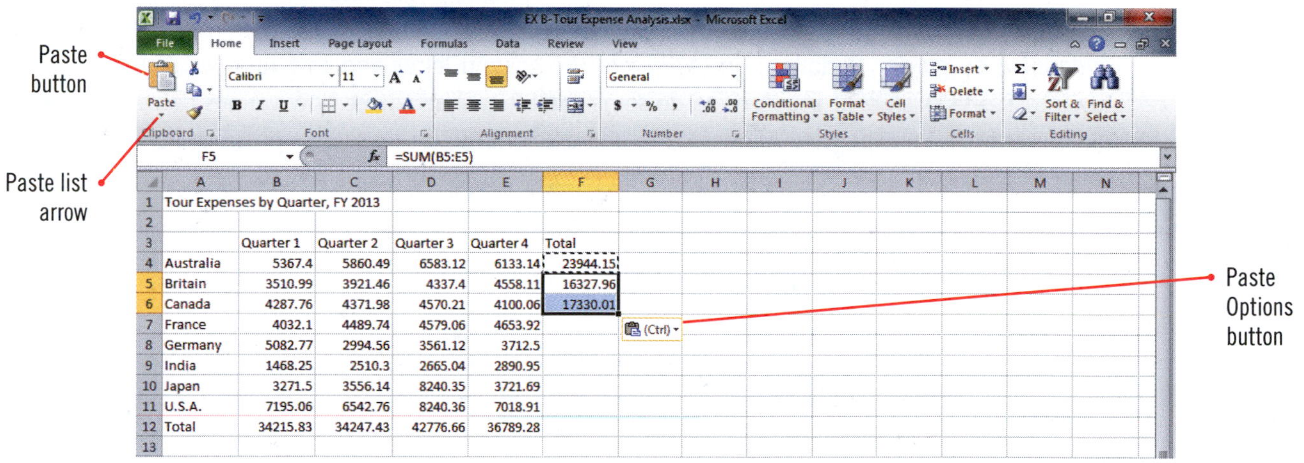

Excel 2010

FIGURE B-16: Formula copied using Fill Down

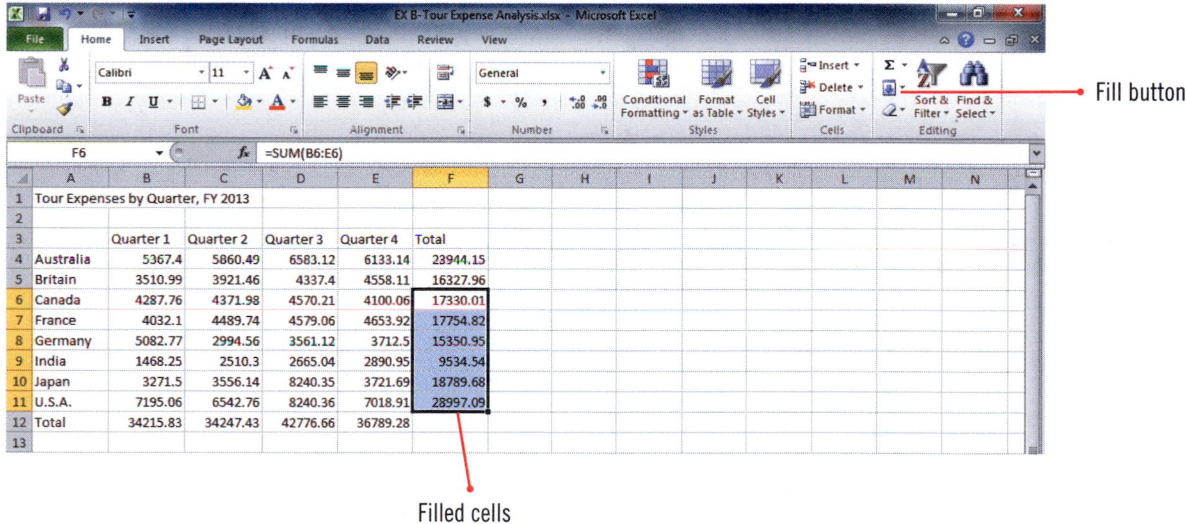

Using Auto Fill options

When you use the fill handle to copy cells, the Auto Fill Options button appears. Auto Fill options differ depending on what you are copying. If you had selected cells containing a series (such as "Monday" and "Tuesday") and then used the fill handle, you would see options for continuing the series (such as "Wednesday" and "Thursday") or for simply pasting the copied cells. Clicking the Auto Fill Options button opens a list that lets you choose from the following options: Copy Cells, Fill Series (if applicable), Fill Formatting Only, or Fill Without Formatting. Choosing Copy Cells means that the cell's contents and its formatting will be copied. The Fill Formatting Only option copies only the formatting attributes, but not cell contents. The Fill Without Formatting option copies the cell contents, but no formatting attributes. Copy Cells is the default option when using the fill handle to copy a cell, so if you want to copy the cell's contents and its formatting, you can ignore the Auto Fill Options button.

Copying Formulas with Absolute Cell References

When copying formulas, you might want one or more cell references in the formula to remain unchanged in relation to the formula. In such an instance, you need to apply an absolute cell reference before copying the formula to preserve the specific cell address when the formula is copied. You create an absolute reference by placing a dollar sign ($) before the column letter and row number of the address (for example, $A$1). You need to do some what-if analysis to see how various percentage increases might affect total expenses. You decide to add a column that calculates a possible increase in the total tour expenses, and then change the percentage to see various potential results.

STEPS

1. **Click cell G1, type Change, then press [Enter]**
2. **Type 1.1, then press [Enter]**

   You store the increase factor that will be used in the what-if analysis in this cell (G2). The value 1.1 can be used to calculate a 10% increase: anything you multiply by 1.1 returns an amount that is 110% of the original amount.
3. **Click cell H3, type What if?, then press [Enter]**
4. **In cell H4, type =, click cell F4, type *, click cell G2, then click the Enter button ✓ on the formula bar**

   The result, 26338.57, appears in cell H4. This value represents the total annual expenses for Australia if there is a 10% increase. You want to perform a what-if analysis for all the tour countries.
5. **Drag the fill handle from cell H4 to cell H11**

   The resulting values in the range H5:H11 are all zeros, which is *not* the result you wanted. Because you used relative cell addressing in cell H4, the copied formula adjusted so that the formula in cell H5 is =F5*G3. Because there is no value in cell G3, the result is 0, an error. You need to use an absolute reference in the formula to keep the formula from adjusting itself. That way, it will always reference cell G2.
6. **Click cell H4, press [F2] to change to Edit mode, then press [F4]**

   When you press [F2], the range finder outlines the arguments of the equation in blue and green. The insertion point appears next to the G2 cell reference in cell H4. When you press [F4], dollar signs are inserted in the G2 cell reference, making it an absolute reference. See Figure B-17.
7. **Click ✓, then drag the fill handle from cell H4 to cell H11**

   Because the formula correctly contains an absolute cell reference, the correct values for a 10% increase appear in cells H4:H11. You now want to see what a 20% increase in expenses looks like.
8. **Click cell G2, type 1.2, then click ✓**

   The values in the range H4:H11 change to reflect the 20% increase. Compare your worksheet to Figure B-18.
9. **Save your work**

QUICK TIP

Before you copy or move a formula, always check to see if you need to use an absolute cell reference.

QUICK TIP

When changing a cell reference to an absolute reference, make sure the reference is selected or the insertion point is next to it in the cell before pressing [F4].

FIGURE B-17: Absolute reference created in formula

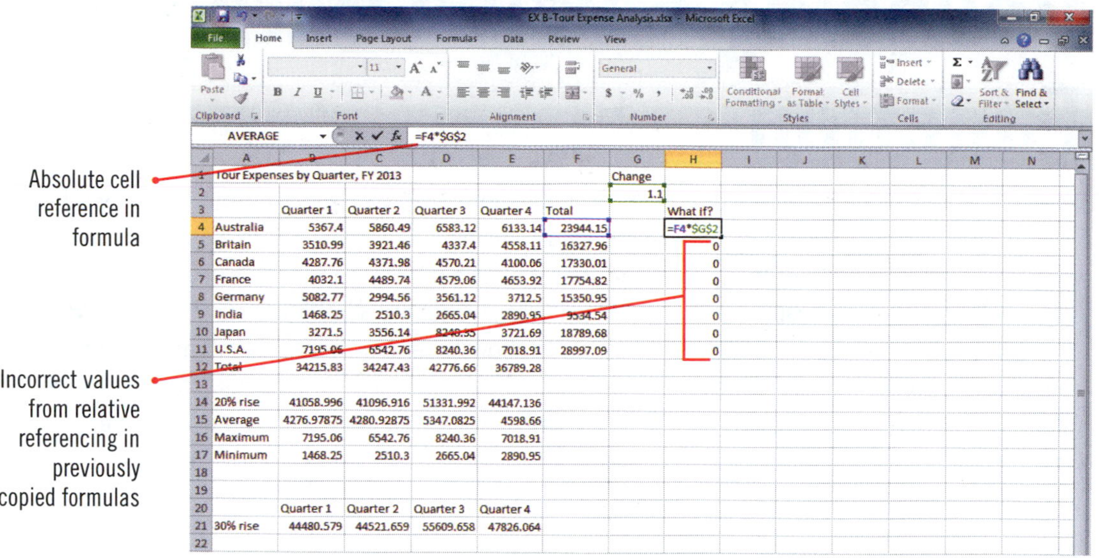

FIGURE B-18: What-if analysis with modified change factor

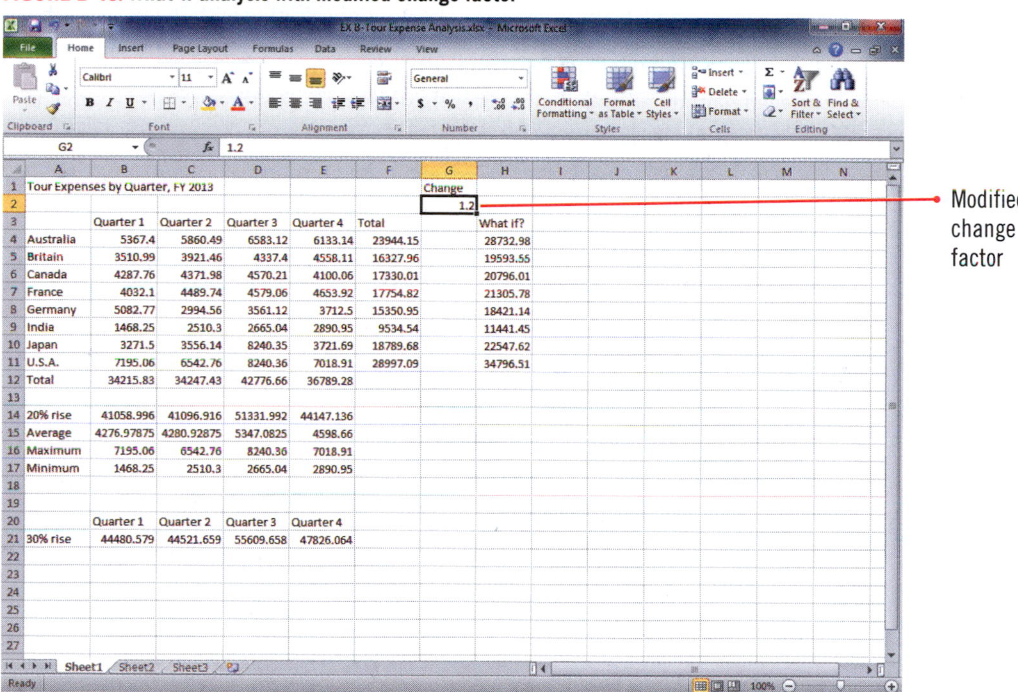

Using the fill handle for sequential text or values

Often, you need to fill cells with sequential text: months of the year, days of the week, years, or text plus a number (Quarter 1, Quarter 2,...). For example, you might want to create a worksheet that calculates data for every month of the year. Using the fill handle, you can quickly and easily create labels for the months of the year just by typing "January" in a cell. Drag the fill handle from the cell containing "January" until you have all the monthly labels you need. You can also easily fill cells with a date sequence by dragging the fill handle on a single cell containing a date. You can fill cells with a number sequence (such as 1, 2, 3,...) by dragging the fill handle on a selection of two or more cells that contain the sequence. To create a number sequence using the value in a single cell, press and hold [Ctrl] as you drag the fill handle of the cell. As you drag the fill handle, Excel automatically extends the existing sequence into the additional cells. (The content of the last filled cell appears in the ScreenTip.) To examine all the fill series options for the current selection, click the Fill button in the Editing group on the Home tab, then click Series to open the Series dialog box.

UNIT
B
Excel 2010

Rounding a Value with a Function

The more you explore features and tools in Excel, the more ways you'll find to simplify your work and convey information more efficiently. For example, cells containing financial data are often easier to read if they contain fewer decimal places than those that appear by default. You can round a value or formula result to a specific number of decimal places by using the ROUND function. In your worksheet, you'd like to round the cells showing the 20% rise in expenses to show fewer digits; after all, it's not important to show cents in the projections, only whole dollars. You want Excel to round the calculated value to the nearest integer. You decide to edit cell B14 so it includes the ROUND function, and then copy the edited formula into the other formulas in this row.

STEPS

1. **Click cell B14, then click to the right of = in the formula bar**

   You want to position the function at the beginning of the formula, before any values or arguments.

2. **Type RO**

   Formula AutoComplete displays a list of functions beginning with RO beneath the formula bar.

3. **Double-click ROUND in the functions list**

   The new function and an opening parenthesis are added to the formula, as shown in Figure B-19. A few additional modifications are needed to complete your edit of the formula. You need to indicate the number of decimal places to which the function should round numbers and you also need to add a closing parenthesis around the set of arguments that comes after the ROUND function.

4. **Press [END], type ,0), then click the Enter button ✓ on the formula bar**

   The comma separates the arguments within the formula, and 0 indicates that you don't want any decimal places to appear in the calculated value. When you complete the edit, the parentheses at either end of the formula briefly become bold, indicating that the formula has the correct number of open and closed parentheses and is balanced.

5. **Drag the fill handle from cell B14 to cell E14**

   The formula in cell B14 is copied to the range C14:E14. All the values are rounded to display no decimal places. Compare your worksheet to Figure B-20.

6. **Click cell A25, type your name, then click ✓ on the formula bar**

7. **Save your work, preview the worksheet in Backstage view, then submit your work to your Instructor as directed**

8. **Exit Excel**

QUICK TIP

In the Insert Function dialog box, the ROUND function is in the Math & Trig category.

TROUBLE

If you have too many or too few parentheses, the extraneous parenthesis is displayed in green, or a warning dialog box opens with a suggested solution to the error.

FIGURE B-19: ROUND function added to an existing formula

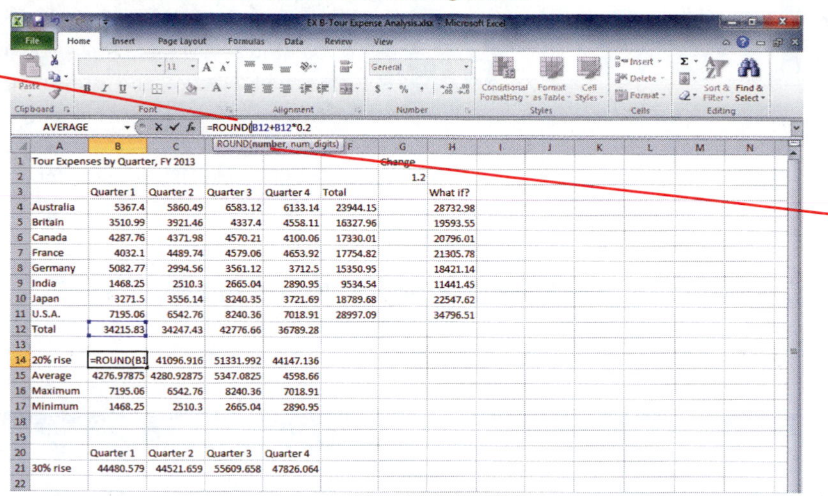

FIGURE B-20: Completed worksheet

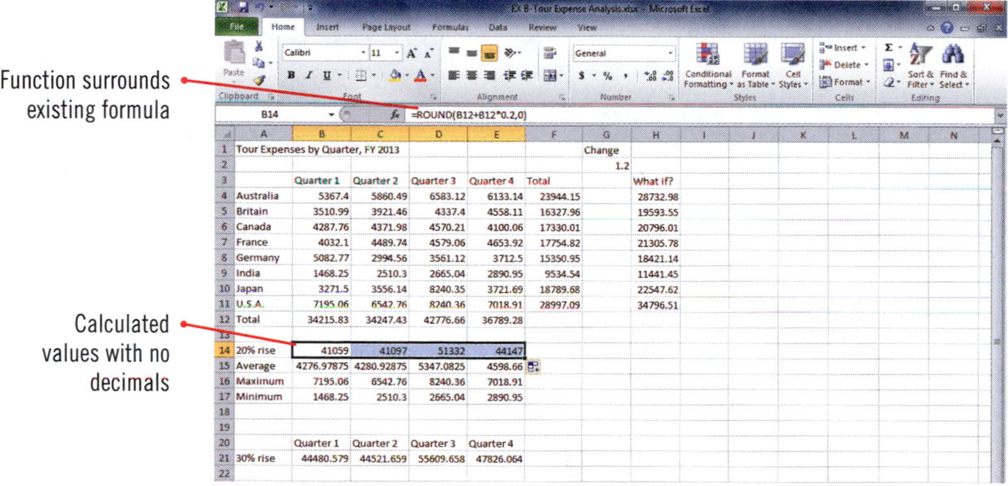

Creating a new workbook using a template

Excel **templates** are predesigned workbook files intended to save time when you create common documents such as balance sheets, budgets, or time cards. Templates contain labels, values, formulas, and formatting, so all you have to do is customize them with your own information. Excel comes with many templates, and you can also create your own or find additional templates on the Web. Unlike a typical workbook, which has the file extension .xlsx, a template has the extension .xltx. To create a workbook using a template, click the File tab, then click New on the navigation bar. The Available Templates pane in Backstage view lists templates installed on your computer and templates available through Office.com. The Blank Workbook template is selected by default and is used to create a blank workbook with no content or special formatting. A preview of the selected template appears to the right of the Available Templates pane. To select a template, click a category in the Available Templates pane, select the template you want in the category, then click Create (if you've selected an installed template) or Download (if you've selected an Office.com template). Figure B-21 shows a template selected in the Budgets category of Office.com templates. (Your list of templates may differ.) When you click Create or Download, a new workbook is created based on the template; when you save the new file in the default format, it has the regular .xlsx extension. To save a workbook of your own as a template, open the Save As dialog box, click the Save as type list arrow, then change the file type to Excel Template.

FIGURE B-21: Budget template selected in Backstage view

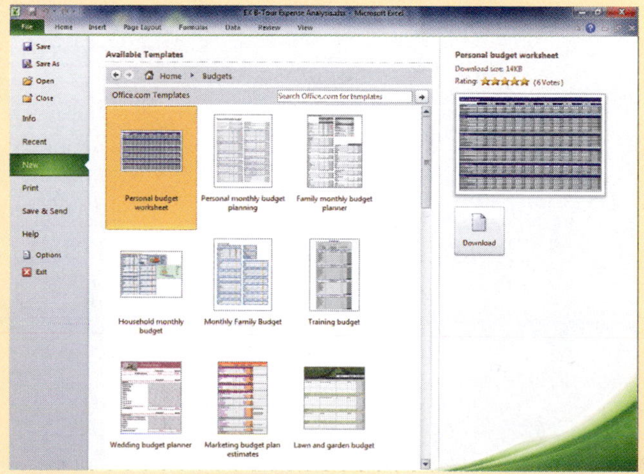

Excel 2010

Practice

Concepts Review

For current SAM information, including versions and content details, visit SAM Central (http://www.cengage.com/samcentral). If you have a SAM user profile, you may have access to hands-on instruction, practice, and assessment of the skills covered in this unit. Since various versions of SAM are supported throughout the life of this text, check with your instructor for the correct instructions and URL/Web site for accessing assignments.

Label each element of the Excel worksheet window shown in Figure B-22.

FIGURE B-22

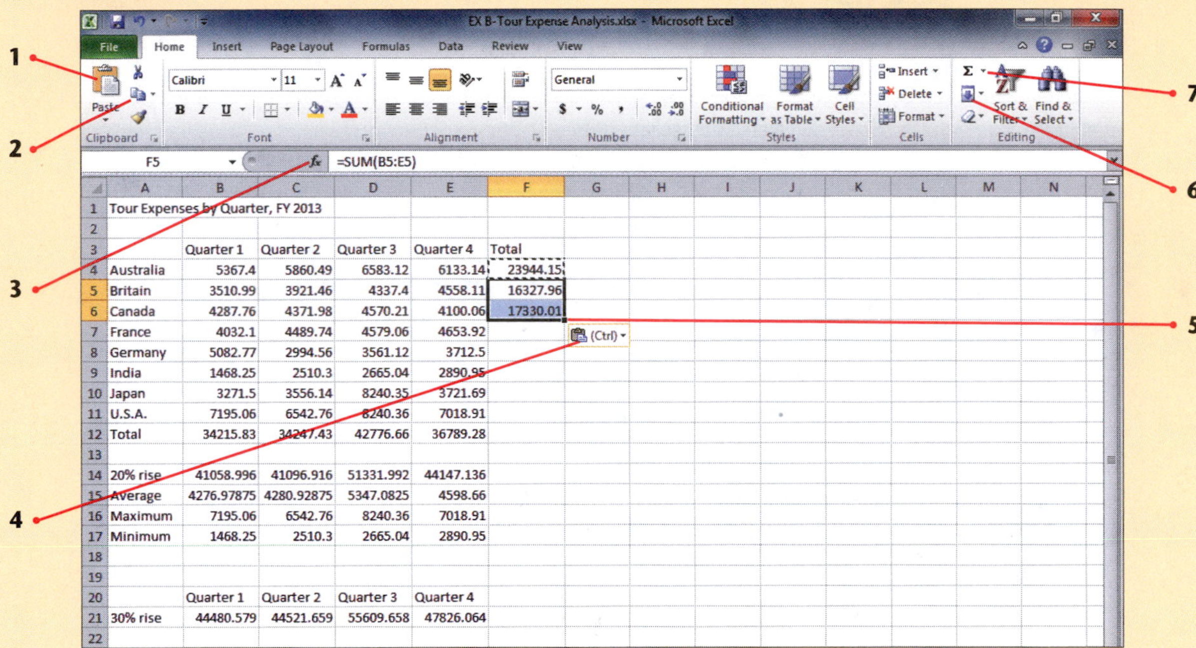

1
2
3
4
5
6
7
EX B-Tour Expense Analysis.xlsx - Microsoft Excel
F5
=SUM(B5:E5)
Tour Expenses by Quarter, FY 2013
Quarter 1 Quarter 2 Quarter 3 Quarter 4 Total
Australia 5367.4 5860.49 6583.12 6133.14 23944.15
Britain 3510.99 3921.46 4337.4 4558.11 16327.96
Canada 4287.76 4371.98 4570.21 4100.06 17330.01
France 4032.1 4489.74 4579.06 4653.92
Germany 5082.77 2994.56 3561.12 3712.5
India 1468.25 2510.3 2665.04 2890.95
Japan 3271.5 3556.14 8240.35 3721.69
U.S.A. 7195.06 6542.76 8240.36 7018.91
Total 34215.83 34247.43 42776.66 36789.28
20% rise 41058.996 41096.916 51331.992 44147.136
Average 4276.97875 4280.92875 5347.0825 4598.66
Maximum 7195.06 6542.76 8240.36 7018.91
Minimum 1468.25 2510.3 2665.04 2890.95
Quarter 1 Quarter 2 Quarter 3 Quarter 4
30% rise 44480.579 44521.659 55609.658 47826.064

Match each term or button with the statement that best describes it.

8. Fill handle
9. Dialog box launcher
10. Drag-and-drop method
11. [Delete]
12. Formula AutoComplete

a. Clears the contents of selected cells
b. Item on the Ribbon that opens a dialog box or task pane
c. Lets you move or copy data from one cell to another without using the Clipboard
d. Displays an alphabetical list of functions from which you can choose
e. Lets you copy cell contents or continue a series of data into a range of selected cells

Select the best answer from the list of choices.

13. Which key do you press to copy while dragging and dropping selected cells?

a. [Alt]
b. [Ctrl]
c. [F2]
d. [Tab]

14. What type of cell reference is C$19?

a. Relative
b. Absolute
c. Mixed
d. Certain

15. What type of cell reference changes when it is copied?

a. Circular
b. Absolute
c. Relative
d. Specified

16. Which key do you press to convert a relative cell reference to an absolute cell reference?

a. [F2]
b. [F4]
c. [F5]
d. [F6]

17. You can use any of the following features to enter a function *except*:

a. Insert Function button.
b. Formula AutoComplete.
c. Sum list arrow.
d. Clipboard.

Skills Review

1. Create a complex formula.

a. Open the file EX B-2.xlsx from the drive and folder where you store your Data Files, then save it as **EX B-Baking Supply Company Inventory**.
b. In cell B11, create a complex formula that calculates a 30% decrease in the total number of cases of cake pans.
c. Use the fill handle to copy this formula into cell C11 through cell E11.
d. Save your work.

2. Insert a function.

a. Use the Sum list arrow to create a formula in cell B13 that averages the number of cases of cake pans in each storage area.
b. Use the Insert Function button to create a formula in cell B14 that calculates the maximum number of cases of cake pans in a storage area.
c. Use the Sum list arrow to create a formula in cell B15 that calculates the minimum number of cases of cake pans in a storage area.
d. Save your work.

3. Type a function.

a. In cell C13, type a formula that includes a function to average the number of cases of pie pans in each storage area. (*Hint*: Use Formula AutoComplete to enter the function.)
b. In cell C14, type a formula that includes a function to calculate the maximum number of cases of pie pans in a storage area.
c. In cell C15, type a formula that includes a function to calculate the minimum number of cases of pie pans in a storage area.
d. Save your work.

Skills Review (continued)

4. **Copy and move cell entries.**
   a. Select the range B3:F3.
   b. Copy the selection to the Clipboard.
   c. Open the Clipboard task pane, then paste the selection into cell B17.
   d. Close the Clipboard task pane, then select the range A4:A9.
   e. Use the drag-and-drop method to copy the selection to cell A18. (*Hint*: The results should fill the range A18:A23.)
   f. Save your work.
5. **Understand relative and absolute cell references.**
   a. Write a brief description of the difference between relative and absolute references.
   b. List at least three situations in which you think a business might use an absolute reference in its calculations. Examples can include calculations for different types of worksheets, such as time cards, invoices, and budgets.
6. **Copy formulas with relative cell references.**
   a. Calculate the total in cell F4.
   b. Use the Fill button to copy the formula in cell F4 down to cells F5:F8.
   c. Select the range C13:C15.
   d. Use the fill handle to copy these cells to the range D13:F15.
   e. Save your work.
7. **Copy formulas with absolute cell references.**
   a. In cell H1, enter the value **1.575**.
   b. In cell H4, create a formula that multiplies F4 and an absolute reference to cell H1.
   c. Use the fill handle to copy the formula in cell H4 to cells H5 and H6.
   d. Use the Copy and Paste buttons to copy the formula in cell H4 to cells H7 and H8.
   e. Change the amount in cell H1 to **2.3**.
   f. Save your work.
8. **Round a value with a function.**
   a. Click cell H4.
   b. Edit this formula to include the ROUND function showing zero decimal places.
   c. Use the fill handle to copy the formula in cell H4 to the range H5:H8.
   d. Enter your name in cell A25, then compare your work to Figure B-23.
   e. Save your work, preview the worksheet in Backstage view, then submit your work to your instructor as directed.
   f. Close the workbook, then exit Excel.

FIGURE B-23

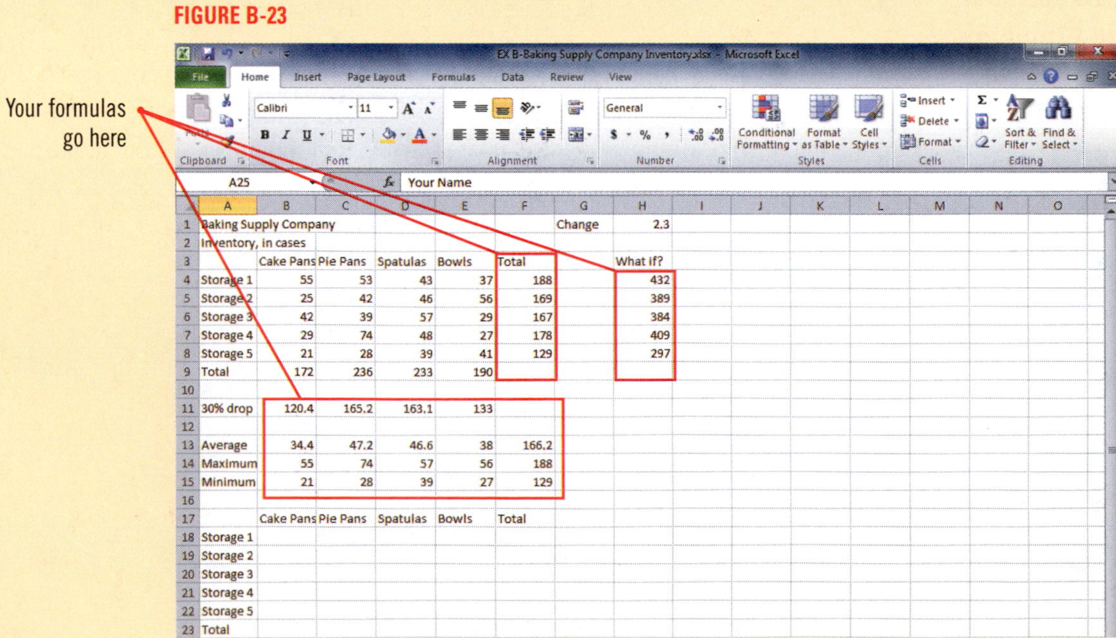

Independent Challenge 1

You are thinking of starting a small express oil change service center. Before you begin, you need to evaluate what you think your monthly expenses will be. You've started a workbook, but need to complete the entries and add formulas.

If you have a SAM 2010 user profile, an autogradable SAM version of this assignment may be available at http://www.cengage.com/sam2010. Check with your instructor to confirm that this assignment is available in SAM. To use the SAM version of this assignment, log into the SAM 2010 Web site and download the instruction and start files.

a. Open the file EX B-3.xlsx from the drive and folder where you store your Data Files, then save it as **EX B-Express Oil Change Expenses**.

b. Make up your own expense data, and enter it in cells B4:B10. (Monthly sales are already included in the worksheet.)

c. Create a formula in cell C4 that calculates the annual rent.

d. Copy the formula in cell C4 to the range C5:C10.

e. Move the label in cell A15 to cell A14.

f. Create formulas in cells B11 and C11 that total the monthly and annual expenses.

g. Create a formula in cell C13 that calculates annual sales.

h. Create a formula in cell B14 that determines whether you will make a profit or loss, then copy the formula into cell C14.

i. Copy the labels in cells B3:C3 to cells E3:F3.

j. Type **Projected Increase** in cell G1, then type **.2** in cell H2.

k. Create a formula in cell E4 that calculates an increase in the monthly rent by the amount in cell H2. You will be copying this formula to other cells, so you'll need to use an absolute reference.

l. Create a formula in cell F4 that calculates the increased annual rent expense based on the calculation in cell E4.

m. Copy the formulas in cells E4:F4 into cells E5:F10 to calculate the remaining monthly and annual expenses.

n. Create a formula in cell E11 that calculates the total monthly expenses, then copy that formula to cell F11.

o. Copy the contents of cells B13:C13 into cells E13:F13.

p. Create formulas in cells E14 and F14 that calculate profit/loss based on the projected increase in monthly and annual expenses.

q. Change the projected increase to **.15**, then compare your work to the sample in Figure B-24.

r. Enter your name in a cell in the worksheet.

s. Save your work, preview the worksheet in Backstage view, submit your work to your instructor as directed, close the workbook, and exit Excel.

FIGURE B-24

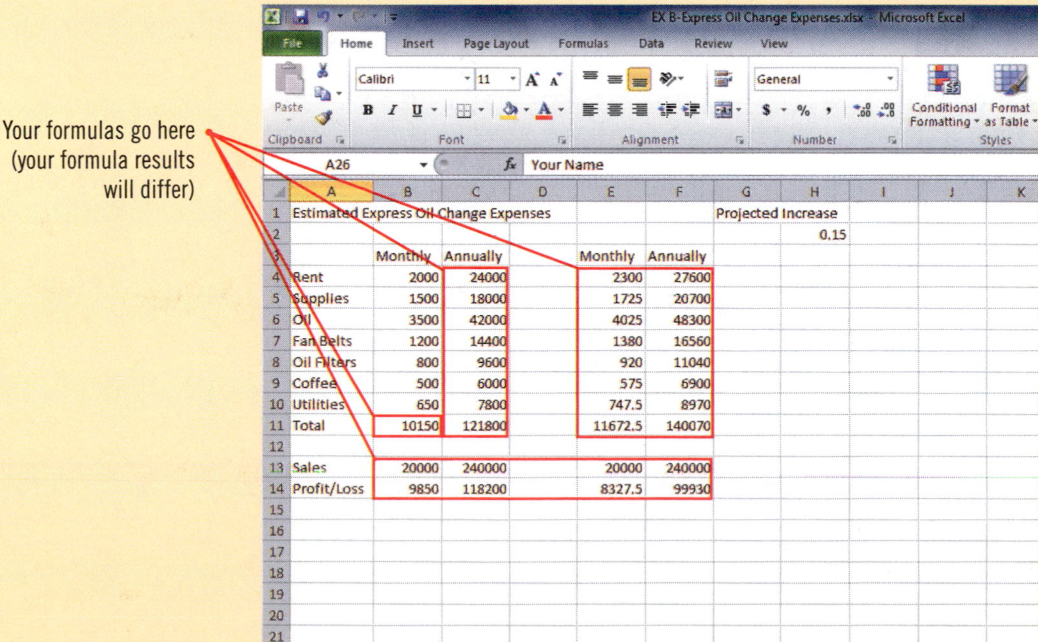

	A	B	C	D	E	F	G	H
1	Estimated Express Oil Change Expenses						Projected Increase	
2								0.15
3		Monthly	Annually		Monthly	Annually		
4	Rent	2000	24000		2300	27600		
5	Supplies	1500	18000		1725	20700		
6	Oil	3500	42000		4025	48300		
7	Fan Belts	1200	14400		1380	16560		
8	Oil Filters	800	9600		920	11040		
9	Coffee	500	6000		575	6900		
10	Utilities	650	7800		747.5	8970		
11	Total	10150	121800		11672.5	140070		
12								
13	Sales	20000	240000		20000	240000		
14	Profit/Loss	9850	118200		8327.5	99930		

Independent Challenge 2

The Dog Days Daycare Center is a small, growing pet care center that has hired you to organize its accounting records using Excel. The owners want you to track the company's expenses. Before you were hired, one of the bookkeepers began entering last year's expenses in a workbook, but the analysis was never completed.

- **a.** Start Excel, open the file EX B-4.xlsx from the drive and folder where you store your Data Files, then save it as **EX B-Dog Days Daycare Center Finances**. The worksheet includes labels for functions such as the average, maximum, and minimum amounts of each of the expenses in the worksheet.
- **b.** Think about what information would be important for the bookkeeping staff to know.
- **c.** Using the SUM function, create formulas for each expense in the Total column and each quarter in the Total row.
- **d.** Create formulas for each expense and each quarter in the Average, Maximum, and Minimum columns and rows using the method of your choice.
- **e.** Save your work, then compare your worksheet to the sample shown in Figure B-25.

FIGURE B-25

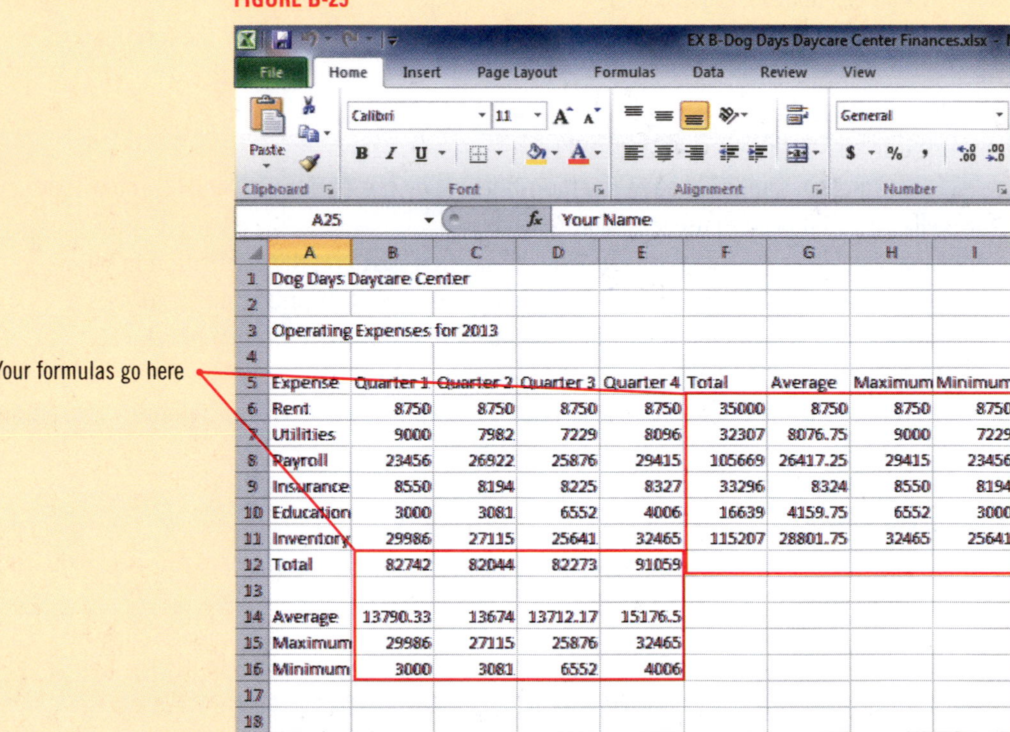

	A	B	C	D	E	F	G	H	I
1	Dog Days Daycare Center								
2									
3	Operating Expenses for 2013								
4									
5	Expense	Quarter 1	Quarter 2	Quarter 3	Quarter 4	Total	Average	Maximum	Minimum
6	Rent	8750	8750	8750	8750	35000	8750	8750	8750
7	Utilities	9000	7982	7229	8096	32307	8076.75	9000	7229
8	Payroll	23456	26922	25876	29415	105669	26417.25	29415	23456
9	Insurance	8550	8194	8225	8327	33296	8324	8550	8194
10	Education	3000	3081	6552	4006	16639	4159.75	6552	3000
11	Inventory	29986	27115	25641	32465	115207	28801.75	32465	25641
12	Total	82742	82044	82273	91059				
13									
14	Average	13790.33	13674	13712.17	15176.5				
15	Maximum	29986	27115	25876	32465				
16	Minimum	3000	3081	6552	4006				
17									
18									

Advanced Challenge Exercise

- Create the label **Expense categories** in cell B19.
- In cell A19, create a formula using the COUNT function that determines the total number of expense categories listed per quarter.
- Save the workbook.

- **f.** Enter your name in cell A25.
- **g.** Preview the worksheet, then submit your work to your instructor as directed.
- **h.** Close the workbook and exit Excel.

Independent Challenge 3

As the accounting manager of a locally owned business, it is your responsibility to calculate accrued sales tax payments on a monthly basis and then submit the payments to the state government. You've decided to use an Excel workbook to make these calculations.

a. Start Excel, then save a new, blank workbook to the drive and folder where you store your Data Files as **EX B-Sales Tax Calculations**.

b. Decide on the layout for all columns and rows. The worksheet will contain data for six stores, which you can name by store number, neighborhood, or another method of your choice. For each store, you will calculate total sales tax based on the local sales tax rate. You'll also calculate total tax owed for all six stores.

c. Make up sales data for all six stores.

d. Enter the rate to be used to calculate the sales tax, using your own local rate.

e. Create formulas to calculate the sales tax owed for each store. If you don't know the local tax rate, use **6.5%**.

f. Create a formula to total all the owed sales tax, then compare your work to the sample shown in Figure B-26.

FIGURE B-26

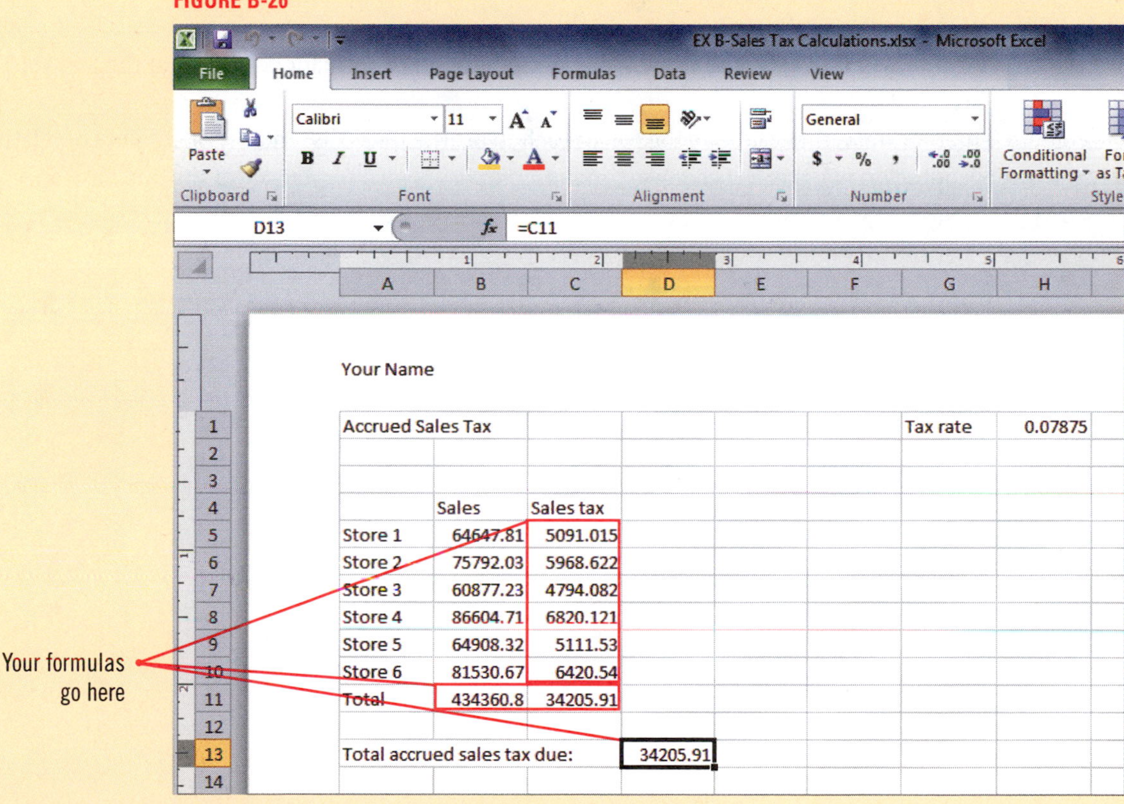

Advanced Challenge Exercise

- Use the ROUND function to eliminate any decimal places in the sales tax figures for each store and the total due.
- Save the workbook.

g. Add your name to the header.

h. Save your work, preview the worksheet, and submit your work to your instructor as directed.

i. Close the workbook and exit Excel.

Real Life Independent Challenge

Since your recent promotion at work, you have started thinking about purchasing a home. As you begin the round of open houses and realtors' listings, you notice that there are many fees associated with buying a home. Some fees are based on a percentage of the purchase price, and others are a flat fee; overall, they seem to represent a substantial amount above the purchase prices you see listed. You've seen five houses so far that interest you; one is easily affordable, and the remaining four are all nice, but increasingly more expensive. Although you will be financing the home, the bottom line is still important to you, so you decide to create an Excel workbook to figure out the real cost of buying each one.

a. Find out the typical cost or percentage rate of at least three fees that are usually charged when buying a home and taking out a mortgage. (*Hint*: If you have access to the Internet you can research the topic of home buying on the Web, or you can ask friends about standard rates or percentages for items such as title insurance, credit reports, and inspection fees.)

b. Start Excel, then save a new, blank workbook to the drive and folder where you store your Data Files as **EX B-Home Purchase Costs**.

c. Create labels and enter data for at least three homes. If you enter this information across the columns in your worksheet, you should have one column for each house, with the purchase price in the cell below each label. Be sure to enter a different purchase price for each house.

d. Create labels for the Fees column and for an Amount or Rate column. Enter the information for each of the fees you have researched.

e. In each house column, enter formulas that calculate the fee for each item. The formulas (and use of absolute or relative referencing) will vary depending on whether the charges are a flat fee or based on a percentage of the purchase price.

Real Life Independent Challenge (continued)

f. Total the fees for each house, then create formulas that add the total fees to the purchase price. A sample of what your workbook might look like is shown in Figure B-27.

g. Enter a title for the worksheet in the header.

h. Enter your name in the header, save your work, preview the worksheet, then submit your work to your instructor as directed.

i. Close the file and exit Excel.

FIGURE B-27

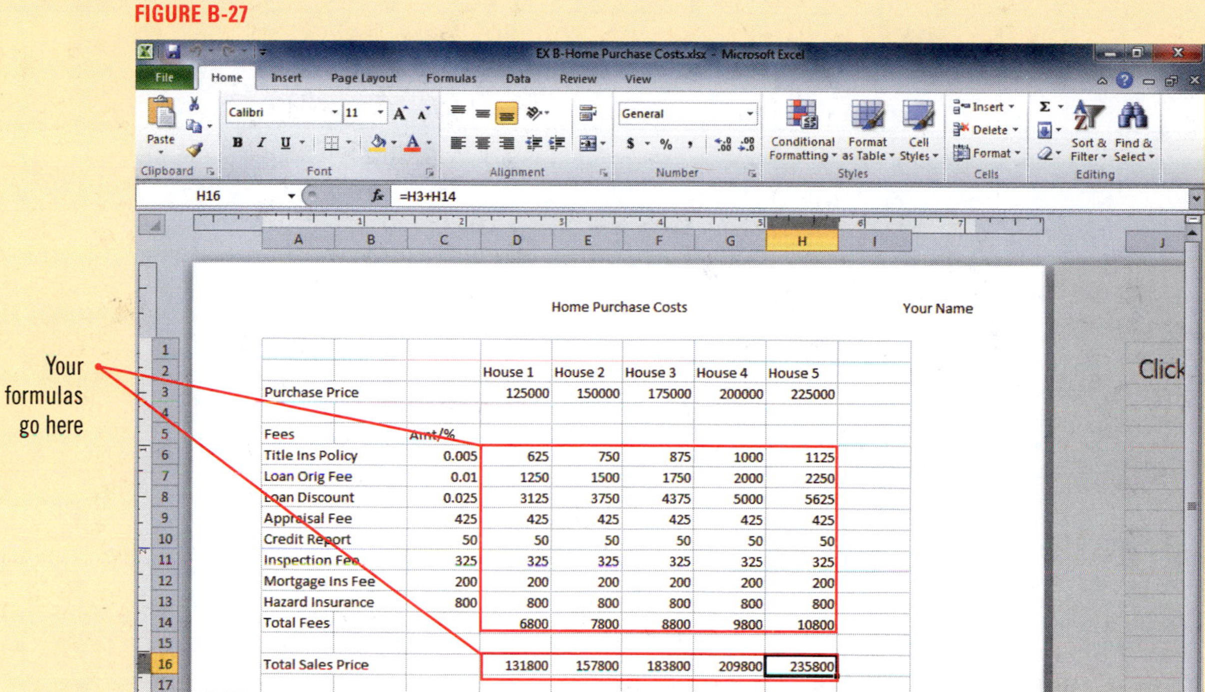

Excel 2010

Visual Workshop

Create the worksheet shown in Figure B-28 using the skills you learned in this unit. Save the workbook as **EX B-Expense Analysis** to the drive and folder where you store your Data Files. Enter your name in the header as shown, hide the gridlines, preview the worksheet, and then submit your work to your instructor as directed.

FIGURE B-28

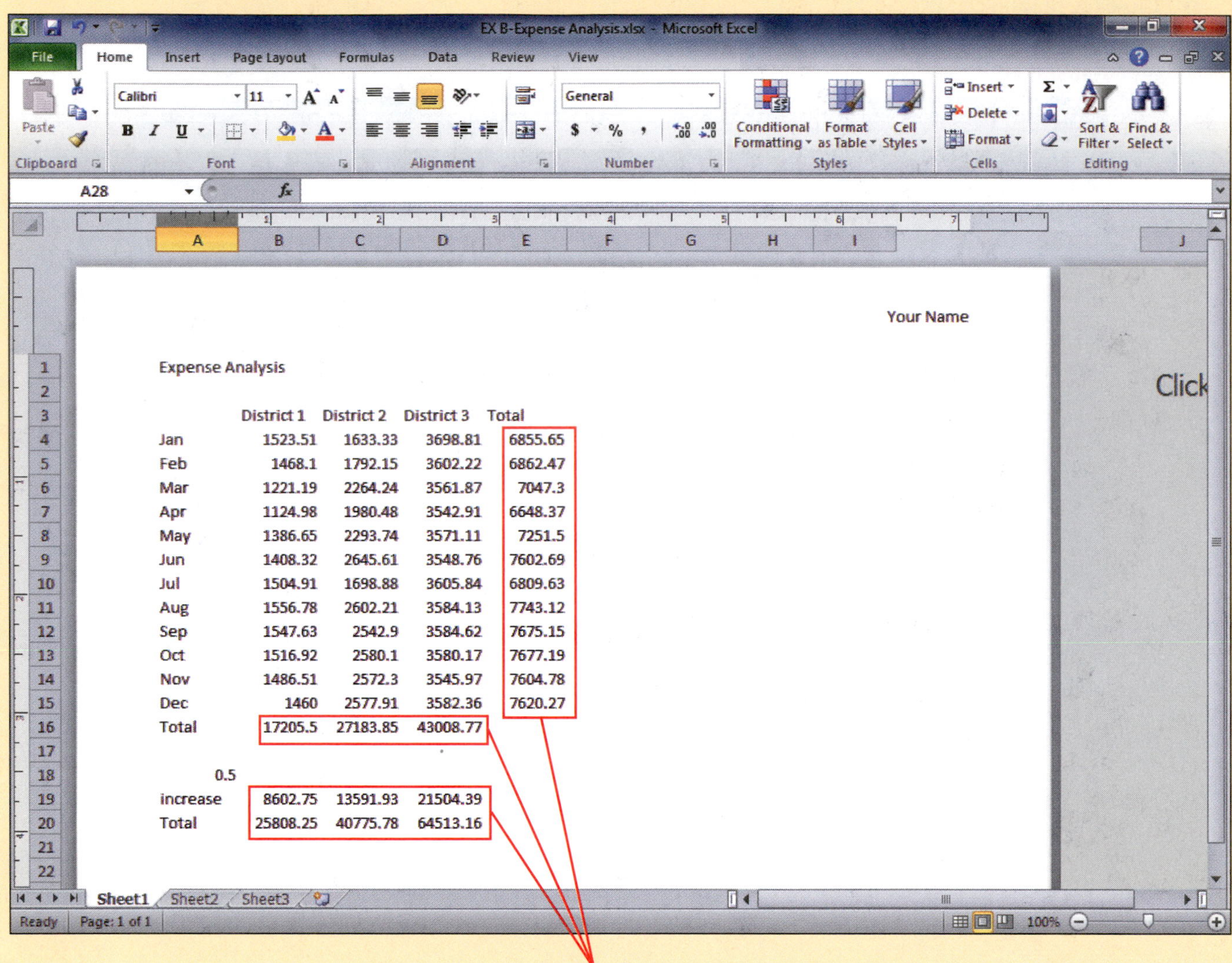

Your Name

Expense Analysis

	District 1	District 2	District 3	Total
Jan	1523.51	1633.33	3698.81	6855.65
Feb	1468.1	1792.15	3602.22	6862.47
Mar	1221.19	2264.24	3561.87	7047.3
Apr	1124.98	1980.48	3542.91	6648.37
May	1386.65	2293.74	3571.11	7251.5
Jun	1408.32	2645.61	3548.76	7602.69
Jul	1504.91	1698.88	3605.84	6809.63
Aug	1556.78	2602.21	3584.13	7743.12
Sep	1547.63	2542.9	3584.62	7675.15
Oct	1516.92	2580.1	3580.17	7677.19
Nov	1486.51	2572.3	3545.97	7604.78
Dec	1460	2577.91	3582.36	7620.27
Total	17205.5	27183.85	43008.77	
0.5				
increase	8602.75	13591.93	21504.39	
Total	25808.25	40775.78	64513.16	

Enter formulas and not values in these cells

Formatting a Worksheet

Files You Will Need:

EX C-1.xlsx
EX C-2.xlsx
EX C-3.xlsx
EX C-4.xlsx
EX C-5.xlsx

You can use formatting features to make a worksheet more attractive or easier to read, and to emphasize key data. You can apply different formatting attributes such as colors, font styles, and font sizes to the cell contents; you can adjust column width and row height; and you can insert or delete columns and rows. You can also apply conditional formatting so that cells meeting certain conditions are formatted differently from other cells. This makes it easy to emphasize selected information, such as sales that exceed or fall below a certain threshold. The corporate marketing managers at QST have requested data from all QST locations for advertising expenses incurred during the first quarter of this year. Grace Wong has created a worksheet listing this information. She asks you to format the worksheet to make it easier to read and to call attention to important data.

OBJECTIVES

- Format values
- Change font and font size
- Change font styles and alignment
- Adjust column width
- Insert and delete rows and columns
- Apply colors, patterns, and borders
- Apply conditional formatting
- Rename and move a worksheet
- Check spelling

UNIT C
Excel 2010

Formatting Values

The **format** of a cell determines how the labels and values look—for example, whether the contents appear boldfaced, italicized, or with dollar signs and commas. Formatting changes only the appearance of a value or label; it does not alter the actual data in any way. To format a cell or range, first you select it, then you apply the formatting using the Ribbon, Mini toolbar, or a keyboard shortcut. You can apply formatting before or after you enter data in a cell or range. Grace has provided you with a worksheet that lists individual advertising expenses, and you're ready to improve its appearance and readability. You decide to start by formatting some of the values so they are displayed as currency, percentages, and dates.

STEPS

QUICK TIP
You can use a different type of currency, such as Euros or British pounds, by clicking the Accounting Number Format list arrow, then clicking a different currency type.

QUICK TIP
Select any range of contiguous cells by clicking the upper-left cell of the range, pressing and holding [Shift], then clicking the lower-right cell of the range. Add a row to the selected range by continuing to hold down [Shift] and pressing ↓; add a column by pressing →.

QUICK TIP
Make sure you examine formatted data to confirm that you have applied the appropriate formatting; for example, dates should not have a currency format, and monetary values should not have a date format.

1. **Start Excel, open the file EX C-1.xlsx from the drive and folder where you store your Data Files, then save it as EX C-QST Advertising Expenses**
   This worksheet is difficult to interpret because all the information is crowded and looks the same. In some columns, the contents appear cut off because there is too much data to fit given the current column width. You decide not to widen the columns yet, because the other changes you plan to make might affect column width and row height. The first thing you want to do is format the data showing the cost of each ad.
2. **Select the range D4:D32, then click the Accounting Number Format button $ in the Number group on the Home tab**
   The default Accounting **number format** adds dollar signs and two decimal places to the data, as shown in Figure C-1. Formatting this data in Accounting format makes it clear that its values are monetary values. Excel automatically resizes the column to display the new formatting. The Accounting and Currency number formats are both used for monetary values, but the Accounting format aligns currency symbols and decimal points of numbers in a column.
3. **Select the range F4:H32, then click the Comma Style button in the Number group**
   The values in columns F, G, and H display the Comma Style format, which does not include a dollar sign but can be useful for some types of accounting data.
4. **Select the range J4:J32, click the Number Format list arrow, click Percentage, then click the Increase Decimal button in the Number group**
   The data in the % of Total column is now formatted with a percent sign (%) and three decimal places. The Number Format list arrow lets you choose from popular number formats and shows an example of what the selected cell or cells would look like in each format (when multiple cells are selected, the example is based on the first cell in the range). Each time you click the Increase Decimal button, you add one decimal place; clicking the button twice would add two decimal places.
5. **Click the Decrease Decimal button in the Number group twice**
   Two decimal places are removed from the percentage values in column J.
6. **Select the range B4:B31, then click the dialog box launcher in the Number group**
   The Format Cells dialog box opens with the Date category already selected on the Number tab.
7. **Select the first 14-Mar-01 format in the Type list box as shown in Figure C-2, then click OK**
   The dates in column B appear in the 14-Mar-01 format. The second 14-Mar-01 format in the list displays all days in two digits (it adds a leading zero if the day is only a single-digit number), while the one you chose displays single-digit days without a leading zero.
8. **Select the range C4:C31, right-click the range, click Format Cells on the shortcut menu, click 14-Mar in the Type list box in the Format Cells dialog box, then click OK**
   Compare your worksheet to Figure C-3.
9. **Press [Ctrl][Home], then save your work**

FIGURE C-1: Accounting number format applied to range

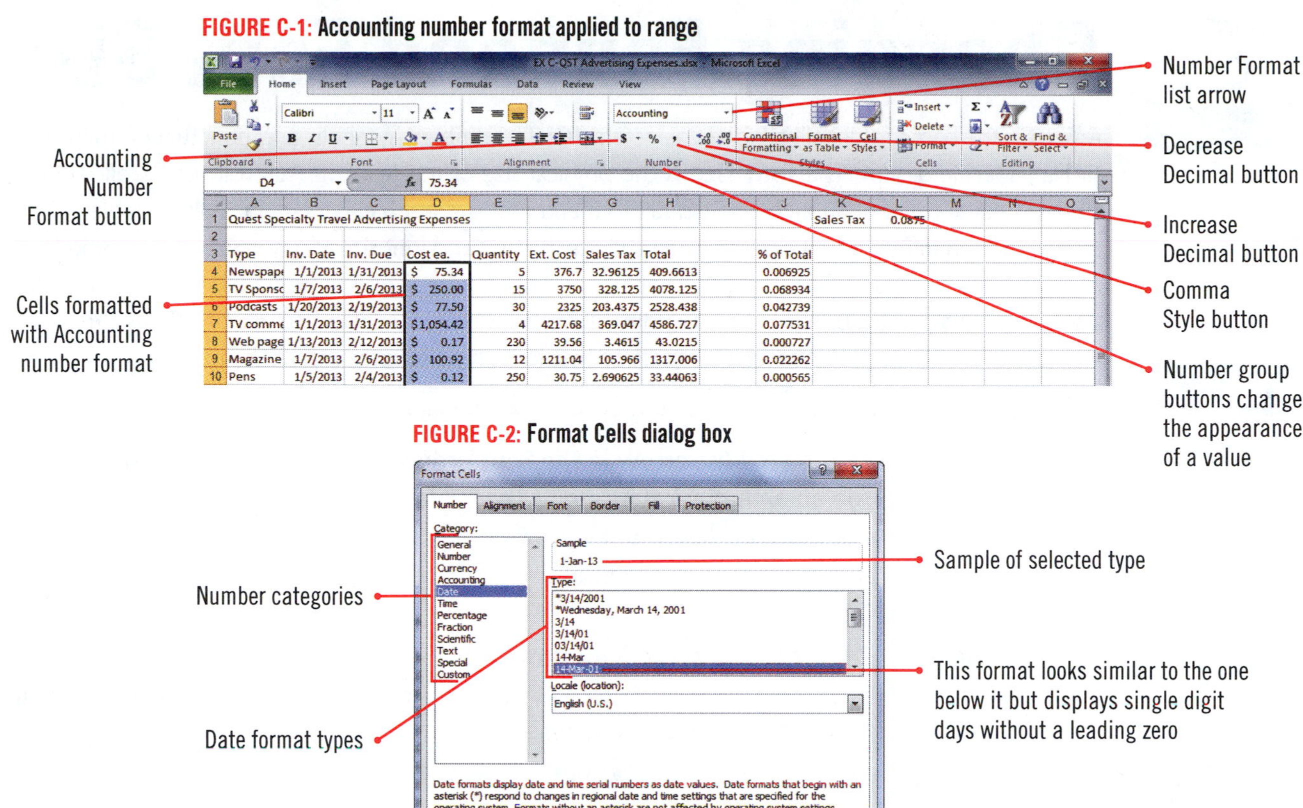

FIGURE C-2: Format Cells dialog box

FIGURE C-3: Worksheet with formatted values

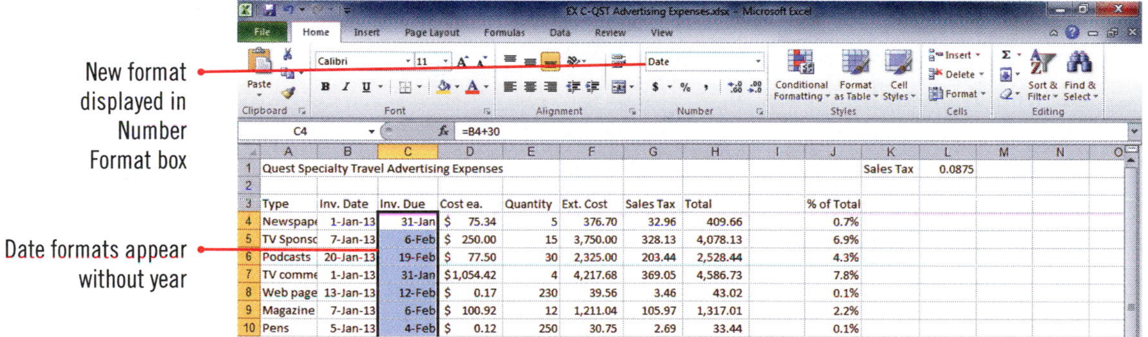

Formatting as a table

Excel includes 60 predefined **table styles** to make it easy to format selected worksheet cells as a table. You can apply table styles to any range of cells that you want to format quickly, or even to an entire worksheet, but they're especially useful for those ranges with labels in the left column and top row, and totals in the bottom row or right column. To apply a table style, select the data to be formatted or click anywhere within the intended range (Excel can automatically detect a range of cells filled with data), click the Format as Table button in the Styles group on the Home tab, then click a style in the gallery, as shown in Figure C-4. Table styles are organized in three categories: Light, Medium, and Dark. Once you click a style, Excel asks you to confirm the range selection, then applies the style. Once you have formatted a range as a table, you can use Live Preview to preview the table in other styles by pointing to any style in the Table Styles gallery.

FIGURE C-4: Table Styles gallery

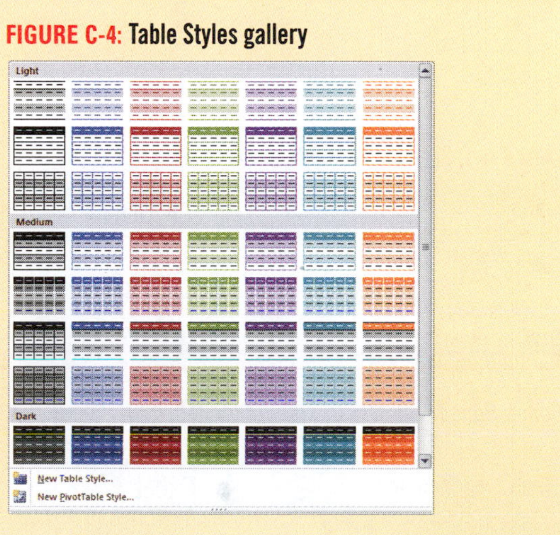

UNIT C

Excel 2010

Changing Font and Font Size

A **font** is the name for a collection of characters (letters, numbers, symbols, and punctuation marks) with a similar, specific design. The **font size** is the physical size of the text, measured in units called points. A **point** is equal to 1/72 of an inch. The default font and font size in Excel is 11-point Calibri. Table C-1 shows several fonts in different font sizes. You can change the font and font size of any cell or range using the Font and Font Size list arrows. The Font and Font Size list arrows appear on the Home tab on the Ribbon and on the Mini toolbar, which opens when you right-click a cell or range. You want to change the font and font size of the labels and the worksheet title so that they stand out more from the data.

STEPS

QUICK TIP
To quickly move to a font in the Font list, type the first few characters of its name.

1. **Click cell A1, click the Font list arrow in the Font group on the Home tab, scroll down in the Font list to see an alphabetical listing of the fonts available on your computer, then click Times New Roman, as shown in Figure C-5**

   The font in cell A1 changes to Times New Roman. Notice that the font names on the list are displayed in the font they represent.

QUICK TIP
When you point to an option in the Font or Font Size list, Live Preview shows the selected cells with the option temporarily applied.

2. **Click the Font Size list arrow in the Font group, then click 20**

   The worksheet title appears in 20-point Times New Roman, and the Font and Font Size list boxes on the Home tab display the new font and font size information.

3. **Click the Increase Font Size button A in the Font group twice**

   The font size of the title increases to 24 point.

4. **Select the range A3:J3, right-click, then click the Font list arrow in the Font group on the Mini toolbar**

   The Mini toolbar includes the most commonly used formatting tools, so it's great for making quick formatting changes.

QUICK TIP
You can format an entire row by clicking the row indicator button to select the row before formatting (or select an entire column by clicking the column indicator button before formatting).

5. **Scroll down in the Font list and click Times New Roman, click the Font Size list arrow on the Mini toolbar, then click 14**

   The Mini toolbar closes when you move the pointer away from the selection. Compare your worksheet to Figure C-6. Notice that some of the column labels are now too wide to appear fully in the column. Excel does not automatically adjust column widths to accommodate cell formatting; you have to adjust column widths manually. You'll learn to do this in a later lesson.

6. **Save your work**

TABLE C-1: Examples of fonts and font sizes

font	12 point	24 point
Calibri	Excel	Excel
Playbill	Excel	Excel
Comic Sans MS	Excel	Excel
Times New Roman	Excel	Excel

FIGURE C-5: Font list

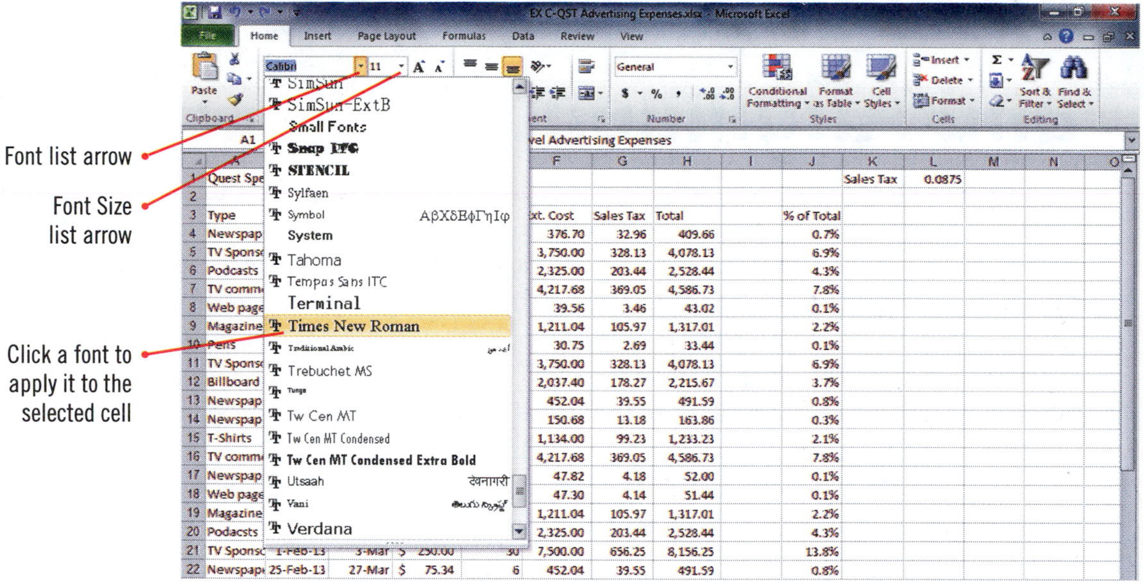

FIGURE C-6: Worksheet with formatted title and column labels

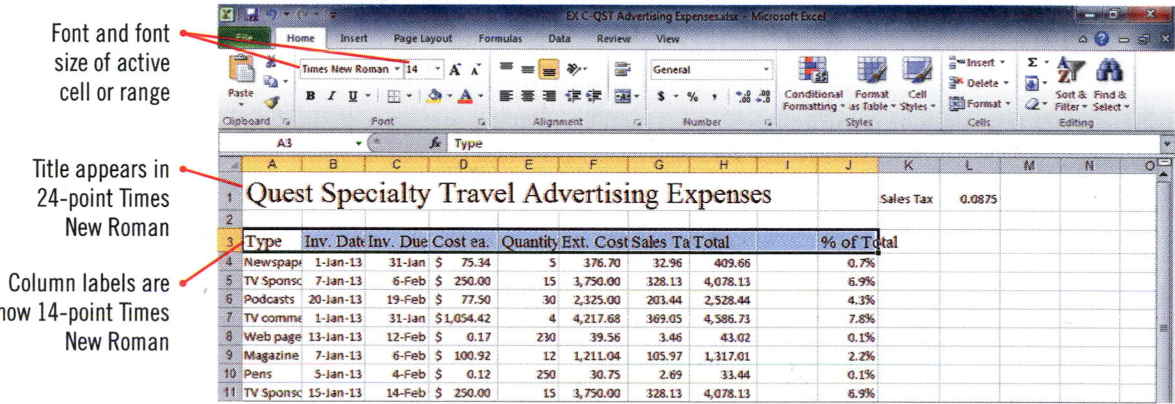

Inserting and adjusting clip art and other images

You can illustrate your worksheets using clip art and other images. A **clip** is an individual media file, such as a graphic, sound, animation, or a movie. **Clip art** refers to images such as a corporate logo, a picture, or a photo. Microsoft Office comes with many clips available for your use. To add a clip to a worksheet, click the Clip Art button in the Illustrations group on the Insert tab. The Clip Art task pane opens. Here you can search for clips by typing one or more keywords (words related to your subject) in the Search for text box, then click Go. Clips that relate to your keywords appear in the Clip Art task pane, as shown in Figure C-7. (If you have a standard Office installation and an active Internet connection, click the Include Office.com content check box to see clips available through Office.com in addition to those on your computer.) When you click the image you want in the Clip Art task pane, the image is inserted at the location of the active cell. To add your own images to a worksheet, click the Insert tab on the Ribbon, then click the Picture button. Navigate to the file you want, then click Insert. To resize an image, drag any corner sizing handle. To move an image, point inside the clip until the pointer changes to ✥, then drag it to a new location.

FIGURE C-7: Results of Clip Art search

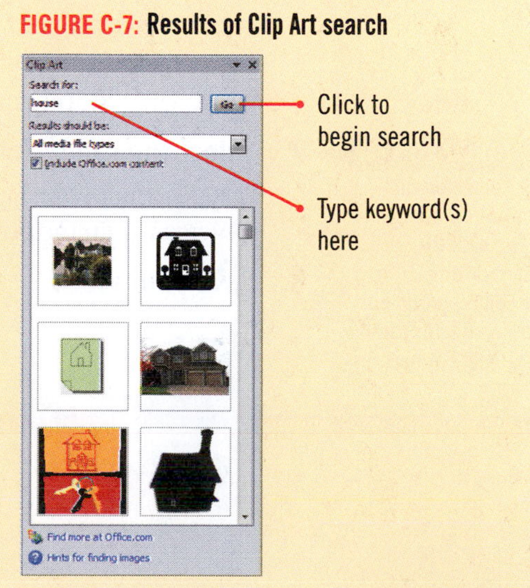

Changing Font Styles and Alignment

Font styles are formats such as bold, italic, and underlining that you can apply to affect the way text and numbers look in a worksheet. You can also change the **alignment** of labels and values in cells to position them in relation to the cells' edges—such as left-aligned, right-aligned, or centered. You can apply font styles and alignment options using the Home tab, the Format Cells dialog box, or the Mini toolbar. See Table C-2 for a description of common font style and alignment buttons that are available on the Home tab and the Mini toolbar. Once you have formatted a cell the way you want it, you can "paint" or copy the cell's formats into other cells by using the Format Painter button in the Clipboard group on the Home tab. This is similar to using copy and paste, but instead of copying cell contents, it copies only the cell's formatting. You want to further enhance the worksheet's appearance by adding bold and underline formatting and centering some of the labels.

STEPS

1. **Press [Ctrl][Home], then click the Bold button in the Font group on the Home tab**
   The title in cell A1 appears in bold.

> **QUICK TIP**
> You can use the following keyboard shortcuts to format a selected cell or range: [Ctrl][B] to bold, [Ctrl][I] to italicize, and [Ctrl][U] to underline.

2. **Click cell A3, then click the Underline button in the Font group**
   The column label is now underlined, though this may be difficult to see with the cell selected.

3. **Click the Italic button in the Font group, then click**
   The heading now appears in boldface, underlined, italic type. Notice that the Bold, Italic, and Underline buttons in the Font group are all selected.

> **QUICK TIP**
> Overuse of any font style and random formatting can make a workbook difficult to read. Be consistent and add the same formatting to similar items throughout a worksheet or in related worksheets.

4. **Click the Italic button to deselect it**
   The italic font style is removed from cell A3, but the bold and underline font styles remain.

5. **Click the Format Painter button in the Clipboard group, then select the range B3:J3**
   The formatting in cell A3 is copied to the rest of the column labels. To paint the formats on more than one selection, double-click the Format Painter button to keep it activated until you turn it off. You can turn off the Format Painter by pressing [Esc] or by clicking . You decide the title would look better if it were centered over the data columns.

6. **Select the range A1:H1, then click the Merge & Center button in the Alignment group**
   The Merge & Center button creates one cell out of the eight cells across the row, then centers the text in that newly created, merged cell. The title "Quest Specialty Travel Advertising Expenses" is centered across the eight columns you selected. To split a merged cell into its original components, select the merged cell, then click the Merge & Center button to deselect it. The merged and centered text might look awkward now, but you'll be changing the column widths shortly.

> **QUICK TIP**
> To clear all formatting from a selected range, click the Clear button in the Editing group on the Home tab, then click Clear Formats.

7. **Select the range A3:J3, right-click, then click the Center button on the Mini toolbar**
   Compare your screen to Figure C-8. Although they may be difficult to read, notice that all the headings are centered within their cells.

8. **Save your work**

FIGURE C-8: Worksheet with font styles and alignment applied

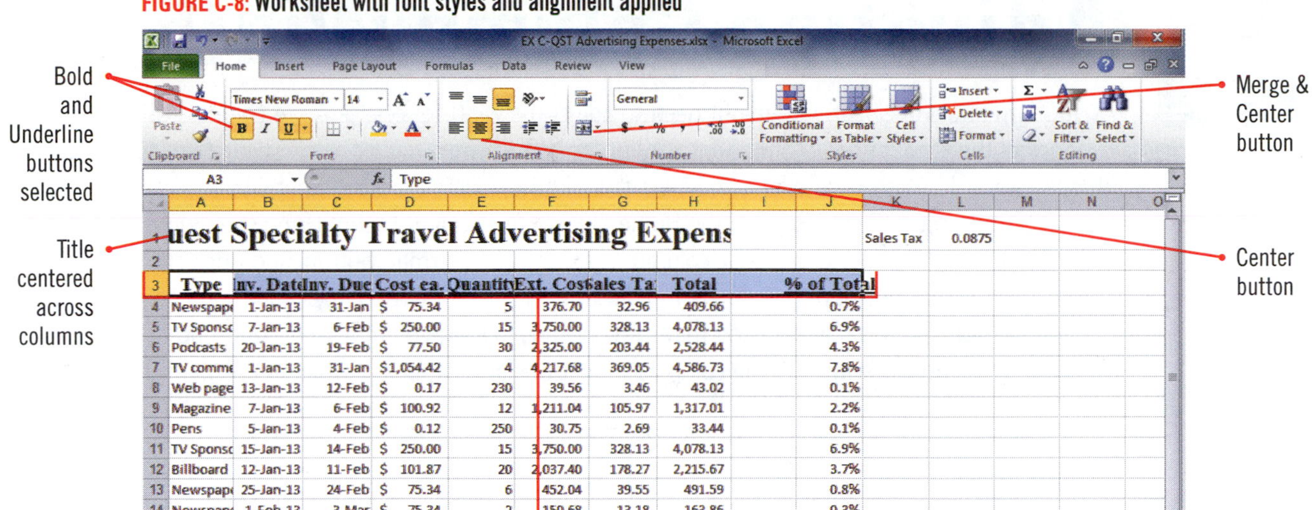

TABLE C-2: Common font style and alignment buttons

button	description	button	description
B	Bolds text		Aligns text at the left edge of the cell
I	Italicizes text		Centers text horizontally within the cell
U	Underlines text		Aligns text at the right edge of the cell
	Centers text across columns, and combines two or more selected, adjacent cells into one cell		

Rotating and indenting cell entries

In addition to applying fonts and font styles, you can rotate or indent data within a cell to further change its appearance. You can rotate text within a cell by altering its alignment. To change alignment, select the cells you want to modify, then click the dialog box launcher in the Alignment group to open the Alignment tab of the Format Cells dialog box. Click a position in the Orientation box or type a number in the Degrees text box to rotate text from its default horizontal orientation, then click OK. You can indent cell contents using the Increase Indent button in the Alignment group, which moves cell contents to the right one space, or the Decrease Indent button, which moves cell contents to the left one space.

Adjusting Column Width

As you format a worksheet, you might need to adjust the width of one or more columns to accommodate changes in the amount of text, the font size, or font style. The default column width is 8.43 characters, a little less than 1". With Excel, you can adjust the width of one or more columns by using the mouse, the Format button in the Cells group on the Home tab, or the shortcut menu. Using the mouse, you can drag or double-click the right edge of a column heading. The Format button and shortcut menu include commands for making more precise width adjustments. Table C-3 describes common column formatting commands. You have noticed that some of the labels in columns A through J don't fit in the cells. You want to adjust the widths of the columns so that the labels appear in their entirety.

STEPS

1. **Position the mouse pointer on the line between the column A and column B headings until it changes to ✛**

   See Figure C-9. The **column heading** is the box at the top of each column containing a letter. Before you can adjust column width using the mouse, you need to position the pointer on the right edge of the column heading for the column you want to adjust. The cell entry "TV commercials" is the widest in the column.

> **QUICK TIP**
> If "#######" appears after you adjust a column of values, the column is too narrow to display the values completely; increase the column width until the values appear.

2. **Click and drag the ✛ to the right until the column displays the "TV commercials" cell entries fully (approximately 13.86 characters, 1.06", or 102 pixels)**

   As you change the column width, a ScreenTip is displayed listing the column width. In Normal view, the ScreenTip lists the width in characters and pixels; in Page Layout view, the ScreenTip lists the width in inches and pixels.

3. **Position the pointer on the line between columns B and C until it changes to ✛, then double-click**

   Double-clicking the right edge of a column heading activates the **AutoFit** feature, which automatically resizes the column to accommodate the widest entry in the column. Column B automatically widens to fit the widest entry, which is the column label "Inv. Date".

4. **Use AutoFit to resize columns C, D, and J**

5. **Select the range E5:H5**

   You can change the width of multiple columns at once, by first selecting either the column headings or at least one cell in each column.

> **QUICK TIP**
> If an entire column rather than a column cell is selected, you can change the width of the column by right-clicking the column heading, then clicking Column Width on the shortcut menu.

6. **Click the Format button in the Cells group, then click Column Width**

   The Column Width dialog box opens. Column width measurement is based on the number of characters that will fit in the column when formatted in the Normal font and font size (in this case, 11 pt Calibri).

7. **Drag the dialog box by its title bar if its placement obscures your view of the worksheet, type 11 in the Column width text box, then click OK**

   The widths of columns E, F, G, and H change to reflect the new setting. See Figure C-10.

8. **Save your work**

TABLE C-3: Common column formatting commands

command	description	available using
Column Width	Sets the width to a specific number of characters	Format button; shortcut menu
AutoFit Column Width	Fits to the widest entry in a column	Format button; mouse
Hide & Unhide	Hides or displays hidden column(s)	Format button; shortcut menu
Default Width	Resets column to worksheet's default column width	Format button

FIGURE C-9: Preparing to change the column width

Resize pointer

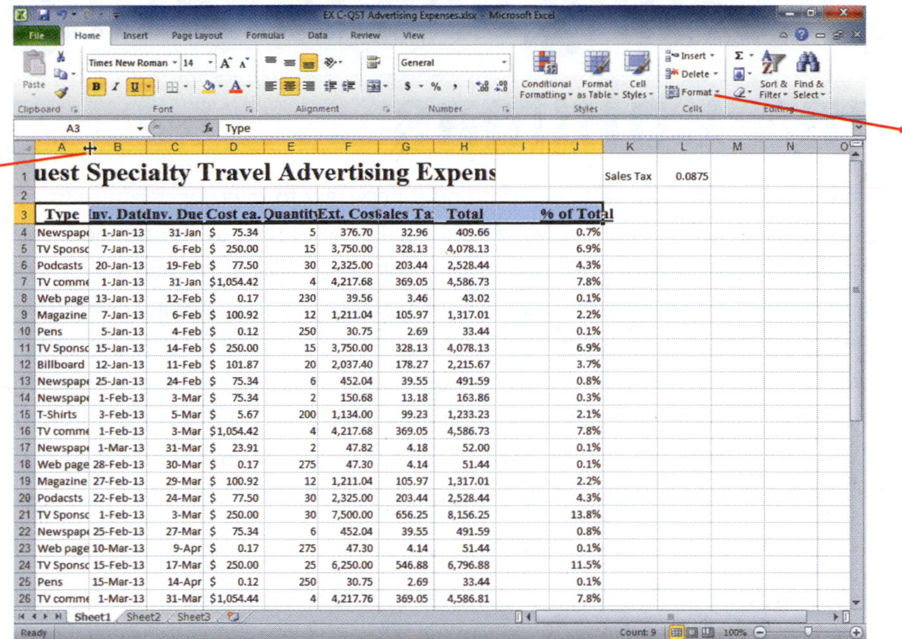

	A	B	C	D	E	F	G	H	I	J	K	L
1	uest Specialty Travel Advertising Expens										Sales Tax	0.0875
2												
3	Type	nv. Dat	dnv. Due	Cost ea.	Quantit	Ext. Cost	Sales Ta	Total		% of Total		
4	Newspap	1-Jan-13	31-Jan	$ 75.34	5	376.70	32.96	409.66		0.7%		
5	TV Sponsc	7-Jan-13	6-Feb	$ 250.00	15	3,750.00	328.13	4,078.13		6.9%		
6	Podcasts	20-Jan-13	19-Feb	$ 77.50	30	2,325.00	203.44	2,528.44		4.3%		
7	TV comme	1-Jan-13	31-Jan	$1,054.42	4	4,217.68	369.05	4,586.73		7.8%		
8	Web page	13-Jan-13	12-Feb	$ 0.17	230	39.56	3.46	43.02		0.1%		
9	Magazine	7-Jan-13	6-Feb	$ 100.92	12	1,211.04	105.97	1,317.01		2.2%		
10	Pens	5-Jan-13	4-Feb	$ 0.12	250	30.75	2.69	33.44		0.1%		
11	TV Sponsc	15-Jan-13	14-Feb	$ 250.00	15	3,750.00	328.13	4,078.13		6.9%		
12	Billboard	12-Jan-13	11-Feb	$ 101.87	20	2,037.40	178.27	2,215.67		3.7%		
13	Newspap	25-Jan-13	24-Feb	$ 75.34	6	452.04	39.55	491.59		0.8%		
14	Newspap	1-Feb-13	3-Mar	$ 75.34	2	150.68	13.18	163.86		0.3%		
15	T-Shirts	3-Feb-13	5-Mar	$ 5.67	200	1,134.00	99.23	1,233.23		2.1%		
16	TV comme	1-Feb-13	3-Mar	$1,054.42	4	4,217.68	369.05	4,586.73		7.8%		
17	Newspap	1-Mar-13	31-Mar	$ 23.91	2	47.82	4.18	52.00		0.1%		
18	Web page	28-Feb-13	30-Mar	$ 0.17	275	47.30	4.14	51.44		0.1%		
19	Magazine	27-Feb-13	29-Mar	$ 100.92	12	1,211.04	105.97	1,317.01		2.2%		
20	Podacsts	22-Feb-13	24-Mar	$ 77.50	30	2,325.00	203.44	2,528.44		4.3%		
21	TV Sponsc	1-Feb-13	3-Mar	$ 250.00	30	7,500.00	656.25	8,156.25		13.8%		
22	Newspap	25-Feb-13	27-Mar	$ 75.34	6	452.04	39.55	491.59		0.8%		
23	Web page	10-Mar-13	9-Apr	$ 0.17	275	47.30	4.14	51.44		0.1%		
24	TV Sponsc	15-Feb-13	17-Mar	$ 250.00	25	6,250.00	546.88	6,796.88		11.5%		
25	Pens	15-Mar-13	14-Apr	$ 0.12	250	30.75	2.69	33.44		0.1%		
26	TV comme	1-Mar-13	31-Mar	$1,054.44	4	4,217.76	369.05	4,586.81		7.8%		

Format button

FIGURE C-10: Worksheet with column widths adjusted

Columns widened to display text

Columns widened to same width

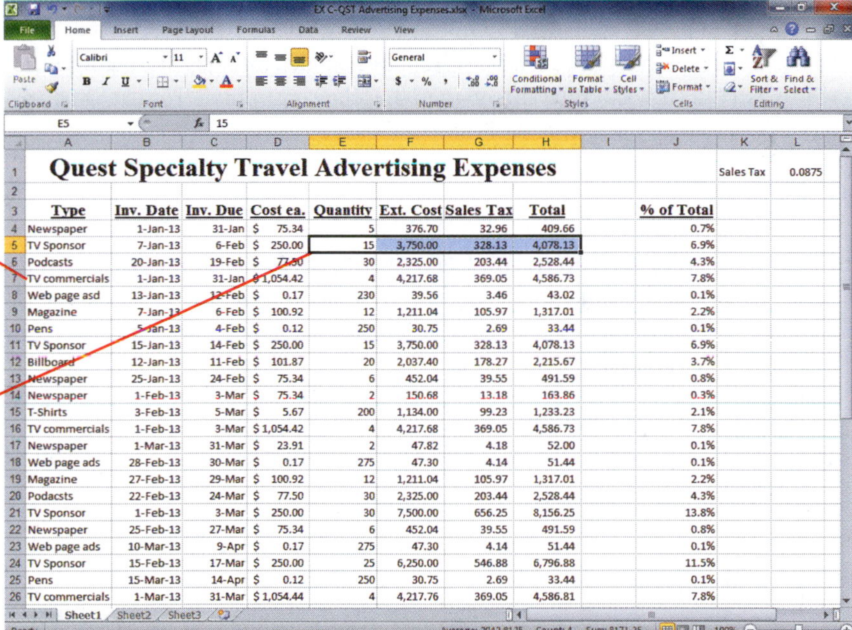

	A	B	C	D	E	F	G	H	I	J	K	L
1	Quest Specialty Travel Advertising Expenses										Sales Tax	0.0875
2												
3	Type	Inv. Date	Inv. Due	Cost ea.	Quantity	Ext. Cost	Sales Tax	Total		% of Total		
4	Newspaper	1-Jan-13	31-Jan	$ 75.34	5	376.70	32.96	409.66		0.7%		
5	TV Sponsor	7-Jan-13	6-Feb	$ 250.00	15	3,750.00	328.13	4,078.13		6.9%		
6	Podcasts	20-Jan-13	19-Feb	$ 77.50	30	2,325.00	203.44	2,528.44		4.3%		
7	TV commercials	1-Jan-13	31-Jan	$ 1,054.42	4	4,217.68	369.05	4,586.73		7.8%		
8	Web page asd	13-Jan-13	12-Feb	$ 0.17	230	39.56	3.46	43.02		0.1%		
9	Magazine	7-Jan-13	6-Feb	$ 100.92	12	1,211.04	105.97	1,317.01		2.2%		
10	Pens	5-Jan-13	4-Feb	$ 0.12	250	30.75	2.69	33.44		0.1%		
11	TV Sponsor	15-Jan-13	14-Feb	$ 250.00	15	3,750.00	328.13	4,078.13		6.9%		
12	Billboard	12-Jan-13	11-Feb	$ 101.87	20	2,037.40	178.27	2,215.67		3.7%		
13	Newspaper	25-Jan-13	24-Feb	$ 75.34	6	452.04	39.55	491.59		0.8%		
14	Newspaper	1-Feb-13	3-Mar	$ 75.34	2	150.68	13.18	163.86		0.3%		
15	T-Shirts	3-Feb-13	5-Mar	$ 5.67	200	1,134.00	99.23	1,233.23		2.1%		
16	TV commercials	1-Feb-13	3-Mar	$ 1,054.42	4	4,217.68	369.05	4,586.73		7.8%		
17	Newspaper	1-Mar-13	31-Mar	$ 23.91	2	47.82	4.18	52.00		0.1%		
18	Web page ads	28-Feb-13	30-Mar	$ 0.17	275	47.30	4.14	51.44		0.1%		
19	Magazine	27-Feb-13	29-Mar	$ 100.92	12	1,211.04	105.97	1,317.01		2.2%		
20	Podacsts	22-Feb-13	24-Mar	$ 77.50	30	2,325.00	203.44	2,528.44		4.3%		
21	TV Sponsor	1-Feb-13	3-Mar	$ 250.00	30	7,500.00	656.25	8,156.25		13.8%		
22	Newspaper	25-Feb-13	27-Mar	$ 75.34	6	452.04	39.55	491.59		0.8%		
23	Web page ads	10-Mar-13	9-Apr	$ 0.17	275	47.30	4.14	51.44		0.1%		
24	TV Sponsor	15-Feb-13	17-Mar	$ 250.00	25	6,250.00	546.88	6,796.88		11.5%		
25	Pens	15-Mar-13	14-Apr	$ 0.12	250	30.75	2.69	33.44		0.1%		
26	TV commercials	1-Mar-13	31-Mar	$ 1,054.44	4	4,217.76	369.05	4,586.81		7.8%		

Changing row height

Changing row height is as easy as changing column width. Row height is calculated in points, the same units of measure used for fonts. The row height must exceed the size of the font you are using. Normally, you don't need to adjust row heights manually, because row heights adjust automatically to accommodate font size changes. If you format something in a row to be a larger point size, Excel adjusts the row to fit the largest point size in the row. However, you have just as many options for changing row height as you do column width. Using the mouse, you can place the ‡ pointer on the line dividing a row heading from the heading below, and then drag to the desired height; double-clicking the line AutoFits the row height where necessary. You can also select one or more rows, then use the Row Height command on the shortcut menu, or click the Format button on the Home tab and click the Row Height or AutoFit Row Height command.

Excel 2010

UNIT C
Excel 2010

Inserting and Deleting Rows and Columns

As you modify a worksheet, you might find it necessary to insert or delete rows and columns to keep your worksheet current. For example, you might need to insert rows to accommodate new inventory products or remove a column of yearly totals that are no longer necessary. When you insert a new row, the row is inserted above the cell pointer and the contents of the worksheet shift down from the newly inserted row. When you insert a new column, the column is inserted to the left of the cell pointer and the contents of the worksheet shift to the right of the new column. To insert multiple rows, select the same number of row headings as you want to insert before using the Insert command. You want to improve the overall appearance of the worksheet by inserting a row between the last row of data and the totals. Also, you have learned that row 27 and column J need to be deleted from the worksheet.

STEPS

QUICK TIP
To insert a single row or column, right-click the row heading immediately below where you want the new row, or right-click the column heading to the right of where you want the new column, then click Insert on the shortcut menu.

1. **Right-click cell A32, then click Insert on the shortcut menu**
   The Insert dialog box opens. See Figure C-11. You can choose to insert a column or a row; insert a single cell and shift the cells in the active column to the right; or insert a single cell and shift the cells in the active row down. An additional row between the last row of data and the totals will visually separate the totals.

2. **Click the Entire row option button, then click OK**
   A blank row appears between the Billboard data and the totals, and the formula result in cell E33 has not changed. The Insert Options button appears beside cell A33. Pointing to the button displays a list arrow, which you can click and then choose from the following options: Format Same As Above (the default setting, already selected), Format Same As Below, or Clear Formatting.

3. **Click the row 27 heading**
   All of row 27 is selected, as shown in Figure C-12.

QUICK TIP
If you inadvertently click the Delete list arrow instead of the button itself, click Delete Sheet Rows in the menu that opens.

4. **Click the Delete button in the Cells group; *do not click the list arrow***
   Excel deletes row 27, and all rows below it shift up one row. You must use the Delete button or the Delete command on the shortcut menu to delete a row or column; pressing [Delete] on the keyboard removes only the *contents* of a selected row or column.

5. **Click the column J heading**
   The percentage information is calculated elsewhere and is no longer necessary in this worksheet.

QUICK TIP
After inserting or deleting rows or columns in a worksheet, be sure to proof formulas that contain relative cell references.

6. **Click the Delete button in the Cells group**
   Excel deletes column J. The remaining columns to the right shift left one column.

7. **Save your work**

Hiding and unhiding columns and rows

When you don't want data in a column or row to be visible, but you don't want to delete it, you can hide the column or row. To hide a selected column, click the Format button in the Cells group on the Home tab, point to Hide & Unhide, then click Hide Columns. A hidden column is indicated by a dark black vertical line in its original position. This black line disappears when you click elsewhere in the worksheet. You can display a hidden column by selecting the columns on either side of the hidden column, clicking the Format button in the Cells group, pointing to Hide & Unhide, and then clicking Unhide Columns. (To hide or unhide one or more rows, substitute Hide Rows and Unhide Rows for the Hide Columns and Unhide Columns commands.)

FIGURE C-11: Insert dialog box

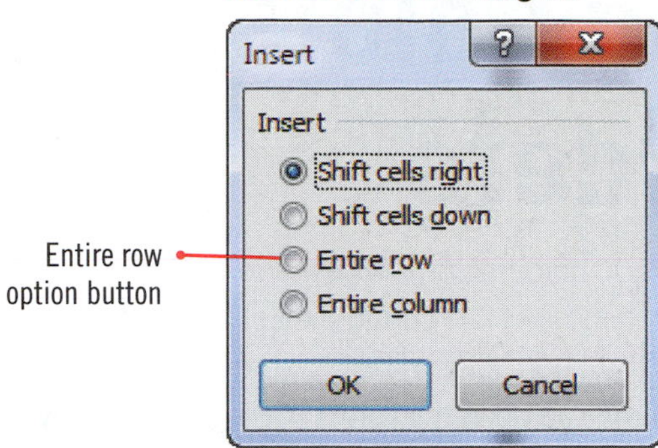

FIGURE C-12: Worksheet with row 27 selected

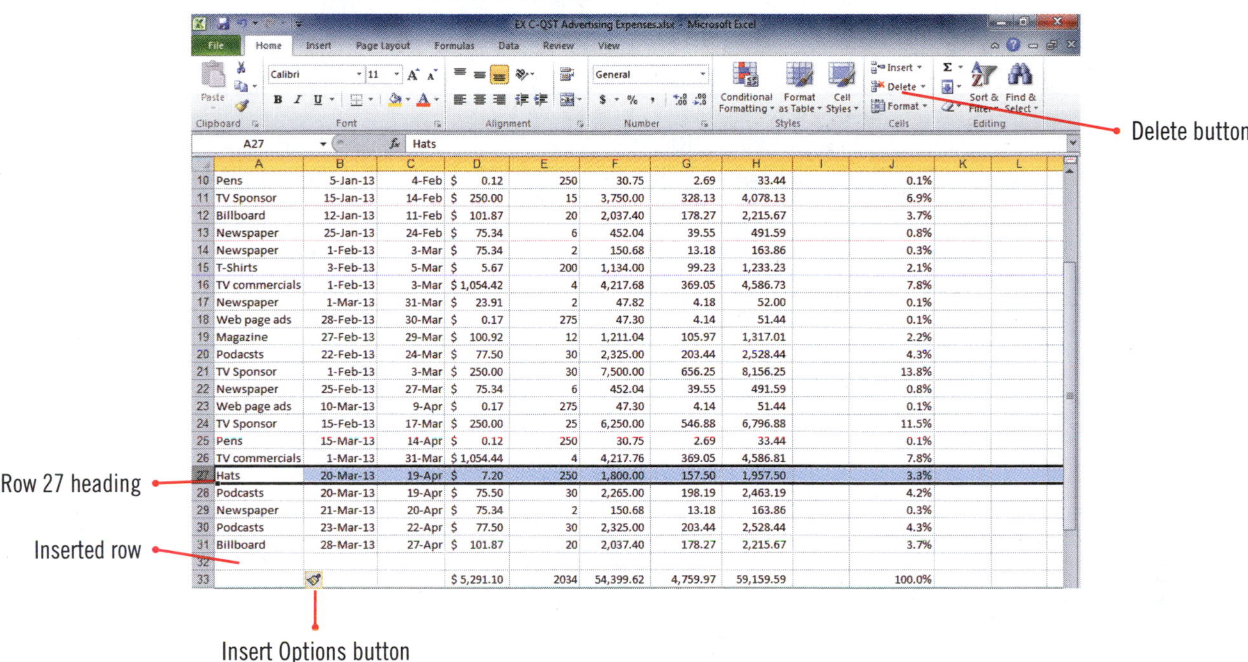

	A	B	C	D	E	F	G	H	I	J	K	L
10	Pens	5-Jan-13	4-Feb	$ 0.12	250	30.75	2.69	33.44		0.1%		
11	TV Sponsor	15-Jan-13	14-Feb	$ 250.00	15	3,750.00	328.13	4,078.13		6.9%		
12	Billboard	12-Jan-13	11-Feb	$ 101.87	20	2,037.40	178.27	2,215.67		3.7%		
13	Newspaper	25-Jan-13	24-Feb	$ 75.34	6	452.04	39.55	491.59		0.8%		
14	Newspaper	1-Feb-13	3-Mar	$ 75.34	2	150.68	13.18	163.86		0.3%		
15	T-Shirts	3-Feb-13	5-Mar	$ 5.67	200	1,134.00	99.23	1,233.23		2.1%		
16	TV commercials	1-Feb-13	3-Mar	$ 1,054.42	4	4,217.68	369.05	4,586.73		7.8%		
17	Newspaper	1-Mar-13	31-Mar	$ 23.91	2	47.82	4.18	52.00		0.1%		
18	Web page ads	28-Feb-13	30-Mar	$ 0.17	275	47.30	4.14	51.44		0.1%		
19	Magazine	27-Feb-13	29-Mar	$ 100.92	12	1,211.04	105.97	1,317.01		2.2%		
20	Podacsts	22-Feb-13	24-Mar	$ 77.50	30	2,325.00	203.44	2,528.44		4.3%		
21	TV Sponsor	1-Feb-13	3-Mar	$ 250.00	30	7,500.00	656.25	8,156.25		13.8%		
22	Newspaper	25-Feb-13	27-Mar	$ 75.34	6	452.04	39.55	491.59		0.8%		
23	Web page ads	10-Mar-13	9-Apr	$ 0.17	275	47.30	4.14	51.44		0.1%		
24	TV Sponsor	15-Feb-13	17-Mar	$ 250.00	25	6,250.00	546.88	6,796.88		11.5%		
25	Pens	15-Mar-13	14-Apr	$ 0.12	250	30.75	2.69	33.44		0.1%		
26	TV commercials	1-Mar-13	31-Mar	$ 1,054.44	4	4,217.76	369.05	4,586.81		7.8%		
27	Hats	20-Mar-13	19-Apr	$ 7.20	250	1,800.00	157.50	1,957.50		3.3%		
28	Podcasts	20-Mar-13	19-Apr	$ 75.50	30	2,265.00	198.19	2,463.19		4.2%		
29	Newspaper	21-Mar-13	20-Apr	$ 75.34	2	150.68	13.18	163.86		0.3%		
30	Podcasts	23-Mar-13	22-Apr	$ 77.50	30	2,325.00	203.44	2,528.44		4.3%		
31	Billboard	28-Mar-13	27-Apr	$ 101.87	20	2,037.40	178.27	2,215.67		3.7%		
32												
33				$ 5,291.10	2034	54,399.62	4,759.97	59,159.59		100.0%		

Adding and editing comments

Much of your work in Excel may be in collaboration with teammates with whom you share worksheets. You can share ideas with other worksheet users by adding comments within selected cells. To include a comment in a worksheet, click the cell where you want to place the comment, click the Review tab on the Ribbon, then click the New Comment button in the Comments group. You can type your comments in the resizable text box that opens containing the computer user's name. A small, red triangle appears in the upper-right corner of a cell containing a comment. If comments are not already displayed in a workbook, other users can point to the triangle to display the comment. To see all worksheet comments, as shown in Figure C-13, click the Show All Comments button in the Comments group. To edit a comment, click the cell containing the comment, then click the Edit Comment button in the Comments group. To delete a comment, click the cell containing the comment, then click the Delete button in the Comments group.

FIGURE C-13: Comments displayed in a worksheet

20	Podcasts	22-Feb-13	24-Mar	iPodAds	$ 75.50
21	TV Sponsor	1-Feb-13	3-Mar	Food Networ	
22	Newspaper	25-Feb-13	27-Mar	Village Reade	
23	Web page ads	10-Mar-13	9-Apr	Advertising C	
24	TV Sponsor	15-Feb-13	17-Mar	Food Networ	
25	Pens	15-Mar-13	14-Apr	Mass Appeal, Inc.	$ 0.12
26	TV commercials	1-Mar-13	31-Mar	Discovery Ch	
27	Podcasts	20-Mar-13	19-Apr	iPodAds	
28	Newspaper	1-Apr-13	1-May	University Vo	
29	Podcasts	10-Apr-13	10-May	iPodAds	
30	Billboard	28-Mar-13	27-Apr	Advertising Concepts	$ 101.87
31					
32					$5,166.04
33					
34					

Grace Wong:
Should we continue with this market, or expand to other publications?

Grace Wong:
I think this will turn out to be a very good decision.

Applying Colors, Patterns, and Borders

You can use colors, patterns, and borders to enhance the overall appearance of a worksheet and make it easier to read. You can add these enhancements by using the Borders, Font Color, and Fill Color buttons in the Font group on the Home tab of the Ribbon and on the Mini toolbar, or by using the Fill tab and the Border tab in the Format Cells dialog box. You can open the Format Cells dialog box by clicking the dialog box launcher in the Font, Alignment, or Number group on the Home tab, or by right-clicking a selection, then clicking Format Cells on the shortcut menu. You can apply a color to the background of a cell or a range or to cell contents (such as letters and numbers), and you can apply a pattern to a cell or range. You can apply borders to all the cells in a worksheet or only to selected cells to call attention to selected information. To save time, you can also apply **cell styles**, predesigned combinations of formats. You want to add a pattern, a border, and color to the title of the worksheet to give the worksheet a more professional appearance.

STEPS

1. **Select cell A1, click the Fill Color list arrow in the Font group, then hover the pointer over the Turquoise, Accent 2 color (first row, sixth column from the left)**
   See Figure C-14. Live Preview shows you how the color will look *before* you apply it. (Remember that cell A1 spans columns A through H because the Merge & Center command was applied.)
2. **Click the Turquoise, Accent 2 color**
   The color is applied to the background (or fill) of this cell. When you change fill or font color, the color on the Fill Color or Font Color button changes to the last color you selected.
3. **Right-click cell A1, then click Format Cells on the shortcut menu**
   The Format Cells dialog box opens.
4. **Click the Fill tab, click the Pattern Style list arrow, click the 6.25% Gray style (first row, sixth column from the left), then click OK**
5. **Click the Borders list arrow in the Font group, then click Thick Bottom Border**
   Unlike underlining, which is a text-formatting tool, borders extend to the width of the cell, and can appear at the bottom of the cell, at the top, on either side, or on any combination of the four sides. It can be difficult to see a border when the cell is selected.
6. **Select the range A3:H3, click the Font Color list arrow in the Font group, then click the Blue, Accent 1 color (first Theme color row, fifth column from the left) on the palette**
   The new color is applied to the labels in the selected range.
7. **Select the range J1:K1, click the Cell Styles button in the Styles group, then click the Neutral cell style (first row, fourth column from the left) in the gallery**
   The font and color change in the range, as shown in Figure C-15.
8. **Save your work**

QUICK TIP

Use fill colors and patterns sparingly. Too many colors can be distracting or make it hard to see which information is important.

QUICK TIP

You can also create custom cell borders. Click the Borders list arrow in the Font group, click More Borders, then click the individual border buttons to apply the borders you want to the selected cell(s).

FIGURE C-14: Live Preview of fill color

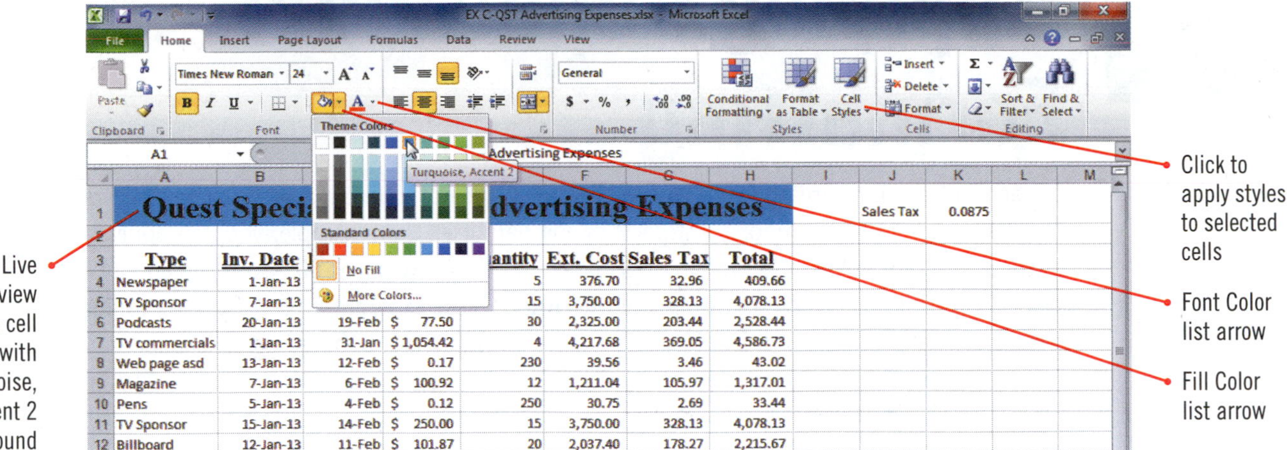
Live Preview shows cell A1 with Turquoise, Accent 2 background
Click to apply styles to selected cells
Font Color list arrow
Fill Color list arrow

FIGURE C-15: Worksheet with color, patterns, border, and cell style applied

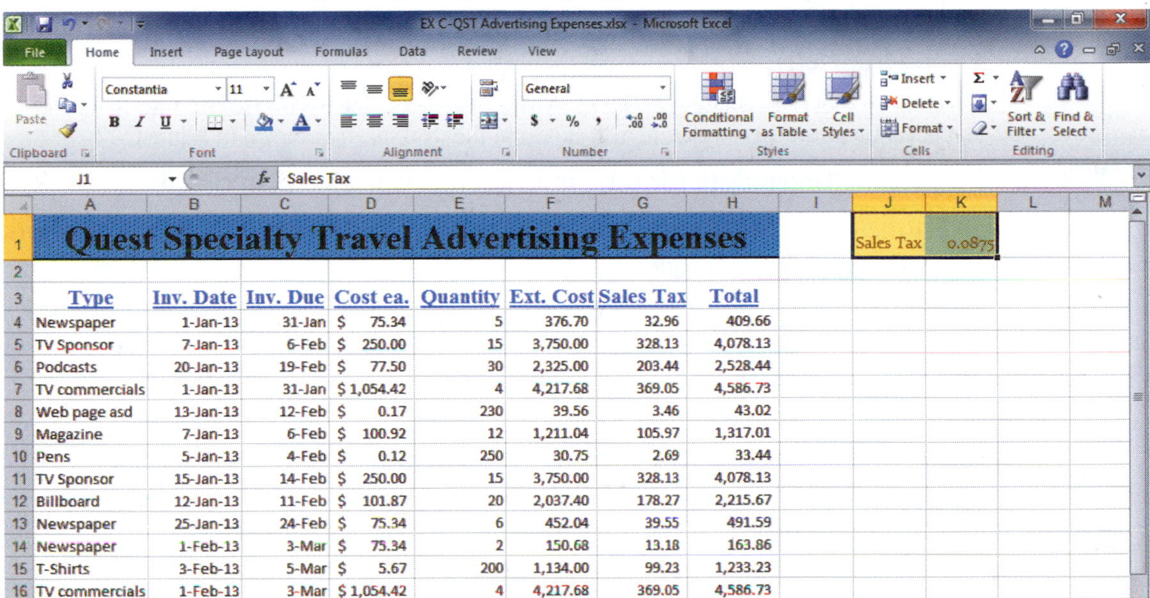

Working with themes and cell styles

Using themes and cell styles makes it easier to ensure that your worksheets are consistent. A **theme** is a predefined set of formats that gives your Excel worksheet a professional look. Formatting choices included in a theme are colors, fonts, and line and fill effects. To apply a theme, click the Themes button in the Themes group on the Page Layout tab to open the Themes gallery, as shown in Figure C-16, then click a theme in the gallery. **Cell styles** are sets of cell formats based on themes, so they are automatically updated if you change a theme. For example, if you apply the 20% - Accent1 cell style to cell A1 in a worksheet that has no theme applied, the fill color changes to light blue and the font changes to Constantia. If you change the theme of the worksheet to Metro, cell A1's fill color changes to light green and the font changes to Corbel, because these are the new theme's associated formats.

FIGURE C-16: Themes gallery

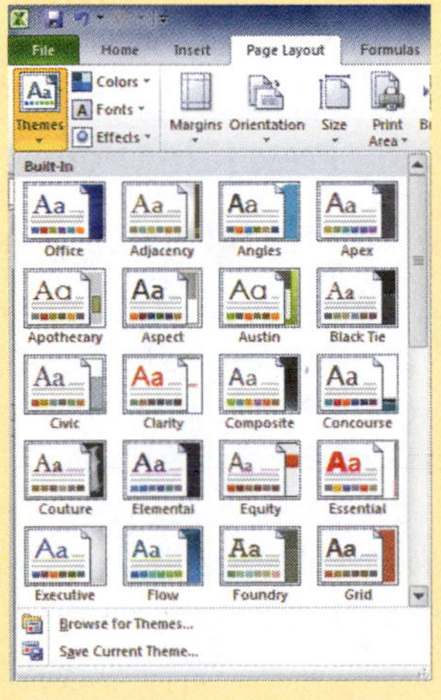

UNIT C Excel 2010

Applying Conditional Formatting

So far, you've used formatting to change the appearance of different types of data, but you can also use formatting to highlight important aspects of the data itself. For example, you can apply formatting that changes the font color to red for any cells where ad costs exceed $100 and to green where ad costs are below $50. This is called **conditional formatting** because Excel automatically applies different formats to data if the data meets conditions you specify. The formatting is updated if you change data in the worksheet. You can also copy conditional formats the same way you copy other formats. Grace is concerned about advertising costs exceeding the yearly budget. You decide to use conditional formatting to highlight certain trends and patterns in the data so that it's easy to spot the most expensive advertising.

STEPS

1. **Select the range H4:H30, click the Conditional Formatting button in the Styles group on the Home tab, point to Data Bars, then point to the Light Blue Data Bar (second row, second from left)**
   Data bars are colored horizontal bars that visually illustrate differences between values in a range of cells. Live Preview shows how this formatting will appear in the worksheet, as shown in Figure C-17.
2. **Point to the Green Data Bar (first row, second from left), then click it**
3. **Select the range F4:F30, click the Conditional Formatting button in the Styles group, then point to Highlight Cells Rules**
   The Highlight Cells Rules submenu displays choices for creating different formatting conditions. For example, you can create a rule for values that are greater than or less than a certain amount, or between two amounts.
4. **Click Between on the submenu**
   The Between dialog box opens, displaying input boxes you can use to define the condition and a default format (Light Red Fill with Dark Red Text) selected for cells that meet that condition. Depending on the condition you select in the Highlight Cells Rules submenu (such as "Greater Than" or "Less Than"), this dialog box displays different input boxes. You define the condition using the input boxes and then assign the formatting you want to use for cells that meet that condition. Values used in input boxes for a condition can be constants, formulas, cell references, or dates.
5. **Type 2000 in the first text box, type 4000 in the second text box, click the with list arrow, click Light Red Fill, compare your settings to Figure C-18, then click OK**
   All cells with values between 2000 and 4000 in column F appear with a light red fill.
6. **Click cell F7, type 3975.55, then press [Enter]**
   When the value in cell F7 changes, the formatting also changes because the new value meets the condition you set. Compare your results to Figure C-19.
7. **Press [Ctrl][Home] to select cell A1, then save your work**

QUICK TIP
You can apply an Icon Set to a selected range by clicking the Conditional Formatting button in the Styles group, then pointing to Icon Sets; icons appear within the cells to illustrate differences in values.

QUICK TIP
To define custom formatting for data that meets the condition, click Custom Format at the bottom of the with list, and then use the Format Cells dialog box to set the formatting to be applied.

Managing conditional formatting rules

If you create a conditional formatting rule and then want to change the condition to reflect a different value or format, you don't need to create a new rule; instead, you can modify the rule using the Rules Manager. Select the cell(s) containing conditional formatting, click the Conditional Formatting button in the Styles group, then click Manage Rules. The Conditional Formatting Rules Manager dialog box opens. Select the rule you want to edit, click Edit Rule, and then modify the settings in the Edit the Rule Description area in the Edit Formatting Rule dialog box. To change the formatting for a rule, click the Format button in the Edit the Rule Description area, select the formatting styles you want the text to have, then click OK three times to close the Format Cells dialog box, the Edit Formatting Rule dialog box, and then the Conditional Formatting Rules Manager dialog box. The rule is modified, and the new conditional formatting is applied to the selected cells. To delete a rule, select the rule in the Conditional Formatting Rules Manager dialog box, then click the Delete Rule button.

FIGURE C-17: Previewing data bars in a range

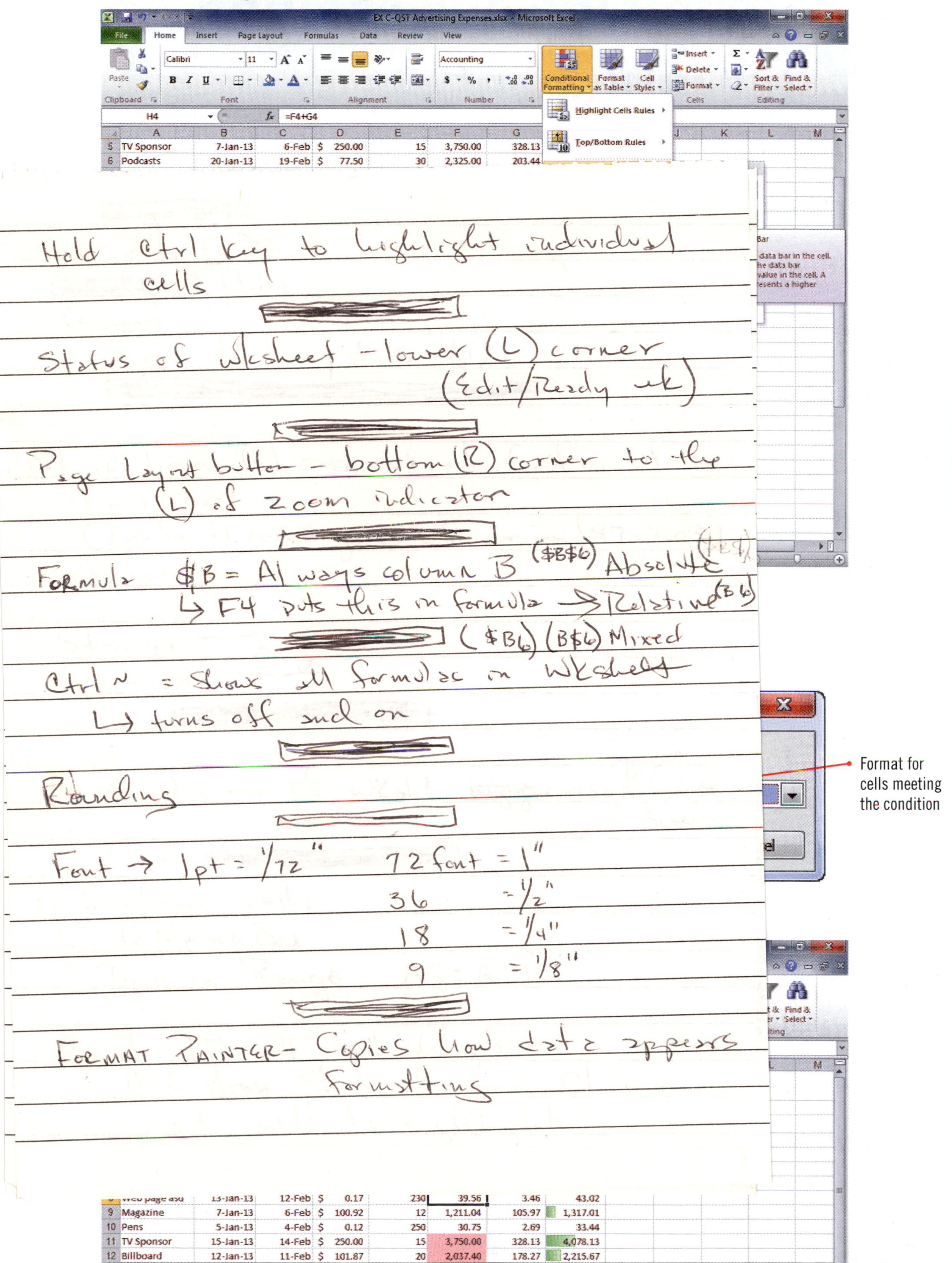

Hold Ctrl key to highlight individual cells
Status of wksheet - lower (L) corner (Edit/Ready ok)
Page Layout button - bottom (R) corner to the (L) of zoom indicator
Formula $B = Always column B ($B$6) Absolute
↳ F4 puts this in formula → Relative (B6)
($B6) (B$6) Mixed
Ctrl ~ = Shows all formulas on Wksheet
↳ turns off and on
Rounding
Font → 1pt = 1/12" 72 font = 1"
36 = 1/2"
18 = 1/4"
9 = 1/8"
FORMAT PAINTER - Copies how data appears formatting

Format for cells meeting the condition

Renaming and Moving a Worksheet

By default, an Excel workbook initially contains three worksheets, named Sheet1, Sheet2, and Sheet3. Each sheet name appears on a sheet tab at the bottom of the worksheet. When you open a new workbook, the first worksheet, Sheet1, is the active sheet. To move from sheet to sheet, you can click any sheet tab at the bottom of the worksheet window. The sheet tab scrolling buttons, located to the left of the sheet tabs, are useful when a workbook contains too many sheet tabs to display at once. To make it easier to identify the sheets in a workbook, you can rename each sheet and add color to the tabs. You can also organize them in a logical way. For instance, to better track performance goals, you could name each workbook sheet for an individual salesperson, and you could move the sheets so they appear in alphabetical order. In the current worksheet, Sheet1 contains information about actual advertising expenses. Sheet2 contains an advertising budget, and Sheet3 contains no data. You want to rename the two sheets in the workbook to reflect their contents, add color to a sheet tab to easily distinguish one from the other, and change their order.

STEPS

QUICK TIP
You can also rename a sheet by right-clicking the tab, clicking Rename on the shortcut menu, typing the new name, then pressing [Enter].

QUICK TIP
To delete a sheet, click its tab, click the Delete list arrow in the Cells group, then click Delete Sheet. To insert a worksheet, click the Insert Worksheet button to the right of the sheet tabs.

QUICK TIP
If you have more sheet tabs than are visible, you can move between sheets by using the tab scrolling buttons to the left of the sheet tabs: the First Worksheet button ; the Last Worksheet button ; the Previous Worksheet button ; and the Next Worksheet button .

1. **Click the Sheet2 tab**
   Sheet2 becomes active, appearing in front of the Sheet1 tab; this is the worksheet that contains the budgeted advertising expenses. See Figure C-20.
2. **Click the Sheet1 tab**
   Sheet1, which contains the actual advertising expenses, becomes active again.
3. **Double-click the Sheet2 tab, type Budget, then press [Enter]**
   The new name for Sheet2 automatically replaces the default name on the tab. Worksheet names can have up to 31 characters, including spaces and punctuation.
4. **Right-click the Budget tab, point to Tab Color on the shortcut menu, then click the Bright Green, Accent 4, Lighter 80% color (second row, third column from the right) as shown in Figure C-21**
5. **Double-click the Sheet1 tab, type Actual, then press [Enter]**
   Notice that the color of the Budget tab changes depending on whether it is the active tab; when the Actual tab is active, the color of the Budget tab changes to the green tab color you selected. You decide to rearrange the order of the sheets, so that the Budget tab is to the left of the Actual tab.
6. **Click the Budget tab, hold down the mouse button, drag it to the left of the Actual tab, as shown in Figure C-22, then release the mouse button**
   As you drag, the pointer changes to , the sheet relocation pointer, and a small, black triangle just above the tabs shows the position the moved sheet will be in when you release the mouse button. The first sheet in the workbook is now the Budget sheet. See Figure C-23.
7. **Click the Actual sheet tab, click the Page Layout button on the status bar to open Page Layout view, enter your name in the left header text box, then click anywhere in the worksheet to deselect the header**
8. **Click the Page Layout tab on the Ribbon, click the Orientation button in the Page Setup group, then click Landscape**
9. **Press [Ctrl][Home], then save your work**

FIGURE C-20: Sheet tabs in workbook

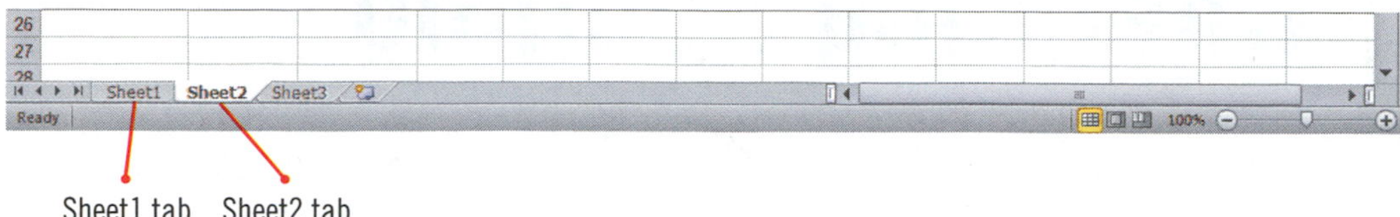

FIGURE C-21: Tab Color palette

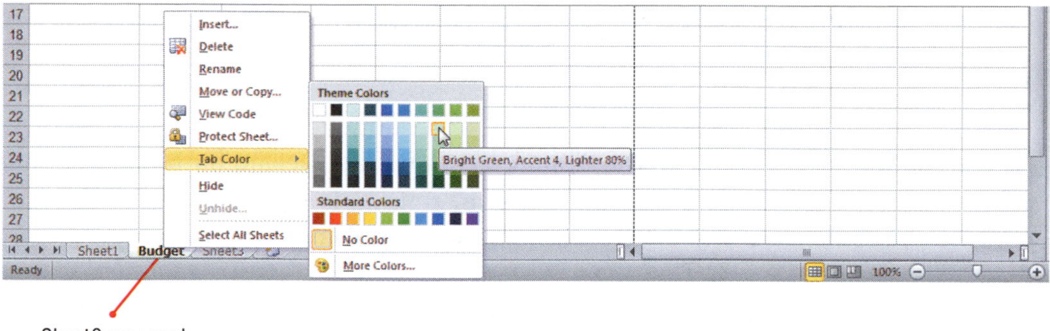

FIGURE C-22: Moving the Budget sheet

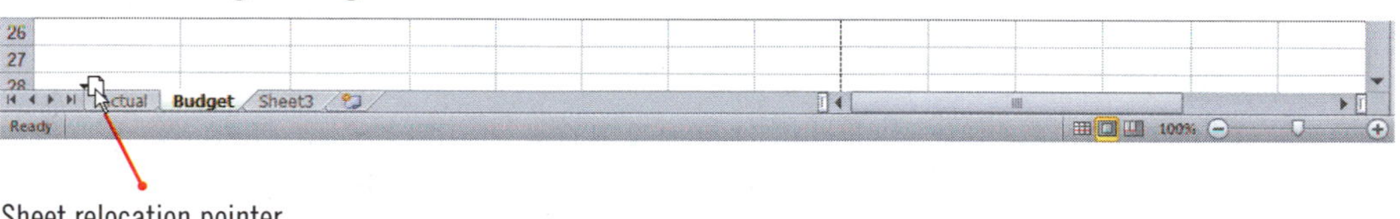

FIGURE C-23: Reordered sheets

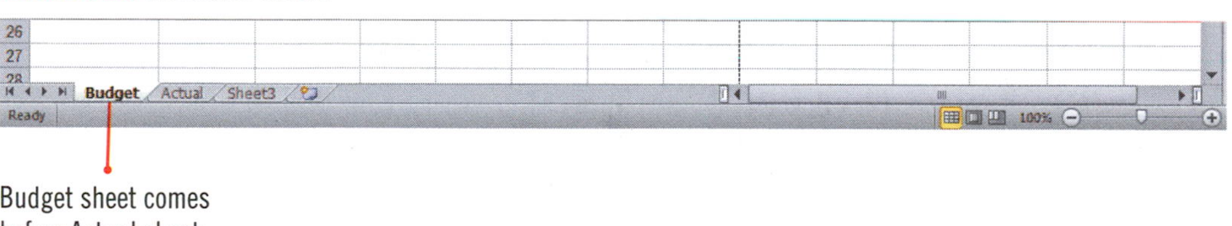

Copying worksheets

There are times when you may want to copy a worksheet. For example, a workbook might contain a sheet with Quarter 1 expenses, and you want to use that sheet as the basis for a sheet containing Quarter 2 expenses. To copy a sheet within the same workbook, press and hold [Ctrl], drag the sheet tab to the desired tab location, release the mouse button, then release [Ctrl]. A duplicate sheet appears with the same name as the copied sheet followed by "(2)" indicating it is a copy. You can then rename the sheet to a more meaningful name. To copy a sheet to a different workbook, both the source and destination workbooks must be open. Select the sheet to copy or move, right-click the sheet tab, then click Move or Copy in the shortcut menu. Complete the information in the Move or Copy dialog box. Be sure to click the Create a copy check box if you are copying rather than moving the worksheet. Carefully check your calculation results whenever you move or copy a worksheet.

Checking Spelling

Excel includes a spell checker to help you ensure that the words in your worksheet are spelled correctly. The spell checker scans your worksheet, displays words it doesn't find in its built-in dictionary, and suggests replacements when they are available. To check all of the sheets in a multiple-sheet workbook, you need to display each sheet individually and run the spell checker for each one. Because the built-in dictionary cannot possibly include all the words that anyone needs, you can add words to the dictionary, such as your company name, an acronym, or an unusual technical term. Once you add a word or term, the spell checker no longer considers that word misspelled. Any words you've added to the dictionary using Word, Access, or PowerPoint are also available in Excel. Before you distribute this workbook to Grace and the marketing managers, you check its spelling.

STEPS

QUICK TIP

The Spelling dialog box lists the name of the language currently being used in its title bar.

1. **Click the Review tab on the Ribbon, then click the Spelling button in the Proofing group**

   The Spelling: English (U.S.) dialog box opens, as shown in Figure C-24, with "asd" selected as the first misspelled word in the worksheet, and with "ads" selected in the Suggestions list as a possible replacement. For any word, you have the option to Ignore this case of the flagged word, Ignore All cases of the flagged word, Change the word to the selected suggestion, Change All instances of the flagged word to the selected suggestion, or add the flagged word to the dictionary using Add to Dictionary.

2. **Click Change**

   Next, the spell checker finds the word "Podacsts" and suggests "Podcasts" as an alternative.

3. **Verify that the word Podcasts is selected in the Suggestions list, then click Change**

   When no more incorrect words are found, Excel displays a message indicating that the spell check is complete.

4. **Click OK**

5. **Click the Home tab, click Find & Select in the Editing group, then click Replace**

   The Find and Replace dialog box opens. You can use this dialog box to replace a word or phrase. It might be a misspelling of a proper name that the spell checker didn't recognize as misspelled, or it could simply be a term that you want to change throughout the worksheet. Grace has just told you that each instance of "Billboard" in the worksheet should be changed to "Sign".

6. **Type Billboard in the Find what text box, press [Tab], then type Sign in the Replace with text box**

   Compare your dialog box to Figure C-25.

7. **Click Replace All, click OK to close the Microsoft Excel dialog box, then click Close to close the Find and Replace dialog box**

   Excel has made two replacements.

8. **Click the File tab, click Print on the navigation bar, click the No Scaling setting in the Settings section on the Print tab, then click Fit Sheet on One Page**

9. **Click the File tab to return to your worksheet, save your work, submit it to your instructor as directed, close the workbook, then exit Excel**

   The completed worksheet is shown in Figure C-26.

E-mailing a workbook

You can send an entire workbook from within Excel using your installed e-mail program, such as Microsoft Outlook. To send a workbook as an e-mail message attachment, open the workbook, click the File tab, then click Save & Send on the navigation bar. With the Send Using E-mail option selected in the Save & Send section in Backstage view, click Send as Attachment in the right pane. An e-mail message opens in your default e-mail program with the workbook automatically attached; the filename appears in the Attached field. Complete the To and optional Cc fields, include a message if you wish, then click Send.

FIGURE C-24: Spelling: English (U.S.) dialog box

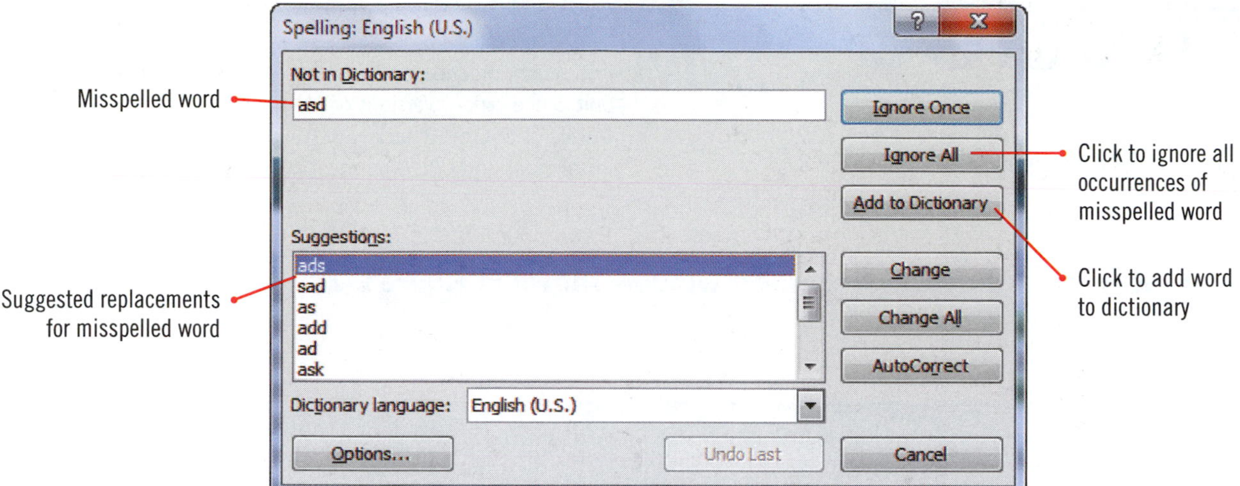

FIGURE C-25: Find and Replace dialog box

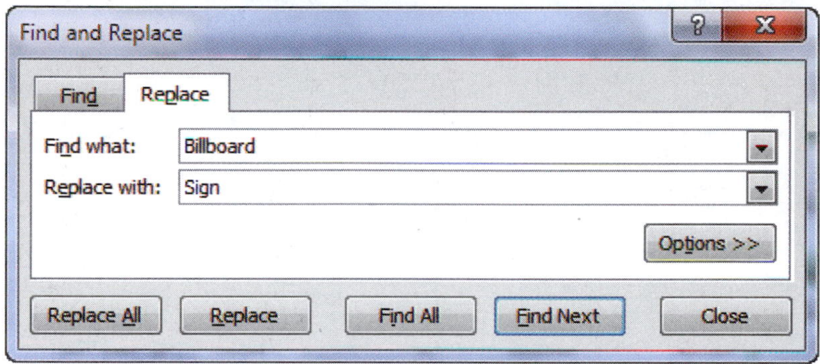

FIGURE C-26: Completed worksheet

Your Name

Quest Specialty Travel Advertising Expenses

Sales Tax 0.0875

Type	Inv. Date	Inv. Due	Cost ea.	Quantity	Ext. Cost	Sales Tax	Total
Newspaper	1-Jan-13	31-Jan	$ 75.34	5	376.70	32.96	409.66
TV Sponsor	7-Jan-13	6-Feb	$ 250.00	15	3,750.00	328.13	4,078.13
Podcasts	20-Jan-13	19-Feb	$ 77.50	30	2,325.00	203.44	2,528.44
TV commercials	1-Jan-13	31-Jan	$ 1,054.42	4	3,975.55	347.86	4,323.41
Web page ads	13-Jan-13	12-Feb	$ 0.17	230	39.56	3.46	43.02
Magazine	7-Jan-13	6-Feb	$ 100.92	12	1,211.04	105.97	1,317.01
Pens	5-Jan-13	4-Feb	$ 0.12	250	30.75	2.69	33.44
TV Sponsor	15-Jan-13	14-Feb	$ 250.00	15	3,750.00	328.13	4,078.13
Sign	12-Jan-13	11-Feb	$ 101.87	20	2,037.40	178.27	2,215.67
Newspaper	25-Jan-13	24-Feb	$ 75.34	6	452.04	39.55	491.59
Newspaper	1-Feb-13	3-Mar	$ 75.34	2	150.68	13.18	163.86
T-Shirts	3-Feb-13	5-Mar	$ 5.67	200	1,134.00	99.23	1,233.23
TV commercials	1-Feb-13	3-Mar	$ 1,054.42	4	4,217.68	369.05	4,586.73
Newspaper	1-Mar-13	31-Mar	$ 23.91	2	47.82	4.18	52.00
Web page ads	28-Feb-13	30-Mar	$ 0.17	275	47.30	4.14	51.44
Magazine	27-Feb-13	29-Mar	$ 100.92	12	1,211.04	105.97	1,317.01
Podcasts	22-Feb-13	24-Mar	$ 77.50	30	2,325.00	203.44	2,528.44
TV Sponsor	1-Feb-13	3-Mar	$ 250.00	30	7,500.00	656.25	8,156.25
Newspaper	25-Feb-13	27-Mar	$ 75.34	6	452.04	39.55	491.59
Web page ads	10-Mar-13	9-Apr	$ 0.17	275	47.30	4.14	51.44
TV Sponsor	15-Feb-13	17-Mar	$ 250.00	25	6,250.00	546.88	6,796.88
Pens	15-Mar-13	14-Apr	$ 0.12	250	30.75	2.69	33.44
TV commercials	1-Mar-13	31-Mar	$ 1,054.44	4	4,217.76	369.05	4,586.81
Podcasts	20-Mar-13	19-Apr	$ 75.50	30	2,265.00	198.19	2,463.19
Newspaper	21-Mar-13	20-Apr	$ 75.34	2	150.68	13.18	163.86
Podcasts	23-Mar-13	22-Apr	$ 77.50	30	2,325.00	203.44	2,528.44
Sign	28-Mar-13	27-Apr	$ 101.87	20	2,037.40	178.27	2,215.67
			$ 5,283.90	1784	52,357.49	4,581.28	56,938.77

Practice

For current SAM information, including versions and content details, visit SAM Central (http://www.cengage.com/samcentral). If you have a SAM user profile, you may have access to hands-on instruction, practice, and assessment of the skills covered in this unit. Since various versions of SAM are supported throughout the life of this text, check with your instructor for the correct instructions and URL/Web site for accessing assignments.

Concepts Review

Label each element of the Excel worksheet window shown in Figure C-27.

FIGURE C-27

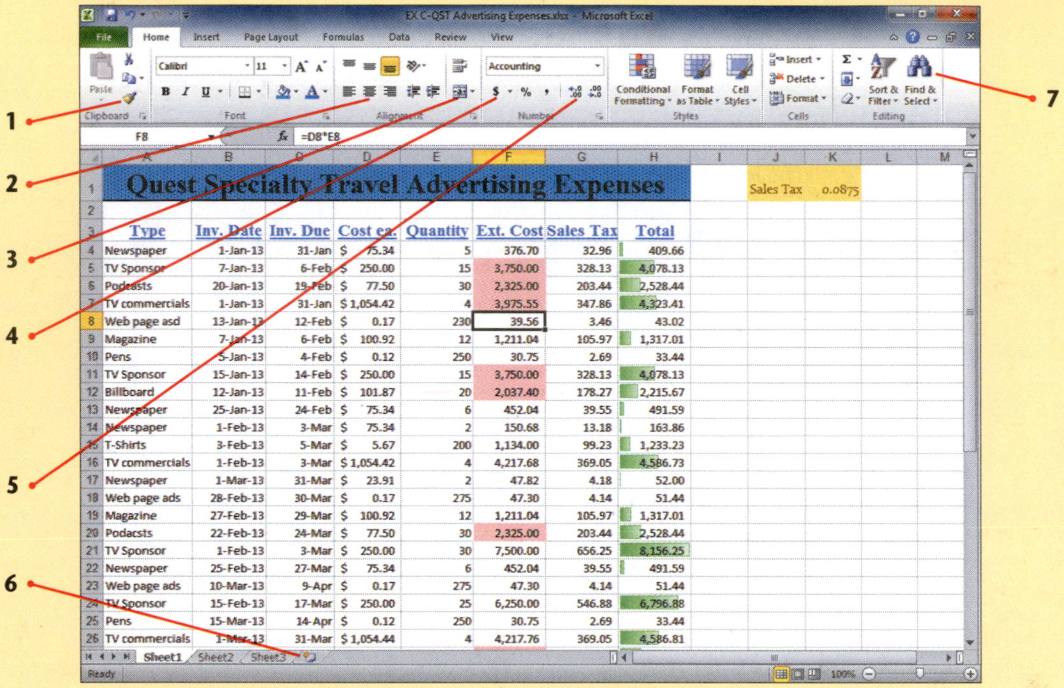

1
2
3
4
5
6
7

Match each command or button with the statement that best describes it.

8. Conditional formatting
9. [button]
10. Spelling button
11. [Ctrl][Home]
12. [button]
13. $

a. Centers cell contents over multiple cells
b. Adds dollar signs and two decimal places to selected data
c. Changes formatting of a cell that meets a certain rule
d. Displays background color options for a cell
e. Moves cell pointer to cell A1
f. Checks for apparent misspellings in a worksheet

Select the best answer from the list of choices.

14. Which of the following is an example of Accounting number format?

- **a.** 5555
- **b.** $5,555.55
- **c.** 55.55%
- **d.** 5,555.55

15. What feature is used to delete a conditional formatting rule?

- **a.** Rules Reminder
- **b.** Conditional Formatting Rules Manager
- **c.** Condition Manager
- **d.** Format Manager

16. Which button removes the italic font style from selected cells?

- **a.** I
- **b.** B
- **c.** ✓
- **d.** I

17. What is the name of the feature used to resize a column to accommodate its widest entry?

- **a.** AutoFormat
- **b.** AutoFit
- **c.** AutoResize
- **d.** AutoRefit

18. Which button increases the number of decimal places in selected cells?

- **a.**
- **b.**
- **c.**
- **d.**

19. Which button copies multiple formats from selected cells to other cells?

- **a.**
- **b.**
- **c.**
- **d.**

Excel 2010

Skills Review

1. Format values.

- **a.** Start Excel, open the file EX C-2.xlsx from the drive and folder where you store your Data Files, then save it as **EX C-Life Insurance Premiums**.
- **b.** Enter a formula in cell B10 that totals the number of employees.
- **c.** Create a formula in cell C5 that calculates the monthly insurance premium for the accounting department. (*Hint*: Make sure you use the correct type of cell reference in the formula. To calculate the department's monthly premium, multiply the number of employees by the monthly premium in cell C14.)
- **d.** Copy the formula in cell C5 to the range C6:C10.
- **e.** Format the range C5:C10 using Accounting number format.
- **f.** Change the format of the range C6:C9 to the Comma Style.
- **g.** Reduce the number of decimals in cell B14 to 0 using a button in the Number group on the Home tab.
- **h.** Save your work.

2. Change font and font sizes.

- **a.** Select the range of cells containing the column labels (in row 4).
- **b.** Change the font of the selection to Times New Roman.
- **c.** Increase the font size of the selection to 12 points.
- **d.** Increase the font size of the label in cell A1 to 14 points.
- **e.** Save your changes.

3. Change font styles and alignment.

- **a.** Apply the bold and italic font styles to the worksheet title in cell A1.
- **b.** Use the Merge & Center button to center the Life Insurance Premiums label over columns A through C.
- **c.** Apply the italic font style to the Life Insurance Premiums label.
- **d.** Add the bold font style to the labels in row 4.
- **e.** Use the Format Painter to copy the format in cell A4 to the range A5:A10.
- **f.** Apply the format in cell C10 to cell B14.

Skills Review (continued)

- **g.** Change the alignment of cell A10 to Align Right using a button in the Alignment group.
- **h.** Select the range of cells containing the column labels, then center them.
- **i.** Remove the italic font style from the Life Insurance Premiums label, then increase the font size to 14.
- **j.** Move the Life Insurance Premiums label to cell A3, then add the bold and underline font styles.
- **k.** Save your changes.

4. Adjust column width.

- **a.** Resize column C to a width of 10.71 characters.
- **b.** Use the AutoFit feature to resize columns A and B.
- **c.** Clear the contents of cell A13 (do not delete the cell).
- **d.** Change the text in cell A14 to **Monthly Insurance Premium**, then change the width of the column to 25 characters.
- **e.** Save your changes.

5. Insert and delete rows and columns.

- **a.** Insert a new row between rows 5 and 6.
- **b.** Add a new department, **Charity**, in the newly inserted row. Enter **6** as the number of employees in the department.
- **c.** Copy the formula in cell C7 to C6.
- **d.** Add the following comment to cell A6: **New department**. Display the comment, then drag to move it out of the way, if necessary.
- **e.** Add a new column between the Department and Employees columns with the title **Family Coverage**, then resize the column using AutoFit.
- **f.** Delete the Legal row from the worksheet.
- **g.** Move the value in cell C14 to cell B14.
- **h.** Save your changes.

6. Apply colors, patterns, and borders.

- **a.** Add Outside Borders around the range A4:D10.
- **b.** Add a Bottom Double Border to cells C9 and D9 (above the calculated employee and premium totals).
- **c.** Apply the Aqua, Accent 5, Lighter 80% fill color to the labels in the Department column (do not include the Total label).
- **d.** Apply the Orange, Accent 6, Lighter 60% fill color to the range A4:D4.
- **e.** Change the color of the font in the range A4:D4 to Red, Accent 2, Darker 25%.
- **f.** Add a 12.5% Gray pattern style to cell A1.
- **g.** Format the range A14:B14 with a fill color of Dark Blue, Text 2, Lighter 40%, change the font color to White, Background 1, then apply the bold font style.
- **h.** Save your changes.

7. Apply conditional formatting.

- **a.** Select the range D5:D9, then create a conditional format that changes cell contents to green fill with dark green text if the value is between 150 and 275.
- **b.** Select the range C5:C9, then create a conditional format that changes cell contents to red text if the number of employees exceeds 10.
- **c.** Apply a blue gradient-filled data bar to the range C5:C9. (*Hint*: Click Blue Data Bar in the Gradient Fill section.)
- **d.** Use the Rules Manager to modify the conditional format in cells C5:C9 to display values greater than 10 in bold dark red text.
- **e.** Merge and center the title (cell A1) over columns A through D.
- **f.** Save your changes.

8. Rename and move a worksheet.

- **a.** Name the Sheet1 tab **Insurance Data**.
- **b.** Name the Sheet3 tab **Employee Data**.
- **c.** Change the Insurance Data tab color to Red, Accent 2, Lighter 40%.
- **d.** Change the Employee Data tab color to Aqua, Accent 5, Lighter 40%.
- **e.** Move the Employee Data sheet so it comes after (to the right of) the Insurance Data sheet.
- **f.** Make the Insurance Data sheet active, enter your name in cell A20, then save your work.

Skills Review (continued)

9. **Check spelling.**
   a. Move the cell pointer to cell A1.
   b. Use the Find & Select feature to replace the Accounting label in cell A5 with Accounting/Legal.
   c. Check the spelling in the worksheet using the spell checker, and correct any spelling errors if necessary.
   d. Save your changes, then compare your Insurance Data sheet to Figure C-28.
   e. Preview the Insurance Data sheet in Backstage view, submit your work to your instructor as directed, then close the workbook and exit Excel.

FIGURE C-28

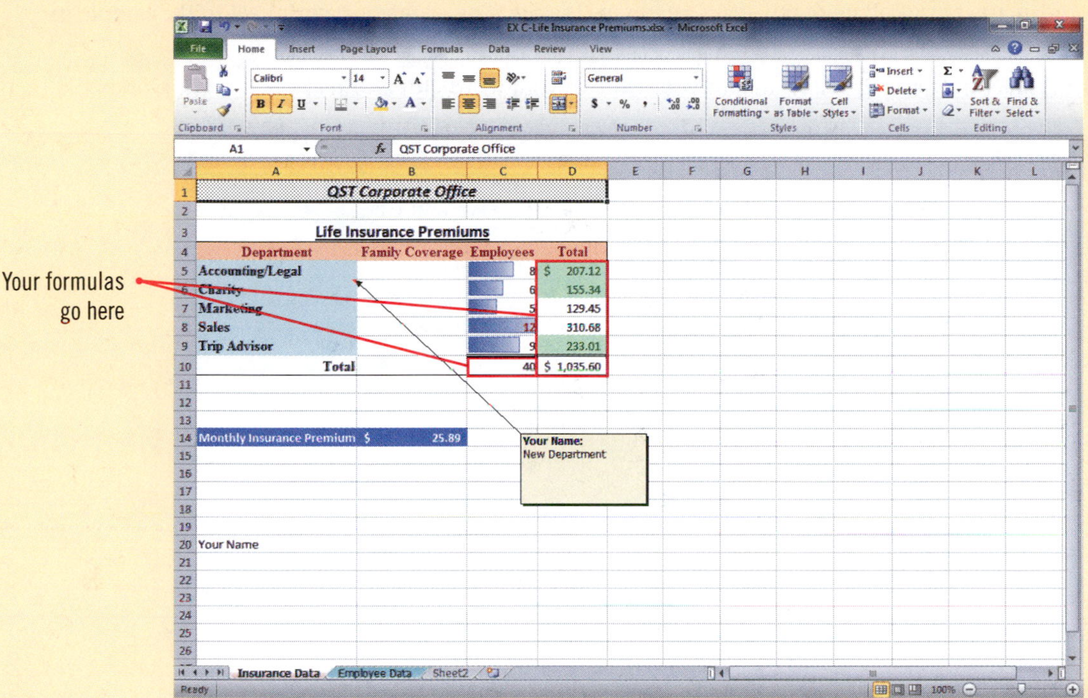

Independent Challenge 1

If you have a SAM 2010 user profile, an autogradable SAM version of this assignment may be available at http://www.cengage.com/sam2010. Check with your instructor to confirm that this assignment is available in SAM. To use the SAM version of this assignment, log into the SAM 2010 Web site and download the instruction and start files.

You run a freelance accounting business, and one of your newest clients is Pen & Paper, a small office supply store. Now that you've converted the store's accounting records to Excel, the manager would like you to work on an analysis of the inventory. Although more items will be added later, the worksheet has enough items for you to begin your modifications.

a. Start Excel, open the file EX C-3.xlsx from the drive and folder where you store your Data Files, then save it as **EX C-Pen & Paper Office Supply Inventory**.
b. Create a formula in cell E4 that calculates the value of the items in stock based on the price paid per item in cell B4. Format the cell in the Comma Style.
c. In cell F4, calculate the sale price of the items in stock using an absolute reference to the markup value shown in cell H1.
d. Copy the formulas created above into the range E5:F14; first convert any necessary cell references to absolute so that the formulas work correctly.
e. Apply bold to the column labels, and italicize the inventory items in column A.
f. Make sure all columns are wide enough to display the data and labels.
g. Format the values in the Sale Price column as Accounting number format with two decimal places.
h. Format the values in the Price Paid column as Comma Style with two decimal places.

Independent Challenge 1 (continued)

i. Add a row under #2 Pencils for **Digital cordless telephones**, price paid **53.45**, sold individually (**each**), with **23** on hand. Copy the appropriate formulas to cells E7:F7.

j. Verify that all the data in the worksheet is visible and formulas are correct. Adjust any items as needed, and check the spelling of the entire worksheet.

k. Use conditional formatting to apply yellow fill with dark yellow text to items with a quantity of less than 25 on hand.

l. Use an icon set of your choosing in the range D4:D15 to illustrate the relative differences between values in the range.

m. Add an outside border around the data in the Item column (do not include the Item column label).

n. Delete the row containing the Thumb tacks entry.

o. Enter your name in an empty cell below the data, then save the file. Compare your worksheet to the sample in Figure C-29.

p. Preview the worksheet in Backstage view, submit your work to your instructor as directed, close the workbook, then exit Excel.

FIGURE C-29

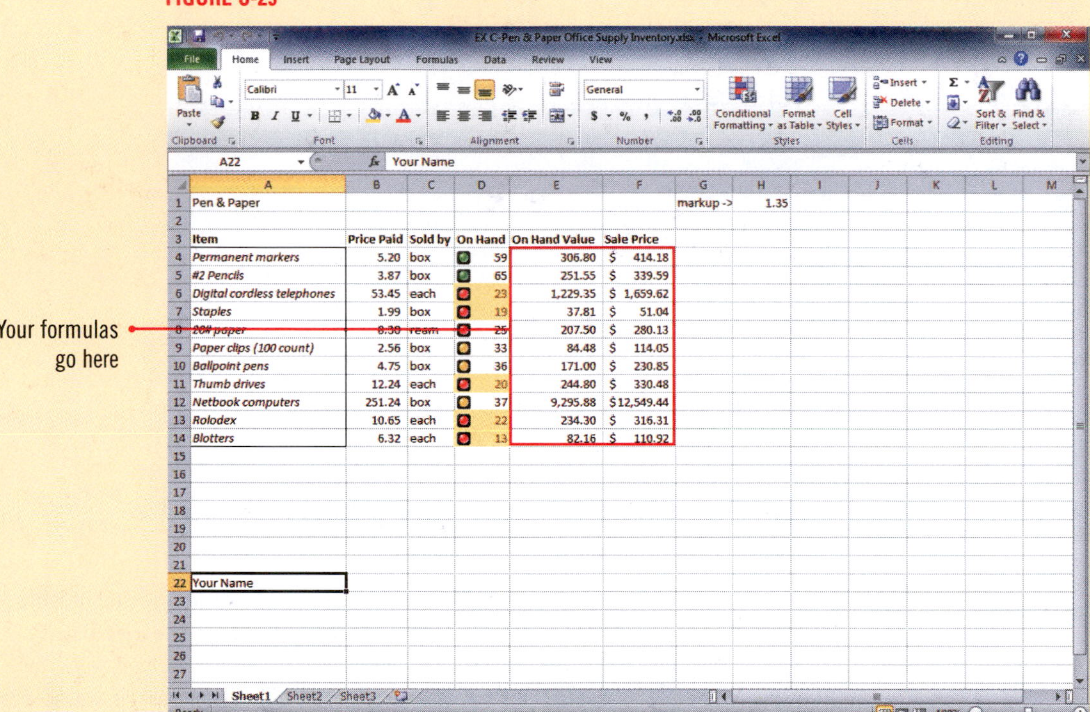

Independent Challenge 2

You volunteer several hours each week with the Assistance League of Boise, and you are in charge of maintaining the membership list. You're currently planning a mailing campaign to members in certain regions of the city. You also want to create renewal letters for members whose membership expires soon. You decide to format the list to enhance the appearance of the worksheet and make your upcoming tasks easier to plan.

a. Start Excel, open the file EX C-4.xlsx from the drive and folder where you store your Data Files, then save it as **EX C-Boise Assistance League**.

b. Remove any blank columns.

c. Create a conditional format in the Zip Code column so that entries greater than 83749 appear in light red fill with dark red text.

d. Make all columns wide enough to fit their data and labels.

e. Use formatting enhancements, such as fonts, font sizes, font styles, and fill colors, to make the worksheet more attractive.

f. Center the column labels.

Independent Challenge 2 (continued)

g. Use conditional formatting so that entries for Year of Membership Expiration that are between 2014 and 2017 appear in green fill with bold black text. (*Hint*: Create a custom format for cells that meet the condition.)

h. Adjust any items as necessary, then check the spelling.

i. Change the name of the Sheet1 tab to one that reflects the sheet's contents, then add a tab color of your choice.

j. Enter your name in an empty cell, then save your work.

k. Preview the worksheet in Backstage view, make any final changes you think necessary, then submit your work to your instructor as directed. Compare your work to the sample shown in Figure C-30.

l. Close the workbook, then exit Excel.

FIGURE C-30

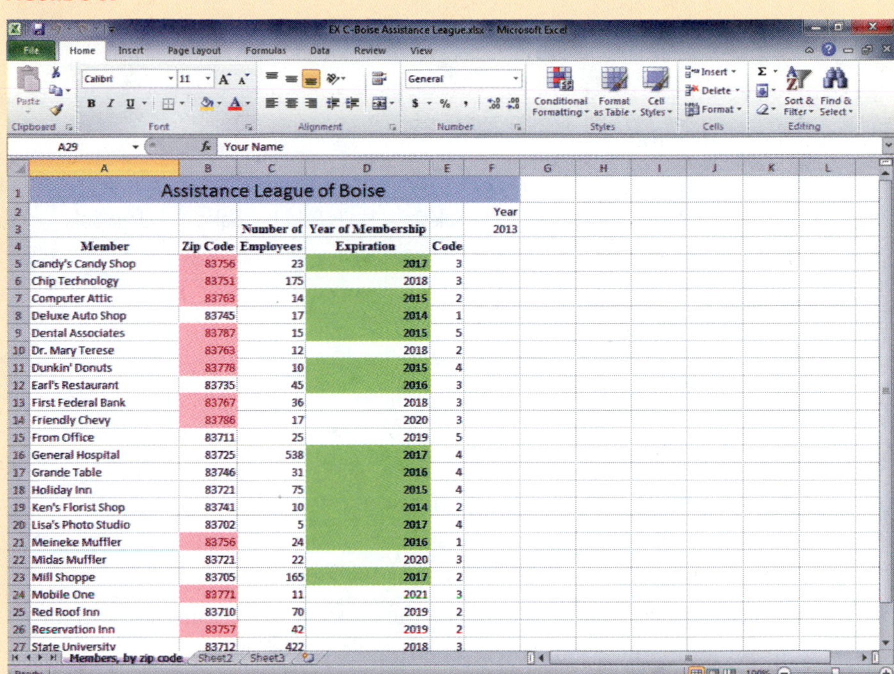

Assistance League of Boise					
					Year
		Number of	Year of Membership		2013
Member	Zip Code	Employees	Expiration	Code	
Candy's Candy Shop	83756	23	2017	3	
Chip Technology	83751	175	2018	3	
Computer Attic	83763	14	2015	2	
Deluxe Auto Shop	83745	17	2014	1	
Dental Associates	83787	15	2015	5	
Dr. Mary Terese	83763	12	2018	2	
Dunkin' Donuts	83778	10	2015	4	
Earl's Restaurant	83735	45	2016	3	
First Federal Bank	83767	36	2018	3	
Friendly Chevy	83786	17	2020	3	
From Office	83711	25	2019	5	
General Hospital	83725	538	2017	4	
Grande Table	83746	31	2016	4	
Holiday Inn	83721	75	2015	4	
Ken's Florist Shop	83741	10	2014	2	
Lisa's Photo Studio	83702	5	2017	4	
Meineke Muffler	83756	24	2016	1	
Midas Muffler	83721	22	2020	3	
Mill Shoppe	83705	165	2017	2	
Mobile One	83771	11	2021	3	
Red Roof Inn	83710	70	2019	2	
Reservation Inn	83757	42	2019	2	
State University	83712	422	2018	3	

Independent Challenge 3

Prestige Press is a Boston-based publisher that manufactures children's books. As the finance manager for the company, one of your responsibilities is to analyze the monthly reports from the five district sales offices. Your boss, Joanne Bennington, has just asked you to prepare a quarterly sales report for an upcoming meeting. Because several top executives will be attending this meeting, Joanne reminds you that the report must look professional. In particular, she asks you to emphasize the company's surge in profits during the last month and to highlight the fact that the Northeastern district continues to outpace the other districts.

a. Plan a worksheet that shows the company's sales during the first quarter. Assume that all books are the same price. Make sure you include the following:
   - The number of books sold (units sold) and the associated revenues (total sales) for each of the five district sales offices. The five sales districts are Northeastern, Midwestern, Southeastern, Southern, and Western.
   - Calculations that show month-by-month totals for January, February, and March, and a 3-month cumulative total.
   - Calculations that show each district's share of sales (percent of Total Sales).
   - Labels that reflect the month-by-month data as well as the cumulative data.
   - Formatting enhancements and data bars that emphasize the recent month's sales surge and the Northeastern district's sales leadership.

b. Ask yourself the following questions about the organization and formatting of the worksheet: What worksheet title and labels do you need, and where should they appear? How can you calculate the totals? What formulas can you copy to save time and keystrokes? Do any of these formulas need to use an absolute reference? How do you show dollar amounts? What information should be shown in bold? Do you need to use more than one font? Should you use more than one point size?

c. Start Excel, then save a new, blank workbook as **EX C-Prestige Press** to the drive and folder where you store your Data Files.

Independent Challenge 3 (continued)

d. Build the worksheet with your own price and sales data. Enter the titles and labels first, then enter the numbers and formulas. You can use the information in Table C-4 to get started.

TABLE C-4

Prestige Press										
1st Quarter Sales Report										
		January		February		March		Total		
Office	Price	Units Sold	Sales	Units Sold	Sales	Units Sold	Sales	Units Sold	Sales	Total % of Sales
Northeastern										
Midwestern										
Southeastern										
Southern										
Western										

e. Add a row beneath the data containing the totals for each column.
f. Adjust the column widths as necessary.
g. Change the height of row 1 to 33 points.
h. Format labels and values to enhance the look of the worksheet, and change the font styles and alignment if necessary.
i. Resize columns and adjust the formatting as necessary.
j. Add data bars for the monthly Units Sold columns.
k. Add a column that calculates a 25% increase in total sales dollars. Use an absolute cell reference in this calculation. (*Hint*: Make sure the current formatting is applied to the new information.)

Advanced Challenge Exercise

- Delete the contents of cells J4:K4 if necessary, then merge and center cell I4 over column I:K.
- Insert a clip art image related to books in an appropriate location, adjusting its size and position as necessary.
- Save your work.

l. Enter your name in an empty cell.
m. Check the spelling in the workbook, change to a landscape orientation, save your work, then compare your work to Figure C-31.
n. Preview the worksheet in Backstage view, then submit your work to your instructor as directed.
o. Close the workbook file, then exit Excel.

FIGURE C-31

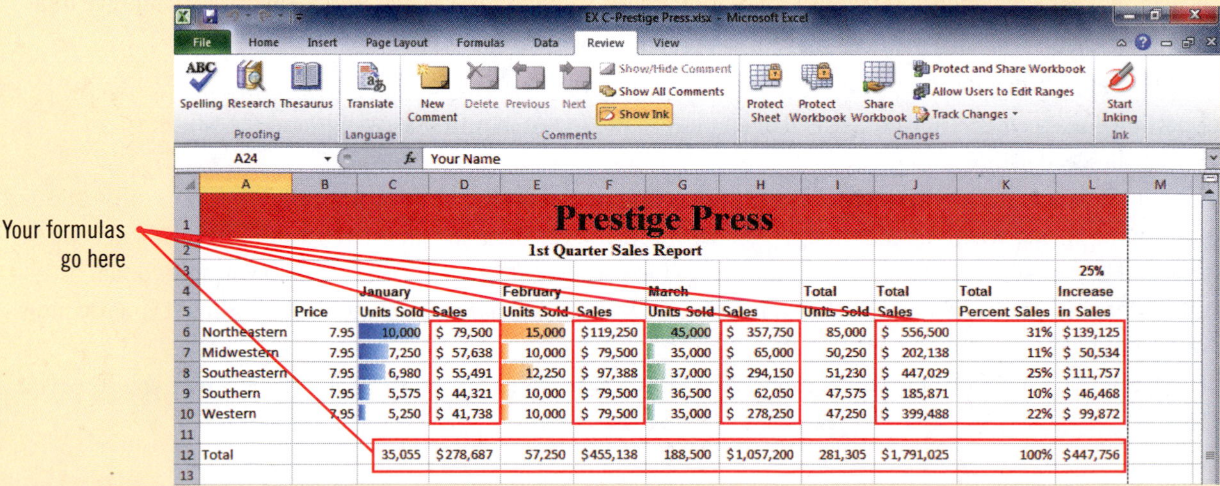

	A	B	C	D	E	F	G	H	I	J	K	L
1	Prestige Press											
2	1st Quarter Sales Report											
3												25%
4			January		February		March		Total	Total	Total	Increase
5		Price	Units Sold	Sales	Units Sold	Sales	Units Sold	Sales	Units Sold	Sales	Percent Sales	in Sales
6	Northeastern	7.95	10,000	$ 79,500	15,000	$119,250	45,000	$ 357,750	85,000	$ 556,500	31%	$139,125
7	Midwestern	7.95	7,250	$ 57,638	10,000	$ 79,500	35,000	$ 65,000	50,250	$ 202,138	11%	$ 50,534
8	Southeastern	7.95	6,980	$ 55,491	12,250	$ 97,388	37,000	$ 294,150	51,230	$ 447,029	25%	$111,757
9	Southern	7.95	5,575	$ 44,321	10,000	$ 79,500	36,500	$ 62,050	47,575	$ 185,871	10%	$ 46,468
10	Western	7.95	5,250	$ 41,738	10,000	$ 79,500	35,000	$ 278,250	47,250	$ 399,488	22%	$ 99,872
11												
12	Total		35,055	$278,687	57,250	$455,138	188,500	$1,057,200	281,305	$1,791,025	100%	$447,756
13												

Real Life Independent Challenge

This project requires an Internet connection.

You are saving money to take an international trip you have always dreamed about. You plan to visit seven different countries over the course of 2 months, and you have budgeted an identical spending allowance in each country. You want to create a worksheet that calculates the amount of native currency you will have in each country based on the budgeted amount. You want the workbook to reflect the currency information for each country.

a. Start Excel, then save a new, blank workbook as **EX C-World Tour Budget** to the drive and folder where you store your Data Files.

b. Add a title at the top of the worksheet.

c. Think of seven countries you would like to visit, then enter column and row labels for your worksheet. (*Hint*: You may wish to include row labels for each country, plus column labels for the country, the $1 equivalent in native currency, the total amount of native currency you'll have in each country, and the name of each country's monetary unit.)

d. Decide how much money you want to bring to each country (for example, $1,000), and enter that in the worksheet.

e. Use your favorite search engine to find your own information sources on currency conversions for the countries you plan to visit.

f. Enter the cash equivalent to $1 in U.S. dollars for each country in your list.

g. Create an equation that calculates the amount of native currency you will have in each country, using an absolute cell reference in the formula.

h. Format the entries in the column containing the native currency $1 equivalent as Number number format with three decimal places, and format the column containing the total native currency budget with two decimal places, using the correct currency number format for each country. (*Hint*: Use the Number tab in the Format cells dialog box; choose the appropriate currency number format from the Symbol list.)

i. Create a conditional format that changes the font style and color of the calculated amount in the $1,000 US column to light red fill with dark red text if the amount exceeds **1000** units of the local currency.

j. Merge and center the worksheet title over the column headings.

k. Add any formatting you want to the column headings, and resize the columns as necessary.

l. Add a background color to the title.

Advanced Challenge Exercise

- Modify the conditional format in the $1,000 US column so that entries between 1500 and 3999 are displayed in red, boldface type; and entries above 4000 appear in blue, boldface type with a light red background.
- Delete all the unused sheets in the workbook.
- Save your work as **EX C-World Tour Budget ACE** to the drive and folder where you store your Data Files.
- If you have access to an e-mail account, e-mail this workbook to your instructor as an attachment.

m. Enter your name in the header of the worksheet.

n. Spell check the worksheet, save your changes, compare your work to Figure C-32, then preview the worksheet in Backstage view, and submit your work to your instructor as directed.

o. Close the workbook and exit Excel.

FIGURE C-32

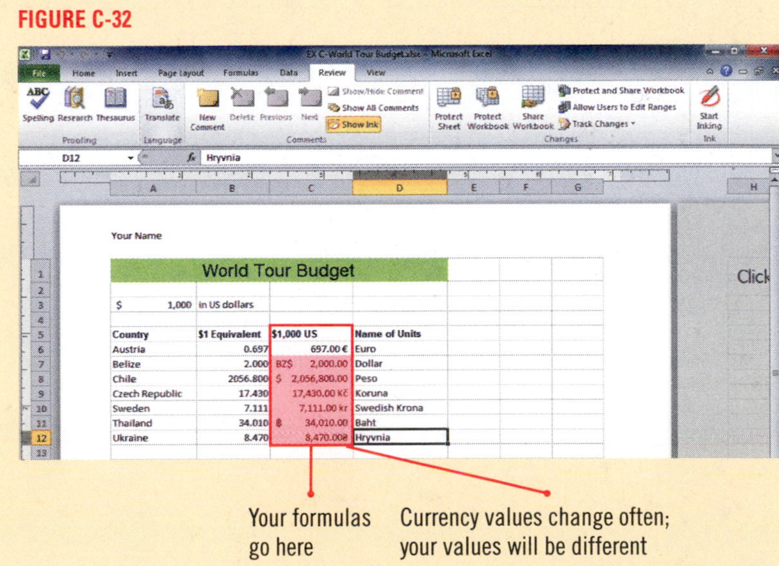

Visual Workshop

Open the file EX C-5.xlsx from the drive and folder where you store your Data Files, then save it as **EX C-Tip-Top Temps**. Use the skills you learned in this unit to format the worksheet so it looks like the one shown in Figure C-33. Create a conditional format in the Level column so that entries greater than 3 appear in red text. Create an additional conditional format in the Review Cycle column so that any value equal to 3 appears in green bold text. Replace the Accounting department label with **Legal**. (*Hint*: The only additional font used in this exercise is 16-point Times New Roman in row 1.) Enter your name in cell A25, check the spelling in the worksheet, save your changes, then submit your work to your instructor as directed.

FIGURE C-33

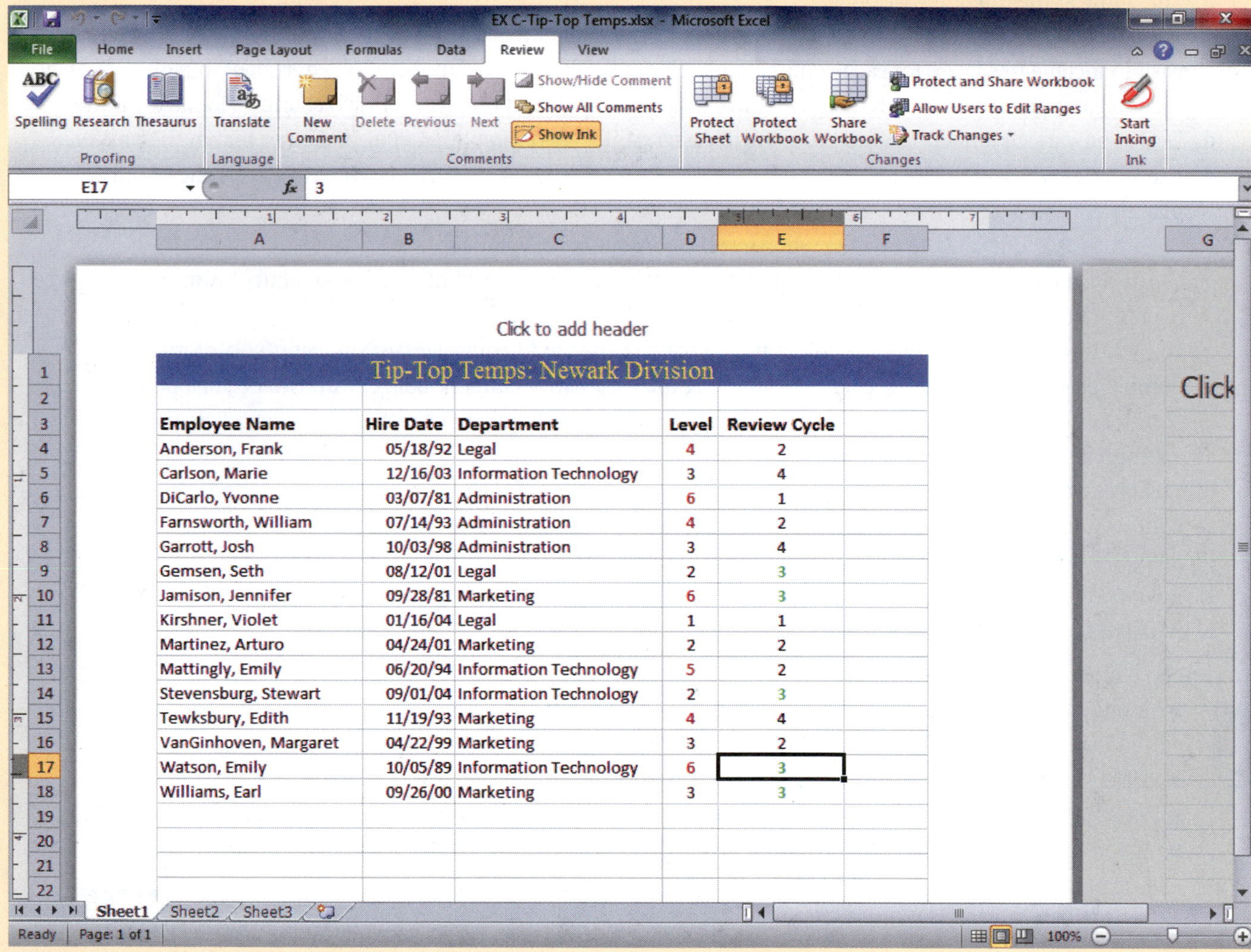

Tip-Top Temps: Newark Division

Employee Name	Hire Date	Department	Level	Review Cycle
Anderson, Frank	05/18/92	Legal	4	2
Carlson, Marie	12/16/03	Information Technology	3	4
DiCarlo, Yvonne	03/07/81	Administration	6	1
Farnsworth, William	07/14/93	Administration	4	2
Garrott, Josh	10/03/98	Administration	3	4
Gemsen, Seth	08/12/01	Legal	2	3
Jamison, Jennifer	09/28/81	Marketing	6	3
Kirshner, Violet	01/16/04	Legal	1	1
Martinez, Arturo	04/24/01	Marketing	2	2
Mattingly, Emily	06/20/94	Information Technology	5	2
Stevensburg, Stewart	09/01/04	Information Technology	2	3
Tewksbury, Edith	11/19/93	Marketing	4	4
VanGinhoven, Margaret	04/22/99	Marketing	3	2
Watson, Emily	10/05/89	Information Technology	6	3
Williams, Earl	09/26/00	Marketing	3	3

UNIT
D
Excel 2010

Working with Charts

Files You Will Need:

EX D-1.xlsx
EX D-2.xlsx
EX D-3.xlsx
EX D-4.xlsx
EX D-5.xlsx
EX D-6.xlsx

Worksheets provide an effective layout for calculating and organizing data, but the grid layout is not always the best format for presenting your work to others. To display information so it's easier to interpret, you can create a chart. **Charts**, sometimes called graphs, present information in a graphic format, making it easier to see patterns, trends, and relationships. In this unit, you learn how to create a chart, how to edit the chart and change the chart type, how to add text annotations and arrows, and how to preview and print the chart. At the upcoming annual meeting, Grace Wong wants to emphasize spending patterns at Quest Specialty Travel. She asks you to create a chart showing the trends in company expenses over the past four quarters.

OBJECTIVES

Plan a chart
Create a chart
Move and resize a chart
Change the chart design
Change the chart layout
Format a chart
Annotate and draw on a chart
Create a pie chart

Planning a Chart

Before creating a chart, you need to plan the information you want your chart to show and how you want it to look. Planning ahead helps you decide what type of chart to create and how to organize the data. Understanding the parts of a chart makes it easier to format and to change specific elements so that the chart best illustrates your data. In preparation for creating the chart for Grace's presentation, you identify your goals for the chart and plan its layout.

DETAILS

Use the following guidelines to plan the chart:

- **Determine the purpose of the chart, and identify the data relationships you want to communicate graphically**

  You want to create a chart that shows quarterly tour expenses for each country where Quest Specialty Travel provides tours. This worksheet data is shown in Figure D-1. You also want the chart to illustrate whether the quarterly expenses for each country increased or decreased from quarter to quarter.

- **Determine the results you want to see, and decide which chart type is most appropriate**

  Different chart types display data in distinctive ways. For example, a pie chart compares parts to the whole, so it's useful for showing what proportion of a budget amount was spent on tours in one country relative to what was spent on tours in other countries. A line chart, in contrast, is best for showing trends over time. To choose the best chart type for your data, you should first decide how you want your data displayed and interpreted. Table D-1 describes several different types of charts you can create in Excel and their corresponding buttons on the Insert tab on the Ribbon. Because you want to compare QST tour expenses in multiple countries over a period of four quarters, you decide to use a column chart.

- **Identify the worksheet data you want the chart to illustrate**

  Sometimes you use all the data in a worksheet to create a chart, while at other times you may need to select a range within the sheet. The worksheet from which you are creating your chart contains expense data for each of the past four quarters and the totals for the past year. You will need to use all the quarterly data contained in the worksheet except the quarterly totals.

- **Understand the elements of a chart**

  The chart shown in Figure D-2 contains basic elements of a chart. In the figure, QST tour countries are on the horizontal axis (also called the **x-axis**) and expense dollar amounts are on the vertical axis (also called the **y-axis**). The horizontal axis is also called the **category axis** because it often contains the names of data groups, such as locations, months, or years. The vertical axis is also called the **value axis** because it often contains numerical values that help you interpret the size of chart elements. (3-D charts also contain a **z-axis**, for comparing data across both categories and values.) The area inside the horizontal and vertical axes is the **plot area**. The **tick marks**, on the vertical axis, and **gridlines** (extending across the plot area) create a scale of measure for each value. Each value in a cell you select for your chart is a **data point**. In any chart, a **data marker** visually represents each data point, which in this case is a column. A collection of related data points is a **data series**. In this chart, there are four data series (Quarter 1, Quarter 2, Quarter 3, and Quarter 4). Each is made up of column data markers of a different color, so a **legend** is included to make it easy to identify them.

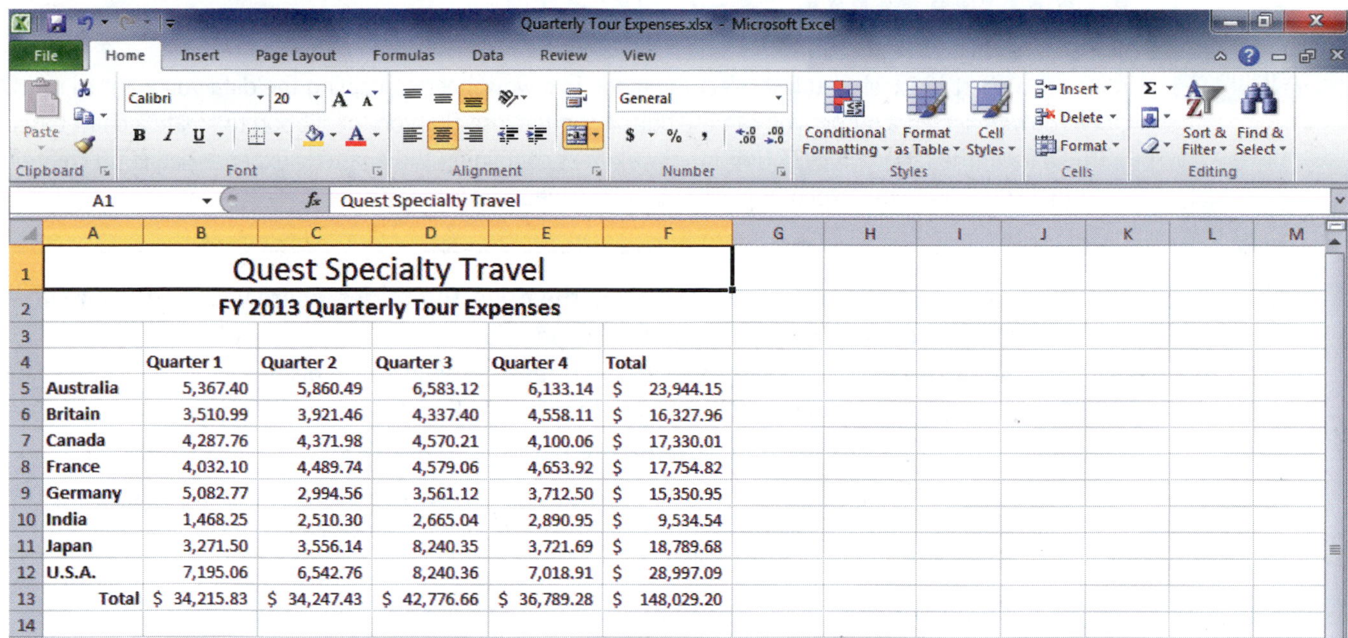

	A	B	C	D	E	F
1	Quest Specialty Travel					
2	FY 2013 Quarterly Tour Expenses					
3						
4		Quarter 1	Quarter 2	Quarter 3	Quarter 4	Total
5	Australia	5,367.40	5,860.49	6,583.12	6,133.14	$ 23,944.15
6	Britain	3,510.99	3,921.46	4,337.40	4,558.11	$ 16,327.96
7	Canada	4,287.76	4,371.98	4,570.21	4,100.06	$ 17,330.01
8	France	4,032.10	4,489.74	4,579.06	4,653.92	$ 17,754.82
9	Germany	5,082.77	2,994.56	3,561.12	3,712.50	$ 15,350.95
10	India	1,468.25	2,510.30	2,665.04	2,890.95	$ 9,534.54
11	Japan	3,271.50	3,556.14	8,240.35	3,721.69	$ 18,789.68
12	U.S.A.	7,195.06	6,542.76	8,240.36	7,018.91	$ 28,997.09
13	Total	$ 34,215.83	$ 34,247.43	$ 42,776.66	$ 36,789.28	$ 148,029.20
14						

FIGURE D-1: Worksheet containing expense data

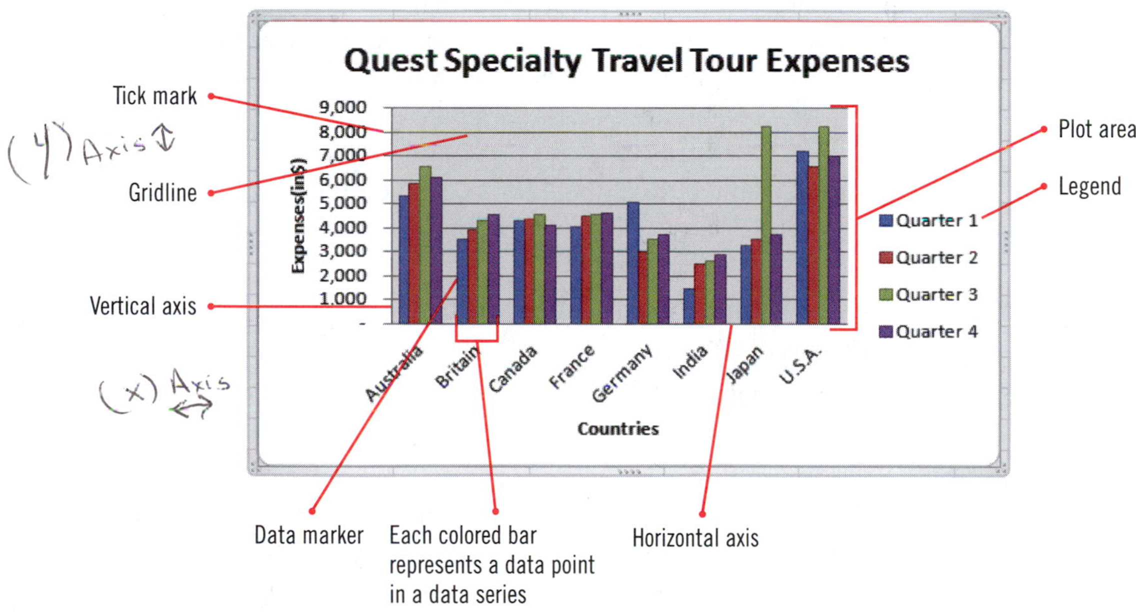

FIGURE D-2: Chart elements

TABLE D-1: Common chart types

type	button	description
Column		Compares data using columns; the Excel default; sometimes referred to as a bar chart in other spreadsheet programs
Line		Compares trends over even time intervals; looks similar to an area chart, but does not emphasize total
Pie		Compares sizes of pieces as part of a whole; used for a single series of numbers
Bar		Compares data using horizontal bars; sometimes referred to as a horizontal bar chart in other spreadsheet programs
Area		Shows how individual volume changes over time in relation to total volume
Scatter		Compares trends over uneven time or measurement intervals; used in scientific and engineering disciplines for trend spotting and extrapolation

Creating a Chart

To create a chart in Excel, you first select the range in a worksheet containing the data you want to chart. Once you've selected a range, you can use buttons on the Insert tab on the Ribbon to create a chart based on the data in the range. Using the worksheet containing the quarterly expense data, you create a chart that shows how the expenses in each country varied across the quarters.

STEPS

QUICK TIP
When charting data for a particular time period, make sure all series are for the same time period.

1. **Start Excel, open the file EX D-1.xlsx from the drive and folder where you store your Data Files, then save it as EX D-Quarterly Tour Expenses**
   You want the chart to include the quarterly tour expenses values, as well as quarter and country labels. You don't include the Total column and row because the figures in these cells would skew the chart.
2. **Select the range A4:E12, then click the Insert tab on the Ribbon**
   The Insert tab contains groups for inserting various types of objects, including charts. The Charts group includes buttons for each major chart type, plus an Other Charts button for additional chart types, such as stock charts for charting stock market data.

QUICK TIP
To base a chart on data in nonadjacent ranges, press and hold [Ctrl] while selecting each range, then use the Insert tab to create the chart.

3. **Click the Column button in the Charts group, then click Clustered Column under 2-D Column in the Column chart gallery, as shown in Figure D-3**
   The chart is inserted in the center of the worksheet, and three contextual Chart Tools tabs appear on the Ribbon: Design, Layout, and Format. On the Design tab, which is currently in front, you can quickly change the chart type, chart layout, and chart style, and you can swap how the columns and rows of data in the worksheet are represented in the chart. Currently, the countries are charted along the horizontal x-axis, with the quarterly expense dollar amounts charted along the y-axis. This lets you easily compare the quarterly expenses for each country.
4. **Click the Switch Row/Column button in the Data group on the Chart Tools Design tab**
   The quarters are now charted along the x-axis. The expense amounts per country are charted along the y-axis, as indicated by the updated legend. See Figure D-4.
5. **Click the Undo button on the Quick Access toolbar**
   The chart returns to its original design.
6. **Click the Chart Tools Layout tab, click the Chart Title button in the Labels group, then click Above Chart**
   A title placeholder appears above the chart.

QUICK TIP
You can also triple-click to select the chart title text.

7. **Click anywhere in the Chart Title text box, press [Ctrl][A] to select the text, type Quarterly Tour Expenses, then click anywhere in the chart to deselect the title**
   Adding a title helps identify the chart. The border around the chart and the chart's **sizing handles**, the small series of dots at the corners and sides of the chart's border, indicate that the chart is selected. See Figure D-5. Your chart might be in a different location on the worksheet and may look slightly different; you will move and resize it in the next lesson. Any time a chart is selected, as it is now, a blue border surrounds the worksheet data range on which the chart is based, a purple border surrounds the cells containing the category axis labels, and a green border surrounds the cells containing the data series labels. This chart is known as an **embedded chart** because it is inserted directly in the current worksheet and doesn't exist in a separate file. Embedding a chart in the current sheet is the default selection when creating a chart, but you can also embed a chart on a different sheet in the workbook, or on a newly created chart sheet. A **chart sheet** is a sheet in a workbook that contains only a chart that is linked to the workbook data.
8. **Save your work**

FIGURE D-3: Column chart gallery

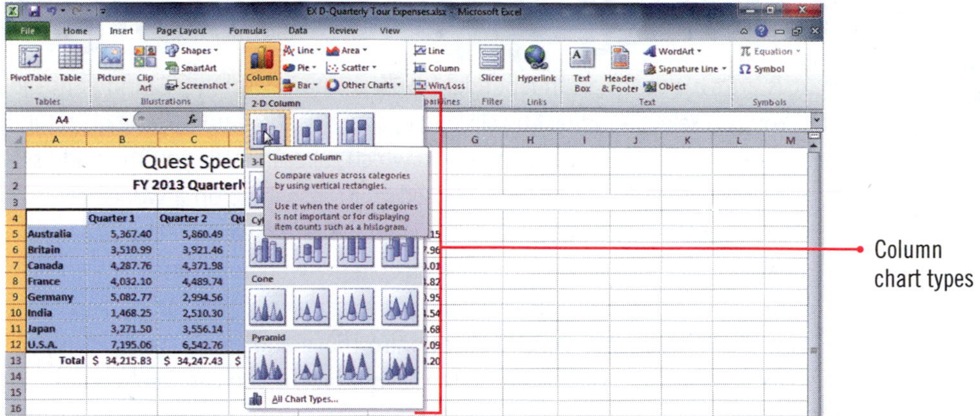

FIGURE D-4: Clustered Column chart with different presentation of data

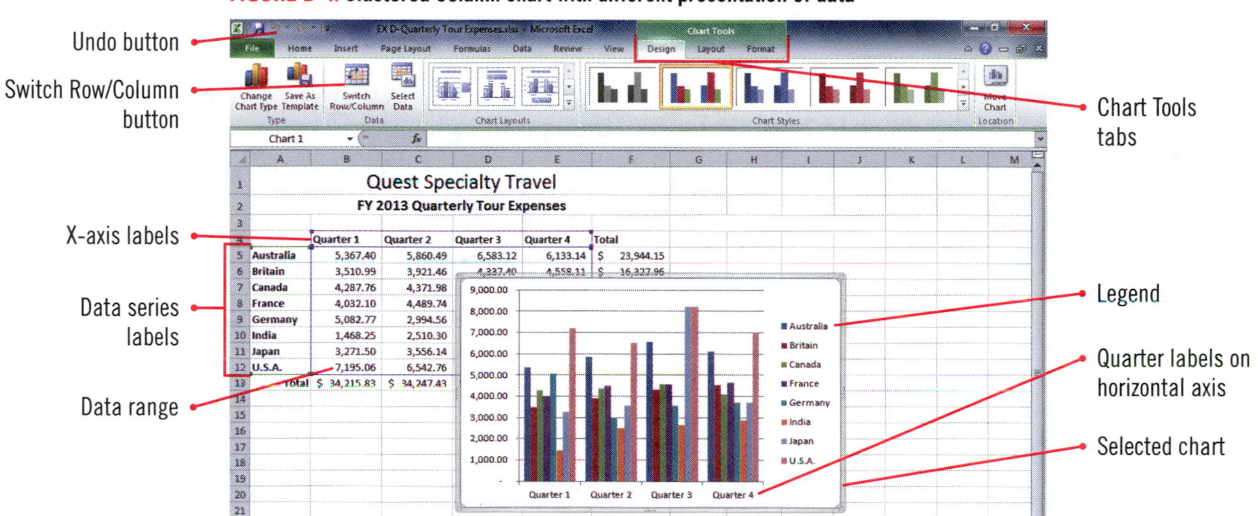

FIGURE D-5: Chart with rows and columns restored and title added

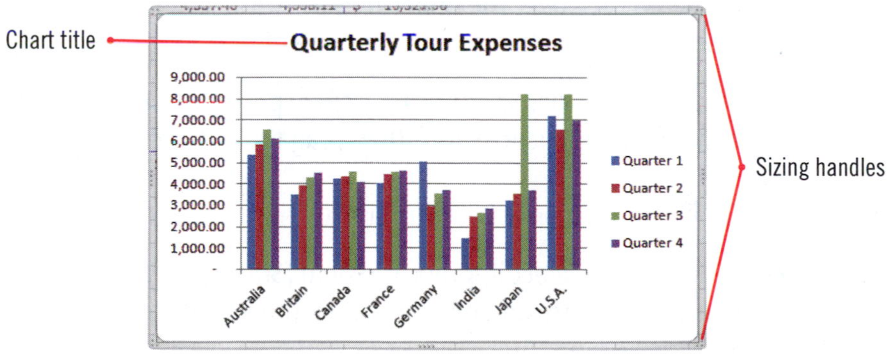

Creating sparklines

You can quickly create a miniature chart called a **sparkline** that serves as a visual indicator of data trends. To do this, select a range of data, click the Insert tab, then click the Line, Column, or Win/Loss button in the Sparklines group. In the Create Sparklines dialog box that opens, enter the cell in which you want the sparkline to appear, then click OK. Figure D-6 shows four sparklines created in four different cells. Any changes to data in the range are reflected in the sparkline. To delete a selected sparkline from a cell, click the Clear button in the Group group on the Sparkline Tools Design tab.

FIGURE D-6: Sparklines in cells

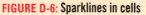

G	H	I	J
Sparklines			
Qtr 1	Qtr 2	Qtr 3	Qtr 4

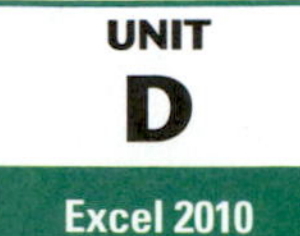

Moving and Resizing a Chart

A chart is an **object**, or an independent element on a worksheet, and is not located in a specific cell or range. You can select an object by clicking it; sizing handles around the object indicate it is selected. (When a chart is selected in Excel, the Name box, which normally tells you the address of the active cell, tells you the chart number.) You can move a selected chart anywhere on a worksheet without affecting formulas or data in the worksheet. However, any data changed in the worksheet is automatically updated in the chart. You can even move a chart to a different sheet in the workbook, and it will still reflect the original data. You can resize a chart to improve its appearance by dragging its sizing handles. A chart contains chart objects, such as a title and legend, which you can also move and resize. You can reposition chart objects to pre-defined locations using commands on the Layout tab, or you can freely move any chart object by dragging it or by cutting and pasting it to a new location. When you point to a chart object, the name of the object appears as a ScreenTip. You want to resize the chart, position it below the worksheet data, and move the legend.

STEPS

QUICK TIP
To delete a selected chart, press [Delete].

1. **Make sure the chart is still selected, then position the pointer over the chart**
   The pointer shape indicates that you can move the chart. For a table of commonly used object pointers, refer to Table D-2.

TROUBLE
If you do not drag a blank area on the chart, you might inadvertently move a chart element instead of the whole chart; if this happens, undo the action and try again.

2. **Position on a blank area near the upper-left edge of the chart, press and hold the left mouse button, drag the chart until its upper-left corner is at the upper-left corner of cell A16, then release the mouse button**
   As you drag the chart, you can see an outline representing the chart's perimeter. The chart appears in the new location.

3. **Position the pointer on the right-middle sizing handle until it changes to ⇔, then drag the right border of the chart to the right edge of column G**
   The chart is widened. See Figure D-7.

QUICK TIP
To resize a selected chart to an exact specification, click the Chart Tools Format tab, then enter the desired height and width in the Size group.

4. **Position the pointer over the upper-middle sizing handle until it changes to ⇕, then drag the top border of the chart to the top edge of row 15**

5. **Scroll down if necessary so row 30 is visible, position the pointer over the lower-middle sizing handle until it changes to ⇕, then drag the bottom border of the chart to the bottom border of row 26**
   You can move any object on a chart. You want to align the top of the legend with the top of the plot area.

QUICK TIP
You can move a legend to the right, top, left, or bottom of a chart by clicking the Legend button in the Labels group on the Chart Tools Layout tab, then clicking a location option.

6. **Click the legend to select it, press and hold [Shift], drag the legend up using so the dotted outline is approximately 1⁄4" above the top of the plot area, then release [Shift]**
   When you click the legend, sizing handles appear around it and "Legend" appears as a ScreenTip when the pointer hovers over the object. As you drag, a dotted outline of the legend border appears. Pressing and holding the [Shift] key holds the horizontal position of the legend as you move it vertically. Although the sizing handles on objects within a chart look different from the sizing handles that surround a chart, they function the same way.

7. **Click cell A12, type United States, click the Enter button ✔ on the formula bar, use AutoFit to resize column A, then press [Ctrl][Home]**
   The axis label changes to reflect the updated cell contents, as shown in Figure D-8. Changing any data in the worksheet modifies corresponding text or values in the chart. Because the chart is no longer selected, the Chart Tools tabs no longer appear on the Ribbon.

8. **Save your work**

FIGURE D-7: Moved and resized chart

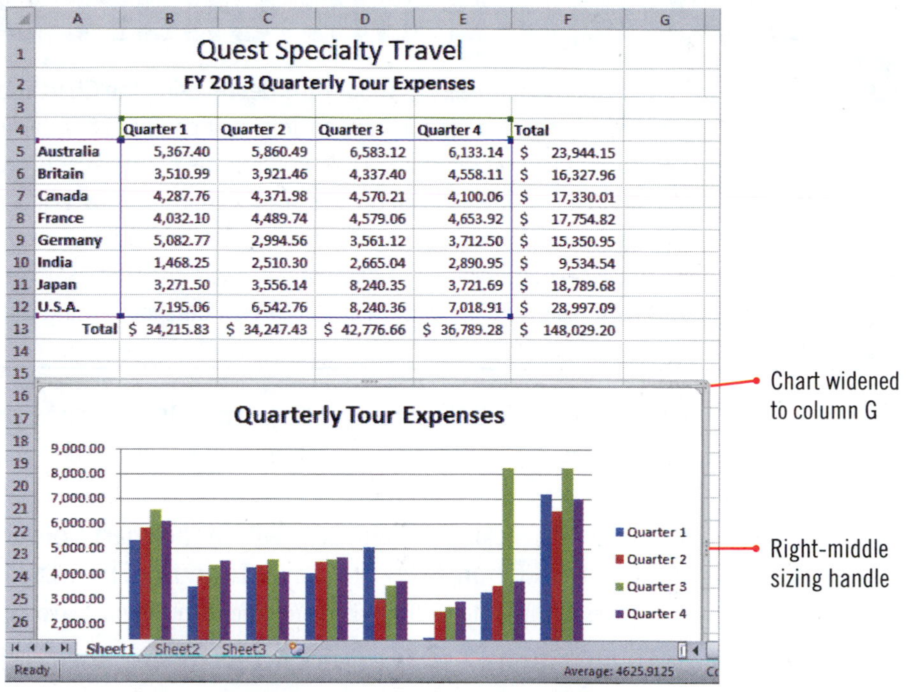

	A	B	C	D	E	F
1	Quest Specialty Travel					
2	FY 2013 Quarterly Tour Expenses					
3						
4		Quarter 1	Quarter 2	Quarter 3	Quarter 4	Total
5	Australia	5,367.40	5,860.49	6,583.12	6,133.14	$ 23,944.15
6	Britain	3,510.99	3,921.46	4,337.40	4,558.11	$ 16,327.96
7	Canada	4,287.76	4,371.98	4,570.21	4,100.06	$ 17,330.01
8	France	4,032.10	4,489.74	4,579.06	4,653.92	$ 17,754.82
9	Germany	5,082.77	2,994.56	3,561.12	3,712.50	$ 15,350.95
10	India	1,468.25	2,510.30	2,665.04	2,890.95	$ 9,534.54
11	Japan	3,271.50	3,556.14	8,240.35	3,721.69	$ 18,789.68
12	U.S.A.	7,195.06	6,542.76	8,240.36	7,018.91	$ 28,997.09
13	Total	$ 34,215.83	$ 34,247.43	$ 42,776.66	$ 36,789.28	$ 148,029.20

FIGURE D-8: Worksheet with modified legend and label

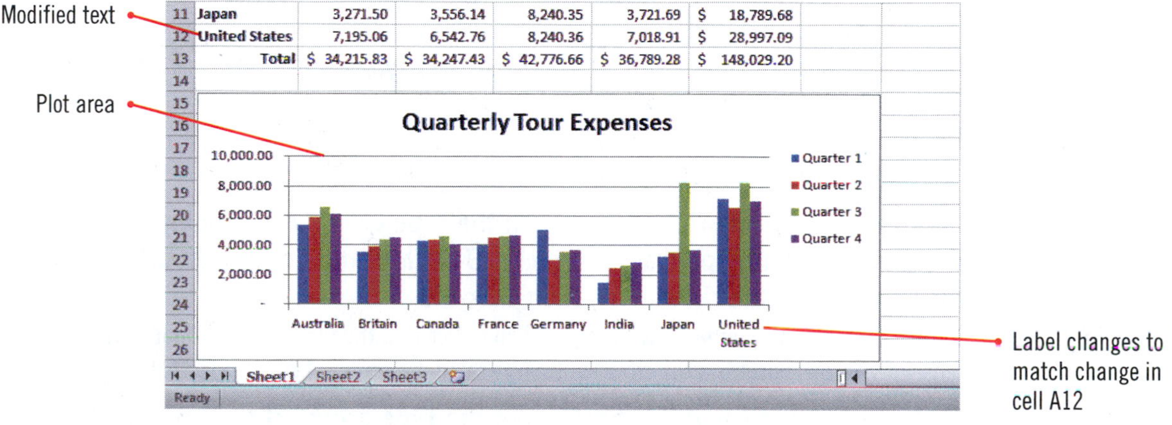

	A	B	C	D	E	F
11	Japan	3,271.50	3,556.14	8,240.35	3,721.69	$ 18,789.68
12	United States	7,195.06	6,542.76	8,240.36	7,018.91	$ 28,997.09
13	Total	$ 34,215.83	$ 34,247.43	$ 42,776.66	$ 36,789.28	$ 148,029.20

TABLE D-2: Common object pointers

name	pointer	use	name	pointer	use
Diagonal resizing	⤢ or ⤡	Change chart shape from corners	I-beam	I	Edit object text
Draw	+	Draw an object	Move	✥	Move object
Horizontal resizing	⇔	Change object width	Vertical resizing	⇕	Change object height

Moving an embedded chart to a sheet

Suppose you have created an embedded chart that you decide would look better on a chart sheet or in a different worksheet. You can make this change without recreating the entire chart. To do so, first select the chart, click the Chart Tools Design tab, then click the Move Chart button in the Location group. The Move Chart dialog box opens. To move the chart to its own chart sheet, click the New sheet option button, type a name for the new sheet if desired, then click OK. If the chart is already on its own sheet, click the Object in option button, select the worksheet to where you want to move it, then click OK.

UNIT
D
Excel 2010

Changing the Chart Design

Once you've created a chart, it's easy to modify the design using the Chart Tools Design tab. You can change the chart type, modify the data range and column/row configuration, apply a different chart style, and change the layout of objects in the chart. The layouts in the Chart Layouts group on the Chart Tools Design tab offer preconfigured arrangements of objects in your chart, such as its legend, title, or gridlines; choosing one of these layouts is an alternative to manually changing how objects are arranged in a chart. You look over your worksheet and realize the data for Japan and the United States in Quarter 3 is incorrect. After you correct this data, you want to see how the corrected data looks using different chart layouts and types.

STEPS

1. **Click cell D11, type 4568.92, press [Enter], type 6107.09, then press [Enter]**
   In the chart, the Quarter 3 data markers for Japan and the United States reflect the adjusted expense figures. See Figure D-9.

> **QUICK TIP**
> You can see more layout choices by clicking the More button in the Chart Layouts group.

2. **Select the chart by clicking a blank area within the chart border, click the Chart Tools Design tab on the Ribbon, then click Layout 3 in the Chart Layouts group**
   The legend moves to the bottom of the chart. You prefer the original layout.
3. **Click the Undo button on the Quick Access toolbar, then click the Change Chart Type button in the Type group**
   The Change Chart Type dialog box opens, as shown in Figure D-10. The left pane of the dialog box lists the available categories, and the right pane shows the individual chart types. An orange border surrounds the currently selected chart type.
4. **Click Bar in the left pane of the Change Chart Type dialog box, confirm that the Clustered Bar chart type is selected in the right pane, then click OK**
   The column chart changes to a clustered bar chart. See Figure D-11. You look at the bar chart, then decide to see how the data looks in a three-dimensional column chart.
5. **Click the Change Chart Type button in the Type group, click Column in the left pane of the Change Chart Type dialog box, click 3-D Clustered Column (fourth from the left in the first row) in the right pane, then click OK**
   A three-dimensional column chart appears. You notice that the three-dimensional column format gives you a sense of volume, but it is more crowded than the two-dimensional column format.

> **QUICK TIP**
> If you plan to print a chart on a black-and-white printer, you may wish to apply a black-and-white chart style to your chart so you can see how the output will look as you work.

6. **Click the Change Chart Type button in the Type group, click Clustered Column (first from the left in the first row) in the right pane of the Change Chart Type dialog box, then click OK**
7. **Click the Style 3 chart style in the Chart Styles group**
   The columns change to shades of blue. You prefer the previous chart style's color scheme.
8. **Click on the Quick Access toolbar, then save your work**

Creating a combination chart

A **combination chart** is two charts in one; a column chart with a line chart, for example. This type of chart (which cannot be used with all data) is helpful when charting dissimilar but related data. For example, you can create a combination chart based on home price and home size data, showing home prices in a column chart, and related home sizes in a line chart. In such a combination chart, a **secondary axis** (such as a vertical axis on the right side of the chart) would supply the scale for the home sizes. To create a combination chart, you can apply a chart type to a data series in an existing chart. Select the chart data series that you want plotted on a secondary axis, then click Format Selection in the Current Selection group on the Chart Tools Layout tab or Format tab to open the Format Data Series dialog box. In the dialog box, click Series Options if necessary, click the Secondary Axis option button under Plot Series On, then click Close. Click the Chart Tools Layout tab if necessary, click the Axes button in the Axes group, then click the type of secondary axis you want and where you want it to appear. To finish, click the Change Chart Type button in the Type group on the Design tab, then select a chart type for the data series.

FIGURE D-9: Worksheet with modified data

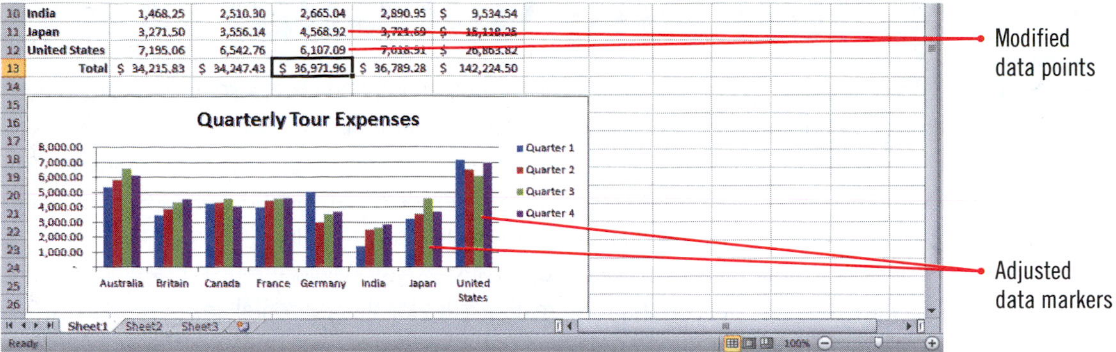

FIGURE D-10: Change Chart Type dialog box

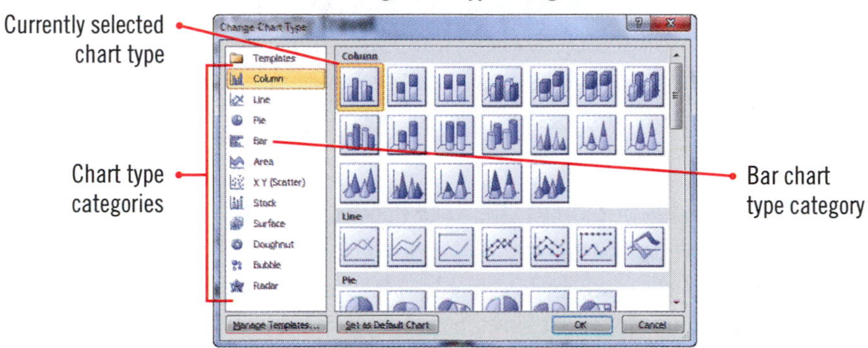

FIGURE D-11: Column chart changed to bar chart

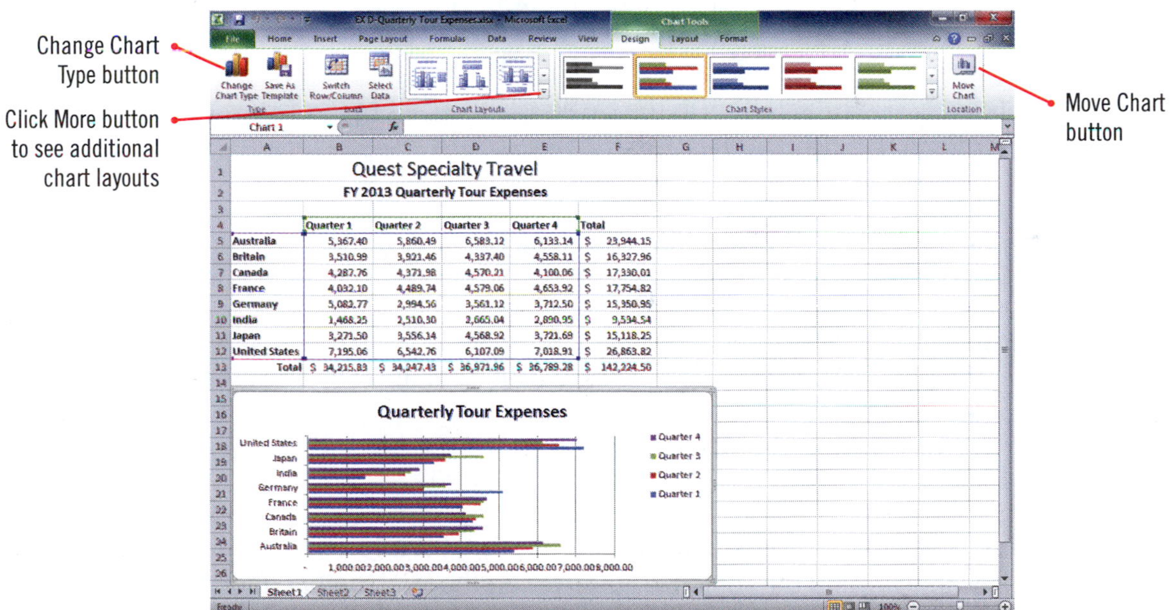

Working with a 3-D chart

Excel includes two kinds of 3-D chart types. In a true 3-D chart, a third axis, called the **z-axis**, lets you compare data points across both categories and values. The z-axis runs along the depth of the chart, so it appears to advance from the back of the chart. To create a true 3-D chart, look for chart types that begin with "3-D," such as 3-D Column. Charts that are formatted in 3-D, but are not true 3-D, contain only two axes but their graphics give the illusion of three-dimensionality. To create a chart that is only formatted in 3-D, look for chart types that end with "in 3-D." In any 3-D chart, data series can sometimes obscure other columns or bars in the same chart, but you can rotate the chart to obtain a better view. Right-click the chart, then click 3-D Rotation. The Format Chart Area dialog box opens with the 3-D Rotation category active. The 3-D Rotation options let you change the orientation and perspective of the chart area, plot area, walls, and floor. The 3-D Format category lets you apply three-dimensional effects to selected chart objects. (Not all 3-D Rotation and 3-D Format options are available on all charts.)

UNIT D Excel 2010

Changing the Chart Layout

While the Chart Tools Design tab contains preconfigured chart layouts you can apply to a chart, the Chart Tools Layout tab makes it easy to add, remove, and modify individual chart objects such as a chart title or legend. Using buttons on this tab, you can also add shapes, pictures, and additional text to a chart, add and modify labels, change the display of axes, modify the fill behind the plot area, create titles for the horizontal and vertical axes, and eliminate or change the look of gridlines. You can format the text in a chart object using the Home tab or the Mini toolbar, just as you would the text in a worksheet. You want to change the layout of the chart by creating titles for the horizontal and vertical axes. To improve the chart's appearance, you'll add a drop shadow to the chart title.

STEPS

1. **With the chart still selected, click the Chart Tools Layout tab on the Ribbon, click the Gridlines button in the Axes group, point to Primary Horizontal Gridlines, then click None**
   The gridlines that extend from the value axis tick marks across the chart's plot area are removed from the chart, as shown in Figure D-12.

2. **Click the Gridlines button in the Axes group, point to Primary Horizontal Gridlines, then click Major & Minor Gridlines**
   Both major and minor gridlines now appear in the chart. **Major gridlines** represent the values at the value axis tick marks, and **minor gridlines** represent the values between the tick marks.

3. **Click the Axis Titles button in the Labels group, point to Primary Horizontal Axis Title, click Title Below Axis, triple-click the axis title, then type Tour Countries**
   Descriptive text on the category axis helps readers understand the chart.

4. **Click the Axis Titles button in the Labels group, point to Primary Vertical Axis Title, then click Rotated Title**
   A placeholder for the vertical axis title is added to the left of the vertical axis.

5. **Triple-click the vertical axis title, then type Expenses (in $)**
   The text "Expenses (in $)" appears to the left of the vertical axis, as shown in Figure D-13.

6. **Right-click the horizontal axis labels ("Australia", "Britain", etc.), click the Font list arrow on the Mini toolbar, click Times New Roman, click the Font Size list arrow on the Mini toolbar, then click 8**
   The font of the horizontal axis labels changes to Times New Roman, and the font size decreases, making more of the plot area visible.

7. **Right-click the vertical axis labels, click the Font list arrow on the Mini toolbar, click Times New Roman, click the Font Size list arrow on the Mini toolbar, then click 8**

8. **Right-click the chart title ("Quarterly Tour Expenses"), click Format Chart Title on the shortcut menu, click Border Color in the left pane of the Format Chart Title dialog box, then click the Solid line option button in the right pane**
   A solid border will appear around the chart title with the default blue color.

9. **Click Shadow in the left pane of the Format Chart Title dialog box, click the Presets list arrow, click Offset Diagonal Bottom Right in the Outer group (first row, first from the left), click Close, then save your work**
   A blue border with a drop shadow surrounds the title. Compare your work to Figure D-14.

QUICK TIP
You can move any title to a new position by clicking one of its edges, then dragging it.

QUICK TIP
You can also edit text in a chart or axis title by positioning the pointer over the selected title until it changes to I, clicking the title, then editing the text.

QUICK TIP
You can also apply a border to a selected chart object by clicking the Shape Outline list arrow on the Chart Tools Format tab, and then selecting from the available options.

QUICK TIP
You can also apply a shadow to a selected chart object by clicking the Shape Effects button on the Chart Tools Layout tab, pointing to Shadow, and then clicking a shadow effect.

FIGURE D-12: Gridlines removed from chart

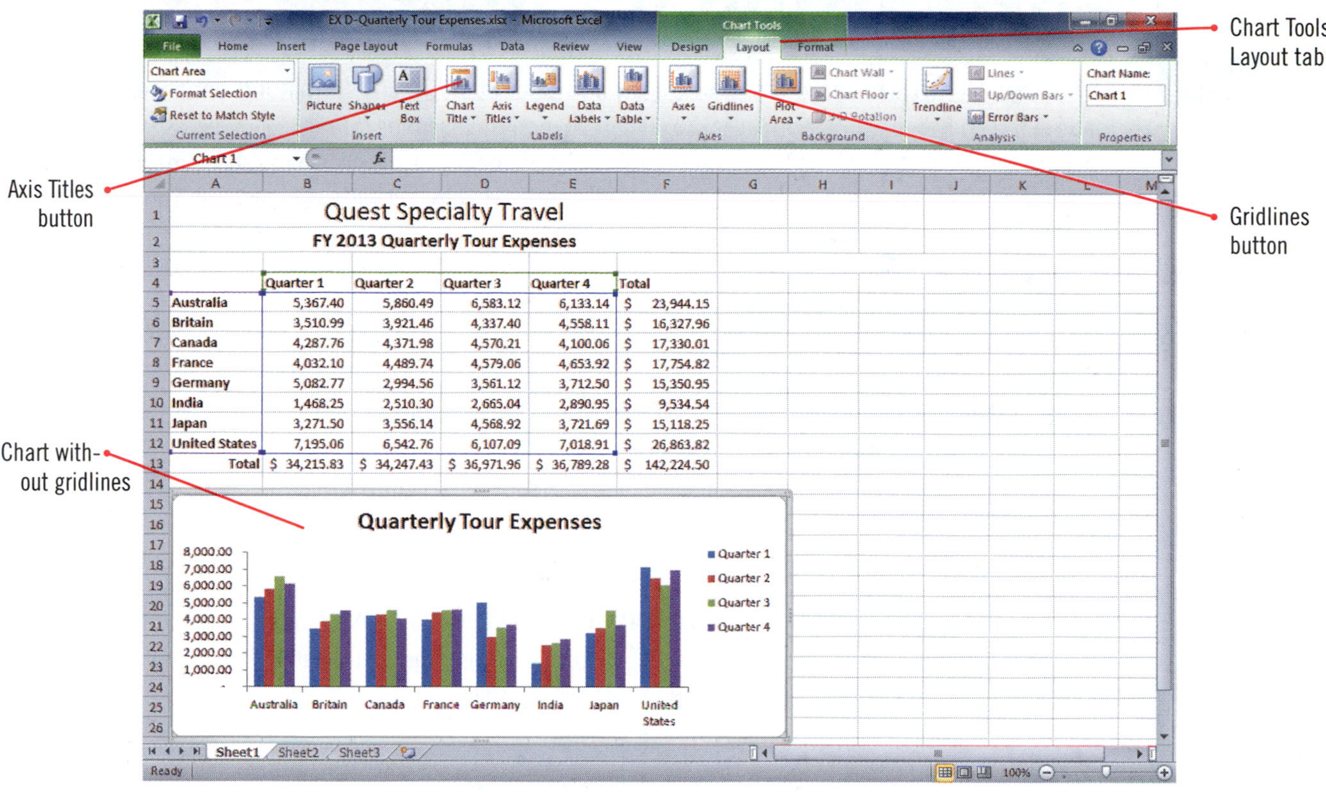

FIGURE D-13: Axis titles added to chart

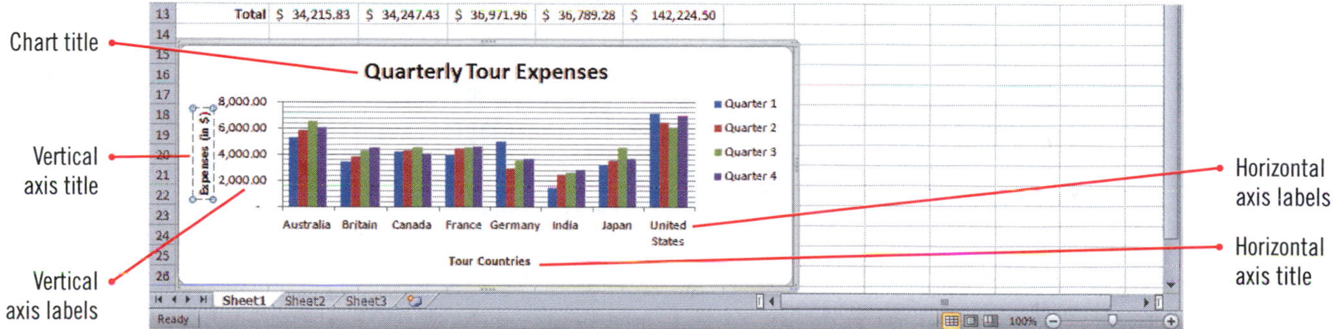

FIGURE D-14: Enhanced chart

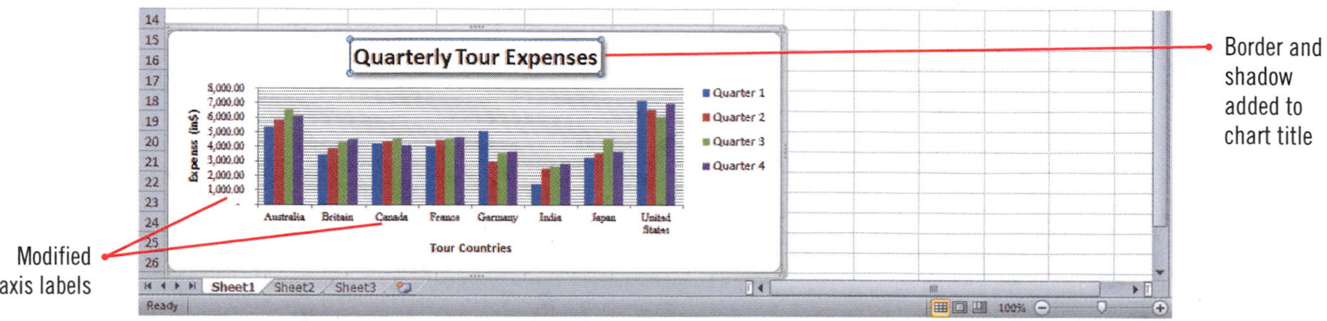

Adding data labels to a chart

There are times when your audience might benefit by seeing data labels on a chart. These labels appear next to the data markers in the chart and can indicate the series name, category name, and/or the value of one or more data points. Once your chart is selected, you can add this information to your chart by clicking the Data Labels button in the Labels group on the Chart Tools Layout tab, and then clicking a display option for the data labels. Once you have added the data labels, you can format them or delete individual data labels. To delete a data label, select it and then press [Delete].

Formatting a Chart

Formatting a chart can make it easier to read and understand. Many formatting enhancements can be made using the Chart Tools Format tab. You can change the fill color for a specific data series, or you can apply a shape style to a title or a data series using the Shape Styles group. Shape styles make it possible to apply multiple formats, such as an outline, fill color, and text color, all with a single click. You can also apply different fill colors, outlines, and effects to chart objects using arrows and buttons in the Shape Styles group. You want to use a different color for one data series in the chart and apply a shape style to another to enhance the look of the chart.

STEPS

1. **With the chart selected, click the Chart Tools Format tab on the Ribbon, then click any column in the Quarter 4 data series**

   The Chart Tools Format tab opens, and handles appear on each column in the Quarter 4 data series, indicating that the entire series is selected.

2. **Click the Shape Fill list arrow in the Shape Styles group on the Chart Tools Format tab**

3. **Click Orange, Accent 6 (first row, 10th from the left) as shown in Figure D-15**

   All the columns for the series become orange, and the legend changes to match the new color. You can also change the color of selected objects by applying a shape style.

4. **Click any column in the Quarter 3 data series**

   Handles appear on each column in the Quarter 3 data series.

5. **Click the More button on the Shape Styles gallery, then hover the pointer over the Moderate Effect – Olive Green, Accent 3 shape style (fifth row, fourth from the left) in the gallery, as shown in Figure D-16**

   Live Preview shows the data series in the chart with the shape style applied.

6. **Click the Subtle Effect – Olive Green, Accent 3 shape style (fourth row, fourth from the left) in the gallery**

   The style for the data series changes, as shown in Figure D-17.

7. **Save your work**

QUICK TIP

To apply a WordArt style to a text object (such as the chart title), select the object, then click a style in the WordArt Styles group on the Chart Tools Format tab.

Changing alignment and angle in axis labels and titles

The buttons on the Chart Tools Layout tab provide a few options for positioning axis labels and titles, but you can customize their position and rotation to exact specifications using the Format Axis dialog box or Format Axis Title dialog box. With a chart selected, right-click the axis text you want to modify, then click Format Axis or Format Axis Title on the shortcut menu. In the dialog box that opens, click Alignment, then select the appropriate Text layout option. You can also create a custom angle by clicking the Custom angle up and down arrows. When you have made the desired changes, click Close.

FIGURE D-15: New shape fill applied to data series

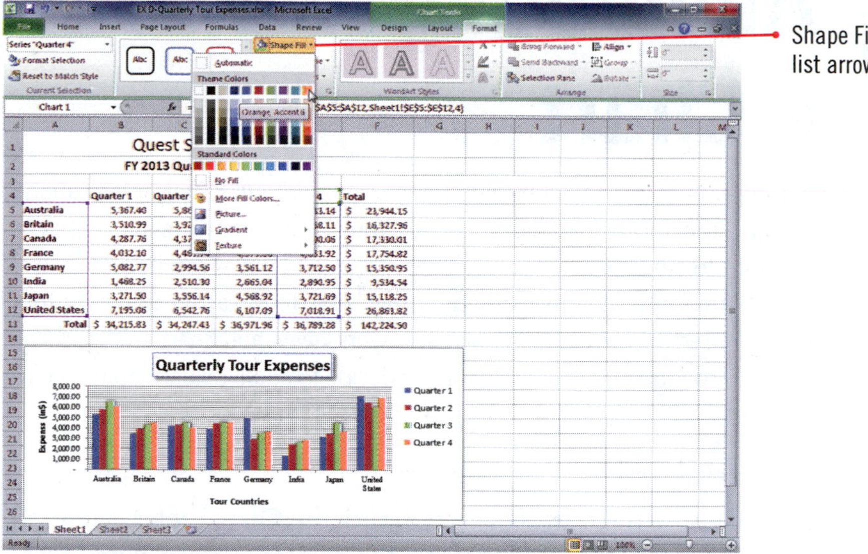

FIGURE D-16: Live Preview of new style applied to data series

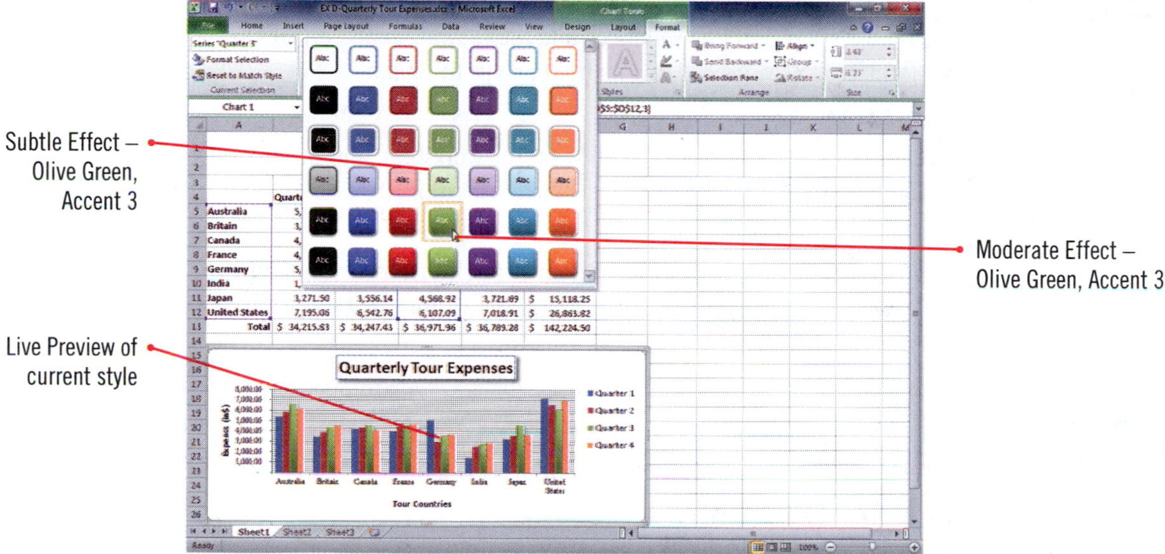

FIGURE D-17: Style of data series changed

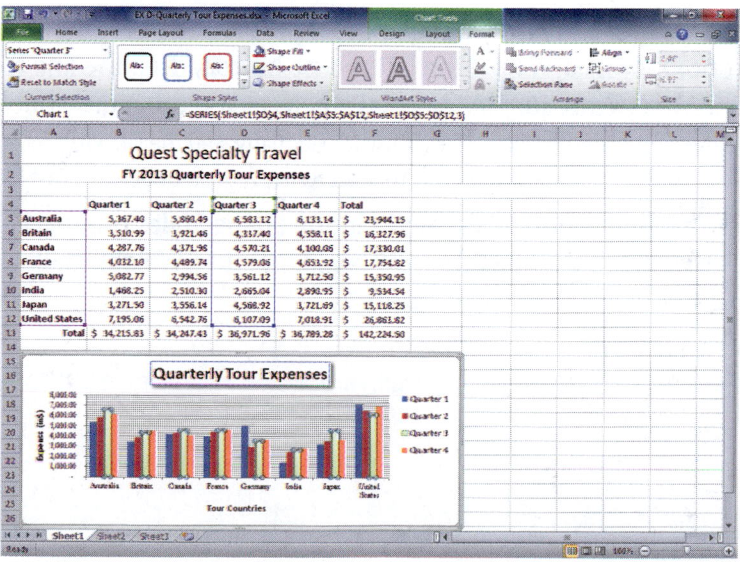

Annotating and Drawing on a Chart

You can use text annotations and graphics to point out critical information in a chart. **Text annotations** are labels that further describe your data. You can also draw lines and arrows that point to the exact locations you want to emphasize. Shapes such as arrows and boxes can be added from the Illustrations group on the Insert tab or from the Insert group on the Chart Tools Layout group on the Ribbon. These groups are also used to insert pictures and clip art into worksheets and charts. You want to call attention to the Germany tour expense decrease, so you decide to add a text annotation and an arrow to this information in the chart.

STEPS

1. **Make sure the chart is selected, click the Chart Tools Layout tab, click the Text Box button in the Insert group, then move the pointer over the worksheet**
   The pointer changes to ↓, indicating that you will insert a text box where you next click.

QUICK TIP
You can also insert a text box by clicking the Text Box button in the Text group in the Insert tab, then clicking in the worksheet.

2. **Click to the right of the chart (anywhere *outside* the chart boundary)**
   A text box is added to the worksheet, and the Drawing Tools Format tab appears on the Ribbon so that you can format the new object. First you need to type the text.
3. **Type Great improvement**
   The text appears in a selected text box on the worksheet, and the chart is no longer selected, as shown in Figure D-18. Your text box may be in a different location; this is not important, because you'll move the annotation in the next step.
4. **Point to an edge of the text box so that the pointer changes to ✥, drag the text box into the chart to the left of the chart title, as shown in Figure D-19, then release the mouse button**
   The text box is a text annotation for the chart. You also want to add a simple arrow shape in the chart.

QUICK TIP
To annotate a chart using a callout, click the Shapes button in either the Illustrations group on the Insert tab or the Insert group on the Chart Tools Layout tab, then click a shape in the Callouts category of the Shapes gallery.

5. **Click the chart to select it, click the Chart Tools Layout tab, click the Shapes button in the Insert group, click the Arrow shape in the Lines category, then move the pointer over the text box on the chart**
   The pointer changes to +, and the status bar displays "Click and drag to insert an AutoShape." When + is over the text box, red handles appear around the text in the text box. A red handle can act as an anchor for the arrow.
6. **Position + on the red handle to the right of the "t" in the word "improvement" (in the text box), press and hold the left mouse button, drag the line to the Quarter 2 column for the Germany category in the chart, then release the mouse button**
   An arrow points to the Quarter 2 expense for Germany, and the Drawing Tools Format tab displays options for working with the new arrow object. You can resize, format, or delete it just like any other object in a chart.
7. **Click the Shape Outline list arrow in the Shape Styles group, click the Automatic color, click the Shape Outline list arrow again, point to Weight, then click 1½ pt**
   Compare your finished chart to Figure D-20.
8. **Save your work**

FIGURE D-18: Text box added

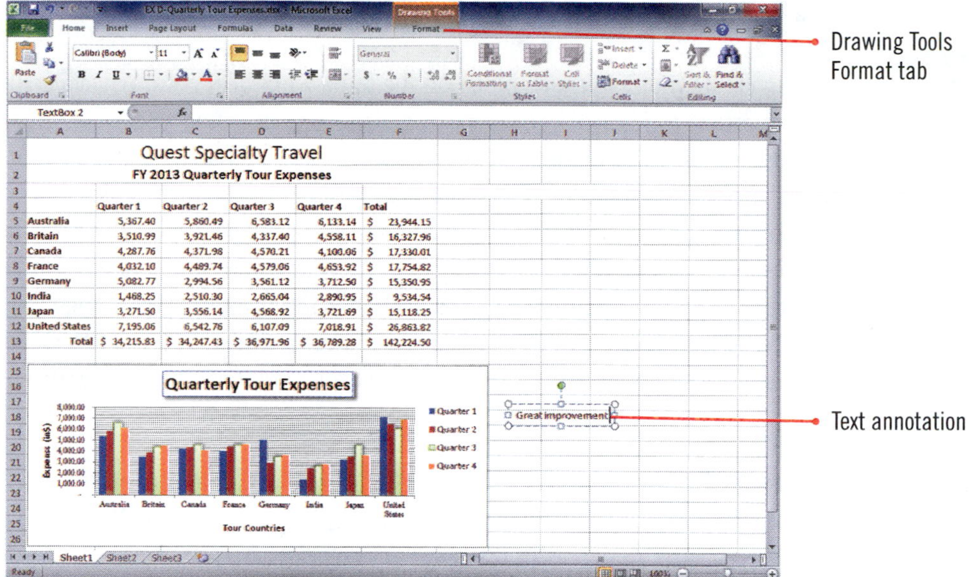

FIGURE D-19: Text annotation on the chart

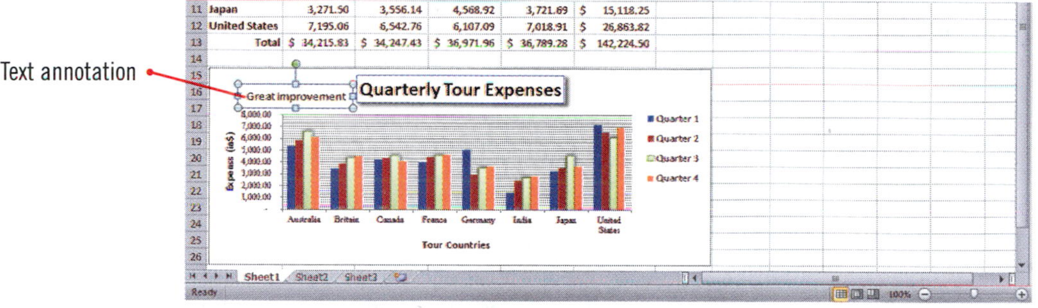

FIGURE D-20: Arrow shape added to chart

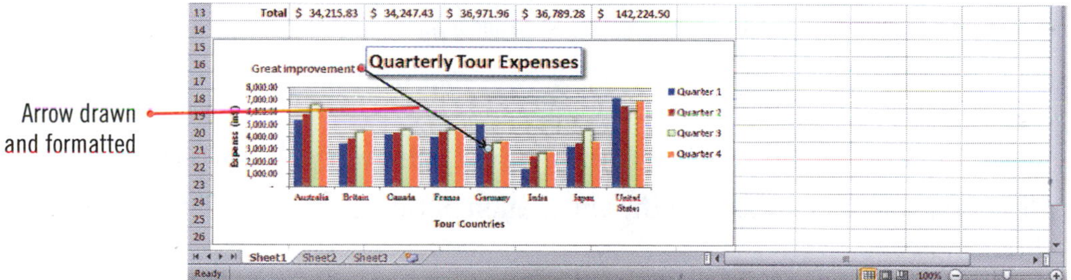

Adding SmartArt graphics

In addition to charts, annotations, and drawn objects, you can create a variety of diagrams using SmartArt graphics. **SmartArt graphics** are available in List, Process, Cycle, Hierarchy, Relationship, Matrix, and Pyramid categories. To insert SmartArt, click the SmartArt button in the Illustrations group on the Insert tab to open the Choose a SmartArt Graphic dialog box. Click a SmartArt category in the left pane, then click the layout for the graphic in the center pane. The right pane shows a sample of the selected SmartArt layout, as shown in Figure D-21. The SmartArt graphic appears in the worksheet as an embedded object with sizing handles. Click the Text Pane button on the SmartArt Tools Design tab to open a text pane next to the graphic; you can enter text into the graphic using the text pane or by typing directly in the shapes in the diagram.

FIGURE D-21: Choose a SmartArt Graphic dialog box

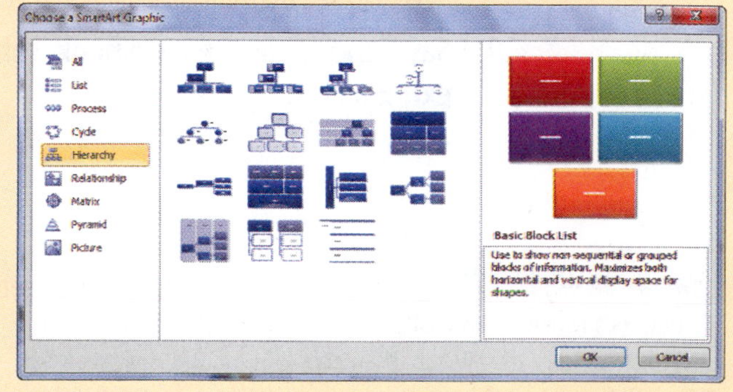

Excel 2010

UNIT
D
Excel 2010

Creating a Pie Chart

You can create multiple charts based on the same worksheet data. While a column chart may illustrate certain important aspects of your worksheet data, you may find you want to create an additional chart to emphasize a different point. Depending on the type of chart you create, you have additional options for calling attention to trends and patterns. For example, if you create a pie chart, you can emphasize one data point by **exploding**, or pulling that slice away from, the pie chart. When you're ready to print a chart, you can preview it just as you do a worksheet to check the output before committing it to paper. You can print a chart by itself or as part of the worksheet. At an upcoming meeting, Grace plans to discuss the total tour expenses and which countries need improvement. You want to create a pie chart she can use to illustrate total expenses. Finally, you want to fit the worksheet and the charts onto one worksheet page.

STEPS

QUICK TIP
The Exploded pie in 3-D button creates a pie chart in which all slices are exploded.

1. **Select the range A5:A12, press and hold [Ctrl], select the range F5:F12, click the Insert tab, click the Pie button in the Charts group, then click Pie in 3-D in the Pie chart gallery**
   The new chart appears in the center of the worksheet. You can move the chart and quickly format it using a chart layout.
2. **Drag the chart so its upper-left corner is at the upper-left corner of cell G1, then click Layout 2 in the Chart Layouts group**
   The chart is repositioned on the page, and its layout changes so that a chart title is added and the legend appears just below the chart title.
3. **Select the chart title text, then type Total Expenses, by Country**
4. **Click the slice for the India data point, click it again so it is the only slice selected, right-click it, then click Format Data Point**
   The Format Data Point dialog box opens, as shown in Figure D-22.You can use the Point Explosion slider to control the distance a pie slice moves away from the pie, or you can type a value in the Point Explosion text box.
5. **Double-click 0 in the Point Explosion text box, type 40, then click Close**
   Compare your chart to Figure D-23. You decide to preview the chart and data before you print.
6. **Click cell A1, switch to Page Layout view, type your name in the left header text box, then click cell A1**
   You decide the chart and data would fit better on the page if they were printed in landscape orientation.
7. **Click the Page Layout tab, click the Orientation button in the Page Setup group, then click Landscape**
8. **Click the File tab, click Print on the navigation bar, click the No Scaling setting in the Settings section on the Print tab, then click Fit Sheet on One Page**
   The data and chart are positioned horizontally on a single page, as shown in Figure D-24. The printer you have selected may affect the appearance of your preview screen.
9. **Save and close the workbook, submit your work to your instructor as directed, then exit Excel**

TROUBLE
If the Format Data Series command appears on the shortcut menu instead of Format Data Point, double-click the slice you want to explode to make sure it is selected by itself, then right-click it again.

Previewing a chart

To print or preview just a chart, select the chart (or make the chart sheet active), click the File tab, then click Print on the navigation bar. To reposition a chart by changing the page's margins, click the Show Margins button in the lower-right corner of the Print tab to display the margins in the preview. You can drag the margin lines to the exact settings you want; as the margins change, the size and placement of the chart on the page changes too.

FIGURE D-22: Format Data Point dialog box

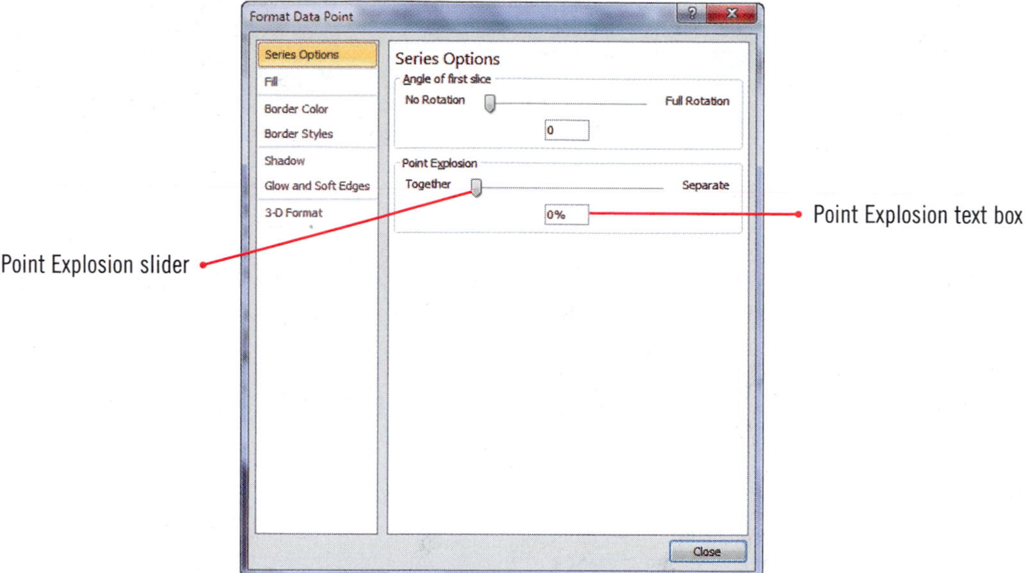

Point Explosion slider

Point Explosion text box

FIGURE D-23: Exploded pie slice

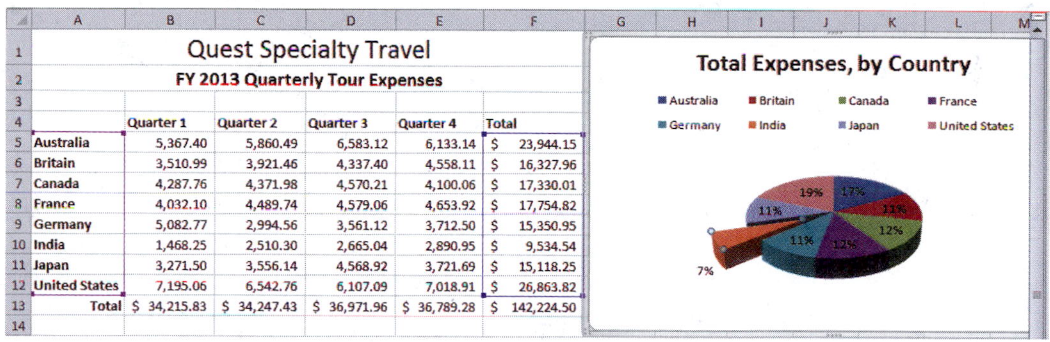

	Quarter 1	Quarter 2	Quarter 3	Quarter 4	Total
Australia	5,367.40	5,860.49	6,583.12	6,133.14	$ 23,944.15
Britain	3,510.99	3,921.46	4,337.40	4,558.11	$ 16,327.96
Canada	4,287.76	4,371.98	4,570.21	4,100.06	$ 17,330.01
France	4,032.10	4,489.74	4,579.06	4,653.92	$ 17,754.82
Germany	5,082.77	2,994.56	3,561.12	3,712.50	$ 15,350.95
India	1,468.25	2,510.30	2,665.04	2,890.95	$ 9,534.54
Japan	3,271.50	3,556.14	4,568.92	3,721.69	$ 15,118.25
United States	7,195.06	6,542.76	6,107.09	7,018.91	$ 26,863.82
Total	$ 34,215.83	$ 34,247.43	$ 36,971.96	$ 36,789.28	$ 142,224.50

FIGURE D-24: Preview of worksheet with charts in Backstage view

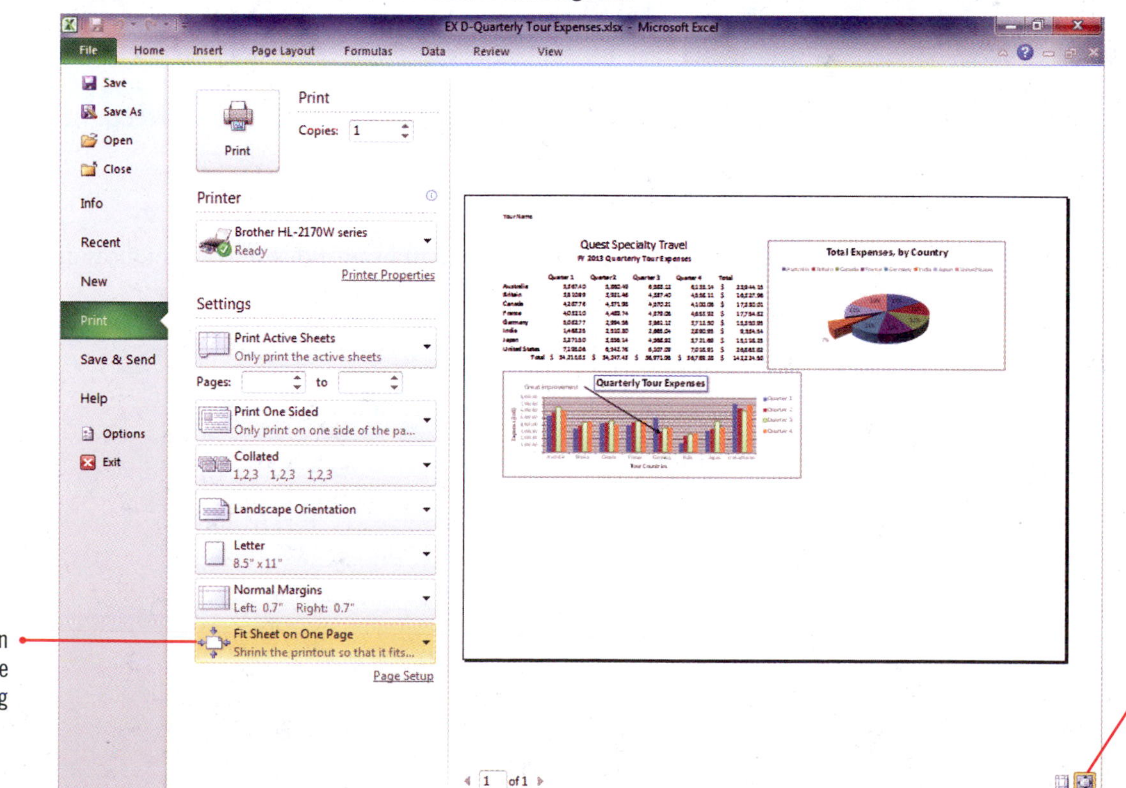

Fit Sheet on One Page setting

Show Margins button

Excel 2010

Practice

Concepts Review

For current SAM information, including versions and content details, visit SAM Central (http://www.cengage.com/samcentral). If you have a SAM user profile, you may have access to hands-on instruction, practice, and assessment of the skills covered in this unit. Since various versions of SAM are supported throughout the life of this text, check with your instructor for the correct instructions and URL/Web site for accessing assignments.

Label each element of the Excel chart shown in Figure D-25.

FIGURE D-25

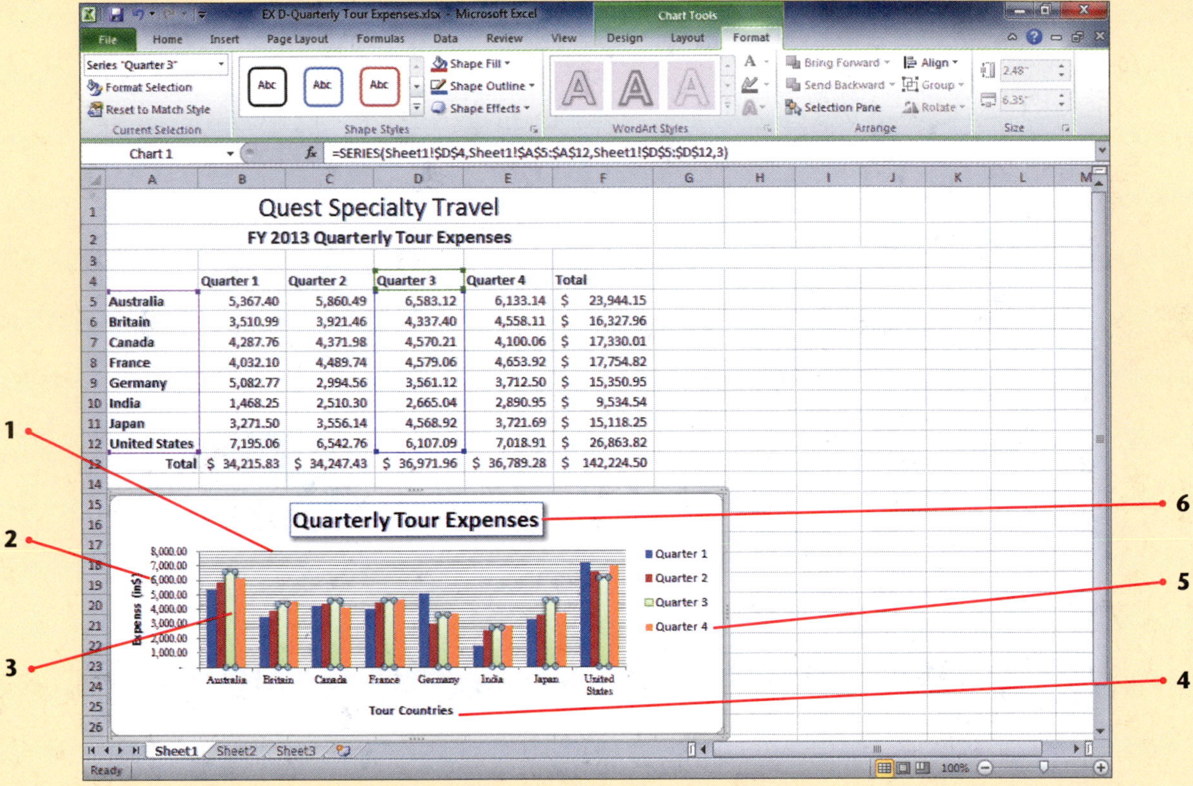

Match each chart type with the statement that best describes it.

7. Column	**a.** Displays a column and line chart using different scales of measurement
8. Line	**b.** Compares trends over even time intervals
9. Combination	**c.** Compares data using columns
10. Pie	**d.** Compares data as parts of a whole
11. Area	**e.** Shows how volume changes over time

Select the best answer from the list of choices.

12. Which pointer do you use to resize a chart?

- **a.** +
- **b.** I
- **c.** ⇕
- **d.** ✥

13. The object in a chart that identifies the colors used for each data series is a(n):

- **a.** Data marker.
- **b.** Data point.
- **c.** Organizer.
- **d.** Legend.

14. Which tab appears only when a chart is selected?

- **a.** Insert
- **b.** Chart Tools Format
- **c.** Review
- **d.** Page Layout

15. How do you move an embedded chart to a chart sheet?

- **a.** Click a button on the Chart Tools Design tab.
- **b.** Drag the chart to the sheet tab.
- **c.** Delete the chart, switch to a different sheet, then create a new chart.
- **d.** Use the Copy and Paste buttons on the Ribbon.

16. Which tab on the Ribbon do you use to create a chart?

- **a.** Design
- **b.** Insert
- **c.** Page Layout
- **d.** Format

17. A collection of related data points in a chart is called a:

- **a.** Data series.
- **b.** Data tick.
- **c.** Cell address.
- **d.** Value title.

Skills Review

If you have a SAM 2010 user profile, an autogradable SAM version of this assignment may be available at http://www.cengage.com/sam2010. Check with your instructor to confirm that this assignment is available in SAM. To use the SAM version of this assignment, log into the SAM 2010 Web site and download the instruction and start files.

1. Plan a chart.

- **a.** Start Excel, open the Data File EX D-2.xlsx from the drive and folder where you store your Data Files, then save it as **EX D-Departmental Software Usage**.
- **b.** Describe the type of chart you would use to plot this data.
- **c.** What chart type would you use to compare the number of Excel users in each department?

2. Create a chart.

- **a.** In the worksheet, select the range containing all the data and headings.
- **b.** Click the Insert tab.
- **c.** Create a Clustered Column chart, then add the chart title **Software Usage, by Department** above the chart.
- **d.** Save your work.

Skills Review (continued)

3. Move and resize a chart.

- **a.** Make sure the chart is still selected.
- **b.** Move the chart beneath the worksheet data.
- **c.** Widen the chart so it extends to the right edge of column H.
- **d.** Use the Chart Tools Layout tab to move the legend below the charted data. (*Hint*: Click the Legend button, then click Show Legend at Bottom.)
- **e.** Resize the chart so its bottom edge is at the top of row 25.
- **f.** Save your work.

4. Change the chart design.

- **a.** Change the value in cell B3 to **15**. Observe the change in the chart.
- **b.** Select the chart.
- **c.** Use the Chart Layouts group on the Chart Tools Design tab to apply the Layout 7 layout to the chart, then undo the change.
- **d.** Use the Change Chart Type button on the Chart Tools Design tab to change the chart to a Clustered Bar chart.
- **e.** Change the chart to a 3-D Clustered Column chart, then change it back to a Clustered Column chart.
- **f.** Save your work.

5. Change the chart layout.

- **a.** Use the Chart Tools Layout tab to turn off the major horizontal gridlines in the chart.
- **b.** Change the font used in the horizontal and vertical axes labels to Times New Roman.
- **c.** Turn on the major gridlines for both the horizontal and vertical axes.
- **d.** Change the chart title's font to Times New Roman if necessary, with a font size of 20.
- **e.** Insert **Departments** as the horizontal axis title.
- **f.** Insert **Number of Users** as the vertical axis title.
- **g.** Change the font size of the horizontal and vertical axis titles to 10 and the font to Times New Roman, if necessary.
- **h.** Change "Personnel" in the worksheet column heading to **Human Resources**, then AutoFit column E.
- **i.** Change the font size of the legend to 14.
- **j.** Add a solid line border in the default color and an Offset Diagonal Bottom Right shadow to the chart title.
- **k.** Save your work.

6. Format a chart.

- **a.** Make sure the chart is selected, then select the Chart Tools Format tab, if necessary.
- **b.** Change the shape fill of the Excel data series to Dark Blue, Text 2.
- **c.** Change the shape style of the Excel data series to Subtle Effect Orange, Accent 6.
- **d.** Save your work.

7. Annotate and draw on a chart.

- **a.** Make sure the chart is selected, then create the text annotation **Needs more users**.
- **b.** Position the text annotation so the word "Needs" is just below the word "Software" in the chart title.
- **c.** Select the chart, then use the Chart Tools Layout tab to create a 1½ pt weight arrow that points from the bottom center of the text box to the Excel users in the Design department.
- **d.** Deselect the chart.
- **e.** Save your work.

Skills Review (continued)

8. Create a pie chart.

- **a.** Select the range A1:F2, then create a Pie in 3-D chart.
- **b.** Drag the 3-D pie chart beneath the existing chart.
- **c.** Change the chart title to **Excel Users**.
- **d.** Apply the Style 42 chart style to the chart.
- **e.** Explode the Human Resources slice from the pie chart at **25%**.
- **f.** In Page Layout view, enter your name in the left section of the worksheet header.
- **g.** Preview the worksheet and charts in Backstage view, make sure all the contents fit on one page, then submit your work to your instructor as directed. When printed, the worksheet should look like Figure D-26.
- **h.** Save your work, close the workbook, then exit Excel.

FIGURE D-26

Your Name

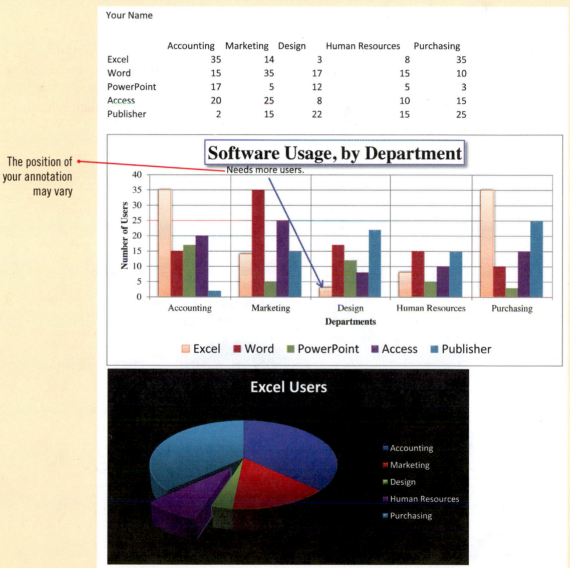

	Accounting	Marketing	Design	Human Resources	Purchasing
Excel	35	14	3	8	35
Word	15	35	17	15	10
PowerPoint	17	5	12	5	3
Access	20	25	8	10	15
Publisher	2	15	22	15	25

The position of your annotation may vary

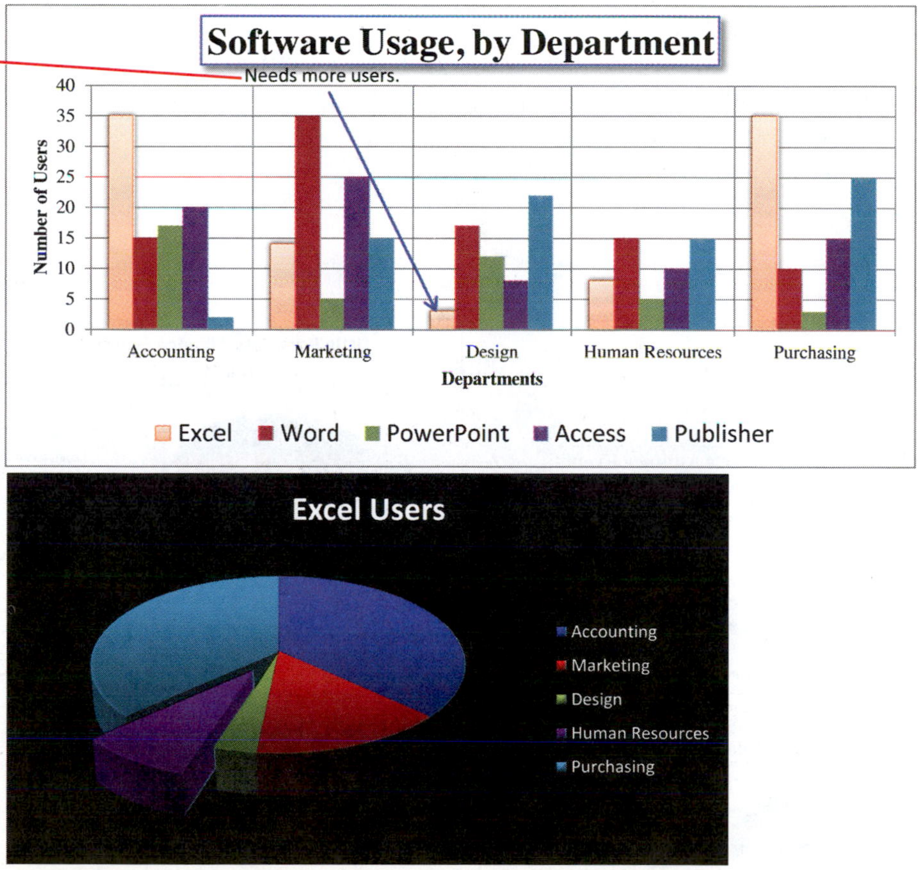

Excel 2010

Independent Challenge 1

You are the operations manager for the Little Rock Arts Alliance in Arkansas. Each year the group applies to various state and federal agencies for matching funds. For this year's funding proposal, you need to create charts to document the number of productions in previous years.

- **a.** Start Excel, open the file EX D-3.xlsx from the drive and folder where you store your Data Files, then save it as **EX D-Little Rock Arts Alliance**.
- **b.** Take some time to plan your charts. Which type of chart or charts might best illustrate the information you need to display? What kind of chart enhancements do you want to use? Will a 3-D effect make your chart easier to understand?
- **c.** Create a Clustered Column chart for the data.
- **d.** Change at least one of the colors used in a data series.
- **e.** Make the appropriate modifications to the chart to make it visually attractive and easier to read and understand. Include a legend to the right of the chart, and add chart titles and horizontal and vertical axis titles using the text shown in Table D-3.

TABLE D-3

title	text
Chart title	Little Rock Arts Alliance Events
Vertical axis title	Number of Events
Horizontal axis title	Types of Events

- **f.** Create at least two additional charts for the same data to show how different chart types display the same data. Reposition each new chart so that all charts are visible in the worksheet. One of the additional charts should be a pie chart; the other is up to you.
- **g.** Modify each new chart as necessary to improve its appearance and effectiveness. A sample worksheet containing three charts based on the worksheet data is shown in Figure D-27.
- **h.** Enter your name in the worksheet header.
- **i.** Save your work. Before printing, preview the worksheet in Backstage view, then adjust any settings as necessary so that all the worksheet data and charts print on a single page.
- **j.** Submit your work to your instructor as directed.
- **k.** Close the workbook, then exit Excel.

FIGURE D-27

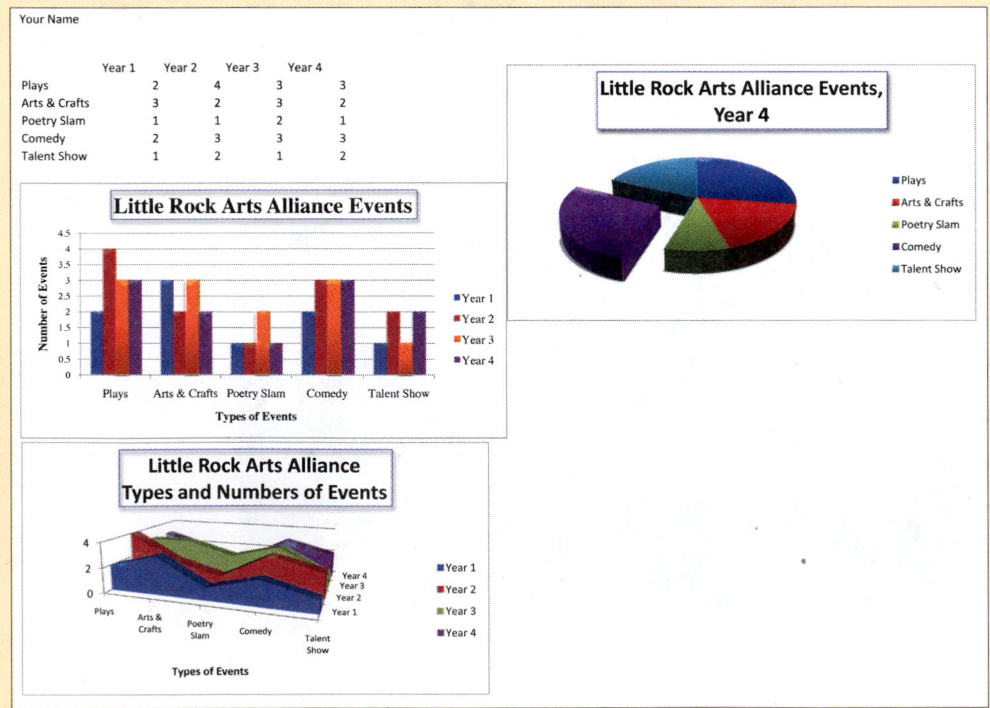

Your Name

	Year 1	Year 2	Year 3	Year 4
Plays	2	4	3	3
Arts & Crafts	3	2	3	2
Poetry Slam	1	1	2	1
Comedy	2	3	3	3
Talent Show	1	2	1	2

Independent Challenge 2

You work at Bark Bark Bark, a locally owned day spa for dogs. One of your responsibilities at the day spa is to manage the company's sales and expenses using Excel. Another is to convince the current staff that Excel can help them make daily operating decisions more easily and efficiently. To do this, you've decided to create charts using the previous year's operating expenses including rent, utilities, and payroll. The manager will use these charts at the next monthly meeting.

- **a.** Start Excel, open the Data File EX D-4.xlsx from the drive and folder where you store your Data Files, then save it as **EX D-Bark Bark Bark Doggie Day Spa Analysis**.
- **b.** Decide which data in the worksheet should be charted. What chart types are best suited for the information you need to show? What kinds of chart enhancements are necessary?
- **c.** Create a 3-D Clustered Column chart in the worksheet showing the expense data for all four quarters. (*Hint*: The expense categories should appear on the x-axis. Do not include the totals.)
- **d.** Change the vertical axis labels (Expenses data) so that no decimals are displayed. (*Hint*: Right-click the axis labels you want to modify, click Format Axis, click the Number category in the Format Axis dialog box, change the number of decimal places, then click Close.)
- **e.** Using the sales data, create two charts on this worksheet that compare the sales amounts. (*Hint*: Move each chart to a new location on the worksheet, then deselect it before creating the next one.)
- **f.** In one chart of the sales data, add data labels, then add chart titles as you see fit.
- **g.** Make any necessary formatting changes to make the charts look more attractive, then enter your name in a worksheet cell.
- **h.** Save your work.
- **i.** Preview each chart in Backstage view, and adjust any items as needed. Fit the worksheet to a single page, then submit your work to your instructor as directed. A sample of a printed worksheet is shown in Figure D-28.
- **j.** Close the workbook, then exit Excel.

FIGURE D-28

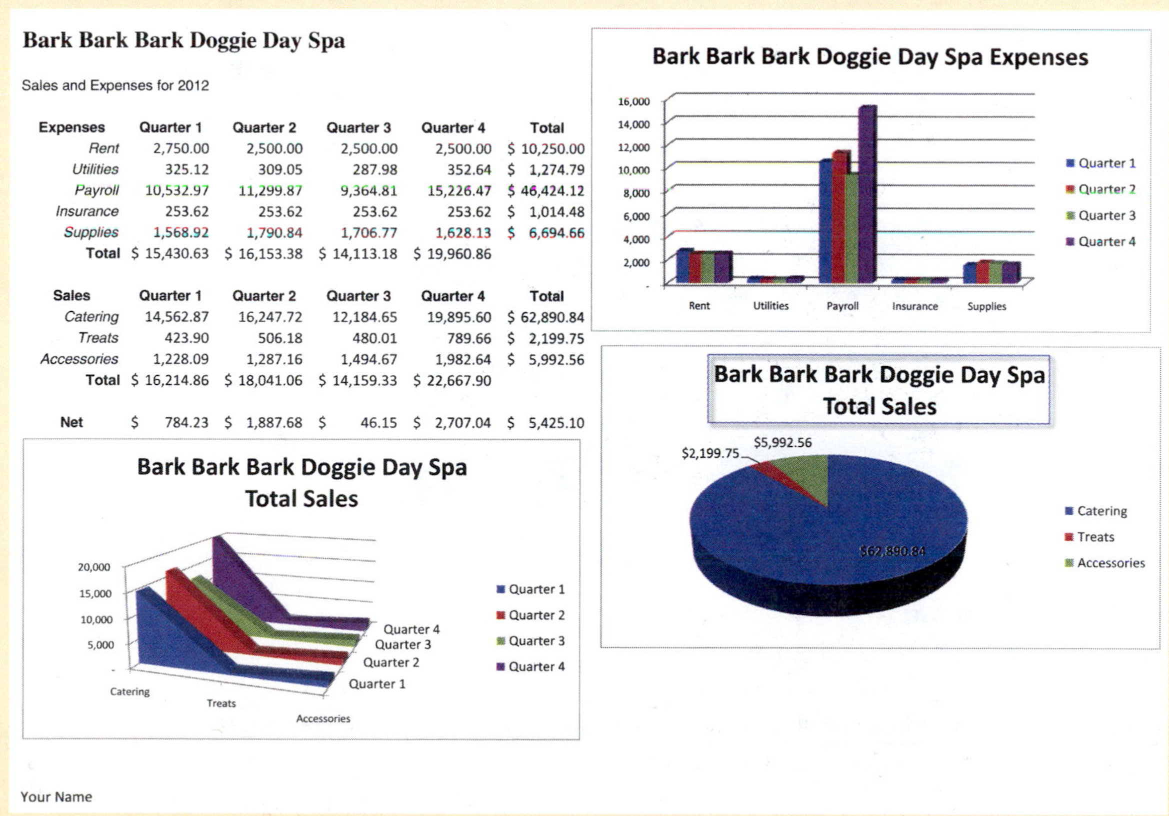

Bark Bark Bark Doggie Day Spa

Sales and Expenses for 2012

Expenses	Quarter 1	Quarter 2	Quarter 3	Quarter 4	Total
Rent	2,750.00	2,500.00	2,500.00	2,500.00	$ 10,250.00
Utilities	325.12	309.05	287.98	352.64	$ 1,274.79
Payroll	10,532.97	11,299.87	9,364.81	15,226.47	$ 46,424.12
Insurance	253.62	253.62	253.62	253.62	$ 1,014.48
Supplies	1,568.92	1,790.84	1,706.77	1,628.13	$ 6,694.66
Total	$ 15,430.63	$ 16,153.38	$ 14,113.18	$ 19,960.86	

Sales	Quarter 1	Quarter 2	Quarter 3	Quarter 4	Total
Catering	14,562.87	16,247.72	12,184.65	19,895.60	$ 62,890.84
Treats	423.90	506.18	480.01	789.66	$ 2,199.75
Accessories	1,228.09	1,287.16	1,494.67	1,982.64	$ 5,992.56
Total	$ 16,214.86	$ 18,041.06	$ 14,159.33	$ 22,667.90	
Net	$ 784.23	$ 1,887.68	$ 46.15	$ 2,707.04	$ 5,425.10

Independent Challenge 3

You are working as an account representative at a magazine called *Creativity*. You have been examining the expenses incurred recently. The CEO wants to examine expenses designed to increase circulation and has asked you to prepare charts that can be used in this evaluation. In particular, you want to see how dollar amounts compare among the different expenses, and you also want to see how expenses compare with each other proportional to the total budget.

- **a.** Start Excel, open the Data File EX D-5.xlsx from the drive and folder where you store your Data Files, then save it as **EX D-Creativity Magazine**.
- **b.** Identify three types of charts that seem best suited to illustrate the data in the range A16:B24. What kinds of chart enhancements are necessary?
- **c.** Create at least two different types of charts that show the distribution of circulation expenses. (*Hint*: Move each chart to a new location on the same worksheet.) One of the charts should be a 3-D pie chart.
- **d.** In at least one of the charts, add annotated text and arrows highlighting important data, such as the largest expense.
- **e.** Change the color of at least one data series in at least one of the charts.
- **f.** Add chart titles and category and value axis titles where appropriate. Format the titles with a font of your choice. Apply a shadow to the chart title in at least one chart.
- **g.** Add your name to a section of the header, then save your work.
- **h.** Preview the worksheet in Backstage view. Adjust any items as needed. Be sure the charts are all visible on one page. Compare your work to the sample in Figure D-29.

FIGURE D-29

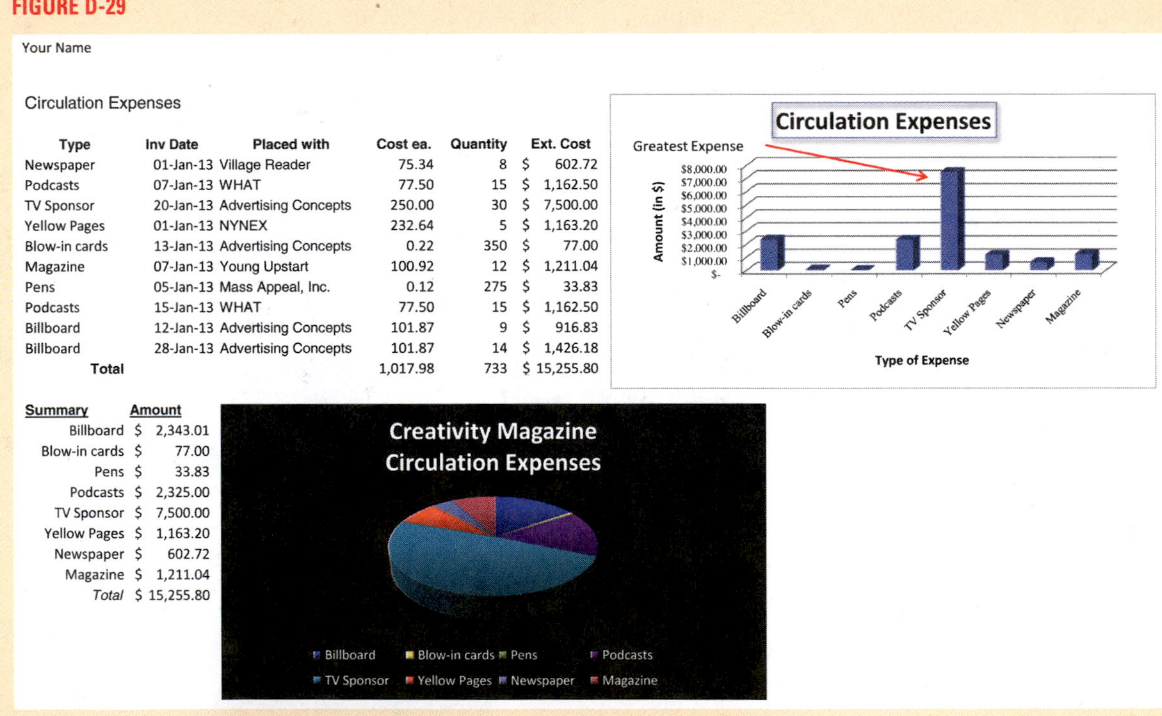

Your Name

Circulation Expenses

Type	Inv Date	Placed with	Cost ea.	Quantity	Ext. Cost
Newspaper	01-Jan-13	Village Reader	75.34	8	$ 602.72
Podcasts	07-Jan-13	WHAT	77.50	15	$ 1,162.50
TV Sponsor	20-Jan-13	Advertising Concepts	250.00	30	$ 7,500.00
Yellow Pages	01-Jan-13	NYNEX	232.64	5	$ 1,163.20
Blow-in cards	13-Jan-13	Advertising Concepts	0.22	350	$ 77.00
Magazine	07-Jan-13	Young Upstart	100.92	12	$ 1,211.04
Pens	05-Jan-13	Mass Appeal, Inc.	0.12	275	$ 33.83
Podcasts	15-Jan-13	WHAT	77.50	15	$ 1,162.50
Billboard	12-Jan-13	Advertising Concepts	101.87	9	$ 916.83
Billboard	28-Jan-13	Advertising Concepts	101.87	14	$ 1,426.18
Total			1,017.98	733	$ 15,255.80

Summary	Amount
Billboard	$ 2,343.01
Blow-in cards	$ 77.00
Pens	$ 33.83
Podcasts	$ 2,325.00
TV Sponsor	$ 7,500.00
Yellow Pages	$ 1,163.20
Newspaper	$ 602.72
Magazine	$ 1,211.04
Total	$ 15,255.80

Advanced Challenge Exercise

- Explode a slice from the 3-D pie chart.
- Add a data label to the exploded pie slice.
- Change the number format of labels in the non-pie chart so no decimals are displayed.
- Save your work, then preview it in Backstage view.

- **i.** Submit your work to your instructor as directed, close the workbook, then exit Excel.

Real Life Independent Challenge

This project requires an Internet connection.

A cash inheritance from a distant relative has finally been deposited in your bank account, and you have decided to purchase a home. You have a good idea where you'd like to live, and you decide to use the Web to find out more about houses that are currently available.

a. Start Excel, then save a new, blank workbook as **EX D-My Dream House** to the drive and folder where you save your Data Files.

b. Decide on where you would like to live, and use your favorite search engine to find information sources on homes for sale in that area. (*Hint*: Try using realtor.com or other realtor-sponsored sites.)

c. Determine a price range and features within the home. Find data for at least five homes that meet your location and price requirements, and enter them in the worksheet. See Table D-4 below for a suggested data layout.

TABLE D-4

suggested data layout					
Location					
Price range					
	House 1	House 2	House 3	House 4	House 5
Asking price					
Bedrooms					
Bathrooms					
Year built					
Size (in sq. ft.)					

d. Format the data so it looks attractive and professional.

e. Create any type of column chart using only the House and Asking Price data. Place it on the same worksheet as the data. Include a descriptive title.

f. Change the colors in the chart using the chart style of your choice.

g. Enter your name in a section of the header.

h. Save the workbook. Preview the worksheet in Backstage view and make adjustments if necessary to fit all of the information on one page. See Figure D-30 for an example of what your worksheet might look like.

i. Submit your work to your instructor as directed.

FIGURE D-30

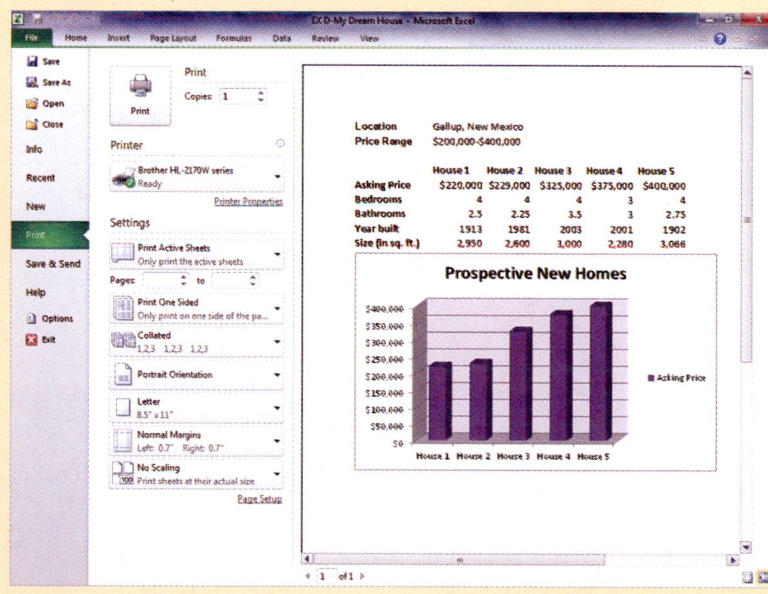

Advanced Challenge Exercise

- If necessary, change the chart type to a Clustered Column chart.
- Change the data used for the chart to include the size data in cells A9:F9.
- Create a combination chart that plots the asking price on one axis and the size of the home on the other axis. (*Hint*: Use Help to get tips on how to chart with a secondary axis.)

j. Close the workbook, then exit Excel.

Visual Workshop

Open the Data File EX D-6.xlsx from the drive and folder where you store your Data Files, then save it as **EX D-Projected Project Expenses**. Format the worksheet data so it looks like Figure D-31, then create and modify two charts to match the ones shown in the figure. You will need to make formatting, layout, and design changes once you create the charts. (*Hint*: The shadow used in the 3-D pie chart title is made using the Outer Offset Diagonal Top Right shadow.) Enter your name in the left text box of the header, then save and preview the worksheet. Submit your work to your instructor as directed, then close the workbook and exit Excel.

FIGURE D-31

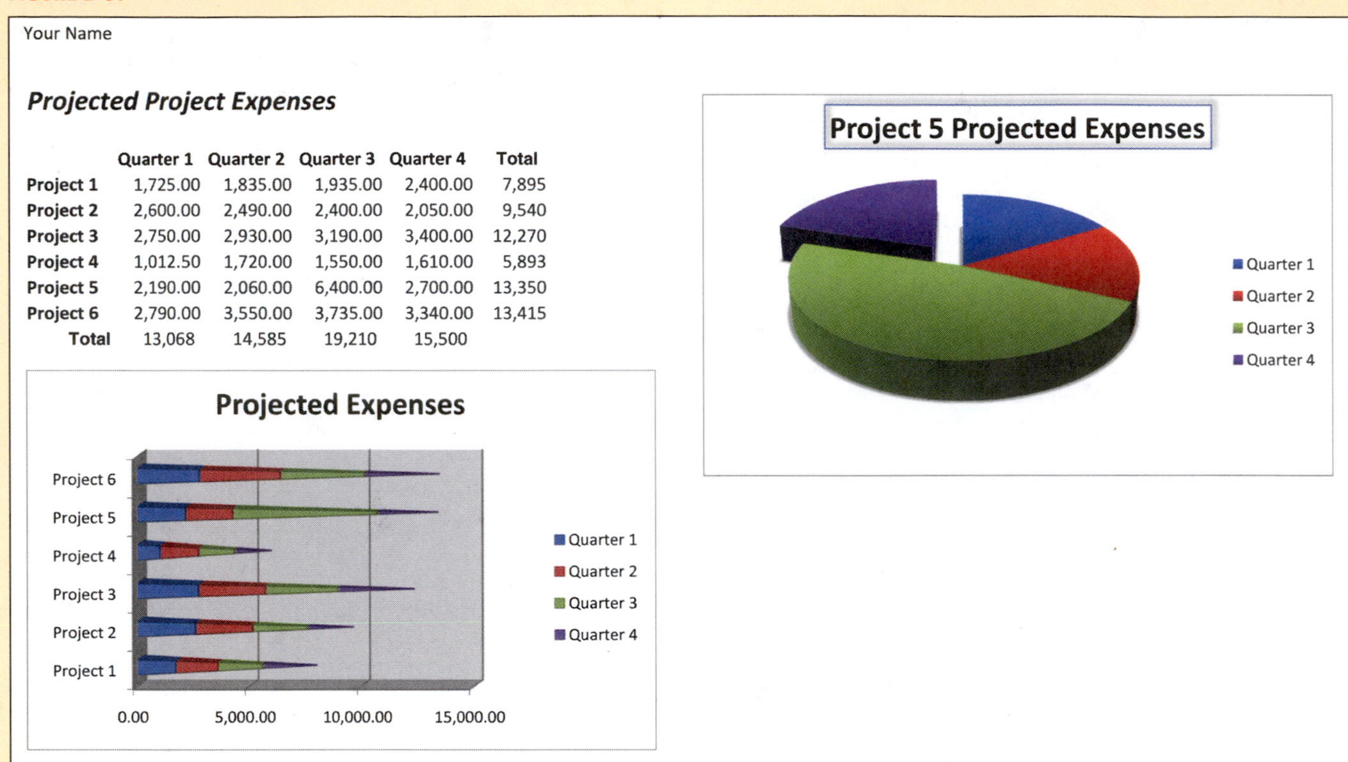

Your Name

Projected Project Expenses

	Quarter 1	Quarter 2	Quarter 3	Quarter 4	Total
Project 1	1,725.00	1,835.00	1,935.00	2,400.00	7,895
Project 2	2,600.00	2,490.00	2,400.00	2,050.00	9,540
Project 3	2,750.00	2,930.00	3,190.00	3,400.00	12,270
Project 4	1,012.50	1,720.00	1,550.00	1,610.00	5,893
Project 5	2,190.00	2,060.00	6,400.00	2,700.00	13,350
Project 6	2,790.00	3,550.00	3,735.00	3,340.00	13,415
Total	13,068	14,585	19,210	15,500	

Analyzing Data Using Formulas

Files You Will Need:

- EX E-1.xlsx
- EX E-2.xlsx
- EX E-3.xlsx
- EX E-4.xlsx
- EX E-5.xlsx
- EX E-6.xlsx
- EX E-7.xlsx

As you have learned, formulas and functions help you to analyze worksheet data. As you learn how to use different types of formulas and functions, you will discover more valuable uses for Excel. In this unit, you will gain a deeper understanding of Excel formulas and learn how to use several Excel functions. Kate Morgan, Quest's vice president of sales, uses Excel formulas and functions to analyze sales data for the U.S. region and to consolidate sales data from several worksheets. Because management is considering adding a new regional branch, Kate asks you to estimate the loan costs for a new office facility and to compare tour sales in the existing U.S. offices.

OBJECTIVES

- Format data using text functions
- Sum a data range based on conditions
- Consolidate data using a formula →Concatenation
- Check formulas for errors
- Construct formulas using named ranges
- Build a logical formula with the IF function
- Build a logical formula with the AND function
- Calculate payments with the PMT function

UNIT

E

Excel 2010

Formatting Data Using Text Functions

Often, you need to import data into Excel from an outside source, such as another program or the Internet. Sometimes you need to reformat this data to make it understandable and attractive. Instead of handling these tasks manually in each cell, you can save time by using Excel text functions to perform these tasks automatically for a range of cell data. The Convert Text to Columns feature breaks data fields in one column into separate columns. The text function PROPER capitalizes the first letter in a string of text as well as any text following a space. You can use the CONCATENATE function to join two or more strings into one text string. Kate has received the U.S. sales representatives' data from the Human Resources Department. She asks you to use text formulas to format the data into a more useful layout.

STEPS

1. **Start Excel, open the file EX E-1.xlsx from the drive and folder where you store your Data Files, then save it as EX E-Sales**
2. **On the Sales Reps sheet, select the range A4:A15, click the Data tab, then click the Text to Columns button in the Data Tools group**

   The Convert Text to Columns Wizard opens, as shown in Figure E-1. The data fields on your worksheet are separated by commas, which will act as delimiters. A **delimiter** is a separator, such as a space, comma, or semicolon that should separate your data. Excel separates your data into columns at the delimiter.
3. **If necessary, click the Delimited option button to select it, click Next, in the Delimiters area of the dialog box click the Comma check box to select it if necessary, click any other selected check boxes to deselect them, then click Next**

   You instructed Excel to separate your data at the comma delimiter.
4. **Click the Text option button in the Column data format area, click the second column with the city data to select it in the Data preview area, click the Text option button again in the Column data format area, observe the column headings and data in the Data preview area, then click Finish**

   The data are separated into three columns of text. You want to format the letters in the names and cities to the correct cases.
5. **Click cell D4, click the Formulas tab, click the Text button in the Function Library group, click PROPER, with the insertion point in the Text text box, click cell A4, then click OK**

   The name is copied from cell A4 to cell D4 with the correct uppercase letters for proper names. The remaining names and the cities are still in lowercase letters.
6. **Drag the fill handle to copy the formula in cell D4 to cell E4, then copy the formulas in cells D4:E4 into the range D5:E15**

   You want to format the years data to be more descriptive.
7. **Click cell F4, click the Text button in the Function Library group, click CONCATENATE, with the insertion point in the Text1 text box, click cell C4, press [Tab], with the insertion point in the Text2 text box, press [Spacebar], type Years, then click OK**
8. **Copy the formula in cell F4 into the range F5:F15, compare your work to Figure E-2, click the Insert tab, click the Header & Footer button in the Text group, click the Go to Footer button in the Navigation group, enter your name in the center text box, click on the worksheet, scroll up and click cell A1, then click the Normal button in the status bar**
9. **Save your file, then preview the worksheet**

QUICK TIP

You can move the Function Arguments dialog box if it overlaps a cell or range that you need to click. You can also click the Collapse Dialog Box button, select the cell or range, then click the Expand Dialog box button to return to the Function Arguments dialog box.

QUICK TIP

Excel automatically inserts quotation marks to enclose the space and the Years text.

FIGURE E-1: Convert Text to Columns dialog box

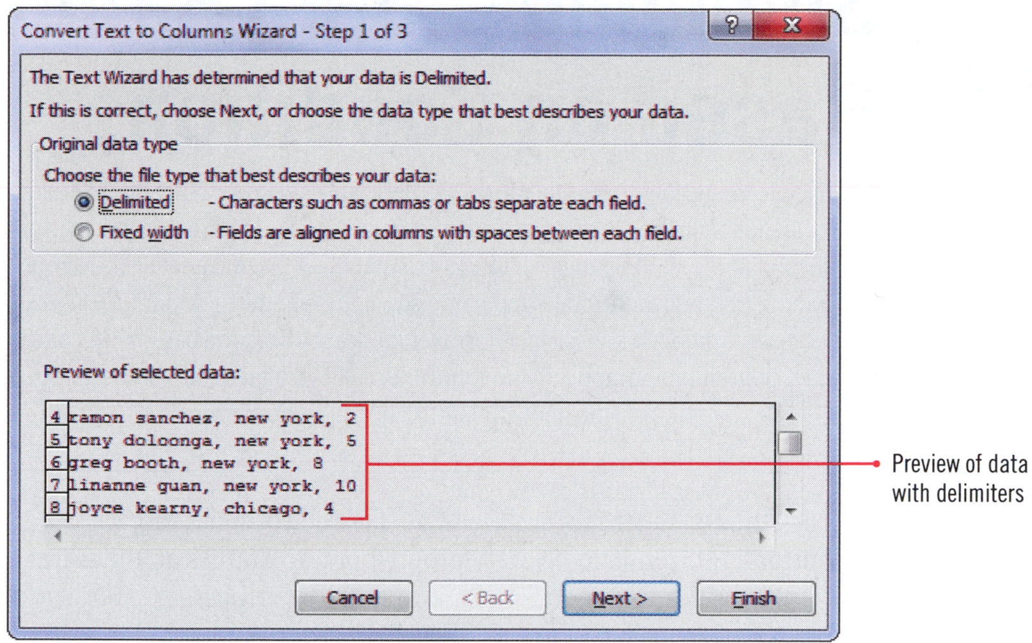

FIGURE E-2: Worksheet with data formatted in columns

	A	B	C	D	E	F
1					Quest	
2					Sales Representatives	
3				Name	Office	Years of Service
4	ramon sanchez	new york	2	Ramon Sanchez	New York	2 Years
5	tony doloonga	new york	5	Tony Doloonga	New York	5 Years
6	greg booth	new york	8	Greg Booth	New York	8 Years
7	linanne guan	new york	10	Linanne Guan	New York	10 Years
8	joyce kearny	chicago	4	Joyce Kearny	Chicago	4 Years
9	garrett cunnea	chicago	7	Garrett Cunnea	Chicago	7 Years
10	kathy jaques	chicago	5	Kathy Jaques	Chicago	5 Years
11	alyssa maztta	chicago	4	Alyssa Maztta	Chicago	4 Years
12	ann tadka	miami	6	Ann Tadka	Miami	6 Years
13	jose costello	miami	7	Jose Costello	Miami	7 Years
14	joan hanley	miami	4	Joan Hanley	Miami	4 Years
15	spring zola	miami	7	Spring Zola	Miami	7 Years
16						

Using text functions

Other useful text functions include UPPER, LOWER, and SUBSTITUTE. The UPPER function converts text to all uppercase letters, the LOWER function converts text to all lowercase letters, and SUBSTITUTE replaces text in a text string. For example, if cell A1 contains the text string "Today is Wednesday", then =LOWER(A1) would produce "today is wednesday"; =UPPER(A1) would produce "TODAY IS WEDNESDAY"; and =SUBSTITUTE(A1, "Wednesday", "Tuesday") would result in "Today is Tuesday".

If you want to copy and paste data that you have formatted using text functions, you need to select Values Only from the Paste Options drop-down list to paste the cell values rather than the text formulas.

Summing a Data Range Based on Conditions

You have learned how to use the SUM, COUNT, and AVERAGE functions for data ranges. You can also use Excel functions to sum, count, and average data in a range based on criteria, or conditions, you set. The SUMIF function totals only the cells in a range that meet given criteria. For example, you can total the values in a column of sales where a sales rep name equals Joe Smith (the criterion). Similarly, the COUNTIF function counts cells and the AVERAGEIF function averages cells in a range based on a specified condition. The format for the SUMIF function appears in Figure E-3. Kate asks you to analyze the New York branch's January sales data to provide her with information about each tour.

STEPS

1. **Click the NY sheet tab, click cell G7, click the Formulas tab, click the More Functions button in the Function Library group, point to Statistical, then click COUNTIF**

   The Function Arguments dialog box opens, as shown in Figure E-4. You want to count the number of times Pacific Odyssey appears in the Tour column. The formula you use will say, in effect, "Examine the range I specify, then count the number of cells in that range that contain "Pacific Odyssey." You will specify absolute addresses for the range so you can copy the formula.

2. **With the insertion point in the Range text box, select the range A6:A25, press [F4], press [Tab], with the insertion point in the Criteria text box, click cell F7, then click OK**

   Your formula asks Excel to search the range A6:A25, and where it finds the value shown in cell F7 (that is, when it finds the value "Pacific Odyssey"), add one to the total count. The number of Pacific Odyssey tours, 4, appears in cell G7. You want to calculate the total sales revenue for the Pacific Odyssey tours.

QUICK TIP

You can also sum, count, and average ranges with multiple criteria using the functions SUMIFS, COUNTIFS, and AVERAGEIFS

3. **Click cell H7, click the Math & Trig button in the Function Library group, scroll down the list of functions, then click SUMIF**

   The Function Arguments dialog box opens. You want to enter two ranges and a criterion; the first range is the one where you want Excel to search for the criteria entered. The second range contains the corresponding cells that Excel will total when it finds the criterion you specify in the first range.

4. **With the insertion point in the Range text box, select the range A6:A25, press [F4], press [Tab], with the insertion point in the Criteria text box, click cell F7, press [Tab], with the insertion point in the Sum_range text box, select the range B6:B25, press [F4], then click OK**

   Your formula asks Excel to search the range A6:A25, and where it finds the value shown in cell F7 (that is, when it finds the value "Pacific Odyssey"), add the corresponding amounts from column B. The revenue for the Pacific Odyssey tours, $4,403, appears in cell H7. You want to calculate the average price paid for the Pacific Odyssey tours.

5. **Click cell I7, click the More Functions button in the Function Library group, point to Statistical, then click AVERAGEIF**

6. **With the insertion point in the Range text box, select the range A6:A25, press [F4], press [Tab], with the insertion point in the Criteria text box, click cell F7, press [Tab], with the insertion point in the Average_range text box, select the range B6:B25, press [F4], then click OK**

   The average price paid for the Pacific Odyssey tours, $1,101, appears in cell I7.

7. **Select the range G7:I7, then drag the fill handle to fill the range G8:I10**

   Compare your results with those in Figure E-5.

TROUBLE

Follow the same steps that you used to add a footer to the Sales Reps worksheet in the previous lesson.

8. **Add your name to the center of the footer, save the workbook, then preview the worksheet**

FIGURE E-3: Format of SUMIF function

SUMIF(range, criteria, [sum_range])

The range the function searches

The condition that must be satisfied in the range

The range where the cells that meet the condition will be totaled

FIGURE E-4: COUNTIF function in the Function Arguments dialog box

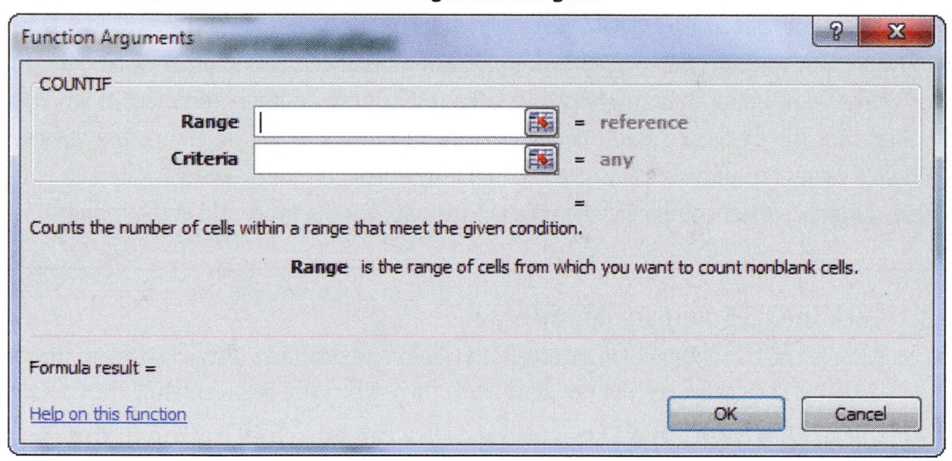

Range is the range of cells from which you want to count nonblank cells.

Help on this function

FIGURE E-5: Worksheet with conditional statistics

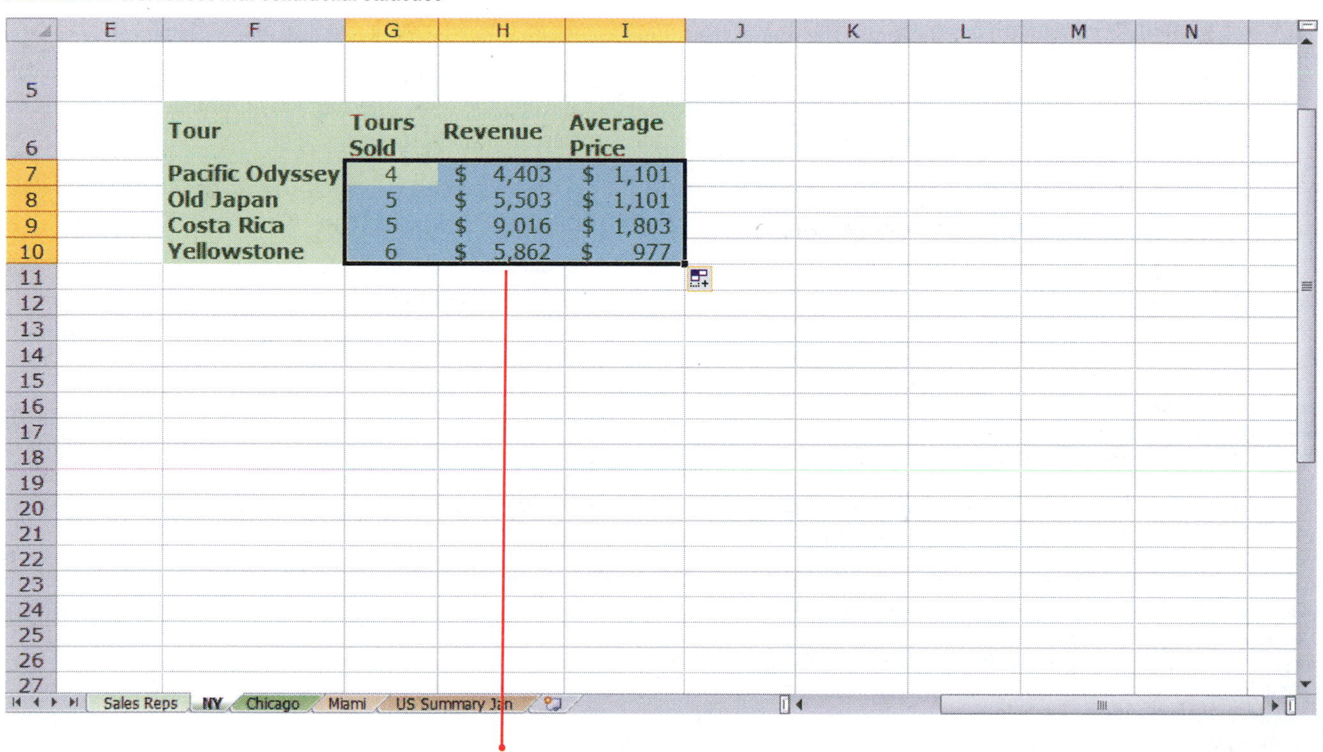

Tour
Tours Sold
Revenue
Average Price
Pacific Odyssey 4 $ 4,403 $ 1,101
Old Japan 5 $ 5,503 $ 1,101
Costa Rica 5 $ 9,016 $ 1,803
Yellowstone 6 $ 5,862 $ 977
Sales Reps
NY
Chicago
Miami
US Summary Jan

Conditional statistics

Excel 2010

Consolidating Data Using a Formula

When you want to summarize similar data that exists in different sheets or workbooks, you can **consolidate**, or combine and display, the data in one sheet. For example, you might have entered departmental sales figures on four different store sheets that you want to consolidate on one summary sheet, showing total departmental sales for all stores. Or, you may have quarterly sales data on separate sheets that you want to total for yearly sales on a summary sheet. The best way to consolidate data is to use cell references to the various sheets on a consolidation, or summary, sheet. Because they reference other sheets that are usually behind the summary sheet, such references effectively create another dimension in the workbook and are called **3-D references**, as shown in Figure E-6. You can reference, or **link** to, data in other sheets and in other workbooks. Linking to a worksheet or workbook is better than retyping calculated results from another worksheet or workbook because the data values that the calculated totals depend on might change. If you reference the values, any changes to the original values are automatically reflected in the consolidation sheet. Kate asks you to prepare a January sales summary sheet comparing the total U.S. revenue for the tours sold in the month.

STEPS

1. **Click the US Summary Jan sheet tab**

   Because the US Summary Jan sheet (which is the consolidation sheet) will contain the reference to the data in the other sheets, the cell pointer must reside there when you begin entering the reference.

2. **Click cell B7, click the Formulas tab, click the AutoSum button in the Function Library group, click the NY sheet tab, press and hold [Shift] and click the Miami sheet tab, scroll up if necessary and click cell G7, then click the Enter button on the formula bar**

   The US Summary Jan sheet becomes active, and the formula bar reads =SUM(NY:Miami!G7), as shown in Figure E-7. "NY:Miami" references the NY, Chicago, and Miami sheets. The exclamation point (!) is an **external reference indicator**, meaning that the cells referenced are outside the active sheet; G7 is the actual cell reference you want to total in the external sheets. The result, 12, appears in cell B7 of the US Summary Jan sheet; it is the sum of the number of Pacific Odyssey tours sold and referenced in cell G7 of the NY, Chicago, and Miami sheets. Because the Revenue data is in the column to the right of the Tours Sold column on the NY, Chicago, and Miami sheets, you can copy the tours sold summary formula, with its relative addresses, into the cell that holds the revenue summary information.

3. **Drag the fill handle to copy the formula in cell B7 to cell C7, click the Auto Fill options list arrow, then click the Fill Without Formatting option button**

   The result, $13,404, appears in cell C7 of the US Summary Jan sheet, showing the sum of the Pacific Odyssey tour revenue referenced in cell H7 of the NY, Chicago, and Miami sheets.

4. **In the US Summary Jan sheet, with the range B7:C7 selected, drag the fill handle to fill the range B8:C10**

   You can test a consolidation reference by changing one cell value on which the formula is based and seeing if the formula result changes.

5. **Click the Chicago sheet tab, edit cell A6 to read Pacific Odyssey, then click the US Summary Jan sheet tab**

   The number of Pacific Odyssey tours sold is automatically updated to 13, and the revenue is increased to $15,279, as shown in Figure E-8.

6. **Save the workbook, then preview the worksheet**

QUICK TIP

You can preview your worksheet with the worksheet gridlines and column and row headings for printing at a later time. Click the Print check boxes under Gridlines and Headings in the Sheet Options group of the Page Layout tab.

FIGURE E-6: Consolidating data from three worksheets

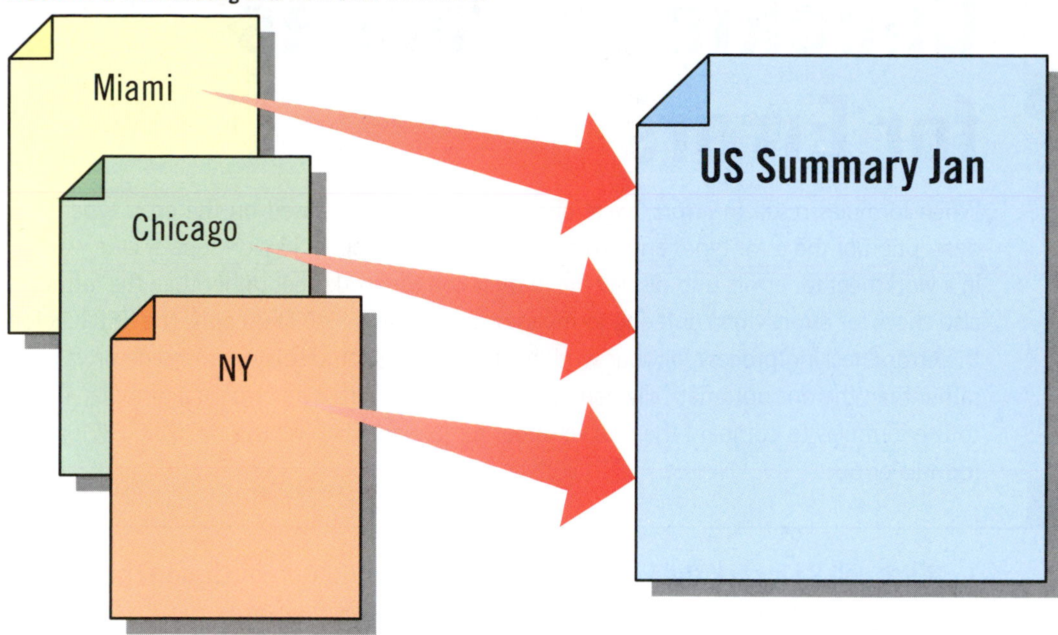

Excel 2010

FIGURE E-7: Worksheet showing total Pacific Odyssey tours sold

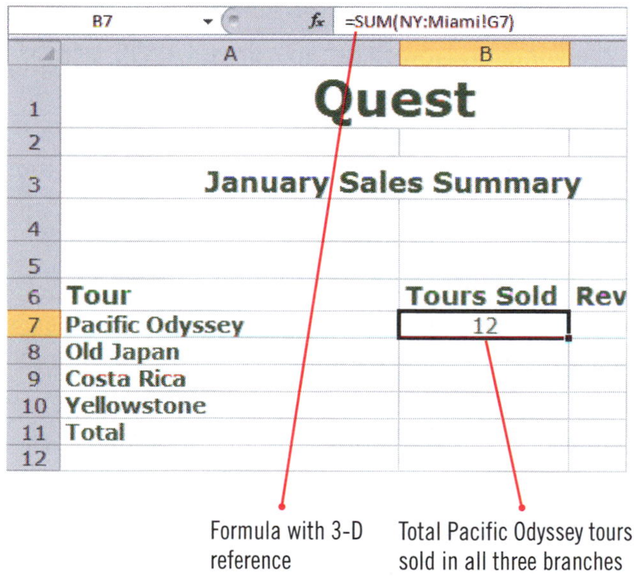

FIGURE E-8: US Summary Jan worksheet with updated totals

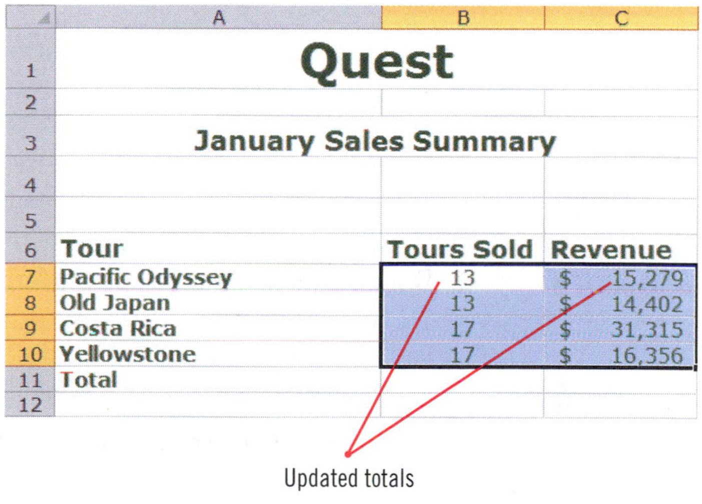

Linking data between workbooks

Just as you can link data between cells in a worksheet and between sheets in a workbook, you can link workbooks so that changes made in referenced cells in one workbook are reflected in the consolidation sheet in the other workbook. To link a single cell between workbooks, open both workbooks, select the cell to receive the linked data, type the equal sign (=), select the cell in the other workbook containing the data to be linked, then press [Enter]. Excel automatically inserts the name of the referenced workbook in the cell reference. For example, if the linked data is contained in cell C7 of the Sales worksheet in the Product workbook, the cell entry reads =[Product.xlsx]Sales!$C$7. To perform calculations, enter formulas on the consolidation sheet using cells in the supporting sheets.

UNIT E

Excel 2010

Checking Formulas for Errors

When formulas result in errors, Excel displays an error value based on the error type. See Table E-1 for a description of the error types and error codes that might appear in worksheets. One way to check formulas in a worksheet for errors is to display the formulas on the worksheet rather than the formula results. You can also check for errors when entering formulas by using the IFERROR function. The IFERROR function simplifies the error-checking process for your worksheets. This function displays a message or value that you specify, rather than the one automatically generated by Excel, if there is an error in a formula. Kate asks you to use formulas to compare the tour revenues for January. You will use the IFERROR function to help catch formula errors.

STEPS

1. **Click cell B11, click the Formulas tab, click the AutoSum button in the Function Library group, then click the Enter button on the formula bar**

   The number of tours sold, 60, appears in cell B11.

2. **Drag the fill handle to copy the formula in cell B11 into cell C11, click the Auto Fill options list arrow, then click the Fill Without Formatting option button**

   The tour revenue total of $77,352 appears in cell C11. You decide to enter a formula to calculate the percentage of revenue the Pacific Odyssey tour represents by dividing the individual tour revenue figures by the total revenue figure. To help with error checking, you decide to enter the formula using the IFERROR function.

3. **Click cell D7, click the Logical button in the Function Library group, click IFERROR, with the insertion point in the Value text box, click cell C7, type /, click cell C11, press [Tab], in the Value_if_error text box, type ERROR, then click OK**

   The Pacific Odyssey tour revenue percentage of 19.75% appears in cell D7. You want to be sure that your error message will be displayed properly, so you decide to test it by intentionally creating an error. You copy and paste the formula—which has a relative address in the denominator, where an absolute address should be used.

TROUBLE

You will fix the ERROR codes in cells D8:D10 in the next step.

4. **Drag the fill handle to copy the formula in cell D7 into the range D8:D10**

   The ERROR value appears in cells D8:D10, as shown in Figure E-9. The errors are a result of the relative address for C11 in the denominator of the copied formula. Changing the relative address of C11 in the copied formula to an absolute address of $C$11 will correct the errors.

QUICK TIP

You can also check formulas for errors using the buttons in the Formula Auditing group on the Formulas tab.

5. **Double-click cell D7, select C11 in the formula, press [F4], then click on the formula bar**

   The formula now contains an absolute reference to cell C11.

6. **Copy the corrected formula in cell D7 into the range D8:D10**

   The tour revenue percentages now appear in all four cells, without error messages, as shown in Figure E-10. You want to check all of your worksheet formulas by displaying them on the worksheet.

QUICK TIP

You can also display worksheet formulas by holding [Ctrl] and pressing [`].

7. **Click the Show Formulas button in the Formula Auditing group**

   The formulas appear in columns B, C, and D. You want to display the formula results again. The Show Formulas button works as a toggle, turning the feature on and off with each click.

8. **Click the Show Formulas button in the Formula Auditing group**

   The formula results appear on the worksheet.

9. **Add your name to the center section of the footer, save the workbook, preview the worksheet, close the workbook, then submit the workbook to your instructor**

FIGURE E-9: Worksheet with error codes

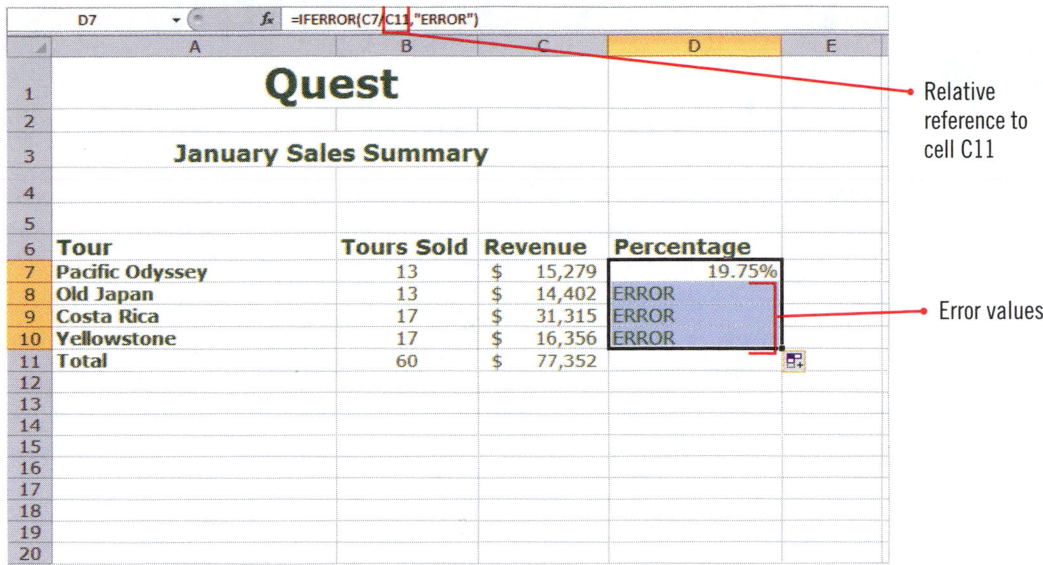

FIGURE E-10: Worksheet with tour percentages

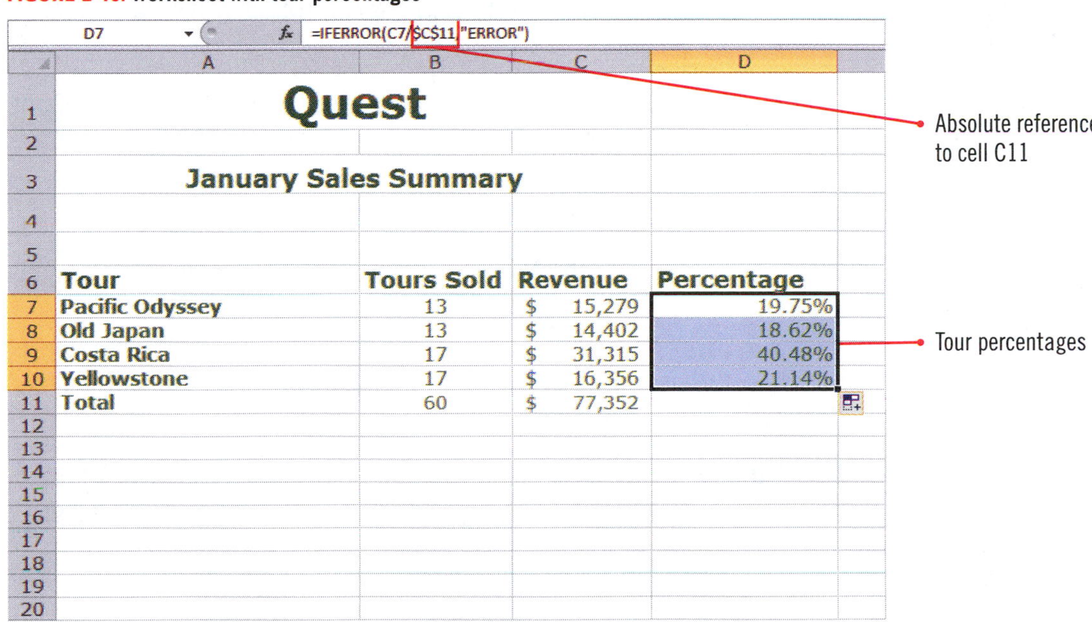

TABLE E-1: Understanding error values

error value	cause of error	error value	cause of error
#DIV/0!	A number is divided by 0	#NAME?	Formula contains text error
#NA	A value in a formula is not available	#NULL!	Invalid intersection of areas
#NUM!	Invalid use of a number in a formula	#REF!	Invalid cell reference
#VALUE!	Wrong type of formula argument or operand	#####	Column is not wide enough to display data

Correcting circular references

A cell with a circular reference contains a formula that refers to its own cell location. If you accidentally enter a formula with a circular reference, a warning box opens, alerting you to the problem. Click OK to open a Help window explaining how to find the circular reference. In simple formulas, a circular reference is easy to spot. To correct it, edit the formula to remove any reference to the cell where the formula is located.

UNIT
E
Excel 2010

Constructing Formulas Using Named Ranges

To make your worksheet easier to follow, you can assign names to cells and ranges. You can also use names in formulas to make them easier to build and to reduce formula errors. For example, the formula "revenue-cost" is easier to understand than the formula "A5-A8". Cell and range names can use uppercase or lowercase letters as well as digits, but cannot have spaces. After you name a cell or range, you can define its **scope**, or the worksheets where you will be able to use it. When defining a name's scope, you can limit its use to a worksheet or make it available to the entire workbook. If you move a named cell or range, its name moves with it, and if you add or remove rows or column to the worksheet the ranges are adjusted to their new position in the worksheet. When used in formulas, names become absolute cell references by default. Kate asks you to calculate the number of days before each tour departs. You will use range names to construct the formula.

STEPS

QUICK TIP
You can create range names by selecting a cell or range, typing a name in the Name Box, then pressing [Enter]. By default, its scope will be the workbook.

QUICK TIP
Because names cannot contain spaces, underscores are often used between words to replace spaces.

QUICK TIP
Named cells and ranges can be used as a navigational tool in a worksheet by selecting the name in the Name Box. The named cell or range becomes active.

1. **Open the file EX E-2.xlsx from the drive and folder where you store your Data Files, then save it as EX E-Tours**

2. **Click cell B4, click the Formulas tab if necessary, click the Define Name button in the Defined Names group**

   The New Name dialog box opens, as shown in Figure E-11. You can give a cell that contains a date a name that will make it easier to build formulas that perform date calculations.

3. **Type current_date in the Name text box, click the Scope list arrow, click April Tours, then click OK**

   The name assigned to cell B4, current_date, appears in the Name Box. Because its scope is the April Tours worksheet, the range name current_date will appear on the name list only on that worksheet. You can also name ranges that contain dates.

4. **Select the range B7:B13, click the Define Name button in the Defined Names group, enter tour_date in the Name text box, click the Scope list arrow, click April Tours, then click OK**

   Now you can use the named cell and named range in a formula. The formula =tour_date–current_date is easier to understand than =B7-$B$4.

5. **Click cell C7, type =, click the Use in Formula button in the Defined Names group, click tour_date, type –, click the Use in Formula button, click current_date, then click the Enter button ✓ on the formula bar**

   The number of days before the Costa Rica tour departs, 10, appears in cell C7. You can use the same formula to calculate the number of days before the other tours depart.

6. **Drag the fill handle to copy the formula in cell C7 into the range C8:C13, then compare your formula results with those in Figure E-12**

7. **Save the workbook**

Consolidating data using named ranges

You can consolidate data using named cells and ranges. For example, you might have entered team sales figures using the names team1, team2, and team3 on different sheets that you want to consolidate on one summary sheet. As you enter the summary formula you can click the Formulas tab, click the Use in Formula button in the Defined Names group, and select the cell or range name.

FIGURE E-11: New Name dialog box

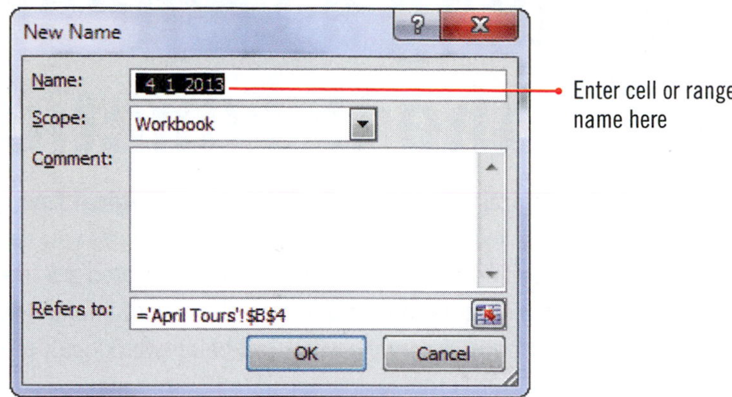

FIGURE E-12: Worksheet with days before departure

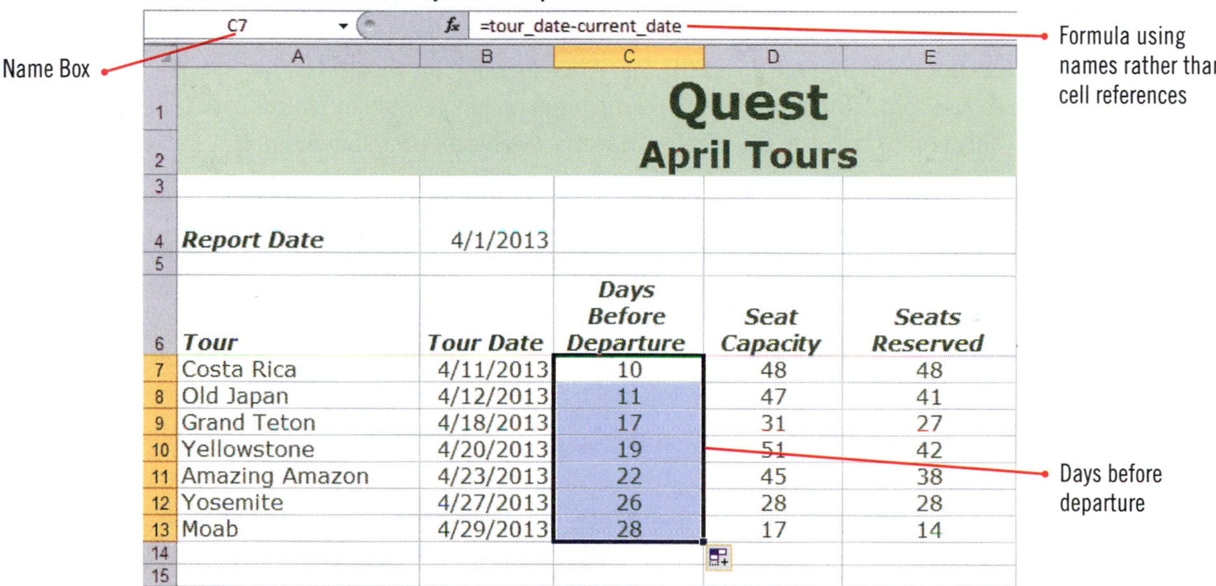

	A	B	C	D	E
6	*Tour*	*Tour Date*	*Days Before Departure*	*Seat Capacity*	*Seats Reserved*
7	Costa Rica	4/11/2013	10	48	48
8	Old Japan	4/12/2013	11	47	41
9	Grand Teton	4/18/2013	17	31	27
10	Yellowstone	4/20/2013	19	51	42
11	Amazing Amazon	4/23/2013	22	45	38
12	Yosemite	4/27/2013	26	28	28
13	Moab	4/29/2013	28	17	14

Managing workbook names

You can use the Name Manager to create, delete, and edit names in a workbook. Click the Name Manager button in the Defined Names group on the Formulas tab to open the Name Manager dialog box, as shown in Figure E-13. Click the New button to create a new named cell or range, click Edit to change a highlighted cell name, and click Delete to remove a highlighted name. Click Filter to see options for displaying specific criteria for displaying names.

FIGURE E-13: Name Manager dialog box

Click to create new name

Click to change name

Click to filter names

Click to delete name

Building a Logical Formula with the IF Function

You can build a logical formula using an IF function. A **logical formula** makes calculations based on criteria that you create, called **stated conditions**. For example, you can build a formula to calculate bonuses based on a person's performance rating. If a person is rated a 5 (the stated condition) on a scale of 1 to 5, with 5 being the highest rating, he or she receives an additional 10% of his or her salary as a bonus; otherwise, there is no bonus. A condition that can be answered with a true or false response is called a **logical test**. The IF function has three parts, separated by commas: a condition or logical test, an action to take if the logical test or condition is true, and an action to take if the logical test or condition is false. Another way of expressing this is: IF(test_cond,do_this,else_this). Translated into an Excel IF function, the formula to calculate bonuses might look like this: IF(Rating=5,Salary*0.10,0). In other words, if the rating equals 5, multiply the salary by 0.10 (the decimal equivalent of 10%), then place the result in the selected cell; if the rating does not equal 5, place a 0 in the cell. When entering the logical test portion of an IF statement, you typically use some combination of the comparison operators listed in Table E-2. Kate asks you to use an IF function to calculate the number of seats available for each tour in April.

STEPS

1. **Click cell F7, on the Formulas tab, click the Logical button in the Function Library group, then click IF**

   The Function Arguments dialog box opens. You want the function to calculate the seats available as follows: If the seat capacity is greater than the number of seats reserved, calculate the number of seats that are available (capacity minus number reserved), and place the result in cell F7; otherwise, place the text "None" in the cell.

2. **With the insertion point in the Logical_test text box, click cell D7, type >, click cell E7, then press [Tab]**

   The symbol (>) represents "greater than." So far, the formula reads "If the seating capacity is greater than the number of reserved seats,". The next part of the function tells Excel the action to take if the capacity exceeds the reserved number of seats.

3. **With the insertion point in the Value_if_true text box, click cell D7, type –, click cell E7, then press [Tab]**

   This part of the formula tells the program what you want it to do if the logical test is true. Continuing the translation of the formula, this part means "Subtract the number of reserved seats from the seat capacity." The last part of the formula tells Excel the action to take if the logical test is false (that is, if the seat capacity does not exceed the number of reserved seats).

4. **Enter None in the Value_if_false text box, then click OK**

   The function is complete, and the result, None (the number of available seats), appears in cell F7, as shown in Figure E-14.

5. **Drag the fill handle to copy the formula in cell F7 into the range F8:F13**

   Compare your results with Figure E-15.

6. **Save the workbook**

FIGURE E-14: Worksheet with IF function

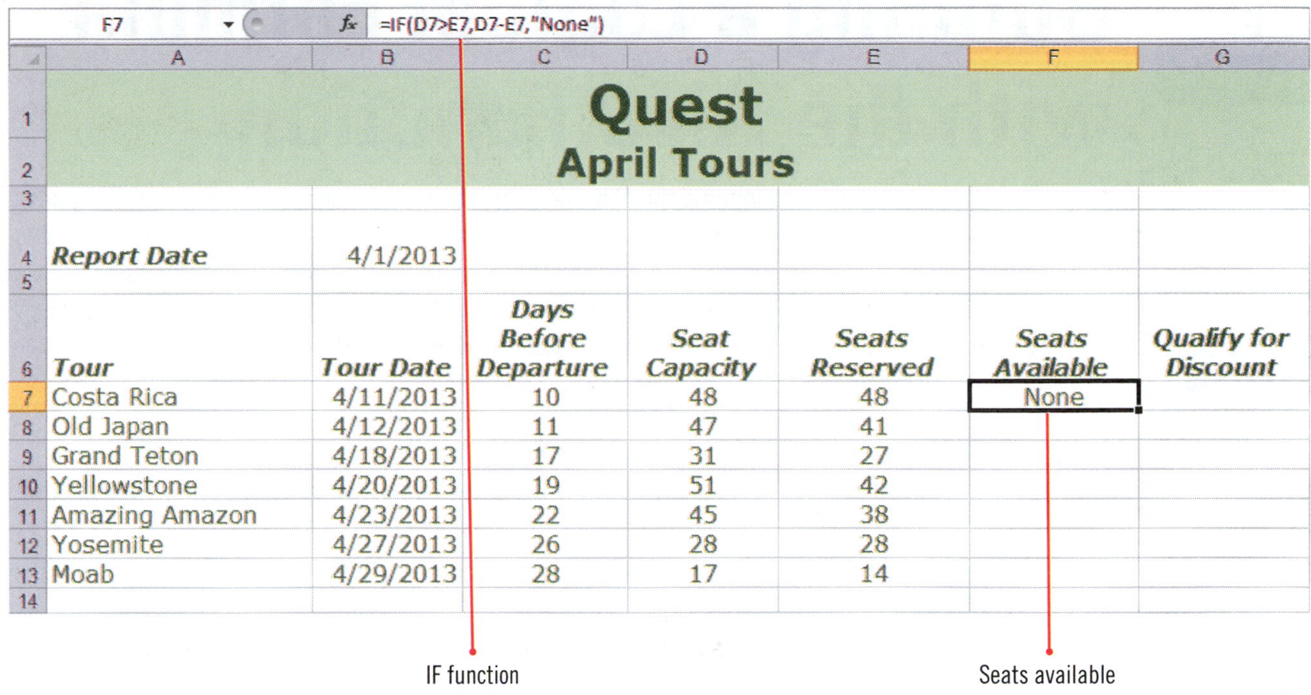

F7 =IF(D7>E7,D7-E7,"None")

	A	B	C	D	E	F	G
1				Quest			
2				April Tours			
3							
4	***Report Date***	4/1/2013					
5							
6	***Tour***	***Tour Date***	***Days Before Departure***	***Seat Capacity***	***Seats Reserved***	***Seats Available***	***Qualify for Discount***
7	Costa Rica	4/11/2013	10	48	48	None	
8	Old Japan	4/12/2013	11	47	41		
9	Grand Teton	4/18/2013	17	31	27		
10	Yellowstone	4/20/2013	19	51	42		
11	Amazing Amazon	4/23/2013	22	45	38		
12	Yosemite	4/27/2013	26	28	28		
13	Moab	4/29/2013	28	17	14		
14							

FIGURE E-15: Worksheet showing seats available

	A	B	C	D	E	F	G
1				Quest			
2				April Tours			
3							
4	***Report Date***	4/1/2013					
5							
6	***Tour***	***Tour Date***	***Days Before Departure***	***Seat Capacity***	***Seats Reserved***	***Seats Available***	***Qualify for Discount***
7	Costa Rica	4/11/2013	10	48	48	None	
8	Old Japan	4/12/2013	11	47	41	6	
9	Grand Teton	4/18/2013	17	31	27	4	
10	Yellowstone	4/20/2013	19	51	42	9	
11	Amazing Amazon	4/23/2013	22	45	38	7	
12	Yosemite	4/27/2013	26	28	28	None	
13	Moab	4/29/2013	28	17	14	3	
14							
15							
16							
17							

Seats available

TABLE E-2: Comparison operators

operator	meaning	operator	meaning
<	Less than	<=	Less than or equal to
>	Greater than	>=	Greater than or equal to
=	Equal to	<>	Not equal to

UNIT E
Excel 2010

Building a Logical Formula with the AND Function

You can also build a logical function using the AND function. The AND function evaluates all of its arguments and **returns**, or displays, TRUE if every logical test in the formula is true. The AND function returns a value of FALSE if one or more of its logical tests is false. The AND function arguments can include text, numbers, or cell references. Kate wants you to analyze the tour data to find tours that qualify for discounting. You will use the AND function to check for tours with seats available and that depart within 21 days.

STEPS

1. **Click cell G7, click the Logical button in the Function Library group, then click AND**
   The Function Arguments dialog box opens. You want the function to evaluate the discount qualification as follows: There must be seats available, and the tour must depart within 21 days.
2. **With the insertion point in the Logical1 text box, click cell F7, type < >, type "None", then press [Tab]**
   The symbol (<>) represents "not equal to." So far, the formula reads "If the number of seats available is not equal to None,"—in other words, if it is an integer. The next logical test checks the number of days before the tour departs.
3. **With the insertion point in the Logical2 text box, click cell C7, type <21, then click OK**
   The function is complete, and the result, FALSE, appears in cell G7, as shown in Figure E-16.
4. **Drag the fill handle to copy the formula in cell G7 into the range G8:G13**
   Compare your results with Figure E-17.
5. **Add your name to the center of the footer, save the workbook, then preview the worksheet**

TROUBLE
If you get a formula error, check to be sure that you typed the quotation marks around None.

TABLE E-3: Examples of AND, OR, and NOT functions with cell values A1=10 and B1=20

function	formula	result
AND	=AND(A1>5,B1>25)	FALSE
OR	=OR(A1>5,B1>25)	TRUE
NOT	=NOT(A1=0)	TRUE

Using the OR and NOT logical functions

The OR logical function has the same syntax as the AND function, but rather than returning TRUE if every argument is true, the OR function will return TRUE if any of its arguments are true. It will only return FALSE if all of its arguments are false. The NOT logical function reverses the value of its argument. For example NOT(TRUE) reverses its argument of TRUE and returns FALSE. This can be used in a worksheet to ensure that a cell is not equal to a particular value. See Table E-3 for examples of the AND, OR, and NOT functions.

FIGURE E-16: Worksheet with AND function

G7 | f_x =AND(F7<>"None",C7<21)

	A	B	C	D	E	F	G
5							
6	Tour	Tour Date	Days Before Departure	Seat Capacity	Seats Reserved	Seats Available	Qualify for Discount
7	Costa Rica	4/11/2013	10	48	48	None	FALSE
8	Old Japan	4/12/2013	11	47	41	6	
9	Grand Teton	4/18/2013	17	31	27	4	
10	Yellowstone	4/20/2013	19	51	42	9	
11	Amazing Amazon	4/23/2013	22	45	38	7	
12	Yosemite	4/27/2013	26	28	28	None	
13	Moab	4/29/2013	28	17	14	3	
14							
15							
16							
17							
18							
19							
20							
21							
22							

AND function

Result of AND function

FIGURE E-17: Worksheet with discount status evaluated

G7 | f_x =AND(F7<>"None",C7<21)

Formula Bar

	A	B	C	D	E	F	G
5							
6	Tour	Tour Date	Days Before Departure	Seat Capacity	Seats Reserved	Seats Available	Qualify for Discount
7	Costa Rica	4/11/2013	10	48	48	None	FALSE
8	Old Japan	4/12/2013	11	47	41	6	TRUE
9	Grand Teton	4/18/2013	17	31	27	4	TRUE
10	Yellowstone	4/20/2013	19	51	42	9	TRUE
11	Amazing Amazon	4/23/2013	22	45	38	7	FALSE
12	Yosemite	4/27/2013	26	28	28	None	FALSE
13	Moab	4/29/2013	28	17	14	3	FALSE
14							
15							
16							
17							
18							
19							
20							
21							
22							

Inserting an equation into a worksheet

If your worksheet contains formulas, you might want to place an equation on the worksheet to document how you arrived at your results. First create a text box to hold the equation: Click the Insert tab, click the Text box button in the Text group, then click on the worksheet location where you want the equation to appear. To place the equation in the text box, click the Insert tab again, then click the Equation button in the Symbols group. When you see "Type equation here," you can build an equation by clicking the mathematical symbols in the Structures group of the Equation Tools Design tab. For example, if you wanted to enter a fraction of 2/7, you click the Fraction button, choose the first option, click the top box, enter 2, press [Tab], enter 7, then click outside of the fraction. To insert the symbol x^2 into a text box, click the Script list arrow in the Structures group of the Equation Tools Design tab, click the first option, click in the lower-left box and enter "x", press [Tab], enter 2 in the upper-right box, then click to the right of the boxes to exit the symbol.You can also add built-in equations to a text box: On the Equation Tools Design tab, click the Equation list arrow in the Tools group, then select the equation. Built-in equations include the equation for the area of a circle, the binomial theorem, Pythagorean theorem, and the quadratic equation.

Calculating Payments with the PMT Function

PMT is a financial function that calculates the periodic payment amount for money borrowed. For example, if you want to borrow money to buy a car, and you know the principal amount, interest rate, and loan term, the PMT function can calculate your monthly payment. Say you want to borrow $20,000 at 6.5% interest and pay the loan off in 5 years. The Excel PMT function can tell you that your monthly payment will be $391.32. The main parts of the PMT function are PMT(rate, nper, pv). See Figure E-18 for an illustration of a PMT function that calculates the monthly payment in the car loan example. For several months, QST's United States region has been discussing opening a new branch in San Francisco. Kate has obtained quotes from three different lenders on borrowing $359,000 to begin the expansion. She obtained loan quotes from a commercial bank, a venture capitalist, and an investment banker. She wants you to summarize the information using the Excel PMT function.

STEPS

1. **Click the Loan sheet tab, click cell F5, click the Formulas tab, click the Financial button in the Function Library group, scroll down the list of functions, then click PMT**

2. **With the insertion point in the Rate text box, click cell D5 on the worksheet, type /12, then press [Tab]**

   You must divide the annual interest by 12 because you are calculating monthly, not annual, payments. You need to be consistent about the units you use for rate and nper. If you express nper as the number of monthly payments, then you must express the interest rate as a monthly rate.

> **QUICK TIP**
> The Fv and Type arguments are optional: The argument Fv is the future value, or the total amount you want to obtain after all payments. If you omit it, Excel assumes you want to pay off the loan completely, so the default Fv is 0. The Type argument indicates when the payments are made; 0 is the end of the period, and 1 is the beginning of the period. The default is the end of the period.

3. **With the insertion point in the Nper text box, click cell E5; click the Pv text box, click cell B5, then click OK**

   The payment of ($7,460.96) in cell F5 appears in red, indicating that it is a negative amount. Excel displays the result of a PMT function as a negative value to reflect the negative cash flow the loan represents to the borrower. To show the monthly payment as a positive number, you can place a minus sign in front of the Pv cell reference in the function.

4. **Double-click cell F5 and edit it so it reads =PMT(D5/12,E5,-B5), then click the Enter button on the formula bar**

   A positive value of $7,460.96 now appears in cell F5, as shown in Figure E-19. You can use the same formula to generate the monthly payments for the other loans.

5. **With cell F5 selected, drag the fill handle to fill the range F6:F7**

   A monthly payment of $11,457.92 for the venture capitalist loan appears in cell F6. A monthly payment of $16,425.54 for the investment banker loan appears in cell F7. The loans with shorter terms have much higher monthly payments. But you will not know the entire financial picture until you calculate the total payments and total interest for each lender.

> **QUICK TIP**
> You can use the keyboard shortcut of [Ctrl][Enter] rather than clicking the Enter button. This enters the formula and leaves the cell selected.

6. **Click cell G5, type =, click cell E5, type *, click cell F5, then press [Tab], in cell H5, type =, click cell G5, type –, click cell B5, then click ✓**

7. **Copy the formulas in cells G5:H5 into the range G6:H7, then click cell A1**

   You can experiment with different interest rates, loan amounts, or terms for any one of the lenders; the PMT function generates a new set of values automatically.

8. **Add your name to the center section of the footer, save the workbook, preview the worksheet, then submit the workbook to your instructor**

   Your worksheet appears as shown in Figure E-20.

9. **Close the workbook and exit Excel**

FIGURE E-18: Example of PMT function for car loan

PMT(0.065/12, 60, 20000) = $391.32

Interest rate per month (rate)

Number of monthly payments

Present value of loan amount (pv)

Monthly payment calculated

FIGURE E-19: PMT function calculating monthly loan payment

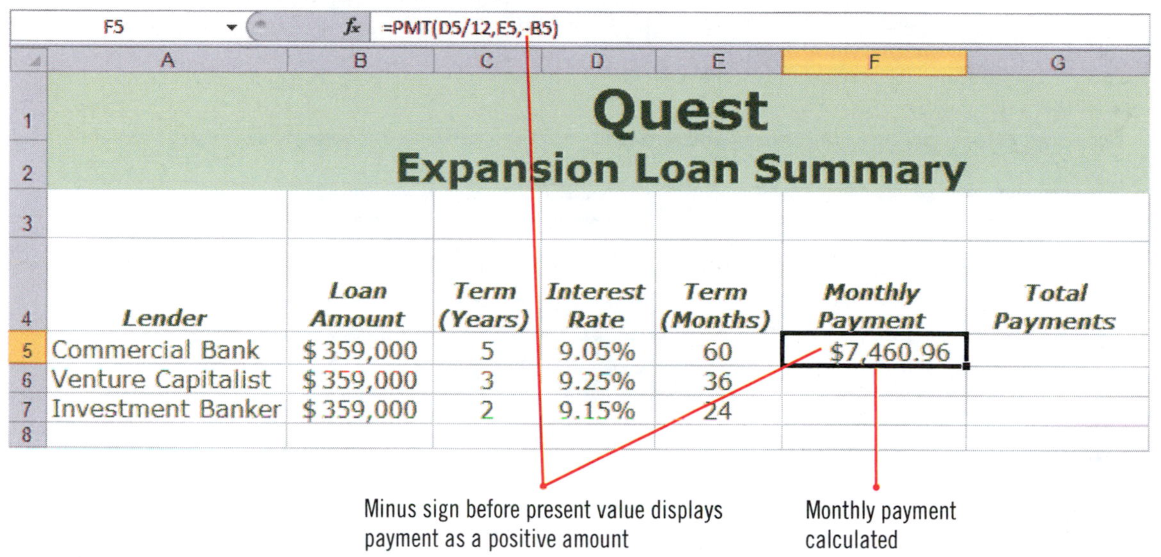

F5 | =PMT(D5/12,E5,-B5)

	A	B	C	D	E	F	G
1	Quest						
2	Expansion Loan Summary						
3							
4	Lender	Loan Amount	Term (Years)	Interest Rate	Term (Months)	Monthly Payment	Total Payments
5	Commercial Bank	$ 359,000	5	9.05%	60	$7,460.96	
6	Venture Capitalist	$ 359,000	3	9.25%	36		
7	Investment Banker	$ 359,000	2	9.15%	24		
8							

Minus sign before present value displays payment as a positive amount
Monthly payment calculated

FIGURE E-20: Completed worksheet

Quest

Expansion Loan Summary

Lender	Loan Amount	Term (Years)	Interest Rate	Term (Months)	Monthly Payment	Total Payments	Total Interest
Commercial Bank	$ 359,000	5	9.05%	60	$7,460.96	$ 447,657.85	$ 88,657.85
Venture Capitalist	$ 359,000	3	9.25%	36	$11,457.92	$ 412,485.14	$ 53,485.14
Investment Banker	$ 359,000	2	9.15%	24	$16,425.54	$ 394,212.98	$ 35,212.98

Copied formula calculates total payments and interest for remaining two loan options

Calculating future value with the FV function

You can use the FV (Future Value) function to determine the amount of money a given monthly investment will amount to, at a given interest rate, after a given number of payment periods. The syntax is similar to that of the PMT function: FV(rate,nper,pmt,pv,type). The rate is the interest paid by the financial institution, the nper is the number of periods, and the pmt is the amount that you deposit. For example, suppose you want to invest $1,000 every month for the next 12 months into an account that pays 2% a year, and you want to know how much you will have at the end of 12 months (that is, its future value). You enter the function FV(.02/12,12,-1000), and Excel returns the value $12,110.61 as the future value of your investment. As with the PMT function, the units for the rate and nper must be consistent.

Practice

For current SAM information, including versions and content details, visit SAM Central (http://www.cengage.com/samcentral). If you have a SAM user profile, you may have access to hands-on instruction, practice, and assessment of the skills covered in this unit. Since various versions of SAM are supported throughout the life of this text, check with your instructor for the correct instructions and URL/Web site for accessing assignments.

Concepts Review

FIGURE E-21

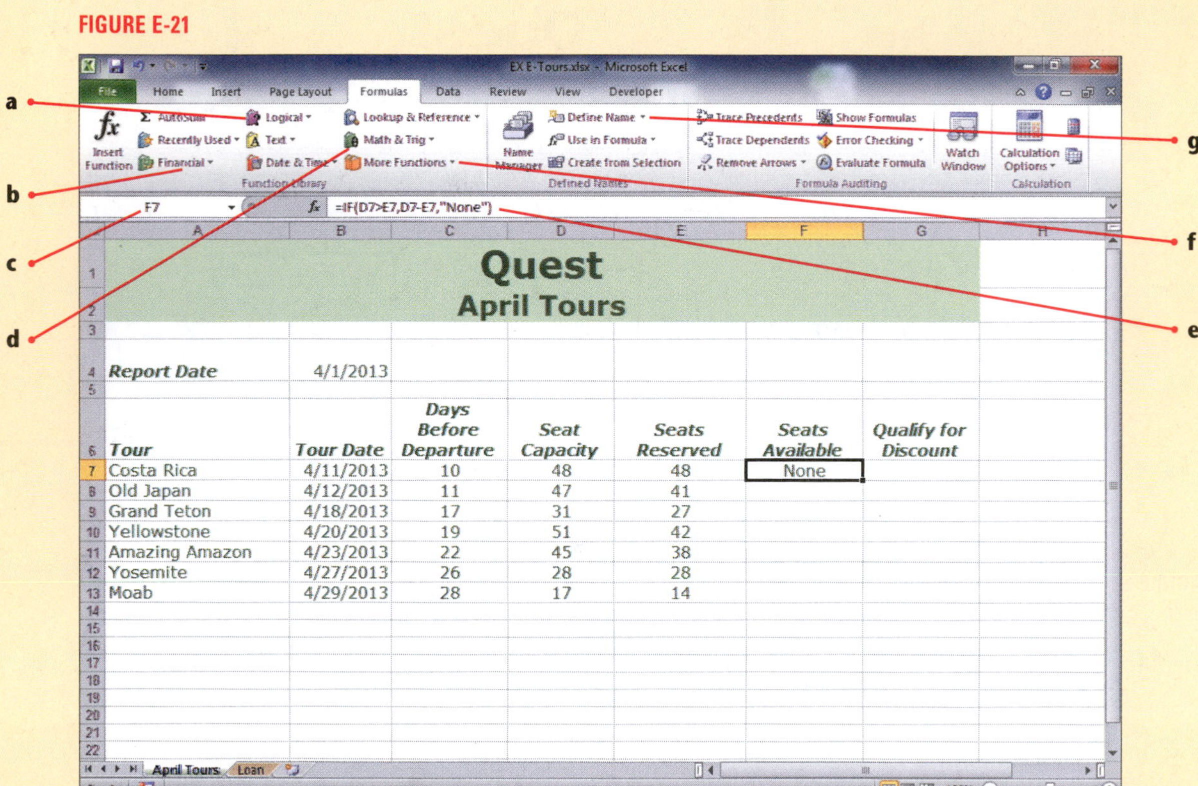

1. **Which element do you click to name a cell or range?**
2. **Which element do you click to add a statistical function to a worksheet?**
3. **Which element points to a logical formula?**
4. **Which element points to the area where the name of a selected cell or range appears?**
5. **Which element do you click to insert a PMT function into a worksheet?**
6. **Which element do you click to add a SUMIF function to a worksheet?**
7. **Which element do you click to add an IF function to a worksheet?**

Match each term with the statement that best describes it.

8. **FV**
9. **PV**
10. **SUMIF**
11. **PROPER**
12. **test_cond**

- **a.** Function used to change the first letter of a string to uppercase
- **b.** Function used to determine the future amount of an investment
- **c.** Part of the PMT function that represents the loan amount
- **d.** Part of the IF function that the conditions are stated in
- **e.** Function used to conditionally total cells

Select the best answer from the list of choices.

13. When you enter the rate and nper arguments in a PMT function, you must:

- **a.** Multiply both units by 12.
- **b.** Be consistent in the units used.
- **c.** Divide both values by 12.
- **d.** Always use annual units.

14. To express conditions such as less than or equal to, you can use a:

- **a.** Comparison operator.
- **b.** Text formula.
- **c.** PMT function.
- **d.** Statistical function.

Skills Review

1. Format data using text functions.

- **a.** Start Excel, open the file EX E-3.xlsx from the drive and folder where you store your Data Files, then save it as **EX E-Reviews**.
- **b.** On the Managers worksheet, select the range A2:A9 and, using the Text to Columns button on the Data tab, separate the names into two text columns. (*Hint*: The delimiter is a space.)
- **c.** In cell D2, enter the text formula to convert the first letter of the department in cell C2 to uppercase, then copy the formula in cell D2 into the range D3:D9.
- **d.** In cell E2, enter the text formula to convert all letters of the department in cell C2 to uppercase, then copy the formula in cell E2 into the range E3:E9.
- **e.** In cell F2, use the text formula to convert all letters of the department in cell C2 to lowercase, then copy the formula in cell F2 into the range F3:F9.
- **f.** In cell G2, use the text formula to substitute "Human Resources" for "hr" if that text exists in cell F2. (*Hint*: In the Function Arguments dialog box, Text is F2, Old_text is "hr", and New_text is "Human Resources".) Copy the formula in cell G2 into the range G3:G9 to change the other cells containing "hr" to "Human Resources". (The marketing and sales entries will not change because the formula searches for the text "hr".)
- **g.** Save your work, then enter your name in the worksheet footer. Compare your screen to Figure E-22.
- **h.** Display the formulas in the worksheet.
- **i.** Redisplay the formula results.

FIGURE E-22

	A	B	C	D	E	F	G
1	Name		Department	PROPER	UPPER	LOWER	SUBSTITUTE
2	Kathy	Kirk	MarkEting	Marketing	MARKETING	marketing	marketing
3	Sallie	Story	hR	Hr	HR	hr	Human Resources
4	Kim	Craven	MarKeting	Marketing	MARKETING	marketing	marketing
5	Albert	Meng	hR	Hr	HR	hr	Human Resources
6	Roberto	Delgado	saLEs	Sales	SALES	sales	sales
7	Harry	Desus	saleS	Sales	SALES	sales	sales
8	Mary	Abbott	hR	Hr	HR	hr	Human Resources
9	Jody	Williams	MarKeTing	Marketing	MARKETING	marketing	marketing

2. Sum a data range based on conditions.

- **a.** Make the HR sheet active.
- **b.** In cell B20, use the COUNTIF function to count the number of employees with a rating of 5.
- **c.** In cell B21, use the AVERAGEIF function to average the salaries of those with a rating of 5.
- **d.** In cell B22, enter the SUMIF function that totals the salaries of employees with a rating of 5.
- **e.** Format cells B21 and B22 with the Number format using commas and no decimals. Save your work, then compare your formula results to Figure E-23.

FIGURE E-23

17		
18	Department Statistics	
19	Top Rating	
20	Number	5
21	Average Salary	31,180
22	Total Salary	155,900
23		

3. Consolidate data using a formula.

- **a.** Make the Summary sheet active.
- **b.** In cell B4, use the AutoSum function to total cell F15 on the HR and Accounting sheets.
- **c.** Format cell B4 with the Accounting Number format if necessary.
- **d.** Enter your name in the worksheet footer, then save your work. Compare your screen to Figure E-24.
- **e.** Display the formula in the worksheet, then redisplay the formula results in the worksheet.

FIGURE E-24

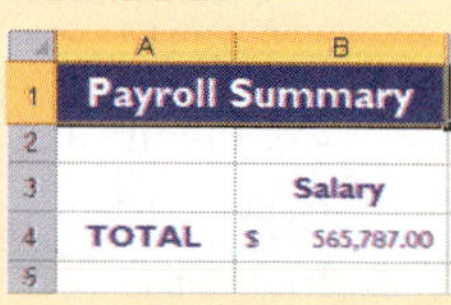

A
B
1 Payroll Summary
2
3 Salary
4 TOTAL $ 565,787.00
5

4. Check formulas for errors.

- **a.** Make the HR sheet active.
- **b.** In cell I6, use the IFERROR function to display "ERROR" in the event that the formula F6/F15 results in a formula error. (*Note*: This formula will generate an intentional error after the next step, which you will correct in a moment.)

Skills Review (continued)

c. Copy the formula in cell I6 into the range I7:I14.

d. Correct the formula in cell I6 by making the denominator, F15, an absolute address.

e. Copy the new formula in cell I6 into the range I7:I14, then save your work.

5. Construct formulas using named ranges.

a. On the HR sheet, name the range C6:C14 **review_date**, and limit the scope of the name to the HR worksheet.

b. In cell E6, enter the formula **=review_date+183**, using the Use in Formula button to enter the cell name.

c. Copy the formula in cell E6 into the range E7:E14.

d. Use the Name Manager to add a comment of **Date of last review** to the review_date name. (*Hint*: In the Name Manager dialog box, click the review_date name, then click Edit to enter the comment.) Save your work.

6. Build a logical formula with the IF function.

a. In cell G6, use the Function Arguments dialog box to enter the formula **=IF(D6=5,F6*0.05,0)**.

b. Copy the formula in cell G6 into the range G7:G14.

c. In cell G15, use AutoSum to total the range G6:G14.

d. Format the range G6:G15 with the Currency number format, using the $ symbol and no decimal places.

e. Save your work.

7. Build a logical formula with the AND function.

a. In cell H6, use the Function Arguments dialog box to enter the formula **=AND(G6>0,B6>5)**.

b. Copy the formula in cell H6 into the range H7:H14.

c. Enter your name in the worksheet footer, save your work, then compare your worksheet to Figure E-25.

d. Make the Accounting sheet active.

e. In cell H6, indicate if the employee needs more development hours to reach the minimum of 5. Use the Function Arguments dialog box for the NOT function to enter **B6>5** in the Logical text box. Copy the formula in cell H6 into the range H7:H14.

f. In cell I6, indicate if the employee needs to enroll in a quality class, as indicated by a rating less than 5 or having fewer than 5 development hours. Use the Function Arguments dialog box for the OR function to enter **D6<5** in the Logical1 text box and **B6<5** in the Logical2 text box. Copy the formula in cell I6 into the range I7:I14.

g. Enter your name in the worksheet footer, save your work, then compare your screen to Figure E-26.

8. Calculate payments with the PMT function.

a. Make the Loan sheet active.

b. In cell B9, determine the monthly payment using the loan information shown: Use the Function Arguments dialog box to enter the formula **=PMT(B5/12,B6,-B4)**.

c. In cell B10, enter a formula that multiplies the number of payments by the monthly payment.

d. In cell B11, enter the formula that subtracts the loan amount from the total payment amount, then compare your screen to Figure E-27.

FIGURE E-25

Human Resources Department
Merit Pay

Last Name	Professional Development Hours	Review Date	Rating	Next Review	Salary	Bonus	Pay Bonus	Percentage of Total
Brack	6	1/5/2013	2	7/7/2013	$ 19,840.00	$0	FALSE	7.21%
Casey	8	4/1/2013	5	10/1/2013	$ 26,700.00	$1,335	TRUE	9.71%
Donnely	1	7/1/2013	4	12/31/2013	$ 33,200.00	$0	FALSE	12.07%
Hemsley	3	4/1/2013	5	10/1/2013	$ 25,500.00	$1,275	FALSE	9.27%
Kim	10	3/1/2013	5	8/31/2013	$ 37,500.00	$1,875	TRUE	13.63%
Maaley	7	5/1/2013	5	10/31/2013	$ 36,500.00	$1,825	TRUE	13.27%
Merry	10	6/1/2013	4	12/1/2013	$ 37,500.00	$0	FALSE	13.63%
Smith	7	1/1/2013	3	7/3/2013	$ 28,600.00	$0	FALSE	10.40%
Storey	3	7/1/2013	5	12/31/2013	$ 29,700.00	$1,485	FALSE	10.80%
Totals					$ 275,040.00	$7,795		

FIGURE E-26

Accounting Department
Merit Pay

Last Name	Professional Development Hours	Review Date	Rating	Next Review	Salary	Bonus	Hours Required	Enroll in Quality Class
Allenson	8	3/10/2013	2	9/9/2013	$ 21,647.00	$0.00	FALSE	TRUE
Greeley	2	5/1/2013	5	10/31/2013	$ 28,600.00	$1,430.00	TRUE	TRUE
LaFonte	6	8/1/2013	3	1/31/2014	$ 33,200.00	$0.00	FALSE	TRUE
Henley	7	6/1/2013	4	12/1/2013	$ 35,500.00	$0.00	FALSE	TRUE
Gosselin	9	3/8/2013	5	9/7/2013	$ 39,500.00	$1,975.00	FALSE	FALSE
Ramerez	6	5/1/2013	5	10/31/2013	$ 36,500.00	$1,825.00	FALSE	FALSE
Marton	10	6/1/2013	4	12/1/2013	$ 36,500.00	$0.00	FALSE	TRUE
Suille	6	1/1/2013	5	7/3/2013	$ 29,600.00	$1,480.00	FALSE	FALSE
Zen	6	9/15/2013	1	3/17/2014	$ 29,700.00	$0.00	FALSE	TRUE
Totals					$ 290,747.00	$6,710.00		

FIGURE E-27

Human Resources
Loan Quote for Infor

Loan Amount	$ 169,000.00
Interest Rate	8.25%
Term in Months	36
Monthly Payment:	$5,315.36
Total Payments:	$ 191,352.89
Total Interest:	$ 22,352.89

Skills Review (continued)

e. Enter your name in the worksheet footer, save the workbook, then submit your workbook to your instructor.
f. Close the workbook, then exit Excel.

Independent Challenge 1

As the accounting manager of World Travel, a travel insurance company, you are reviewing the accounts payable information for your advertising accounts and prioritizing the overdue invoices for your collections service. You will analyze the invoices and use logical functions to emphasize priority accounts.

a. Start Excel, open the file EX E-4.xlsx from the drive and folder where you store your Data Files, then save it as **EX E-Accounts**.
b. Name the range B7:B13 **invoice_date**, and give the name a scope of the accounts payable worksheet.
c. Name the cell B4 **current_date**, and give the name a scope of the accounts payable worksheet.
d. Enter a formula using the named range invoice_date in cell E7 that calculates the invoice due date by adding 30 to the invoice date.
e. Copy the formula in cell E7 to the range E8:E13.
f. In cell F7, enter a formula using the named range invoice_date and the named cell current_date that calculates the invoice age by subtracting the invoice date from the current date.
g. Copy the formula in cell F7 to the range F8:F13.
h. In cell G7, enter an IF function that calculates the number of days an invoice is overdue, assuming that an invoice must be paid in 30 days. (*Hint*: The Logical_test should check to see if the age of the invoice is greater than 30, the Value_if_true should calculate the current date minus the invoice due date, and the Value_if_false should be 0.) Copy the IF function into the range G8:G13.
i. In cell H7, enter an AND function to prioritize the overdue invoices that are more than $1,000 for collection services. (*Hint*: The Logical1 condition should check to see if the number of days overdue is more than 0, and the Logical2 condition should check if the amount is more than 1,000.) Copy the AND function into the range H8:H13.
j. Enter your name in the worksheet footer, save the workbook, preview the worksheet, then submit the workbook to your instructor.

Advanced Challenge Exercise

- Use the "Refers to:" text box in the Name Manager dialog box to verify that the names in the worksheet refer to the correct ranges.
- Use the Filter button in the Name Manager dialog box to verify that your names are scoped to the worksheet and not the workbook.
- Use the Filter button in the Name Manager dialog box to verify that your names are defined, free of errors, and not part of a table. If necessary, clear the Filter.

k. Close the workbook, then exit Excel.

Independent Challenge 2

You are an auditor with a certified public accounting firm. The Green Home, an online seller of environmentally friendly home products, has contacted you to audit its first-quarter sales records. The management is considering expanding and needs its sales records audited to prepare the business plan. Specifically, they want to show what percent of annual sales each category represents. You will use a formula on a summary worksheet to summarize the sales for January, February, and March and to calculate the overall first-quarter percentage of the sales categories.

a. Start Excel, open the file EX E-5.xlsx from the drive and folder where you store your Data Files, then save it as **EX E-Products**.
b. In cell B10 of the Jan, Feb, and Mar sheets, enter the formulas to calculate the sales totals for the month.

Independent Challenge 2 (continued)

c. For each month, in cell C5, create a formula calculating the percent of sales for the Compost Bins sales category. Use a function to display "INCORRECT" if there is a mistake in the formula. Verify that the percent appears with two decimal places. Copy this formula as necessary to complete the % of sales for all sales categories on all sheets. If any cells display "INCORRECT", fix the formulas in those cells.

d. In column B of the Summary sheet, use formulas to total the sales categories for the Jan, Feb, and Mar worksheets.

e. Enter the formula to calculate the first quarter sales total in cell B10 using the sales totals on the Jan, Feb, and Mar worksheets. Calculate the percent of each sales category on the Summary sheet. Use a function to display **MISCALCULATION** if there is a mistake in the formula. Copy this formula as necessary. If any cells display **MISCALCULATION,** fix the formulas in those cells.

f. Enter your name in the Summary worksheet footer, save the workbook, preview the worksheet, then submit it to your instructor.

g. On the Products sheet, separate the product list in cell A1 into separate columns of text data. (*Hint*: The products are delimited with commas.) Widen the columns as necessary. Use the second row to display the products with the first letter of each word in uppercase, as shown in Figure E-28.

FIGURE E-28

	A	B	C	D	E
1	compost bins	green furniture	green bags	solar education materials	natural hot tubs
2	Compost Bins	Green Furniture	Green Bags	Solar Education Materials	Natural Hot Tubs
3					

h. Enter your name in the Products worksheet footer, save the workbook, preview the worksheet, then submit the workbook to your instructor.

Advanced Challenge Exercise

- Add a new sheet to the workbook and name it **Equations**.
- Use the built-in equations to enter the Pythagorean theorem in a text box on the worksheet. (*Hint*: Click the Equation list arrow in the Tools group of the Equation Tools Design tab and click Pythagorean Theorem. Also, see the Clues to Use "Inserting an equation into a worksheet" for more information about adding equations.)
- In a new text box, build the Pythagorean theorem using the mathematical symbols below the built-in equation. (*Hint*: To insert a^2 into a text box, click the Script list arrow in the Structures group of the Equation Tools Design tab, click the first option, click in the lower-left box and enter **a**, press [Tab], enter **2** in the upper-right box, then click to the right of the boxes to exit the symbol.)
- Enter your name in the Equations worksheet footer, save the workbook, preview the worksheet, then submit the workbook to your instructor.

i. Close the workbook, then exit Excel.

Independent Challenge 3

As the owner of Digital Designs, a Web and graphic design firm, you are planning to expand your business. Because you will have to purchase additional equipment and hire a new part-time designer, you decide to take out a $50,000 loan to finance your expansion expenses. You check three loan sources: the Small Business Administration (SBA), your local bank, and a consortium of investors. The SBA will lend you the money at 6.5% interest, but you have to pay it off in 3 years. The local bank offers you the loan at 7.75% interest over 4 years. The consortium offers you an 8% loan, but they require you to pay it back in 2 years. To analyze all three loan options, you decide to build a loan summary worksheet. Using the loan terms provided, build a worksheet summarizing your options.

a. Start Excel, open a new workbook, save it as **EX E-Loan**, then rename Sheet1 **Loan Summary**.

b. Using Figure E-29 as a guide, enter labels and worksheet data for the three loan sources in columns A through D. (*Hint*: The worksheet in the figure uses the

FIGURE E-29

1	Digital Designs						
2	Loan Options						
3							
4	Loan Source	Loan Amount	Interest Rate	# Payments	Monthly Payment	Total Payments	Total Interest
5	SBA	$ 50,000.00	6.50%	36	$ 1,532.45	$ 55,168.21	$ 5,168.21
6	Bank	$ 50,000.00	7.75%	48	$ 1,214.79	$ 58,309.78	$ 8,309.78
7	Investors	$ 50,000.00	8.00%	24	$ 2,261.36	$ 54,272.75	$ 4,272.75
8							

Your formulas go here

Independent Challenge 3 (continued)

Median theme with Orange, Accent 2, Lighter 60%, as the fill color in the first two rows. Rows 1, 2 and 4 are bolded. The labels in column A are also bolded. The worksheet text color is orange, Accent 2, Darker 50%.)

c. Enter the monthly payment formula for your first loan source (making sure to show the payment as a positive amount), copy the formula as appropriate, then name the range containing the monthly payment formulas **Monthly_Payment** with a scope of the workbook.

d. Name the cell range containing the number of payments **Number_Payments** with the scope of the workbook.

e. Enter the formula for total payments for your first loan source using the named ranges Monthly_Payment and Number_Payments, then copy the formula as necessary.

f. Name the cell range containing the formulas for Total payments **Total_Payments**. Name the cell range containing the loan amounts **Loan_Amount**. Each name should have the workbook as its scope.

g. Enter the formula for total interest for your first loan source using the named ranges Total_Payments and Loan_Amount, then copy the formula as necessary.

h. Format the worksheet using appropriate formatting, then enter your name in the worksheet footer.

i. Save the workbook, preview the worksheet and change it to landscape orientation on a single page, then submit the workbook to your instructor.

Advanced Challenge Exercise

- Turn on the print gridlines option for the sheet, then turn on printing of row and column headings.
- Display the worksheet formulas, save the workbook and submit it to your instructor.

j. Close the workbook then exit Excel.

Excel 2010

Real Life Independent Challenge

You decide to create a weekly log of your daily aerobic exercise. As part of this log, you record your aerobic activity along with the number of minutes spent working out. If you do more than one activity in a day, for example, if you bike and walk, record each as a separate event. Along with each activity, you record the location where you exercise. For example, you may walk in the gym or outdoors. You will use the log to analyze the amount of time that you spend on each type of exercise.

a. Start Excel, open the file EX E-6.xlsx from the drive and folder where you store your Data Files, then save it as **EX E-Workout**.

b. Use the structure of the worksheet to record your aerobic exercise activities. Change the data in columns A, B, C, D, and F to reflect your activities, locations, and times. If you do not have any data to enter, use the provided worksheet data.

c. Use a SUMIF function in the column G cells to calculate the total minutes spent on each activity.

d. Enter an AVERAGEIF function in the column H cells to average the number of minutes spent on each activity.

e. Enter a COUNTIF function in the column I cells to calculate the number of times each activity was performed. (*Hint*: The Range of cells to count is $B$2:$B$12 and the criteria is in cell F3.)

f. Format the Average Minutes column as number with two decimal places.

Advanced Challenge Exercise

- Enter one of your activities with a specific location, such as Walk Outdoors, in a column F cell, then enter the SUMIFS function in the adjacent column G cell that calculates the total number of minutes spent on that activity in the specific location.
- Enter the AVERAGEIFS function in the corresponding column H cell that calculates the average number of minutes spent on the activity in the specified location.
- Enter the COUNTIFS function in the corresponding column I cell that calculates the number of days spent on the activity in the specific location.

g. Enter your name in the worksheet footer, save the workbook, preview the worksheet, then submit it to your instructor.

h. Close the workbook, then exit Excel.

Visual Workshop

Open the file EX E-7.xlsx from the drive and folder where you store your Data Files, then save it as **EX E-Summary**. Create the worksheet shown in Figure E-30 using the data in columns B, C, and D along with the following criteria:

- The employee is eligible for a bonus if:
  - The employee has a performance rating of seven or higher.

  AND

  - The employee has sales that exceed the sales quota.
- If the employee is eligible for a bonus, the bonus amount is calculated as one percent of the sales amount. Otherwise the bonus amount is 0.

Enter your name in the worksheet footer, save the workbook, preview the worksheet, then submit the worksheet to your instructor.

(*Hint*: Use an AND formula to determine if a person is eligible for a bonus, and use an IF formula to check eligibility and to enter the bonus amount.)

FIGURE E-30

	A	B	C	D	E	F
1	Bonus Pay Summary					
2						
3	Last Name	Quota	Sales	Performance Rating	Eligible	Bonus Amount
4	Andrews	$175,000	$182,557	7	TRUE	$1,826
5	Green	$95,774	$94,223	3	FALSE	$0
6	Grey	$102,663	$99,887	9	FALSE	$0
7	Hanley	$145,335	$151,887	5	FALSE	$0
8	Kelly	$145,000	$151,228	8	TRUE	$1,512
9	Medway	$130,000	$152,774	5	FALSE	$0
10	Merkel	$152,885	$160,224	7	TRUE	$1,602
11	Star	$98,000	$87,224	3	FALSE	$0
12	Sealey	$90,000	$86,700	9	FALSE	$0

Working with Windows Live and Office Web Apps

Files You Will Need:
WEB-1.pptx
WEB-2.xlsx

If the computer you are using has an active Internet connection, you can go to the Microsoft Windows Live Web site and access a wide variety of services and Web applications. For example, you can check your e-mail through Windows Live, network with your friends and coworkers, and use SkyDrive to store and share files. From SkyDrive, you can also use Office Web Apps to create and edit Word, PowerPoint, Excel, and OneNote files, even when you are using a computer that does not have Office 2010 installed. You work in the Vancouver branch of Quest Specialty Travel. Your supervisor, Mary Lou Jacobs, asks you to explore Windows Live and learn how she can use SkyDrive and Office Web Apps to work with her files online.

(*Note*: SkyDrive and Office Web Apps are dynamic Web pages, and might change over time, including the way they are organized and how commands are performed. The steps and figures in this appendix were accurate at the time this book was published.)

OBJECTIVES

- Explore how to work online from Windows Live
- Obtain a Windows Live ID and sign in to Windows Live
- Upload files to Windows Live
- Work with the PowerPoint Web App
- Create folders and organize files on SkyDrive
- Add people to your network and share files
- Work with the Excel Web App

Appendix
Web Apps
Office 2010

Exploring How to Work Online from Windows Live

You can use your Web browser to upload your files to Windows Live from any computer connected to the Internet. You can work on the files right in your Web browser using Office Web Apps and share your files with people in your Windows Live network. You review the concepts and services related to working online from Windows Live.

DETAILS

- **What is Windows Live?**
  Windows Live is a collection of services and Web applications that you can use to help you be more productive both personally and professionally. For example, you can use Windows Live to send and receive e-mail, to chat with friends via instant messaging, to share photos, to create a blog, and to store and edit files using SkyDrive. Table WEB-1 describes the services available on Windows Live. Windows Live is a free service that you sign up for. When you sign up, you receive a Windows Live ID, which you use to sign in to Windows Live. When you work with files on Windows Live, you are cloud computing.

- **What is Cloud Computing?**
  The term **cloud computing** refers to the process of working with files online in a Web browser. When you save files to SkyDrive on Windows Live, you are saving your files to an online location. SkyDrive is like having a personal hard drive in the cloud.

- **What is SkyDrive?**
  SkyDrive is an online storage and file sharing service. With a Windows Live account, you receive access to your own SkyDrive, which is your personal storage area on the Internet. On your SkyDrive, you are given space to store up to 25 GB of data online. Each file can be a maximum size of 50 MB. You can also use SkyDrive to access Office Web Apps, which you use to create and edit files created in Word, OneNote, PowerPoint, and Excel online in your Web browser.

- **Why use Windows Live and SkyDrive?**
  On Windows Live, you use SkyDrive to access additional storage for your files. You don't have to worry about backing up your files to a memory stick or other storage device that could be lost or damaged. Another advantage of storing your files on SkyDrive is that you can access your files from any computer that has an active Internet connection. Figure WEB-1 shows the SkyDrive Web page that appears when accessed from a Windows Live account. From SkyDrive, you can also access Office Web Apps.

- **What are Office Web Apps?**
  Office Web Apps are versions of Microsoft Word, Excel, PowerPoint, and OneNote that you can access online from your SkyDrive. An Office Web App does not include all of the features and functions included with the full Office version of its associated application. However, you can use the Office Web App from any computer that is connected to the Internet, even if Microsoft Office 2010 is not installed on that computer.

- **How do SkyDrive and Office Web Apps work together?**
  You can create a file in Office 2010 using Word, Excel, PowerPoint, or OneNote and then upload the file to your SkyDrive. You can then open the Office file saved to SkyDrive and edit it using your Web browser and the corresponding Office Web App. Figure WEB-2 shows a PowerPoint presentation open in the PowerPoint Web App. You can also use an Office Web App to create a new file, which is saved automatically to SkyDrive while you work. In addition, you can download a file created with an Office Web App and continue to work with the file in the full version of the corresponding Office application: Word, Excel, PowerPoint, or OneNote. Finally, you can create a SkyDrive network that consists of the people you want to be able to view your folders and files on your SkyDrive. You can give people permission to view and edit your files using any computer with an active Internet connection and a Web browser.

FIGURE WEB-1: SkyDrive on Windows Live

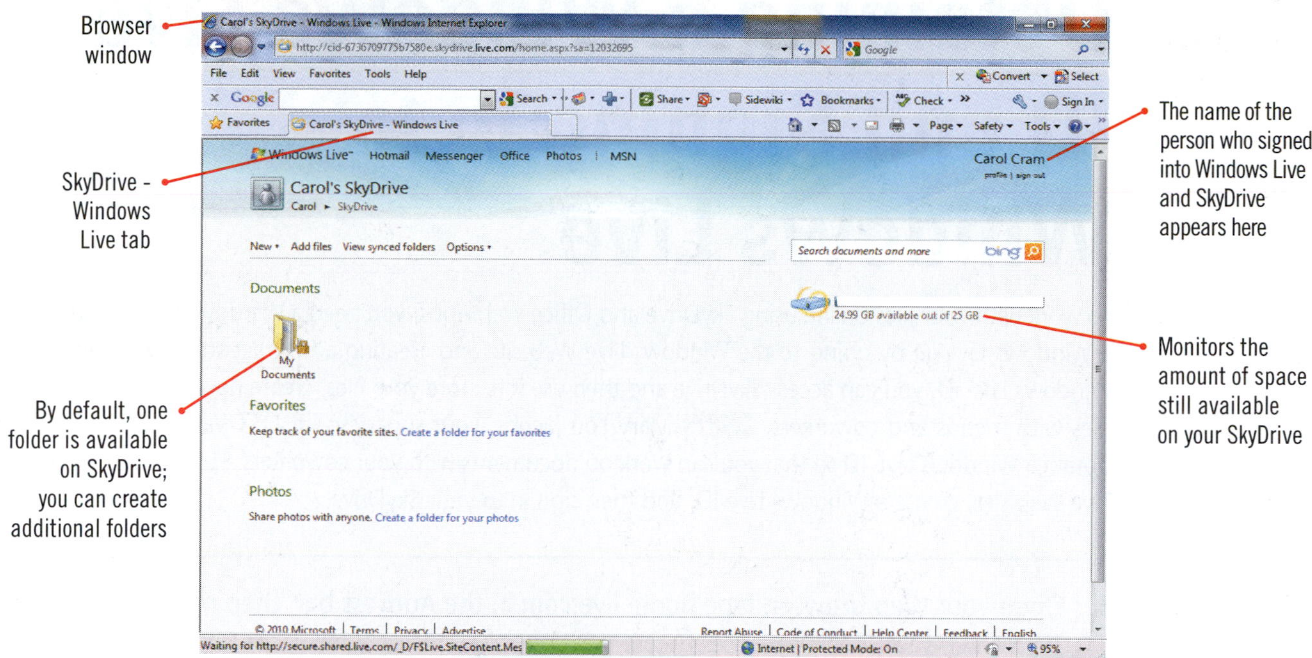
Browser window
SkyDrive - Windows Live tab
By default, one folder is available on SkyDrive; you can create additional folders
The name of the person who signed into Windows Live and SkyDrive appears here
Monitors the amount of space still available on your SkyDrive
Carol's SkyDrive
Documents
Favorites
Photos
24.99 GB available out of 25 GB

FIGURE WEB-2: PowerPoint presentation open in the PowerPoint Web App

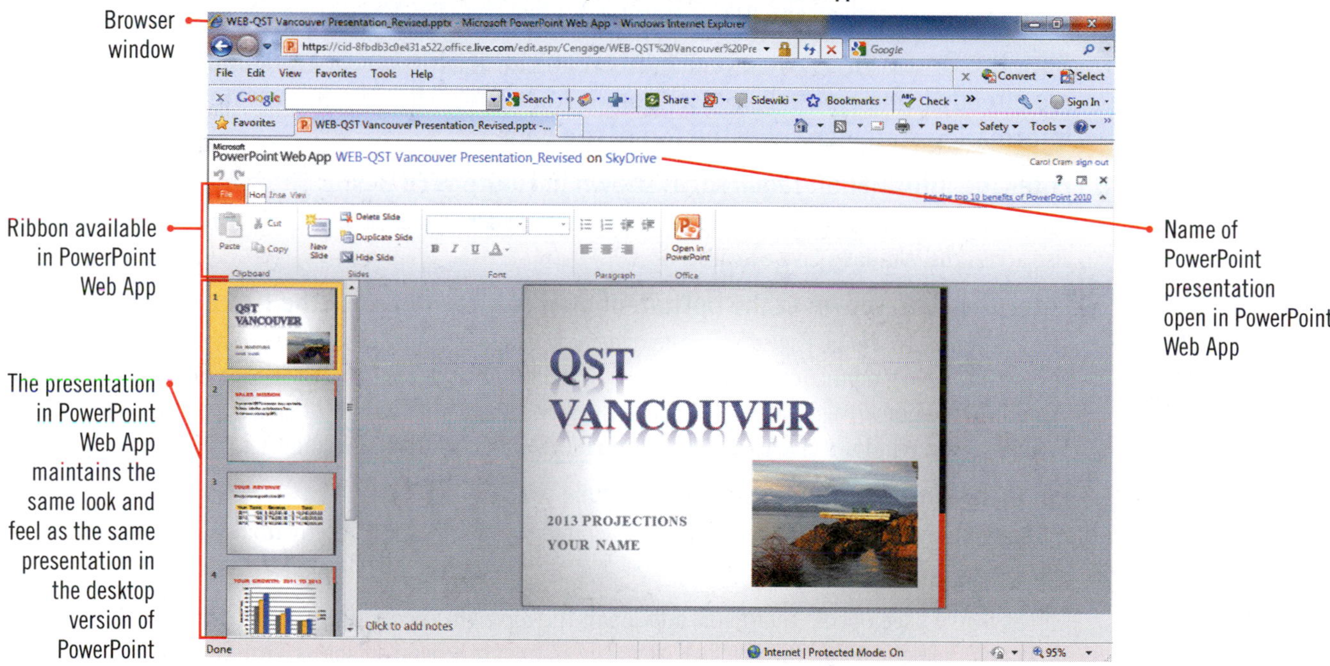
Browser window
Ribbon available in PowerPoint Web App
The presentation in PowerPoint Web App maintains the same look and feel as the same presentation in the desktop version of PowerPoint
Name of PowerPoint presentation open in PowerPoint Web App
PowerPoint Web App WEB-QST Vancouver Presentation_Revised on SkyDrive
QST VANCOUVER
2013 PROJECTIONS
YOUR NAME
Click to add notes

TABLE WEB-1: Services available via Windows Live

service	description
E-mail	Send and receive e-mail using a Hotmail account
Instant Messaging	Use Messenger to chat with friends, share photos, and play games
SkyDrive	Store files, work on files using Office Web Apps, and share files with people in your network
Photos	Upload and share photos with friends
People	Develop a network of friends and coworkers, then use the network to distribute information and stay in touch
Downloads	Access a variety of free programs available for download to a PC
Mobile Device	Access applications for a mobile device: text messaging, using Hotmail, networking, and sharing photos

Appendix
Web Apps
Office 2010

Obtaining a Windows Live ID and Signing In to Windows Live

To work with your files online using SkyDrive and Office Web Apps, you need a Windows Live ID. You obtain a Windows Live ID by going to the Windows Live Web site and creating a new account. Once you have a Windows Live ID, you can access SkyDrive and then use it to store your files, create new files, and share your files with friends and coworkers. Mary Lou Jacobs, your supervisor at QST Vancouver, asks you to obtain a Windows Live ID so that you can work on documents with your coworkers. You go to the Windows Live Web site, create a Windows Live ID, and then sign in to your SkyDrive.

STEPS

QUICK TIP
If you already have a Windows Live ID, go to the next lesson and sign in as directed using your account.

1. **Open your Web browser, type home.live.com in the Address bar, then press [Enter]**
   The Windows Live home page opens. From this page, you can create a Windows Live account and receive your Windows Live ID.
2. **Click the Sign up button** ***(Note: You may see a Sign up link instead of a button)***
   The Create your Windows Live ID page opens.
3. **Click the Or use your own e-mail address link under the Check availability button or if you are already using Hotmail, Messenger, or Xbox LIVE, click the Sign in now link in the Information statement near the top of the page**
4. **Enter the information required, as shown in Figure WEB-3**
   If you wish, you can sign up for a Windows Live e-mail address such as yourname@live.com so that you can also access the Windows Live e-mail services.

TROUBLE
The code can be difficult to read. If you receive an error message, enter the new code that appears.

5. **Enter the code shown at the bottom of your screen, then click the I accept button**
   The Windows Live home page opens. The name you entered when you signed up for your Windows Live ID appears in the top right corner of the window to indicate that you are signed in to Windows Live. From the Windows Live home page, you can access all the services and applications offered by Windows Live. See the Verifying your Windows Live ID box for information on finalizing your account set up.
6. **Point to Windows Live, as shown in Figure WEB-4**
   A list of options appears. SkyDrive is one of the options you can access directly from Windows Live.

TROUBLE
Click I accept if you are asked to review and accept the Windows Live Service Agreement and Privacy Statement.

7. **Click SkyDrive**
   The SkyDrive page opens. Your name appears in the top right corner, and the amount of space available is shown on the right side of the SkyDrive page. The amount of space available is monitored, as indicated by the gauge that fills with color as space is used. Using SkyDrive, you can add files to the existing folder and you can create new folders.
8. **Click sign out in the top right corner under your name, then exit the Web browser**
   You are signed out of your Windows Live account. You can sign in again directly from the Windows Live page in your browser or from within a file created with PowerPoint, Excel, Word, or OneNote.

FIGURE WEB-3: Creating a Windows Live ID

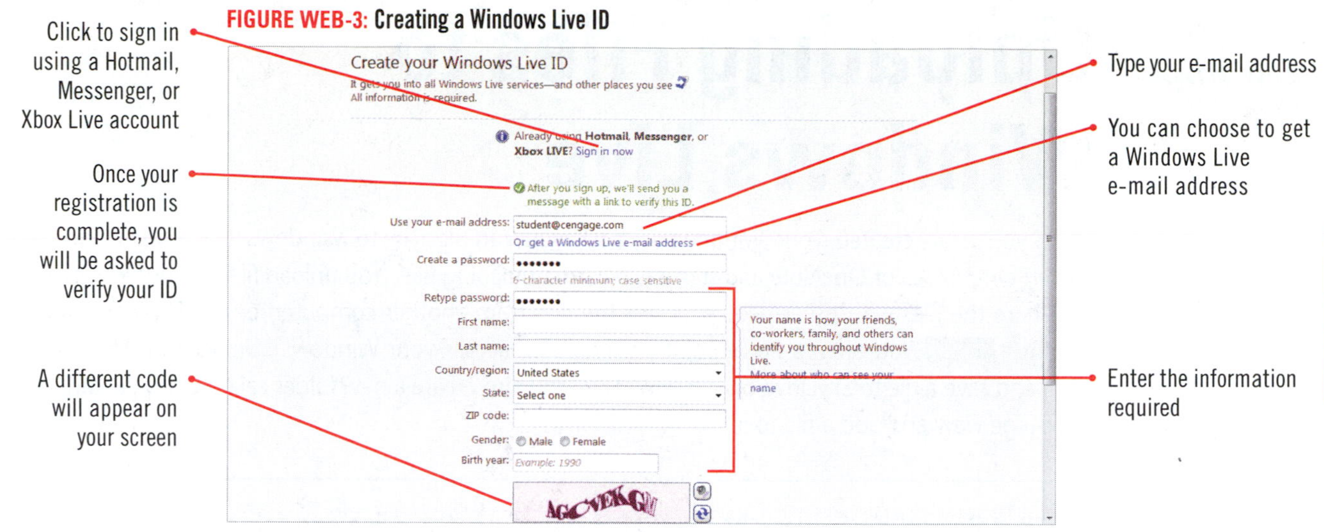

FIGURE WEB-4: Selecting SkyDrive

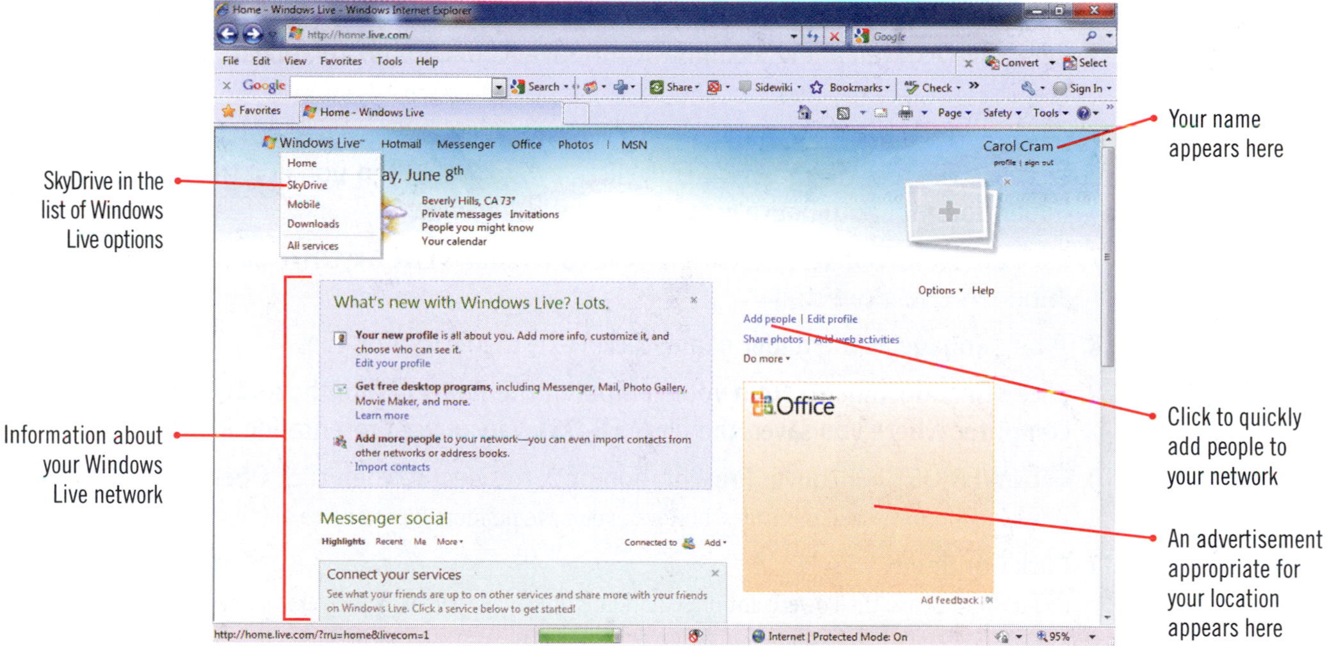

Verifying your Windows Live ID

As soon as you accept the Windows Live terms, an e-mail is sent to the e-mail address you supplied when you created your Windows Live ID. Open your e-mail program, and then open the e-mail from Microsoft with the Subject line: Confirm your e-mail address for Windows Live. Follow the simple, step-by-step instructions in the e-mail to confirm your Windows Live ID. When the confirmation is complete, you will be asked to sign in to Windows Live, using your e-mail address and password. Once signed in, you will see your Windows Live Account page.

Uploading Files to Windows Live

Once you have created your Windows Live ID, you can sign in to Windows Live directly from Word, PowerPoint, Excel, or OneNote and start saving and uploading files. You upload files to your SkyDrive so you can share the files with other people, access the files from another computer, or use SkyDrive's additional storage. You open a PowerPoint presentation, access your Windows Live account from Backstage view, and save a file to SkyDrive on Windows Live. You also create a new folder called Cengage directly from Backstage view and add a file to it.

STEPS

1. **Start PowerPoint, open the file WEB-1.pptx from the drive and folder where you store your Data Files, then save the file as WEB-QST Vancouver Presentation**
2. **Click the File tab, then click Save & Send**
   The Save & Send options available in PowerPoint are listed in Backstage view, as shown in Figure WEB-5.
3. **Click Save to Web**
4. **Click Sign In, type your e-mail address, press [Tab], type your password, then click OK**
   The My Documents folder on your SkyDrive appears in the Save to Windows Live SkyDrive information area.

   QUICK TIP
   Skip this step if the computer you are using signs you in automatically.
5. **Click Save As, wait a few seconds for the Save As dialog box to appear, then click Save**
   The file is saved to the My Documents folder on the SkyDrive that is associated with your Windows Live account. You can also create a new folder and upload files directly to SkyDrive from your hard drive.
6. **Click the File tab, click Save & Send, click Save to Web, then sign in if the My Documents folder does not automatically appear in Backstage view**
7. **Click the New Folder button in the Save to Windows Live SkyDrive pane, then sign in to Windows Live if directed**
8. **Type Cengage as the folder name, click Next, then click Add files**
9. **Click select documents from your computer, then navigate to the location on your computer where you saved the file WEB-QST Vancouver Presentation in Step 1**
10. **Click WEB-QST Vancouver Presentation.pptx to select it, then click Open**
    You can continue to add more files; however, you have no more files to upload at this time.
11. **Click Continue**
    In a few moments, the PowerPoint presentation is uploaded to your SkyDrive, as shown in Figure WEB-6. You can simply store the file on SkyDrive or you can choose to work on the presentation using the PowerPoint Web App.
12. **Click the PowerPoint icon on your taskbar to return to PowerPoint, then close the presentation and exit PowerPoint**

FIGURE WEB-5: Save & Send options in Backstage view

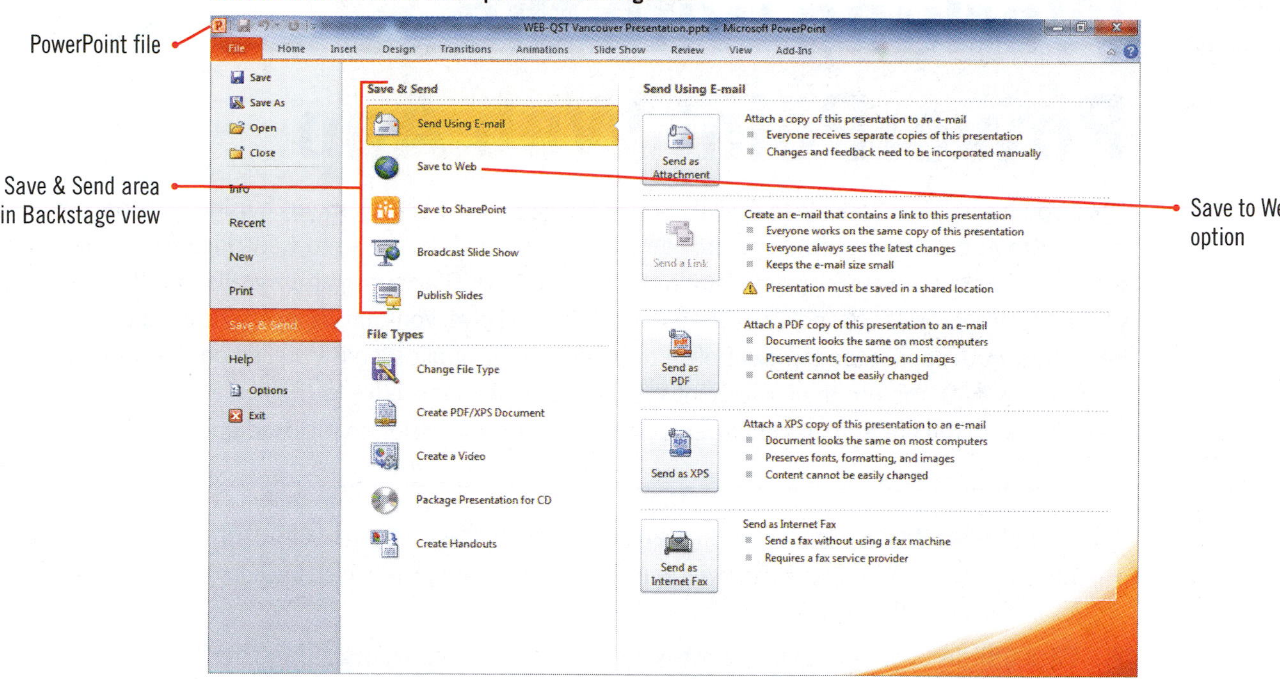

FIGURE WEB-6: File uploaded to the Cengage folder on Windows Live

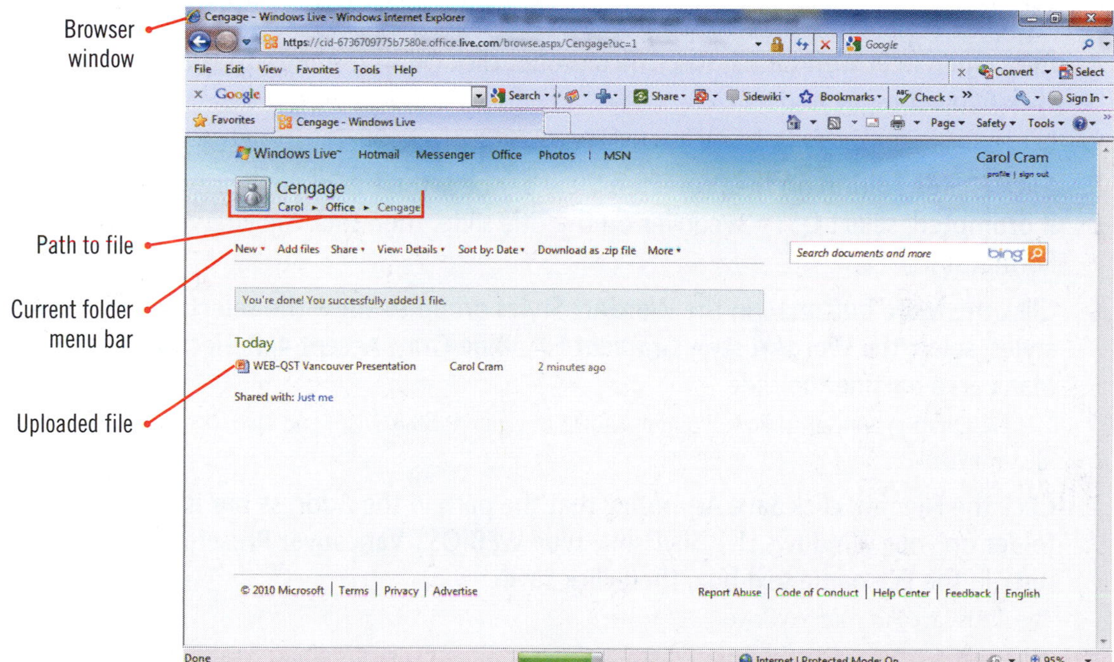

Web Apps

Working with the PowerPoint Web App

Once you have uploaded a file to SkyDrive on Windows Live, you can work on it using its corresponding Office Web App. **Office Web Apps** provide you with the tools you need to view documents online and to edit them right in your browser. You do not need to have Office programs installed on the computer you use to access SkyDrive and Office Web Apps. From SkyDrive, you can also open the document directly in the full Office application (for example, PowerPoint) if the application is installed on the computer you are using. You use the PowerPoint Web App to make some edits to the PowerPoint presentation. You then open the presentation in PowerPoint and use the full version to make additional edits.

STEPS

TROUBLE
Click the browser button on the taskbar, then click the Windows Live SkyDrive window to make it the active window.

1. **Click the WEB-QST Vancouver Presentation file in the Cengage folder on SkyDrive**
   The presentation opens in your browser window. A menu is available, which includes the options you have for working with the file.
2. **Click Edit in Browser, then if a message appears related to installing the Sign-in Assistant, click the Close button to the far right of the message**
   In a few moments, the PowerPoint presentation opens in the PowerPoint Web App, as shown in Figure WEB-7. Table WEB-2 lists the commands you can perform using the PowerPoint Web App.

QUICK TIP
The changes you make to the presentation are saved automatically on SkyDrive.

3. **Enter your name where indicated on Slide 1, click Slide 3 (New Tours) in the Slides pane, then click Delete Slide in the Slides group**
   The slide is removed from the presentation. You decide to open the file in the full version of PowerPoint on your computer so you can apply WordArt to the slide title. You work with the file in the full version of PowerPoint when you want to use functions, such as WordArt, that are not available on the PowerPoint Web App.
4. **Click Open in PowerPoint in the Office group, click OK in response to the message, then click Allow if requested**
   In a few moments, the revised version of the PowerPoint slide opens in PowerPoint on your computer.
5. **Click Enable Editing on the Protected View bar near the top of your presentation window if prompted, select QST Vancouver on the title slide, then click the Drawing Tools Format tab**

QUICK TIP
Use the ScreenTips to help you find the required WordArt style.

6. **Click the More button in the WordArt Styles group to show the selection of WordArt styles, select the WordArt style Gradient Fill - Blue-Gray, Accent 4, Reflection, then click a blank area outside the slide**
   The presentation appears in PowerPoint as shown in Figure WEB-8. Next, you save the revised version of the file to SkyDrive.
7. **Click the File tab, click Save As, notice that the path in the Address bar is to the Cengage folder on your Windows Live SkyDrive, type WEB-QST Vancouver Presentation_Revised.pptx in the File name text box, then click Save**
   The file is saved to your SkyDrive.

TROUBLE
The browser opens to the Cengage folder but the file is not visible. Follow Step 8 to open the Cengage folder and refresh thelist of files in the folder.

8. **Click the browser icon on the taskbar to open your SkyDrive page, then click Office next to your name in the SkyDrive path, view a list of recent documents, then click Cengage in the list to the left of the recent documents list to open the Cengage folder**
   Two PowerPoint files now appear in the Cengage folder.
9. **Exit the Web browser and close all tabs if prompted, then exit PowerPoint**

FIGURE WEB-7: Presentation opened in the PowerPoint Web App from Windows Live

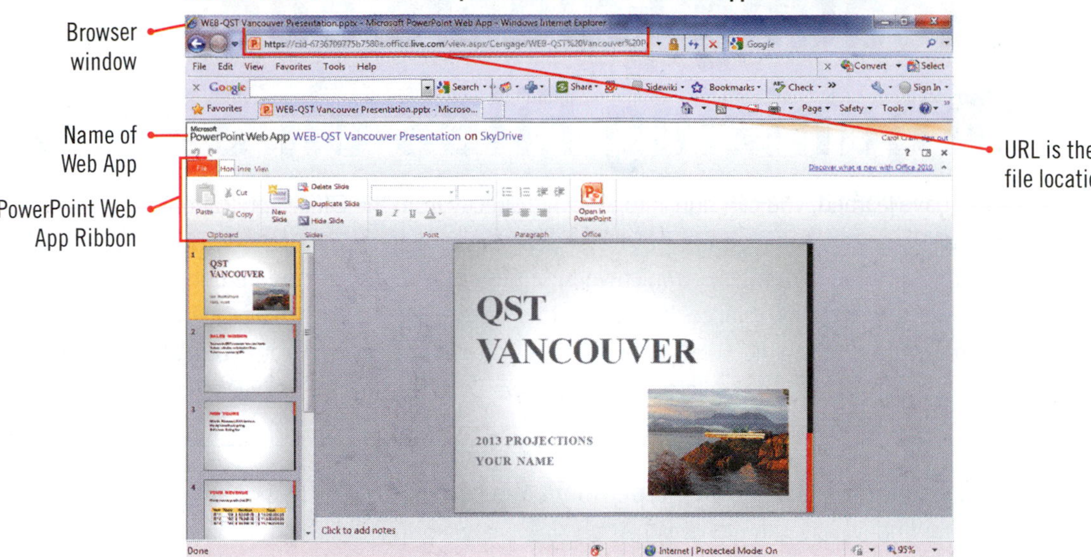

FIGURE WEB-8: Revised PowerPoint presentation

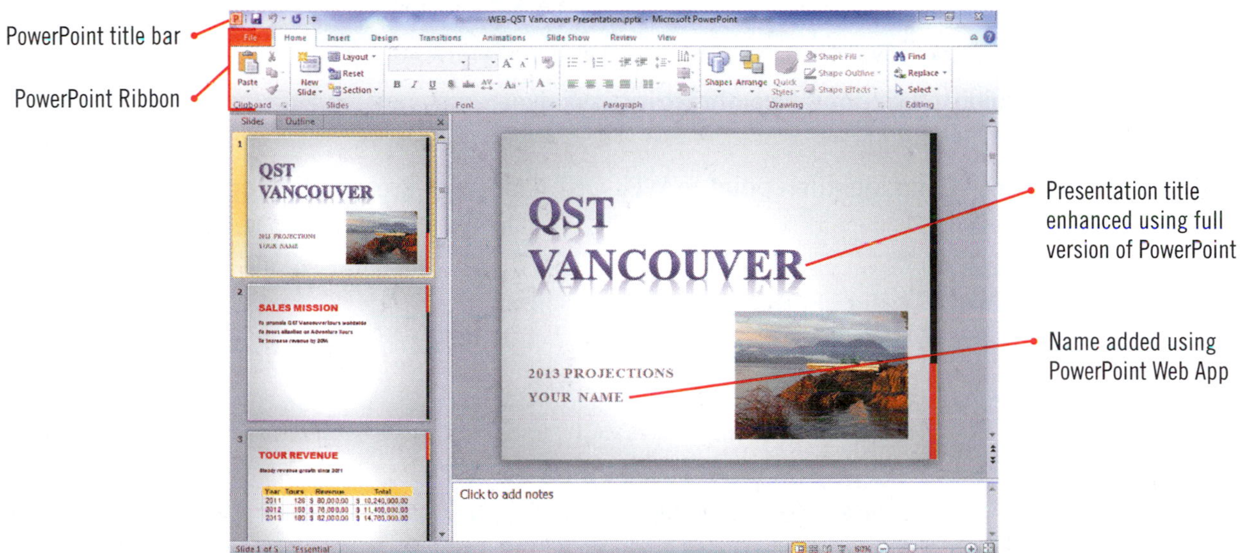

TABLE WEB-2: Commands on the PowerPoint Web App

tab	commands available
File	• Open in PowerPoint: select to open the file in PowerPoint on your computer • Where's the Save Button?: when you click this option, a message appears telling you that you do not need to save your presentation when you are working on it with PowerPoint Web App. The presentation is saved automatically as you work. • Print • Share • Properties • Give Feedback • Privacy • Terms of Use • Close
Home	• Clipboard group: Cut, Copy, Paste • Slides group: Add a New Slide, Delete a Slide, Duplicate a Slide, and Hide a Slide • Font group: Work with text: change the font, style, color, and size of selected text • Paragraph group: Work with paragraphs: add bullets and numbers, indent text, align text • Office group: Open the file in PowerPoint on your computer
Insert	• Insert a Picture • Insert a SmartArt diagram • Insert a link such as a link to another file on SkyDrive or to a Web page
View	• Editing view (the default) • Reading view • Slide Show view • Notes view

Creating Folders and Organizing Files on SkyDrive

As you have learned, you can sign in to SkyDrive directly from the Office applications PowerPoint, Excel, Word, and OneNote, or you can access SkyDrive directly through your Web browser. This option is useful when you are away from the computer on which you normally work or when you are using a computer that does not have Office applications installed. You can go to SkyDrive, create and organize folders, and then create or open files to work on with Office Web Apps. You access SkyDrive from your Web browser, create a new folder called Illustrated, and delete one of the PowerPoint files from the My Documents folder.

STEPS

TROUBLE
Go to Step 3 if you are already signed in.

TROUBLE
Type your Windows Live ID (your e-mail) and password, then click Sign in if prompted to do so.

1. **Open your Web browser, type home.live.com in the Address bar, then press [Enter]**
   The Windows Live home page opens. From here, you can sign in to your Windows Live account and then access SkyDrive.
2. **Sign into Windows Live as directed**
   You are signed in to your Windows Live page. From this page, you can take advantage of the many applications available on Windows Live, including SkyDrive.
3. **Point to Windows Live, then click SkyDrive**
   SkyDrive opens.
4. **Click Cengage, then point to WEB-QST Vancouver Presentation.pptx**
   A menu of options for working with the file, including a Delete button to the far right, appears to the right of the filename.
5. **Click the Delete button, then click OK**
   The file is removed from the Cengage folder on your SkyDrive. You still have a copy of the file on your computer.
6. **Point to Windows Live, then click SkyDrive**
   Your SkyDrive screen with the current selection of folders available on your SkyDrive opens, as shown in Figure WEB-9.
7. **Click New, click Folder, type Illustrated, click Next, click Office in the path under Add documents to Illustrated at the top of the window, then click View all in the list under Personal**
   You are returned to your list of folders, where you see the new Illustrated folder.
8. **Click Cengage, point to WEB-QST Vancouver Presentation_Revised.pptx, click More, click Move, then click the Illustrated folder**
9. **Click Move this file into Illustrated, as shown in Figure WEB-10**
   The file is moved to the Illustrated folder.

FIGURE WEB-9: Folders on your SkyDrive

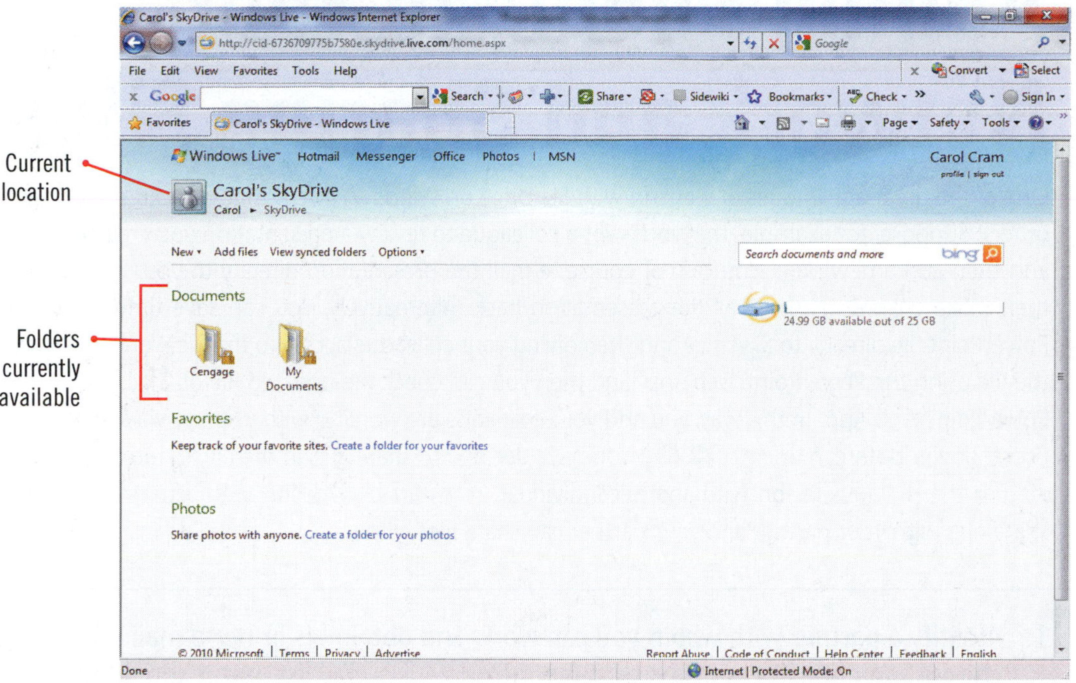
Current location
Folders currently available

FIGURE WEB-10: Moving a file to the Illustrated folder

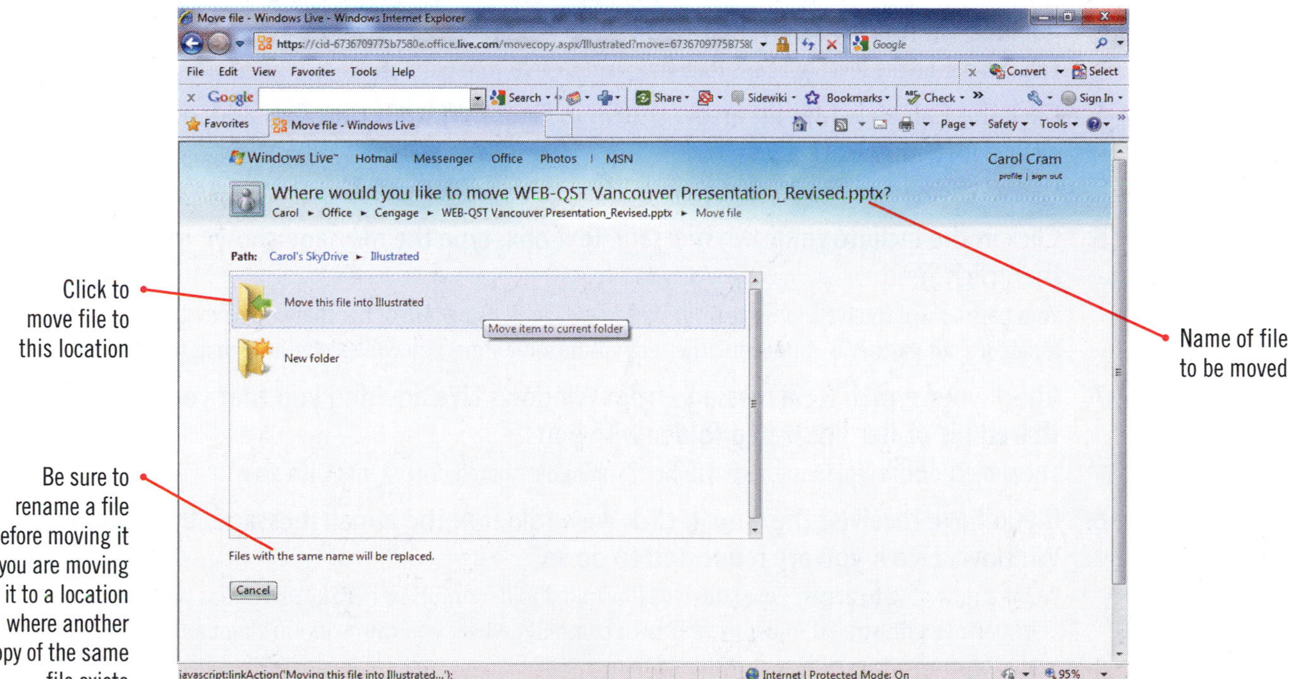
Click to move file to this location
Be sure to rename a file before moving it if you are moving it to a location where another copy of the same file exists
Name of file to be moved

Adding People to Your Network and Sharing Files

One of the great advantages of working with SkyDrive on Windows Live is that you can share your files with others. Suppose, for example, that you want a colleague to review a presentation you created in PowerPoint and then add a new slide. You can, of course, e-mail the presentation directly to your colleague, who can then make changes and e-mail the presentation back. Alternatively, you can save time by uploading the PowerPoint file directly to SkyDrive and then giving your colleague access to the file. Your colleague can edit the file using the PowerPoint Web App, and then you can check the updated file on SkyDrive, also using the PowerPoint Web App. In this way, you and your colleague are working with just one version of the presentation that you both can update. You have decided to share files in the Illustrated folder that you created in the previous lesson with another individual. You start by working with a partner so that you can share files with your partner and your partner can share files with you.

STEPS

TROUBLE
If you cannot find a partner, read the steps so you understand how the process works.

1. **Identify a partner with whom you can work, and obtain his or her e-mail address; you can choose someone in your class or someone on your e-mail list, but it should be someone who will be completing these steps when you are**
2. **From the Illustrated folder, click Share**
3. **Click Edit permissions**

   The Edit permissions page opens. On this page, you can select the individual with whom you would like to share the contents of the Illustrated folder.
4. **Click in the Enter a name or an e-mail address text box, type the e-mail address of your partner, then press [Tab]**

   You can define the level of access that you want to give your partner.
5. **Click the Can view files list arrow shown in Figure WEB-11, click Can add, edit details, and delete files, then click Save**

   You can choose to send a notification to each individual when you grant permission to access your files.
6. **Click in the Include your own message text box, type the message shown in Figure WEB-12, then click Send**

   Your partner will receive a message from Windows Live advising him or her that you have shared your Illustrated folder. If your partner is completing the steps at the same time, you will receive an e-mail from your partner.

TROUBLE
If you do not receive a message from Windows Live, your partner has not yet completed the steps to share the Illustrated folder.

7. **Check your e-mail for a message from Windows Live advising you that your partner has shared his or her Illustrated folder with you**

   The subject of the e-mail message will be "[Name] has shared documents with you."

QUICK TIP
You will know you are on your partner's SkyDrive because you will see your partner's first name at the beginning of the SkyDrive path.

8. **If you have received the e-mail, click View folder in the e-mail message, then sign in to Windows Live if you are requested to do so**

   You are now able to access your partner's Illustrated folder on his or her SkyDrive. You can download files in your partner's Illustrated folder to your own computer where you can work on them and then upload them again to your partner's Illustrated shared folder.
9. **Exit the browser**

FIGURE WEB-11: Editing folder permissions

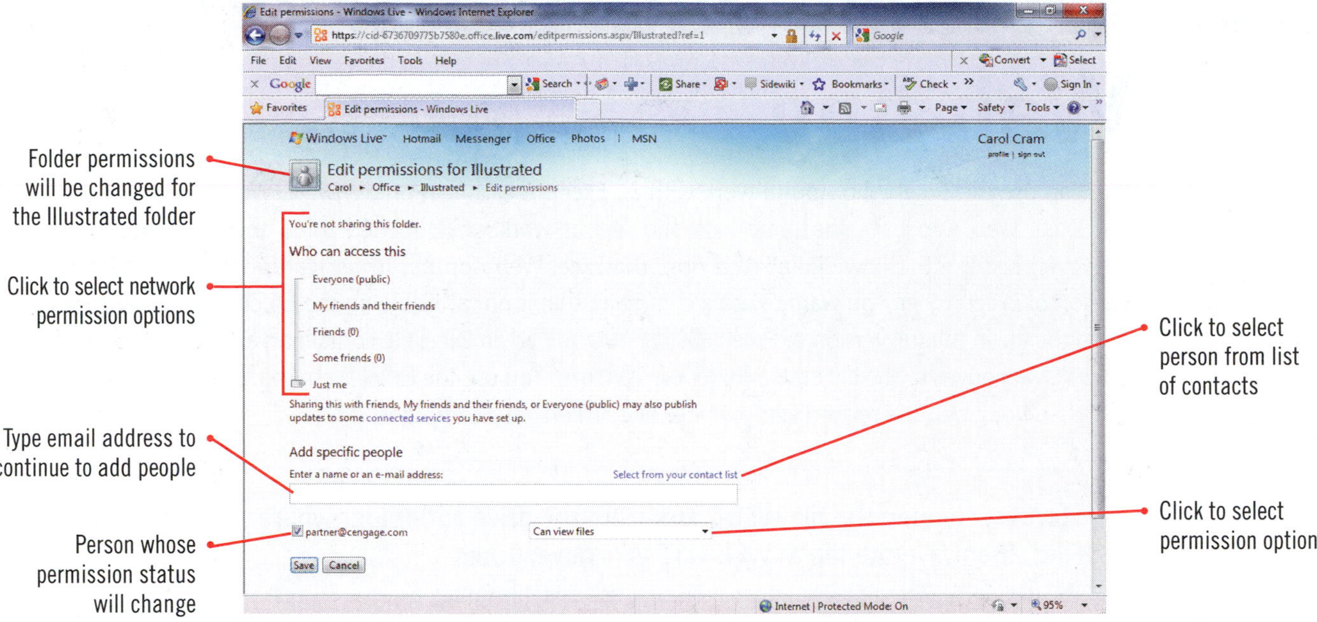

FIGURE WEB-12: Entering a message to notify a person that file sharing permission has been granted

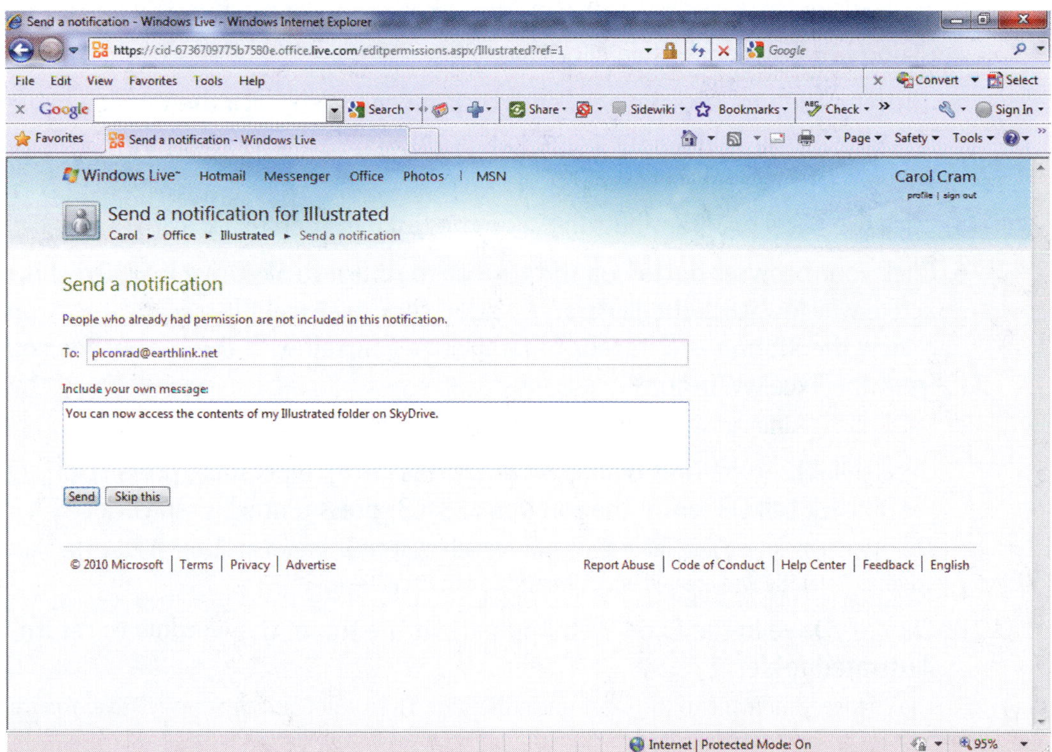

Sharing files on SkyDrive

When you share a folder with other people, the people with whom you share a folder can download the file to their computers and then make changes using the full version of the corresponding Office application. Once these changes are made, each individual can then upload the file to SkyDrive and into a folder shared with you and others. In this way, you can create a network of people with whom you share your files.

Working with the Excel Web App

You can use the Excel Web App to work with an Excel spreadsheet on SkyDrive. Workbooks opened using the Excel Web App have the same look and feel as workbooks opened using the full version of Excel. However, just like the PowerPoint Web App, the Excel Web App has fewer features available than the full version of Excel. When you want to use a command that is not available on the Excel Web App, you need to open the file in the full version of Excel. You upload an Excel file containing a list of the tours offered by QST Vancouver to the Illustrated folder on SkyDrive. You use the Excel Web App to make some changes, and then you open the revised version in Excel 2010 on your computer.

STEPS

TROUBLE
If prompted, sign in to your Windows Live account as directed.

QUICK TIP
Alternately, you can open your Web browser and go to Windows Live to sign in to SkyDrive.

1. **Start Excel, open the file WEB-2.xlsx from the drive and folder where you store your Data Files, then save the file as WEB-QST Vancouver Tours**
   The data in the Excel file is formatted using the Excel table function.
2. **Click the File tab, click Save & Send, then click Save to Web**
   In a few moments, you should see three folders to which you can save spreadsheets. My Documents and Cengage are personal folder that contains files that only you can access. Illustrated is a shared folder that contains files you can share with others in your network. The Illustrated folder is shared with your partner.
3. **Click the Illustrated folder, click the Save As button, wait a few seconds for the Save As dialog box to appear, then click Save**
4. **Click the File tab, click Save & Send, click Save to Web, click the Windows Live SkyDrive link above your folders, then sign in if prompted**
   Windows Live opens to your SkyDrive.
5. **Click the Excel program button on the taskbar, then exit Excel**
6. **Click your browser button on the taskbar to return to SkyDrive if SkyDrive is not the active window, click the Illustrated folder, click the Excel file, click Edit in Browser, then review the Ribbon and its tabs to familiarize yourself with the commands you can access from the Excel Web App**
   Table WEB-3 summarizes the commands that are available.
7. **Click cell A12, type Gulf Islands Sailing, press [TAB], type 3000, press [TAB], type 10, press [TAB], click cell D3, enter the formula =B3*C3, press [Enter], then click cell A1**
   The formula is copied automatically to the remaining rows as shown in Figure WEB-13 because the data in the original Excel file was created and formatted as an Excel table.
8. **Click SkyDrive in the Excel Web App path at the top of the window to return to the Illustrated folder**
   The changes you made to the Excel spreadsheet are saved automatically on SkyDrive. You can download the file directly to your computer from SkyDrive.
9. **Point to the Excel file, click More, click Download, click Save, navigate to the location where you save the files for this book, name the file WEB-QST Vancouver Tours_Updated, click Save, then click Close in the Download complete dialog box**
   The updated version of the spreadsheet is saved on your computer and on SkyDrive.
10. **Exit the Web browser**

FIGURE WEB-13: Updated table in the Excel Web App

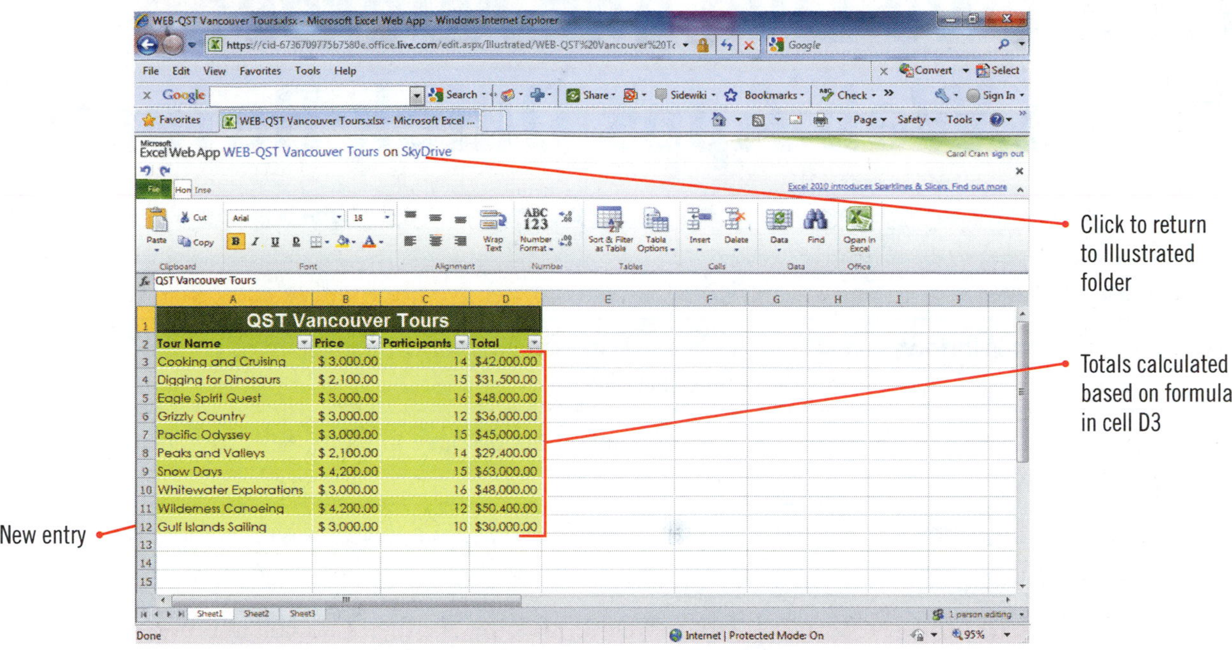

TABLE WEB-3: Commands on the Excel Web App

tab	commands available
File	• Open in Excel: select to open the file in Excel on your computer • Where's the Save Button?: when you click this option, a message appears telling you that you do not need to save your spreadsheet when you are working in it with Excel Web App; the spreadsheet is saved automatically as you work • Save As • Share • Download a Snapshot: a snapshot contains only the values and the formatting; you cannot modify a snapshot • Download a Copy: the file can be opened and edited in the full version of Excel • Give Feedback • Privacy Statement • Terms of Use • Close
Home	• Clipboard group: Cut, Copy, Paste • Font group: change the font, style, color, and size of selected labels and values, as well as border styles and fill colors • Alignment group: change vertical and horizontal alignment and turn on the Wrap Text feature • Number group: change the number format and increase or decrease decimal places • Tables: sort and filter data in a table and modify Table Options • Cells: insert and delete cells • Data: refresh data and find labels or values • Office: open the file in Excel on your computer
Insert	• Insert a Table • Insert a Hyperlink to a Web page

Exploring other Office Web Apps

Two other Office Web Apps are Word and OneNote. You can share files on SkyDrive directly from Word or from OneNote using the same method you used to share files from PowerPoint and Excel. After you upload a Word or OneNote file to SkyDrive, you can work with it in its corresponding Office Web App. To familiarize yourself with the commands available in an Office Web App, open the file and then review the commands on each tab on the Ribbon. If you want to perform a task that is not available in the Office Web App, open the file in the full version of the application.

In addition to working with uploaded files, you can create files from new on SkyDrive. Simply sign in to SkyDrive and open a folder. With a folder open, click New and then select the Web App you want to use to create the new file.

Windows Live and Microsoft Office Web Apps Quick Reference

To Do This	Go Here
Access Windows Live	From the Web browser, type **home.live.com**, then click Sign In
Access SkyDrive on Windows Live	From the Windows Live home page, point to Windows Live, then click SkyDrive
Save to Windows Live from Word, PowerPoint, or Excel	File tab | Save & Send | Save to Web | Select a folder | Save As
Create a New Folder from Backstage view	File tab | Save & Send | Save to Web | New Folder button
Edit a File with a Web App	From SkyDrive, click the file, then click Edit in Browser
Open a File in a desktop version of the application from a Web App: Word, Excel, PowerPoint	Click Open in [Application] in the Office group in each Office Web App
Share files on Windows Live	From SkyDrive, click the folder containing the files to share, click Share on the menu bar, click Edit permissions, enter the e-mail address of the person to share files with, click the Can view files list arrow, click Can add, edit details, and delete files, then click Save

Glossary

3-D reference A worksheet reference that uses values on other sheets or workbooks, effectively creating another dimension to a workbook.

Absolute cell reference In a formula, a cell address that refers to a specific cell and does not change when you copy the formula; indicated by a dollar sign before the column letter and/or row number. *See also* Relative cell reference.

Active The currently available document, program, or object; on the taskbar, when more than one program is open, the button for the active program appears slightly lighter.

Active cell The cell in which you are currently working.

Alignment The placement of cell contents in relation to a cell's edges; for example, left-aligned, centered, or right-aligned.

Argument Information necessary for a formula or function to calculate an answer.

Arithmetic operators In a formula, symbols that perform mathematical calculations, such as addition (+), subraction (–), multiplication (*), division(/), or exponentiation (^).

AutoFill Feature activated by dragging the fill handle; copies a cell's contents or continues a series of entries into adjacent cells.

AutoFill Options button Button that appears after using the fill handle to copy cell contents; enables you to choose to fill cells with specific elements (such as formatting) of the copied cell if desired.

AutoFit A feature that automatically adjusts the width of a column or the height of a row to accommodate its widest or tallest entry.

Backstage view View available in all Microsoft Office programs that allows you to perform many common tasks, such as opening and saving a file, and printing and previewing a document.

Backward-compatible Software feature that enables documents saved in an older version of a program to be opened in a newer version of the program.

Calculation operators Symbols in a formula that indicate what type of calculation to perform on the cells, ranges, or values.

Category axis Horizontal axis in a chart, usually containing the names of data categories; in a 2-dimensional chart, also known as the x-axis.

Cell The intersection of a column and a row in a worksheet or table.

Cell address The location of a cell, expressed by cell coordinates; for example, the cell address of the cell in column A, row 1 is A1.

Cell pointer Dark rectangle that outlines the active cell.

Cell styles Predesigned combinations of formats based on themes that can be applied to selected cells to enhance the look of a worksheet.

Chart sheet A separate sheet in a workbook that contains only a chart, which is linked to the workbook data.

Charts Pictorial representations of worksheet data that make it easier to see patterns, trends, and relationships; *also called* graphs.

Clip A media file, such as a graphic, sound, animation, or movie.

Clip art A graphic image, such as a corporate logo, a picture, or a photo, that can be inserted into a document.

Clipboard A temporary Windows storage area that holds the selections you copy or cut.

Cloud computing When data, applications, and resources are stored on servers accessed over the Internet or a company's internal network rather than on users' computers.

Column heading Box that appears above each column in a worksheet; identifies the column letter, such as A, B, etc.

Combination chart Two charts in one, such as a column chart combined with a line chart, that together graph related but dissimilar data.

Comparison operators In a formula, symbols that compare values for the purpose of true/false results.

Compatibility The ability of different programs to work together and exchange data.

Complex formula A formula that uses more than one arithmetic operator.

Conditional formatting A type of cell formatting that changes based on the cell's value or the outcome of a formula.

Consolidate To combine data on multiple worksheets and display the result on another worksheet.

Data marker A graphical representation of a data point in a chart, such as a bar or column.

Data point Individual piece of data plotted in a chart.

Data series The selected range in a worksheet whose related data points Excel converts into a chart.

Delimiter A separator such as a space, comma, or semicolon between elements in imported data.

Dialog box launcher An icon available in many groups on the Ribbon that you can click to open a dialog box or task pane, offering an alternative way to choose commands.

Document window The portion of a program window in which you create the document; displays all or part of an open document.

Edit To make a change to the contents of an active cell.

Electronic spreadsheet A computer program used to perform calculations and analyze and present numeric data.

Embedded chart A chart displayed as an object in a worksheet.

Exploding Visually pulling a slice of a pie chart away from the whole pie chart in order to add emphasis to the pie slice.

External reference indicator The exclamation point (!) used in a formula to indicate that a referenced cell is outside the active sheet.

File An electronic collection of stored data that has a unique name, distinguishing it from other files, such as a letter, video, or program.

Font The typeface or design of a set of characters (letters, numbers, symbols, and punctuation marks).

Font size The size of characters, measured in units called points.

Font style Format such as bold, italic, and underlining that can be applied to change the way characters look in a worksheet or chart.

Format The appearance of a cell and its contents, including font, font styles, font color, fill color, borders, and shading. *See also* Number format.

Formula A set of instructions used to perform one or more numeric calculations, such as adding, multiplying, or averaging, on values or cells.

Formula bar The area above the worksheet grid where you enter or edit data in the active cell.

Formula prefix An arithmetic symbol, such as the equal sign (=), used to start a formula.

Function A special, predefined formula that provides a shortcut for a commonly used or complex calculation, such as SUM (for calculating a sum) or FV (for calculating the future value of an investment).

Gallery A visual collection of choices you can browse through to make a selection. Often available with Live Preview.

Gridlines Evenly spaced horizontal and/or vertical lines used in a worksheet or chart to make it easier to read.

Group In a Microsoft program window's Ribbon, a section containing related command buttons.

Insertion point A blinking vertical line that appears when you click in the formula bar or in an active cell; indicates where new text will be inserted.

Integrate To incorporate a document and parts of a document created in one program into another program; for example, to incorporate an Excel chart into a PowerPoint slide, or an Access table into a Word document.

Interface The look and feel of a program; for example, the appearance of commands and the way they are organized in the program window.

Labels Descriptive text or other information that identifies data in rows, columns, or charts, but is not included in calculations.

Landscape Page orientation in which the contents of a page span the length of a page rather than its width, making the page wider than it is tall.

Launch To open or start a program on your computer.

Legend In a chart, information that identifies how data is represented by colors or patterns.

Linking The dynamic referencing of data in the same or in other workbooks, so that when data in the other location is changed, the references in the current location are automatically updated.

Live Preview A feature that lets you point to a choice in a gallery or palette and see the results in the document without actually clicking the choice.

Logical formula A formula with calculations that are based on stated conditions.

Logical test The first part of an IF function; if the logical test is true, then the second part of the function is applied; if it is false, then the third part of the function is applied.

Major gridlines In a chart, the gridlines that represent the values at the tick marks on the value axis.

Minor gridlines In a chart, the gridlines that represent the values between the tick marks on the value axis.

Mixed reference Cell reference that combines both absolute and relative cell addressing.

Mode indicator An area on the left end of the status bar that indicates the program's status. For example, when you are changing the contents of a cell, the word 'Edit' appears in the mode indicator.

Name box Box to the left of the formula bar that shows the cell reference or name of the active cell.

Navigate To move around in a worksheet; for example, you can use the arrow keys on the keyboard to navigate from cell to cell, or press [Page Up] or [Page Down] to move one screen at a time.

Normal view Default worksheet view that shows the worksheet without features such as headers and footers; ideal for creating and editing a worksheet, but may not be detailed enough when formatting a document.

Number format A format applied to values to express numeric concepts, such as currency, date, and percentage.

Object Independent element on a worksheet (such as a chart or graphic) that is not located in a specific cell or range; can be moved and resized and displays handles when selected.

Office Web App Versions of the Microsoft Office applications with limited functionality that are available online from Windows Live SkyDrive. Users can view documents online and then edit them in the browser using a selection of functions. Office Web Apps are available for Word, PowerPoint, Excel, and OneNote.

Online collaboration The ability to incorporate feedback or share information across the Internet or a company network or intranet.

Order of precedence Rules that determine the order in which operations are performed within a formula containing more than one arithmetic operator.

Page Break Preview A worksheet view that displays a reduced view of each page in your worksheet, along with page break indicators that you can drag to include more or less information on a page.

Page Layout view Provides an accurate view of how a worksheet will look when printed, including headers and footers.

Paste Options button Button that appears onscreen after pasting content; enables you to choose to paste only specific elements of the copied selection, such as the formatting or values, if desired.

Plot area In a chart, the area inside the horizontal and vertical axes.

Previewing Prior to printing, seeing onscreen exactly how the printed document will look.

Point A unit of measure used for font size and row height. One point is equal to 1/72nd of an inch.

Portrait Page orientation in which the contents of a page span the width of a page, so the page is taller than it is wide.

Print area The portion of a worksheet that will be printed; can be defined by selecting a range and then using the Print Area button on the Page Layout tab.

Quick Access toolbar A small toolbar on the left side of a Microsoft application program window's title bar, containing icons that you click to quickly perform common actions, such as saving a file.

Range A selection of two or more cells, such as B5:B14.

Reference operators In a formula, symbols which enable you to use ranges in calculations.

Relative cell reference In a formula, a cell address that refers to a cell's location in relation to the cell containing the formula and that automatically changes to reflect the new location when the formula is copied or moved; default type of referencing used in Excel worksheets. *See also* Absolute cell reference.

Return In a function, to display a result.

Ribbon Contains command for the current Office program, organized into tabs and groups.

Scope In a named cell or range, the worksheet(s) in which the name can be used.

Screen capture An electronic snapshot of your screen, as if you took a picture of it with a camera, which you can paste into a document.

Scroll bars Bars on the right edge (vertical scroll bar) and bottom edge (horizontal scroll bar) of the document window that allow you to move around in a document that is too large to fit on the screen at once.

Secondary axis In a combination chart, an additional axis that supplies the scale for one of the chart types used.

Sheet tab scrolling buttons Allow you to navigate to additional sheet tabs when available; located to the left of the sheet tabs.

Sheet tabs Identify the sheets in a workbook and let you switch between sheets; located below the worksheet grid.

Sizing handles Small series of dots at the corners and edges of a chart indicating that the chart is selected; drag to resize the chart.

SkyDrive An online storage and file sharing service. Access to SkyDrive is through a Windows Live account. Up to 25 GB of data can be stored in a personal SkyDrive, with each file a maximum size of 50 MB.

SmartArt graphics Predesigned diagram types for the following types of data: List, Process, Cycle, Hierarchy, Relationship, Matrix, and Pyramid.

Sparkline A quick, simple chart located within a cell that serves as a visual indicator of data trends.

Stated conditions In a logical formula, criteria you create.

Status bar Bar at the bottom of the Excel window that provides a brief description about the active command or task in progress.

Suite A group of programs that are bundled together and share a similar interface, making it easy to transfer skills and program content among them.

Tab A page in an application program's Ribbon, or in a dialog box, that contains a group of related settings.

Table An organized collection of rows and columns of similarly structured data on a worksheet.

Table styles Predesigned formatting that can be applied to a range of cells or even to an entire worksheet; especially useful for those ranges with labels in the left column and top row, and totals in the bottom row or right column. *See also* Table.

Template A predesigned, formatted file that serves as the basis for a new workbook; Excel template files have the file extension .xltx.

Text annotations Labels added to a chart to draw attention to or describe a particular area.

Text concatenation operators In a formula, symbols used to join strings of text in different cells.

Theme A predefined set of colors, fonts, line and fill effects, and other formats that can be applied to an Excel worksheet and give it a consistent, professional look.

Tick marks Notations of a scale of measure on a chart axis.

Title bar Bar at the top of every program window that displays the document and program name. In Internet Explorer, usually contains the name of the Web page currently displayed in the Web browser's active tab window.

User interface A collective term for all the ways you interact with a software program.

Value axis In a chart, the axis that contains numerical values; in a 2-dimensional chart, also known as the y-axis.

Values Numbers, formulas, and functions used in calculations.

View In Windows Explorer, the appearance choices for your folder contents, such as Large Icons view or Details view. In an application program, display settings that show or hide selected elements of a document in the document window, to make it easier to focus on a certain task, such as formatting or reading text.

What-if analysis A decision-making tool in which data is changed and formulas are recalculated, in order to predict various possible outcomes.

Windows Live A collection of services and Web applications that people can access through a login. Windows Live services include access to e-mail and instant messaging, storage of files on SkyDrive, sharing and storage of photos, networking with people, downloading software, and interfacing with a mobile device.

Workbook A collection of related worksheets contained within a single file.

Worksheet A single sheet within a workbook file; also, the entire area within an electronic spreadsheet that contains a grid of columns and rows.

Worksheet window Area of the program window that displays part of the current worksheet; the worksheet window displays only a small fraction of the worksheet, which can contain a total of 1,048,576 rows and 16,384 columns.

X-axis The horizontal axis in a chart; because it often shows data categories, such as months or locations, *also called* Category axis.

XML Acronym that stands for eXtensible Markup Language, which is a language used to structure, store, and send information.

Y-axis The vertical axis in a chart; because it often shows numerical values, *also called* Value axis.

Z-axis The third axis in a true 3-D chart, lets you compare data points across both categories and values.

Zooming in A feature that makes a document appear larger but shows less of it on screen at once; does not affect actual document size.

Zooming out A feature that shows more of a document on screen at once but at a reduced size; does not affect actual document size.

Index

KEY TO PAGE NUMBER ABBREVIATIONS

Excel	EX
Office A	OFF
Web Apps	WEB

SPECIAL CHARACTERS